Progress
in
Communication
Sciences
Volume IV

PROGRESS IN COMMUNICATION SCIENCES

An Annual Review

Edited by

BRENDA DERVIN
University of Washington
and
MELVIN J. VOIGT
University of California, San Diego

Melvin J. Voigt and Gerhard J. Hanneman • Progress in Communication Sciences Volume I

Brenda Dervin and Melvin J. Voigt • Progress in Communication Sciences Volume II

Brenda Dervin and Melvin J. Voigt • Progress in Communication Sciences Volume III

Brenda Dervin and Melvin J. Voigt • Progress in Communication Sciences Volume IV

In Preparation:

Brenda Dervin and Melvin J. Voigt · Progress in Communication Sciences Volume V

Brenda Dervin and Melvin J. Voigt · Progress in Communication Sciences Volume VI

Progress
in
Communication
Sciences
Volume IV

edited by

Brenda Dervin

University of Washington

Melvin J. Voigt

University of California, San Diego

 ABLEX Publishing Corporation
Norwood, New Jersey 07648

P
81
.P74
v.4

ISBN: 0–89391–102–X   ISSN: 0163–5689

ABLEX Publishing Corporation
355 Chestnut Street
Norwood, New Jersey 07648

Contents

3 Comparative Communication Research:
A Response to World Problems,
Alex S. Edelstein **43**

4 Critical Perspectives on the State of
Intercultural Communication Research,
Rita Atwood **63**

5 Semiotics and Communications Studies: Points of Contact,
Gertrude J. Robinson and William O. Straw **91**

Contributors

CHARLES K. ATKIN (205), Department of Communication, Michigan State University, East Lansing, Michigan.

RITA ATWOOD (67), Department of Radio-Television-Film, University of Texas, Austin, Texas.

ALEX S. EDELSTEIN (43), School of Communications, University of Washington, Seattle, Washington.

JOSEPH P. FOLGER (115), Department of Communication, University of Michigan, Ann Arbor, Michigan.

DEAN HEWES (115), Department of Speech Communication, University of Illinois, Urbana, Illinois.

ROBIN KENCH (163), School of Librarianship, University of New South Wales, Kensington, New South Wales, Australia.

CARMEL MAGUIRE (163), School of Librarianship, University of New South Wales, Kensington, New South Wales, Australia.

ELIZABETH MAHAN (1), Council on Latin American Studies, New Haven, Connecticut.

THOMAS H. MARTIN (23), School of Information Studies, Syracuse University, Syracuse, New York.

MARSHALL SCOTT POOLE (115), Department of Speech Communication, University of Illinois, Urbana, Illinois.

GERTRUDE J. ROBINSON (91), Graduate Program in Communications, McGill University, Montreal, Quebec.

JORGE REINA SCHEMENT (1), Annenberg School of Communications, University of Southern California, Los Angeles.

WILLIAM O. STRAW (91), Graduate Program in Communications, McGill University, Montreal, Quebec.

Preface

This volume in the *Progress in Communication Sciences* series, like the volumes that preceded it, has as one of its purposes to provide the reader with high quality state of the art reviews of thought and research that represent the diversity of attentions that are being brought to bear to study and understand information-communication processes and, in particular, the areas of: 1) information, information transfer, and information systems; 2) the uses and effects of communication; and 3) the control and regulating of communications and information. This purpose, then, focuses on content and coverage, bringing together in each volume 8-12 state of the art reviews representing work on the "cutting edge" of particular thrusts of effort.

This volume, and its predecessors, has another purpose as well—a purpose which emerges from the seeming contradiction of bringing together such diverse attentions into one volume. This second purpose deals with synthesis and the search for not merely coverage but convergence, for the points of intersection in common between the reviews, for the contributions that a group of such reviews provides collectively for understanding the past, present, and potential future of communication-information scholarship.

Readers who come to this volume may do so for either purpose. An overview of the volume can also take both perspectives. When coverage is the focus, an overview shows that eight state of the art reviews are included in this volume representing a concern for eight quite distinct and on the surface, at least, quite different content areas—broadcast regulation, policy research, comparative research, intercultural communication, semiotics, social interaction, diffusion of technological innovation in industry, and advertising effects. A diversity of research approaches and methods are also represented—quantitative and qualitative, theoretic and applied, conceptual and actuarial. This diversity shows clearly in a roster of brief descriptions of the eight reviews.

1. Mahan and Schement's "The Broadcast Regulatory Process: Toward a New Analytical Framework" proposes that achieving an understanding of "how and why the broadcast regulatory process operates as it does and who benefits from it" will require that institutional perspectives be used in research. By institutional research, they refer to research approaches which seek to identify how and why media institutions function as they do and focus on the influences on actors in regulatory processes and the interrelationships among actors which effect ultimate policy decisions.

2. Martin's "Information and Communication Policy Research in the United States: The Researcher as Advocate, Facilitator, and Staff Member" considers the role of research as a relatively new factor in communication policy making and attempts to break new ground in reviewing and clarifying the role of the researcher as advocate, facilitator, and staff member. Martin sees policy as acting as a bridge which facilitates the convergence of information and communication technologies.

3. Edelstein's "Comparative Communication Research: A Response to World Problems" reviews the kinds of international communication problems which have been addressed by comparative research scholars and what these studies "tell us that we need to know and can learn in no other way." Some major themes of concern to scholars in comparative communication research are analyzed as they relate to world problems: comparative modernization, political and economic development, news flow and the new international information order, values and culture, image construction, and the role of the journalist.

4. Atwood's review of "Critical Perspectives on the State of Intercultural Communication Research" takes a broad look at those studies in the field of communication which have focused on contact among persons from diverse cultures. She notes that while in the past these studies focused primarily on interpersonal contact, recent expansions have included the role of mass communication software and technology in such contacts. Most of the Atwood review identifies the major sources of complexity and confusion in concepts of intercultural research and analyzes alternative concepts and conceptual shifts necessary for a more productive research future. She calls, in particular, for more emphasis on actor definitions and perspectives in intercultural research.

5. Robinson and Straw's "Semiotics and Communication Studies: Points of Contact" starts by contrasting two perspectives currently used to study communication—the transmission perspective given more emphasis in U.S. research and the ritual or cultural perspective given more emphasis in European research. The former focuses on transmitting messages for purposes of control while the latter focuses on the processes by which shared culture is created, modified, and transformed. This review assesses the past and potential future contributions of cultural studies, in particular semiotics (the study of signs or signification) to understanding communication.

6. Folger, Hewes, and Poole's "Coding Social Interaction" start their review by noting that it is "one of the great ironies of the field of communications" that little focus is actually placed on messages. Their review focuses on one class of messages, those produced in social interactions, and is concerned with the methodological problems inherent in studying these communication behaviors empirically. The review collates and assesses what is known about how research can achieve reliability and validity in coding how messages are exchanged and interpreted in face-to-face encounters.

7. Maguire and Kench's "The Introduction and Diffusion of Technological Innovation in Industry: An Information Research Perspective" notes that while the diffusion of new techniques in industry has been studied for some time, "relatively little of the literature has been focused directly on the part played by information in technological innovation and diffusion." The review covers the literature as it has come from various disciplinary bases, including the work of economists and management theorists; empirical studies of multi-disciplinary groups; and studies of information scientists on information seeking behaviors and patterns of information flow. The review notes the lack of synthesis in the innovations literature. It suggests, however, that while the literature "has not produced a critical mass of data which is about to impel new paradigms," it has "amassed much useful data from which sensible guidelines can be extracted."

8. Atkin's "Consumer and Social Effects of Advertising" deals with the impact of the "pervasive stream of commercial messages" reaching the public through newspapers, television, radio, and magazines. The review "examines key concepts and comprehensively reviews research evidence dealing with the effects of advertising on product knowledge, attitudes, and behavior." It also includes a brief review of socially significant consequences of advertising. For this review, advertising is seen as a form of communication involving the classic "sender-oriented perspective" in which interest focuses on how effective sources (advertisers) have been in using "source, message, and channel factors to achieve maximum impact on the audience."

Turning the focus for the overview from coverage to convergence, the eight reviews stand as "state of the art" not only because of their coverage but because individually and collectively they clearly, more so than in preceding years, search for convergence and address the gaps that seem to stand as barriers to that goal. If there is any truth to the idea that any small set of well-chosen articles taken from a field at a point in time are sufficient to show that field's past, present, and future, this set of eight reviews is illustrative of the point.

This search for convergence and grappling with gaps to that goal permeates almost all the reviews in one way or other. The simplest form of its expression is in the echoing call for the need for synthesis heard in virtually all the reviews. More interesting, however, are the complex forms of the search's expression, manifested in a variety of ways.

One symptom of the search is shown in the evident breaking down of traditional barriers. These reviews suggest, for example, that the walls between U.S. and non-U.S. research are beginning to fall. The Robinson and Straw review focuses here most directly, but the bibliographies of other reviews (notably those by Atwood and Edelstein) show the same patterns. Other walls are reported as coming down as well—that between applied and theoretic (see, in particular, the reviews of Atwood, Mahan and Schement, and Martin); between qualitative and quantitative (see, in particular, the reviews of Atwood, and Folger, Hewes, and Poole); between mass and interpersonal (see, in particular, Atwood); and between communication and information (see, in particular, the reviews by Martin, and Maguire and Kench).

More apparant even than the evidence these reviews present of walls beginning to tumble down is the emphasis on discussion of alternative underlying assumptions that pervade virtually all the reviews. If anything, it is clear that the study of information-communication processes has become self-analytic. Almost all the reviews incorporate explicit statements of the assumptions about human beings that guide them. Most devote considerable attention specifically to these assumptions (see, in particular, Mahan and Schement, Robinson and Straw, and Atwood).

These major classes of assumptions receive, by far, the majority of attention. Fittingly, they are the three points which define the "cutting edge" of the study of information-communication processes. The first of these classes of assumptions deals with how human beings are conceptualized as being involved in communication-information processes. One view, that which has predominated Western social science until recently, sees these processes as primarily mechanistic, and human beings as recipients (receivers) of messages transmitted by sources. In this volume, the Atkin review most clearly (and explicitly) rests on this set of assumptions. The alternative view (presented most clearly in this volume by Atwood and Robinson and Straw, but emphasized as well by Edelstein and Mahan and Schement) focuses instead phenomenologically on individual creative cognitive processes or, as Robinson and Straw state it, how people make sense out of their existence and surroundings.

The second class of assumptions, related to the first, deals with the appropriate role of situational and structural contexts in understanding communication-information processes. Virtually all the reviews agree that these processes must be studied in context. Some state explicitly that studying communication-information processes out of context can only produce non-useful or limited results (e.g., Mahan and Schement, Atwood, and Robinson and Straw). What differs between the reviews, however, is how this context receives focus. Some (for example, Atwood) call for assessing how individual actors create understandings of their own context. Others (for example, Mahan and Schement) call for observer assessments of the contexts and imply that these assessments are more comprehensive at a minimum and, in some cases, contain elements not included in actor perspectives. While clearly these two differing approaches to context are growing in strength, they continue in this volume, as they have in the past, to travel separate roads. What differs in this volume, however, is the appearance of explicit discussion of why one approach versus another is more useful for some purposes. Mahan and Schement, for example, discuss explicitly why they see an individual actor perspective as leading to an erroneous view of broadcast regulatory processes. Atwood, in contrast, gives a rationale why individual actors should be asked to define their own cultural context. While the arguments and perspectives differ, the explicit discussion is symptomatic of the beginnings of a search for convergence.

The final set of assumptions deals with the role of behavior in the study of communication-information processes. Continuing a move that has been gaining momentum for the past few years, many of these reviews show a clear commitment to the utility of focusing on behavior. Some (e.g., Atwood, Robinson and Straw, Edelstein) focus on cognitive behaviors (constructing ideas, creating images, making sense) while others focus on face-to-face behaviors (e.g., Folger, Hewes, and Poole) and others focus on ritualized or rule-governed behavior in systems (e.g., Mahan and Schement, Martin). These differences are merely manifestations of differences in points of emphasis. The reviews show a clear move away from studying communication-information processes as if they occurred without involving actors either cognitively, interpersonally, or institutionally.

Perhaps what is most useful in terms of a focus on covergence is the fact that these eight reviews point to the kind of excitement that comes from the tension of thinkers coming to grips with seemingly contradictory notions and making some progress in finding the unities between the contradictions. As several of the reviews note, both information and communication scholarship have been highly descriptive and disparate, with journals filled with seemingly unrelated particulars. Clearly, this is changing. What is beginning to emerge is a focus on the kind of metatheoretic and theoretic ideas that on the surface have nothing to do with particulars but offer hope for creating understandings which unify. More than anything, then, the excitement of these reviews is that one can find above and between the particulars less to learn and more to think about.

Brenda Dervin
Melvin J. Voigt

Contents of Previous Volumes

Volume 3

1 The Broadcast Regulatory Process: Toward a New Analytical Framework

Elizabeth Mahan
Council on Latin American Studies
Yale University
P.O. Box 1881, Yale Station
New Haven, Connecticut 06520

Jorge Reina Schement
Annenberg School of Communications
University of Southern California
Los Angeles, California 90007

I. INTRODUCTION

In this review we propose and illustrate an institutional perspective and framework for the study of the broadcast regulatory process. This approach to the study of regulation allows the consideration of variables which have been minimized or overlooked in previous studies of the FCC, but which have power to explain how and why the broadcast regulatory process operates as it does and who benefits from it. Understanding of the day-to-day workings of the regulatory process differs from knowing the formal procedural requirements of the regulatory system. Such an understanding is essential to the formulation and realization of realistic demands upon the FCC and other regulatory actors.

In 1962, Judge H.J. Friendly summarized the strong criticisms leveled at the Federal Communications Commission (FCC) over time by a number of individuals in and out of government. At that time, the FCC was generally considered to be one of the least adept and successful regulatory agencies in specifying and carrying out its legislative mandate. Studies of the FCC and the broadcast regulatory process since the publication of Friendly's lectures do not reflect a change in opinion. Several of these studies (Besen and Krattenmaker, 1981; Cole and Oettinger, 1978; Krasnow and Longley, 1978; Mosco, 1979; Park, 1973; Robinson, 1978) offer opinions and analyses of why the FCC and broadcast regulation have been inefficient and ineffective. Some also suggest measures to improve the operation of the FCC and, presumably, the effectiveness of broadcast regulation (Robinson, 1978; Schulman, 1979). With the exception of Krasnow and Longley, most studies of broadcast regulation focus on the FCC—primarily upon the actions and decisions of commissioners—often ignoring the political context of regulation and interactions among actors in the regulatory arena. This narrow perspective results in a view of broadcast regulation which implies that the FCC or the commissioners can or should be able to alter and improve the regulatory process.

The broadcast regulatory process, however, reflects the processes of the larger political and administrative environment of the United States. Because of this, the independence and autonomy of the supposedly independent regulatory commission is circumscribed to the extent that it is effectively inhibited from developing, implementing, and enforcing vigorous, rational communication policies (Mahan, 1982).

In the following discussion various approaches to the study of broadcast regulation during the past ten years are reviewed. None of the studies considered provides a complete explanation of the broadcast regulatory process, but their combined perspectives begin to do so. Therefore, the review of these studies is followed by a discussion and illustration of the institutional approach to the study of broadcast regulation—a perspective which integrates and expands the approaches of previous research.

II. APPROACHES TO THE STUDY OF
BROADCAST REGULATION

The literature of U.S. broadcast regulation is vast. Many works focus on one particular regulatory problem or incident (Geller, 1981; Le Duc, 1972; Levin, 1971; Schmidt, 1978). Others, however, attempt to view broadcast regulation as a whole. This literature, which attempts to account for the process and outcomes of broadcast regulation, is reviewed here. The review is not exhaustive, but focuses on works generally acknowledged to be major studies of the FCC, plus others which are significant, if less well known. The review is organized according to a typology of explanations which observers of the FCC have offered to account for the behavior of that agency. These categories of explanation are: (A) no systematic explanation; (B) industry capture; (C) failure to analyze and understand available information; and (D) regulatory paradigm breakdown.

A. No Systematic Explanation

A primary example of this category of broadcast regulatory study is Cole and Oettinger's *Reluctant Regulators* (1978). This study is based largely on observations made by Cole during a five-year association with the FCC, and contains a wealth of descriptive information and a number of details about day-to-day activities at the Commission. It is somewhat impressionistic, however, and lacks a framework for analyzing and explaining the seeming regulatory ineptitude described. Cole and Oettinger are critical of the FCC and the conduct of commissioners, but they also make it clear that the FCC is subject to a number of conflicting pressures from within the organization itself, from other sectors of the government, and from the private sector. There is no attempt, however, to explain how these pressures might be linked to regulatory decisions and actions. This notwithstanding, it would be unfair to minimize the contribution of this study, for it certainly conveys a sense of the complexity of the regulatory environment, a factor which itself goes some distance toward explaining the state of broadcast regulation.

B. Industry Capture

Studies in the second category explain the current state of broadcast regulation in terms of "industry capture"—that is, the control of the FCC by the broadcast industry. Moore (1973) contends that the FCC's tendency to view the public interest in terms of what is profitable to the broadcast industry is evidence that the Commission has been captured by that industry. Owen (1973), although he does not use the term capture, arrives at essentially the same conclusion via a somewhat different route. He holds that regulatory outcomes can be explained as the resolution of bargaining among parties at interest in the regulatory process. It just happens that the broadcast industry is the most powerful contender in the bargaining process; the FCC, therefore, is bound to serve that industry. In other words, the strongest competitor in the regulatory process is able to capture the Commission.

Both Moore and Owen are correct in observing that the broadcast industry often appears to dominate the regulatory process. Neither, however, explains convincingly why this should occur. Moore infers from the fact that regulations have favored existing broadcast industry perquisites that this is due to its capture of the Commission, equating, as it were, effect with cause. Owen touches upon an important aspect of the regulatory process when he explains the apparent dominance of the broadcast industry as the outcome of a bargaining process in which the industry is the strongest bargainer. A great deal of interaction and bargaining does occur among actors in that process. Nevertheless, the connection of the outcome of the process to the bargaining strength of a single actor, while germane, is tenuous. Rarely can regulatory outcomes be shown to be the result of the force, actions, or decisions of a single actor in that process.

Recognizing this, Krasnow and Longley (1978) set out to analyze the interactions between the FCC and other institutional actors in the regulatory process. To do this, they introduce a systems approach represented by David Easton's (1968) input-output model of a political system, which permits the identification and description of the inputs (e.g., the demands of various public and private actors in the regulatory process) and the identification of outcomes or specific FCC regulations and decisions.

There are two main weaknesses in Krasnow and Longley's use of the model. The first concerns the specification of the influence of contextual or environmental factors on the formation of demands and outcomes. This, in fact, is a weakness of the model itself as formulated by Easton (Holt and Richardson, 1970). While Krasnow and Longley note historical and legal precedents and social expectations as contextual factors which affect both demands and outcomes, they do not show how these are related to the specific regulatory decisions which they analyze. This results in the tendency to explain regulatory outcomes in terms of the presumed ability of the actor, which the decision favors, to control the FCC—a tautology similar to Moore's.

A second weakness in their approach is that regulatory outcomes are taken to be the written regulations or formal decisions of the FCC in a particular case. This ignores the considerable amount of interaction occurring during the implementation and enforcement phases of the regulatory process. These interactions often yield a regulatory outcome quite different from the formal decisions and regulations and can, therefore, alter the perception of which input or actor is the most powerful and which, if any, controls the FCC. For example, formal FCC regulations on multiple ownership of broadcast stations indicate that the Commission is able, and at some level has determined, to restrain ownership concentration. In practice, however, the FCC makes exceptions to its regulations, with the result that concentration has increased in spite of the Commission's formal positions.

A general criticism can be directed at works which explain the broadcast regulatory process in terms of the power of the broadcast industry to control the FCC. These works tend to minimize or ignore initiatives and influences which emanate from the FCC itself, and which can affect not only the demands of other actors, but the formulation, implementation, and enforcement of regulations as well. In fairness, it should be noted that the "capture" explanations of the broadcast regulatory process originally appeared before serious competitors to the broadcast industry developed. Broadcast industry capture may have seemed to be a plausible explanation under such conditions, but if such an explanation is to be theoretically sound, then the industry must demonstrably control the Commisison or be replaced by a new, most powerful contender in the regulatory arena, such as the cable TV industry, which would then control the FCC. This has not happened. The past, seeming dominance of the broadcast industry has been challenged, but no single actor has emerged to capture the Commission. Rather, power among industrial actors in the regulatory process has been diffused, requiring an explanation other than the ability of a dominant contender to capture the regulatory agency to account for regulatory outcomes.

C. Failure to Analyze Information

That other factors can be brought into account is illustrated by the third category of study, which relates the inadequacies of the broadcast regulatory process to the failure of the FCC to understand and analyze available information and the long and broad range implications of its decisions. Besen and Krattenmaker (1981) account for FCC decisions concerning the television networks in this way. Their criticism of the FCC is quite strong, almost implying intentional ineptitude on the part of the Commission. The viewpoints expressed by contributors to Park (1973) generally deplore the FCC's failure to analyze regulatory options and implications before reaching decisions. However, contributions by Owen (1973) (noted previously) and Webbink (1973), as well as comments by Park himself, indicate awareness that the environment of broadcast regulation may in certain instances be inhospitable to analysis; even when analysis is conducted, available, and understandable, the FCC is often prevented from acting strictly in terms of it because of political pressures elsewhere in the regulatory arena. Still, Park maintains that the regulatory process might be improved if changes could be made in the evaluation capabilities of the FCC and in the attitudes and training of the commissioners.

A variation on the lack of analysis theme is illustrated by Mosco (1979), who holds that FCC decisions which have tended to perpetuate a status quo favoring the broadcast industry can be explained by the commissioners' inability to cope with the technical and political complexity of the issues that confront them. Commissioners are required to make decisions about technology and economic arrangements they do not understand, while adhering to complicated and cumbersome administrative procedures and being subject to various pressures from parties outside the agency. Decisions which perpetuate the dominant position of the broadcast industry are, therefore, not evidence of the Commission's capture, but of its manner of simplifying its decisionmaking environment.

There is a great deal of merit to an explanation of broadcast regulation which centers upon the Commission's use of information and analysis. However, if used as the sole explanation, it is as misleading as the capture thesis, because it leads ultimately to the conclusion that "better men"—that is, individuals with more and better training than current and past commissioners—could improve the regulatory process. This position, which was advocated by Dean James M. Landis in his report on federal regulatory agencies (1960), overlooks the fact that formal regulatory decisions do not simply reflect commissioner views or expertise, but are a collage of decisions made at many levels within the FCC as individuals respond to organizational pressures, personal motivations, and pressures from the public, the communications industries, and other branches of government. The administrative capacity of a regulatory agency like the FCC consists only in part of its ability to understand and use information. Its ability to maneuver in an intensely political environment is also a factor of great importance.

D. Paradigm Breakdown

The final category of literature centers on the concept of paradigm breakdown and is represented by only one work, a significant study by Singleton (1979). He uses the paradigm concept developed by Kuhn (1970) as the basis for his analysis of FCC handling of cases involving concentration of ownership in the mass media industries. While the idea of a regulatory paradigm is useful and apt, by failing to analyze the behavior of the FCC in terms of the larger phenomenon of economic regulation, Singleton concludes that the failure of FCC application of regulations to operationalize the ideals set forth in the *Communications Act of 1934* indicates a breakdown of the regulatory paradigm. In this case, an analysis, which looked beyond the FCC and its specific mandate to the larger regulatory arena and the experience of other regulatory agencies, would reveal that the existence of a regulatory ideal which is contradicted by day-to-day regulatory practice is a fundamental element of the U.S. regulatory paradigm. This, in turn, is related to societal attitudes toward government intervention in the economy, vague legislative mandates, and the difficulty of coping with competing interest groups. If the broadcast regulatory paradigm is in a state of crisis, it is more likely to be due to the effects of new technologies on the provision of services to audiences than to a lack of fit between ideals expressed in laws and regulations and actual regulatory actions.

III. INTEGRATING AND EXPANDING THE STUDY OF THE BROADCAST REGULATORY PROCESS

As Mosco (1979) explicitly states, as Cole and Oettinger (1978) indicate with their description of daily activities at the FCC, and as Krasnow and Longley (1978) show through their description of how actors outside the FCC participate in the process, the broadcast regulatory process is extremely complex. To understand it, one needs to look not only at the FCC, but at its relationships with other organs of government and the private sector, and, finally, to view all the relationships and interactions in light of the limits imposed on government regulation of private economic enterprise by U.S. political culture. Failure to consider the nature of the interactions between actors in the regulatory process, and how that process relates to the larger political and administrative system, results in a tendency to overemphasize the responsibility of the FCC for the present state of broadcast regulation. Media institutions such as the FCC exist in social and political contexts which need to be taken into account in any explanation of their behavior. Indeed, these factors outside the institution per se may be more powerful determinants of its behavior than are initiatives emanating from within.

What is needed is a research approach which seeks to identify and understand how and why media institutions function as they do. We refer to this type of study as institutional analysis because that designation encompasses both the concern with a specific media organization and the attempt to study the sociopolitical processes and structures which affect the operation and outputs of that organization.

A. The Nature of Institutional Analysis

The term institution can refer to an organization (e.g., the Federal Communications Commission) or a complex of social and economic relationships and concepts (e.g., the institution of slavery). When we speak of institutional analysis we are referring to a perspective which embodies both meanings of the term institution—that is, a research effort which focuses on one or more institution (in the organizational sense) and which analyzes that institution in terms of its social, political, and economic context, with the objective of identifying and explaining processes and relationships between the institution and its environment. Thus, we would distinguish between the study of the FCC as the institution which regulates (among other things) commercial broadcasting, and the study of the institution of broadcast regulation. The former would be the focus of much of the work in the field of organizational research. The latter would entail not only study of the FCC as an organization, but also study of the other groups and organizations involved in broadcast regulation, and the phenomenon of regulated private enterprise which is characteristic of U.S. political and economic culture.

A major assumption underlying institutional analysis is that social phenomena cannot be adequately explained if considered apart from the contextual forces which influence their organization and operation. Because of this, an institutional approach is particularly useful in the study of broadcast regulation, because the regulatory process is carried on at many levels of government and involves private as well as public actors. The broad institutional perspective increases the likelihood of identifying and explaining the relationships among relevant variables in the regulatory process. This knowledge is crucial to an understanding of the regulatory process as a whole, as well as to an explanation of how and why regulations are formulated and implemented and who benefits from them.

B. Level of Analysis

An important difference between institutional analysis and traditional organization research is the level at which the analysis is carried out. Since institutional analysis aims at understanding processes and relationships among institutions as these derive from and manifest a particular social context, it exemplifies what Katz and Kahn (1966) call macro level analysis. Organizational research, on the other hand, with its focus on how individuals within a particular organization affect and are affected by the structure of the organization, can be considered micro level analysis. Note that to designate one approach as macro and the other as micro is not to make any claims for the absolute superiority of one or the other. Each is appropriate in a particular type of study. More importantly, it should not be inferred that a macro analysis makes use of a higher level of abstraction than does a micro analysis.

The macro level institutional analysis we advocate for the study of broadcast regulation has limited deductive power, a characteristic which Bertalanffy (1968) notes in all macro level analysis. However, Bertalanffy (1968, p. 15) emphasizes that the macro approach ''has the advantage that it remains rather close to reality and it can easily be illustrated and verified by examples . . . .'' In addition, Katz and Kahn (1966, p. 11) point out that ''the macro approach is invaluable . . . in calling attention to the significant problem and directing our attention to areas in which variables need more careful formulation.''

The macro level of institutional analysis is thus appropriate for the study of the broadcast regulatory process because the objective is not so much ''mathematical elegance and deductive strength'' (Bertalanffy, 1968, p. 15), as an explanation of how the policies and regulations which have emerged in the past came into being, so as to understand the kinds of regulatory options which exist in the present and are likely in the future. There is a kind of predictive power here, but it results from induction rather than deduction.

C. The General Systems Perspective and Institutional Analysis

In adopting a macro level of analysis, it becomes necessary to employ general systems theory as the principle by which an institution is identified for study. General systems theory accounts for the fact that actors in social systems and the social outputs of those systems are constrained or marked by their cultural, political, and economic context. The systems perspective emphasizes the identification and analysis of the components of a system, such as an organization or a policy arena, and the exchanges or interactions occurring between the components of the system and the environment in which it exists. (A similar perspective, called bureaucratic politics, has been developed by political scientists to account for governmental policy decisions and outcomes (Allison, 1969).)

Briefly defined, "a system is a set of objects, together with relationships between the objects and between their attributes" (Hall and Fagen, 1968, p. 81). This definition reveals three major emphases of the systems perspective which make it appropriate for institutional analysis. First, there is a focus on a set of objects; that is, on parts and a whole. This can refer to a subsystem within a single organization, or to a larger social universe such as a political system. What should be noted in the concept, "set of objects," is that there is no implication that one object is necessarily dominant. This means that a systems perspective does not require a pre-judgement as to which social actors are most important. There are such things as centralized systems in which there is clearly one dominant object, but we would contend that, in the institutional analysis of policy at least, preconceived ideas about which actor (or actors) is dominant might be misleading. Rather, the relative strengths and positions of actors will be discovered in the process of institutional analysis; they may well differ from what the formal organization of the policy arena would lead one to believe.

Second, this perspective is concerend with the attributes or characteristics of objects in the system. In terms of a single organization, this could refer to its formal structure or to the outputs produced. When speaking of a regulatory system, we would note social and cultural attributes: historical precedents and belief patterns which characterize the structure or organization of the system and the interactions among actors in it.

Third, a systems perspective emphasizes relationships among objects in the system. In fact, without relationships, one cannot properly speak of a system at all. Despite the paramount importance of relationships in analyzing social phenomena from a systems perspective, it is again important to note that there need be no prior specification of which relationships are important to the particular analysis at hand. Indeed, in many instances, it is not always apparent, from the simple identification of actors in a policy or regulatory arena, which relationships are strong or crucial to the creation of the various outputs of the policy process. The systems perspective allows the researcher to identify and analyze the interactions which occur in a system and between the system and its environment, and how those interactions are related to the system's outputs. Once this kind of descriptive information has been accumulated, it is possible to specify the key relationships in the system.

An additional aspect of the systems perspective, particularly important for institutional analysis, is the concept of environment. As defined by Hall and Fagen (1968, p. 83), "for a given system, the environment is the set of all objects a change in whose attributes affects the system and also those objects whose attributes are changed by the behavior of the system." This view leaves much discretion to the researcher in delimiting the system and the environment: an organization can be considered to be the environment of its subsystems or an object in a larger social environment. An institutional analysis of policy might well deal with the same organization from both perspectives in a single study.

However, environment as explained above contains a conceptual difficulty in that it implies that it should (or must) be possible to draw a line between the system and its environment, or at least to identify (1) environment-induced changes in the system, and (2) system-induced changes in the environment. This is problematic because, while it is apparent that a change in a social environment will influence a system, it is not as apparent when and how a social system can or will induce permanent changes in its environment. For example, changes in laws, which can be considered part of the environment of policy making organizations, can affect an organization and its policy outputs rather quickly and directly. However, since a policy making organization must stay within the bounds imposed both by law and by the system of social beliefs which supports the policy process, it is less readily apparent how (or if) that organization can induce more than superficial changes in the social environment.

This is because social systems are exposed and react to environments whose characteristics are thoroughly ingrained in the system. The term "ingrained" conveys a sense of the difficulty of separating a social system from its environment. In doing so, it also allows us to account for the seemingly more profound influence of the environment on the system, and for the slowly occurring and slowly manifested changes which the system does induce in the social environment.

IV. AN INSTITUTIONAL APPROACH TO THE STUDY OF BROADCAST REGULATION

The institutional framework for the study of broadcast regulation we propose is based on one suggested by Redford (1969), and involves the identification and analysis of the following components of a regulatory system: (A) environment;

(B) structure; (C) interactions; and (D) policy. (Mahan (1982) provides an in depth case study of the broadcast regulatory process using this approach.)

A. The Environment of Regulation

Hall and Fagen (1968, p. 86) state that "to specify completely an environment one needs to know all the factors that affect or are affected by a system." Clearly this is no easy task, if indeed it is possible at all with regard to a social system. When considering broadcast regulation, however, we can begin to delineate the environment of the regulatory process when we answer the question: What factors external to the regulatory agency shape or predetermine the procedures, policies, and regulations resulting from the process?

Thus, technology imposes some requirements on industry organization and operation, as do laws passed in response to social factors related to broadcasting. Beyond that, the organization of the broadcast industry in one society reflects the particular economic arrangements usually prevalent in that society. Historical and cultural factors, furthermore, provide a set of belief patterns which influence the perspectives and options of actors in the regulatory arena and, therefore, the regulations which are eventually implemeted. Environment, therefore, consists of the technical, legal, historical, and cultural bases for the provision of broadcast services, the organization of those services, and their regulation by government. The research reviewed previously has tended to overlook or minimize the impact of these factors in explaining the broadcast regulatory process.

1. Beliefs About Regulation

The concept of the public interest is foremost among the beliefs which underlie all regulatory activity in the United States, whether this be the creation of a new agency by Congress or the formulation of regulations within an agency. There is, however, no operational definition of the public interest which is applicable in all cases. Mitnick (1980) discusses the development of the public interest concept in the United States and presents a typology of public interest concepts which have been used to justify regulation and the behavior of regulatory agencies. He makes it absolutely clear that there is no single operational concept of the public interest in the United States and that a view of the public interest which places broad social values and benefits above the interests of individual private businessmen, for example, is merely one of the various public interest concepts used from time to time to justify regulatory action.

Nevertheless, despite considerable evidence that regulation has been instituted at the request of business interests pursuing their own interests (Mitnick, 1980; Wilson, 1980), it is the presumed benefits of regulation, which are supposed to accrue to the general public from the activities of regulated businesses, which continue to justify this type of intervention by the government in the economy. Thus, for example, the *Radio Act of 1927* justified government intervention in private broadcasting operations on the basis of the "public interest, convenience, or necessity,'' even though the law was drafted and passed in response to demands from commercial broadcasters, who saw it as the only way to reduce the chaos on the overcrowded radio spectrum. What the *Radio Act* did by justifying regulation of the radio industry in the name of the public interest was, in effect, to identify the interests of the industry with those of the public at large and, thus, the protection of radio business interests with the protection of radio audiences. From the outset, then, a tension has existed between the interests of business and those of the public, a tension which makes almost any FCC action subject to criticism from segments of the public (which includes businessmen) who see their interests being slighted or injured.

A second major belief which has affected the operation of regulatory commissions in the United States is that "regulation should be fair and this requires judicial process" (Redford, 1969, p. 33; Woll, 1977). Thus, the laws under which regulatory agencies have been created usually grant broad powers to those agencies and "establish processes for on-going legal adjustments rather than ordain legal outcomes . . . ."(Schmidt, 1978, p. 196). It is questionable, then, to speak of the regulatory process in the United States as a rational policy making activity, since the case-by-case approach to regulation implicit in the belief in the necessity and efficacy of judicial process (an approach which relies heavily on the idea of precedent and the flexibility implicit in that concept) virtually precludes the conscious formulation *and* implementation of overarching or long range policies. Regulation thus becomes a "pragmatic process of searching for the appropriate answer in each particular case with only vaguely defined policy guides" (Redford, 1969, p. 37).

2. The Goals of Broadcast Regulation

It was not the commercial nature of broadcasting or questions of program content, but the limitations of the radio spectrum, which provided the initial rationale for government regulation of broadcasting. Because of the physical nature of the electromagnetic spectrum, only one station can broadcast over a given frequency at a given time in a given location. Thus, the conventional reasoning in the United States is that government regulation must be concerned at the very least with the technical aspects of broadcast operations.

The objective of technical regulation is to protect the rights and interests of competing broadcasters by managing spectrum allocation and the technical aspects of broadcasting which impinge upon signal quality. The right of the audience to good radio reception has been acknowledged in this way since the early days of broadcast regulation, but the primary concern in formulating regulations seems to have been the well-being of broadcasters (Friendly, 1962; Le Duc, 1972; U.S. Federal Radio Commission, 1928).

The *Communications Act of 1934* and programming-related FCC regulations also reveal regulatory goals, beyond that of spectrum management, which have been summarized by Levin (1980). These are (1) diversity of ideas, standards, and values in program content; (2) localism, or programming responsive to local needs, tastes, and interests which is supplied and originated as much as possible by local stations; (3) wide geographic availability of service which is also fairly and efficiently distributed; and (4) competition among stations as the means to promote diversity in programming.

Despite the apparent coherence of these goals and their consistency with basic U.S. economic philosophy, they did (and do) not taken into account the economics of broadcasting nor the development of technologies which compete with broadcasting to provide information and entertainment to the public. Furthermore, the experience of almost 50 years has revealed that these goals are inherently contradictory, that insisting on local ownership of stations leads neither to diversity in programming nor to an efficient distribution of stations.

In sum, government regulation of commercial broadcasting in the United States derives its legitimacy from the physical limitations of the radio spectrum and the ideal of the primacy of the public interest. This is not as straightforward as it might seem, however, since the public interest standard is at best vague, permitting no clear determination of when or if the public interest differs from the interests of private broadcasters, who are, after all, also part of the public.

Thus, in the United States, political and economic traditions which limit the legitimate role of the government in the economy combine with a judicial tradition that insists upon a case-by-case approach to the regulation of economic interests. Together they create a regulatory environment in which the public interest tends to become identified with the interests of private businessmen. The *Communications Act of 1934* embodies the conflicts between the public and private interests and extends them to the formal goals of broadcast regulation.

B. The Structure of the Regulatory Arena

In specifying the structure of the regulatory arena, we are drawing something analogous to a formal organization chart. Therefore, to determine structure, we ask: Who is formally involved in the regulatory process and in what capacity? The emphasis on formal involvement is important. Some actors who might not actually play a prominent role in the regulatory process could be included because of formal procedural requirements of the regulatory system. Others might not appear in the chart because their involvement might not be formally or legally recognized. (This was the case of the "public" in licence renewal proceedings before the Circuit Court granted it standing.)

The U.S. commercial broadcast regulatory arena consists of public and private actors. The public or federal actors include the FCC, Congress, agencies of the executive branch (including the President), and the courts, with Congress and the FCC being the primary communications policy making bodies. Of these, the first three are active in all phases of the regulatory process. The courts, on the other hand, become involved only when formal regulatory decisions have been challenged. Private sector participants include the broadcast industry and the public, which is usually represented by citizens' groups. Similarly, the broadcast industry is often represented by organized groups, the largest and most powerful of which is the National Association of Broadcasters.

The formal structure of the regulatory arena, as well as the philosophical underpinnings of regulation in the United States, gives Congress, the executive branch, and the broadcast industry the most direct access to decisionmaking at the FCC. Congress and the executive branch are able to affect regulatory decisionmaking in a number of formal ways, for example, through the appointment and appropriations processes. The broadcast industry becomes involved partly as a result of its role as an FCC information source and partly because broadcasters are subject to the authority of the FCC. The formal involvement of the broadcast audience (also known as the public) in the regulatory process is more recent than that of federal actors and the broadcast industry. Because of this, and because citizens' groups tend to be less broadly based and to lack the economic resources of the broadcast industry, public participation in regulatory decisionmaking at the FCC or through Congress appears more limited.

C. Interactions in the Regulatory Arena

The formal structure of a regulatory or policy arena might not necessarily reveal all the actors who are involved in the regulatory process, nor their relative strengths as power contenders. Formal structure does not necessarily do this because "a social system is a structuring of events or happenings rather than of physical parts and it therefore has no structure apart from its functioning" (Katz and Kahn, p. 31). It is, therefore, important to study the interactions which occur during the formulation, implementation, and enforcement of regulations. When we examine interactions among regulatory actors, we are asking: Who interacts with whom? Through what channels? At what times? How often? Do these interactions reveal any particularly strong or sensitive relationships which influence the regulatory process? Answers to these questions can clarify the structure of the regulatory arena and indicate which groups and/or individuals will tend to prevail in the regulatory process.

The U.S. regulatory system is quite open, with the result that virtually any party at interest can approach the FCC and Congress in some manner at will. Analysis of interactions in the U.S. broadcast regulatory arena, therefore, does not reveal any actors unaccounted for by the formal structure of the arena. This does not mean, however, that all interactions have the same purpose or impact.

Interactions between public and private regulatory actors occur in a number of contexts: formal filings with the FCC; lobbying by broadcasters and citizens (both as groups or individuals) before the Commission and Congress; participation in commissioner appointment proceedings; or public relations gatherings, such as meetings of broadcasting or citizens' organizations which are attended by

FCC staff or Congressmen. Much of the interaction between public and private regulatory actors is informal—that is, occurring outside of the formal procedures specified in the *Administrative Procedure Act* (Woll, 1977). It occasionally happens that such informal interactions, particularly those between broadcasters and FCC officials, result in on-the-spot policy formulation (Carey, 1967; Cole and Oettinger, 1978).

Despite the fact that many different actors representing many different interests (both public and private) are involved in the broadcast regulatory process, it appears that the broadcast industry and Congress are the strongest participants, at least from the perspective of being able to influence the FCC. This is primarily because of the number of points at which direct and indirect pressures can be exerted on the Commission, and because the formal procedures of the regulatory process are so expensive and time consuming as to make it difficult for many citizens' groups to sustain their participation.

Analysis of interactions among regulatory actors thus confirms the distribution of power and influence which the formal structure of the regulatory arena implies. The broadcast industry, the FCC, and Congress dominate the process, but they are not always united in their stands. The broadcast industry, from many perspectives, is the most active participant in the regulatory process. Its interactions with the FCC and Congress occur frequently and under a variety of circumstances, and ultimately reveal a reciprocity of demands and interests.

It becomes apparent that the broadcast regulatory process is above all an intermingling of public and private initiatives and influences which tends to perpetuate the dominance of the broadcast industry as a regulatory actor, but not at the expense of Congressional access to the media. The FCC begins with a legislative mandate which is unclear as to the distinction between public and private interests. It operates in an environment in which on-going formal and informal interactions with other regulatory actors serve further to blur the distinctions between public and private, both in terms of the interests to be served and the actions to be taken.

D. Regulatory Policy

An examination of policy reveals the rules governing the day-to-day operations of the broadcast industry and, perhaps more importantly, the beneficiaries of the outcomes of regulatory interactions. Policy, however, can be seen from two perspectives: explicit policy as stated in laws and regulations, and policy which emerges through analysis of the implementation and enforcement of regulations. The need to consider differences between explicit and implemented policy can be explained partially by the existence of administrative procedures which virtually preordain that implemented policy will diverge to some extent from explicit policy as stated in laws. Laws passed by Congress are often vague statements of social goals and values. It is left to administrative agencies (of which the FCC is one) to write the regulations which make the government policy, as expressed in legislation, operational.

Regulations which are to be implemented, therefore, often look quite different from policies expressed in laws. However, it would be misleading only to consider the differences between laws and formal regulations. The considerable amount of non-compliance with regulations in the United States requires that day-to-day industry practice be analyzed in order to ascertain just what policies seem to underlie the operations of the broadcast industry and its relationship with the government.

The conflicts in broadcast regulatory goals noted earlier lead one to expect that not all goals can or will be met. Nevertheless, the FCC has attempted, from time to time, to establish norms to guide the conduct of broadcasters and to permit its staff to evaluate that conduct. Technical rules and programming minimums which provide guidelines for both broadcasters and FCC staff in licensing cases, for example, would appear to be explicit enough, but pressure from broadcasters, particularly those with strong economic interests and political ties, have inhibited FCC attempts to enforce the regulations (Cole and Oettinger, 1978). The media ownership concentration issue provides another example of clearly delineated policies which are unevenly applied (Singleton, 1979). The strength of the broadcast interests involved, no doubt, partially explains FCC behavior in this regard, but the Commission's recognition of the conflict between the goals of local ownership of broadcast facilities and program diversity is also a factor (Noll et al., 1973).

The cable TV case (Geller, 1981; Mosco, 1979) illustrates, not just the dilemma a legislative mandate to regulate broadcasting has posed for the Commission, but the fact that the objectives of regulation—both explicit ones which deal with service to the public and the implicit goal of protecting the regulated industry—have been established without much regard for existing or possible alternatives in regulatory procedures or for possible innovations in the regulated industry which might render current arrangements obsolete. The FCC's initial reaction to cable TV, which was to inhibit its growth (Mosco, 1979), can be seen in light of its legislative mandate to regulate broadcasting. Its more recent moves, which have the effect of promoting the interests of cable TV operators at the expense of a number of over-the-air broadcasters (Geller, 1981), reflect the ability of the FCC to impose conditions counter to the wishes of Congress and the broadcast industry. They also indicate that the economic balance in the electronic communications field is shifting and that, as a result, the balance in the regulatory arena is shifting as well.

E. The Institutional View of the Broadcast Regulatory Process

We see that FCC decisions emerge not only from actions within the Commission. There are influences and inputs from sources in the larger administrative and political environment of the FCC which also carry considerable weight. Within the sphere of government per se, the FCC must interact with, and often accommodate itself to, the demands of Congress, pressures from the executive branch, the judgement of the courts, and rules issued by other administrative agencies with overlapping jurisdiction. Outside of government, pressures are exerted by the broadcast and other regulated industries, as well as by citizens' groups, all of which might espouse different positions.

Formal channels of communication and procedures have been devised to facilitate the regulation of broadcasting by the FCC. Nevertheless, the scope of the interests involved in the regulatory process, not to mention the expense in terms of time and money of operating through the established channels, has resulted in the predominance of informal decisionmaking—something which is characteristic of the entire U.S. regulatory system (Woll, 1977).

That regulatory system, and therefore the broadcast regulatory system, is "one which combines . . . private and public activity in the supply of an economic service" (Redford, 1969, p. 25). A number of conflicts are inherent in this system. With regard to the regulation of commercial broadcasting, the most striking are (1) the juxtaposition of the belief in private ownership of broadcast stations with the stated public ownership of the airwaves; (2) the implicit conflict between the rights and responsibilities of private broadcasters to conduct business in their own interests, and the idea that broadcasting should serve the public interest; and (3) the existence of a regulatory agency charged with policy making in a system whose judicial and political underpinnings seem to preclude long term policy formulation and implementation.

These conflicts are not unique to broadcast regulation, but are also evident in other spheres of regulated economic activity. The U.S. regulatory system is designed to place an agency like the FCC apart from and largely above the other actors in the regulatory process, particularly those with explicitly political roles. Therefore, the FCC's formal position in the federal establishment would appear to assure its capacity for independent action. However, the process by which commissioners are selected, the reliance of the commissioners and other FCC staff members on the broadcast industry for technical information and expertise, and the nature of the interactions among all active participants in the process serve to bring the FCC into the regulatory arena to find its footing among the other contending parties.

What lies at the heart of the question of the meaning of FCC regulations, of the role and position of the Commission, and, indeed, of the regulatory process itself is the conflict between public and private interests. On the one hand, there is a semantic problem—the idea that the "public" interest has to do with people in general and is, therefore, of a higher order than the supposedly "private" interests of broadcasters, which are usually reduced to a matter of profit or loss.

On the other hand, the broadcast industry, relations between that industry, competing communications industries, and citizens' groups, broadcast regulatory goals, and the regulatory process itself all embody the ideal of competition—a key element of U.S. economic culture. In doing so, they under-line another aspect of U.S. culture—the belief that the public interest is served when private interests are allowed to compete. The public interest, thus, is often conceptualized as what results from the resolution of conflict among competing private interests. Note that this in itself does not necessitate that what results be "fair" or equally beneficial to all members of society, or even agreed upon by all members of society. The result of competition among interests is presumed to be in the public interest because the process of competition is presumed to be in the public interest (McConnell, 1966). The concern for establishing processes which are intended to assure that the public interest can emerge, rather than preor-daining regulatory outcomes which embody an essentially static concept of the public interest, is reflected in the language of legislation and in the belief that adherence to judicial type procedures will result in fair regulation.

From this perspective, it is problematic to characterize broadcast regula-tions in terms of consensus. Challenges to regulations through the courts, through non-compliance, and through pressure on the FCC, Congress, or the ex-ecutive branch, coupled with the success of those challenges in altering the con-tent and enforcement of regulations, emphasize the lack of consensus inherent in those regulations. We can speak of regulations reflecting compromise among in-terests, but it is still important to recognize that regulations and policies generally embody the demands of the most powerful competitor, given the particular issue at the particular time they are formulated. Alterations, for what ever reason, in the substance of regulations are indicative of the flexibility of the regulatory sys-tem in accommodating a new "majority" or most powerful contender. Thus, what Redford (1952) has called a "moving balance" among actors in the regulatory area is perpetuated.

To a very large extent, then, the regulatory system mirrors the general po-litical system, which is relatively stable and predictable in spite of changes in the power and positions of actors. The moving balance which is established reflects the practical consideration that actors in the regulatory arena depend upon each other for cooperation, or for at least a minimum of outright defiance. At some point, each will need another or the others to win a position it seeks.

Thus, a judicial tradition which promotes case-by-case regulation merges with both a political tradition which limits the legitimate power of government to direct the operations of businessmen, and an economic tradition which promotes competition among private interests as *the* means of determining and promoting the public interst. From this perspective, the broadcast regulatory system—even if it is, as Krasnow and Longley (1978, p. 92) contend, deficient—is consistent with the social, economic, and political system within it exists.

One might still argue that this regulatory system has not led to the develop-ment of a commercial broadcasting system that operates in the public interest, however defined. This notwithstanding, however, to expect the regulatory sys-tem, as presently conceived and structured, consisently to promote anything other than the interests of the most powerful actor in the broadcast regulatory arena at any one time is probably asking more than the system can deliver.

V. SUMMARY

Thus far we have attempted to define and illustrate institutional analysis as a research approach which seeks to explain how and why social institutions function as they do. The relationship between institutional analysis and general systems theory was discussed in order to explain how institutional analysis has been developed and how it can be applied. We have argued that the systems perspective implicit in institutional analysis is pertinent to the study of the broadcast regulatory process because it allows the researcher to consider how actors in that process interact, how they are influenced by the broader social, political, and economic culture in which they exist, and, finally, how policy, in terms of implemented outcomes, reflects and reinforces interrelationships among actors in the regulatory arena and in the broader political system.

The framework for studying broadcast regulation which was discussed enables the researcher to identify and analyze the dynamics of the regulatory process: that is, (A) the organization of the regulatory arena as revealed by the interactions among actors; (B) the process through which these interactions are transformed into formal regulations; (C) how these regulations might be further transformed through the implementation process, and (D) how these final regulatory outcomes are related to the broader social and political environment.

This approach to the study of the broadcast regulatory process generates a great deal of information which describes and accounts for arrangements, procedures, and outcomes. Understanding how a regulatory system is organized and operates is essential to the formulation of realistic demands on that system for policies and programs, whether they are aimed at industry control, protecting the rights of the audience, or settling international communications issues.

VI. REFERENCES

Allison, G. T. (1969). Conceptual models and the Cuban missile crisis. *American Political Science Review 63,* 689–718.

Bertalanffy, L. (1968). General systems theory—a critical review. *In* W. Buckley (Ed.), "Modern Systems Research for the Behavioral Scientist," pp. 11–30. Chicago, Illinois: Aldine.

Besen, S. M., and Krattenmaker, T. G. (1981). Regulating network television: Dubious premises and doubtful solutions. *Regulation* (May-June), 27–34.

Carey, W. L. (1967). "Politics and the Regulatory Agencies." New York: McGraw-Hill.

Cole, B., and Oettinger, M. (1978). "Reluctant Regulators." 2nd ed. Reading, Massachusetts: Addison-Wesley.

Easton, D. (1968). A systems analysis of political life. *In* W. Buckley (Ed.), "Modern Systems Research for the Behavioral Scientist," pp. 428–436. Chicago, Illinois: Aldine.

Friendley, H. J. (1962). "The Federal Administrative Agencies." Cambridge, Massachusetts: Harvard University Press.

Geller, H. (1981). Making cable TV pay? *Regulation* (May-June), 35–39; 58.

Hall, A. D., and Fagen, R. F. (1968). Definition of system. *In* W. Buckley (Ed.), "Modern Systems Research for the Behavioral Scientist," pp. 81–92. Chicago, Illinois: Aldine.

Holt, R. T., and Richardson, J. M. (1970). Competing paradigms in comparative politics. *In* R. T. Holt and J. E. Turner (Eds.), "The Methodology of Comparative Research," pp. 21–71. New York: Free Press.

Katz, D., and Kahn, R. L. (1966). "The Social Psychology of Organizations." New York: John Wiley & Sons.

Krasnow, E. G., and Longley, L. D. (1978). "The Politics of Broadcast Regulation," 2nd ed. New York: St. Martin's Press.

Kuhn, T. S. (1970). "The Structure of Scientific Revolutions," 2nd ed. Chicago, Illinois: University of Chicago Press.

Landis, J. M. (1960). "Report on Regulatory Agencies to the President Elect." Washington, D.C.: Government Printing Office.

Le Duc, D. R. (1972). The cable question: Evolution or revolution in electronic mass communications. *Annals of the Academy of Political and Social Science 400*, 127–139.

Levin, H. J. (1971). "The Invisible Resource: Use and Regulation of the Radio Spectrum." Baltimore, Maryland: Johns Hopkins University Press.

Levin, H. J. (1980). "Fact and Fancy in Television Regulation." New York: Russell Sage.

Mahan, M. E. (1982). "Commercial Broadcast Regulation: Structures and Processes in Mexico and the United States." Unpublished dissertation, University of Texas at Austin.

McConnell, G. (1966). "Private Power and American Democracy." New York: Vintage.

Mitnick, B. M. (1980). "The Political Economy of Regulation." New York: Columbia University Press.

Moore, B. C., Jr. (1973). The FCC: Competition and communications. +iIn M. J. Green (Ed.), "The Monopoly Makers: Ralph Nader's Study Group Report on Regulation and Competition," pp. 35–73. New York: Grossman Publishers.

Mosco, V. (1979). "Broadcasting in the United States: Innovative Challenge and Organizational Control." Norwood, New Jersey: Ablex.

Noll, R. G., Peck, M. J., and McGowan, J. J. (1973). "Economic Aspects of Television Regulation." Washington, D.C.: Brookings Institution.

Owen, B. M. (1973). A view from the president's office of telecommunications policy. *In* R. E. Park (Ed.), "The Role of Analysis in Regulatory Decisionmaking: The Case of Cable Television," pp. 3–14. Lexington, Massachusetts: Lexington Books.

Park, R. E. (1973). "The Role of Analysis in Regulatory Decisionmaking: The Case of Cable Television." Lexington, Massachusetts: Lexington Books.

Redford, E. S. (1952). "Administrative of National Economic Control." New York: Macmillan.

Redford, E. S. (1969). "The Regulatory Process," Austin, Texas: University of Texas Press.

Robinson, G. O. (1978). The Federal Communications Commission. *In* G. O. Robinson (Ed.), "Communications for Tomorrow," pp. 353–400. New York: Praeger.

Schmidt, B. (1978). Pluralistic programming and regulatory policy. *In* G. O. Robinson (Ed.), "Communications for Tomorrow," pp. 191–228. New York: Praeger.

Schulman, H. J. (1979). Is structural and procedural change a better answer for consumers than the "reform" of abolishing the FCC? *In* T. R. Haight (Ed.), "Telecommunications Policy and the Citizen," pp. 65–94. New York: Praeger.

Singleton, L. A. (1979). "An Analysis of Television Station Multiple Ownership As an Example of the Passing of the Dominant Paradigm in Commercial Broadcast Regulation." Unpublished dissertation, University of Texas at Austin.

U.S. Federal Radio Commission. (1928). "Statement Made by the Commission on August 23, 1928, Relative to Public Interest, Convenience, or Necessity." Reprinted in F. J. Kahn. (1978). "Documents of American Broadcasting," 3rd ed. New York: Appleton-Century-Crofts.

Webbink, D. W. (1973). A view from the Federal Communications Commission. *In* R. E. Park (Ed.), "The Role of Analysis in Regulatory Decisionmaking: The Case of Cable Television," pp. 35–41. Lexington, Massachusetts: Lexington Books.

Wilson, J. Q. (Ed.) (1980). "The Politics of Regulation." New York: Basic Books.

Woll, P. (1977). "American Bureaucracy," 2nd ed. New York: W. W. Norton & Co.

2 Information and Communication Policy Research in the United States: The Researcher as Advocate, Facilitator, and Staff Member

Thomas H. Martin
School of Information Studies
Syracuse University
Syracuse, New York 13210

I. INTRODUCTION

Policy research is a relatively new interest for information scientists and communication researchers. Policymakers are often unaware that research can or has played a role in policy formulation, while academics often scoff at the policy researchers as being opportunistic or doing work which does not contribute to the advancement of the field. Researchers vacillate from studying the policymaking process to actively attempting to enter research results into policy arenas. There is a great amount of confusion, misunderstanding, and wasted effort. The focus of this review will be a commentary on the efforts of researchers who have successfully entered into the information/communication policymaking process from the vantage point of a sympathetic observer. It is the contention of this chapter that research has a role to play in national policy formulation, and that information and communication scientists have much to learn from the contributions by their colleagues.

The review is organized around a model of the policy process. The model suggests that (1) policymakers supported by (2) staff find themselves surrounded by (3) facilitators representing (4) interest groups. The staff and facilitators work together to understand the problem area and to negotiate a compromise policy. The researcher can take and has taken on most of these roles and has had various levels of success in each. The review starts out with a discussion of research on policy research impacts in general, distinguishes it from communication/ information policy research, then focuses on advocacy and demonstration research, then shifts to staff research, then to facilitating research, provides examples of where the model works and does not work, and then sums up by suggesting what policy research has to offer the information and communication sciences. The experiences from both areas are brought together in the chapter not just because the author's and editors' interests are broad, but more importantly because information and communication technologies are converging, and policy research acts as one of the bridges connecting the fields.

The review does not do what is often expected in a policy chapter: that is, to lay out the substance or new changes in policy. Many other authors have done this recently. The U. S. National Telecommunications and Information Administration (1981) has compiled six reviews of information policy issues under the supervision of Jane Yurow. The reviews focus on dissemination of information, access to information, information privacy, information market economics, property rights or subsidies as creation incentives, and information management. Communication policies have been dealt with in Robinson (1978), where issues of industry structures, new electronic media, and policymaking institutions are described. Zimmerman and Brimmer (1981) and Brimmer (1982), in two *Annual Review of Information Science and Technology* chapters, describe the interest groups, issues, and policy activities which are involved in the data communication/AT&T reorganization arena. McDonald (1982) covers policymaking related to governmental/private sector competition in information dissemination. Henry (1980), in a five volume series of source documents, describes the evolution of the copyright act. The U.S. Office of Technology Assessment (1981) is in the process of issuing a series of studies on the impact of national computerized information systems.

The chapter does not cry out either for new policy or more research. The classic plea for a coherent policy is the *National Information Policy* report issued by the U.S. Domestic Council Committee on the Right of Privacy (1976). Currently, Congressman Glenn English of the House Committee on Government Operations is seeking to reorganize policymaking related to U.S. international information policy activities. The intent of the bill (HR 1957) (U.S. Congress, 1981b) is to help the United States present an organized and unified front in negotiations abroad. Congressman George Brown in a different bill (HR 3137) (U.S. Congress, 1981a) has proposed setting up a national information policy research institute. There is no question but that there is a need for more coherent information/communication policy, and that research is needed to guarantee that the policy makes sense. It is clear, however, that, currently, policymaking attention is focused on budget reductions, economic recovery, and military preparedness. The National Telecommunications and Information Administration has been significantly cut back. The Reagan administration is the first in four administrations to have no one on the White House staff who is responsible for information and communication policy questions. Research funding is being cut back significantly, and a great many former policy researchers have taken jobs as consultants to industry or as corporate researchers. In discussions with policy researchers, it has become clear that a decade of intense activity is over, and that a new generation of researchers, most likely working from within academia or the private sector, will have to renew the campaign to inform policymakers.

II. RESEARCH ON POLICY RESEARCH IMPACTS

Given federal funding of researchers during the 1960s and 1970s to carry out policy-relevant research, there have been attempts by some individuals to assess the success of this activity. In one of six volumes (National Research Council. Study Project on Social Research and Development, 1978-1979), Sundquist (1978) develops a model of the chain through which social science information passes. The researcher typically operates in an academic setting where constraints of tenure, publishing, and teaching influence projects. When results have policy implications, established and politically visible academics promote the results and interpret them to their friends in government. The people in government most attuned to the research facilitators tend to be former students or staff members who have a special interest in new ideas. They know particular policymakers and the constraints within which the policymakers work, and so can broker research in a form and at a time that fits the biases of the policymakers. Sundquist points out that, traditionally, the research broker is the least understood member of the chain and the most likely not to exist when he is needed.

One of the concerns of the evaluators of policy research impact is what factors make research results interesting to policymakers and so increase the likelihood that information will pass through the chain. Weiss and Bucuvalas (1977) describe a survey they carried out of mental health policymakers regarding features they felt were important in research they utilized. The features assessed were (1) relevance of the research to a policy issue, (2) extent to which the topic or study fit the decisionmaker's interests, (3) the basis of trust established between researcher and policymaker, (4) quality of the research, (5) conformity of results to expectations, (6) action implications, and (7) extent to which the status quo was challenged. Upon factor analyzing survey results, it became clear that the quality of the research was quite important for mobilizing support and changing ways of thinking. A surprising result was that studies challenging the status quo appeared to be very highly valued.

Caplan (1977), in another study, found that five factors needed to be present for research to have much impact on policymaking: (1) the decision-makers had to have an appreciation of scientific contributions, (2) the policymakers had a conscious sense of social direction and responsibility, (3) the policy issues had to be well-defined and of such a nature that a best solution required research inputs, (4) the research findings had to match intuition, be believably objective, and have feasible action implications, and (5) the policymakers and knowledge producers had to be linked via facilitators who could couple scientific inputs to policy goals. Weiss (1980) perhaps best summarizes the relationship as "knowledge creep," with the academic researchers establishing a framework for thinking that policymakers gradually fall into. The benefit of social science may be in clarifying the nature of the questions rather than in coming up with the solutions.

The researcher as viewed by these studies is essentially an outsider, perhaps assisted by a facilitator. However, many researchers have shifted over to the facilitator or even staff roles. What they do may not look like empirical or theory-based research. They may summarize the positions of parties, propose alternate policies, assess the potential impacts of policies, or attempt to educate policy-makers. Their contributions are often original and significant in terms of deriving policy which is grounded in theory and consensus of the interest groups. In this chapter these individuals are treated as still being researchers, and their impacts are also considered.

III. INFORMATION/COMMUNICATION POLICY CHARACTERISTICS

The information and communication policy arenas are somewhat unlike the social welfare policy arenas that Weiss studied. Typically, policymakers respond to crises. There are so many problems competing for their attention that they focus on new problems only when they are forced to. In addition, policymakers are used to well-organized interest groups pushing for slight changes in policy which will be of direct financial benefit for the interest group. Most of the social welfare issues of the 1970s met these criteria. The information and communication policy arena is not one characterized by crisis. The new technology industries are some of the fastest growing ones in the economy. The United States retains a competitive edge in international trade in these fields. There are few well-organized constituencies outraged by what is happening to them. Because of the convergence of the technologies, industries find themselves in new markets or confused as to what is in their best interest. For example, the telephone company finds itself in the computer industry battling publishers and cable television companies over whether or not the proposed unregulated subsidiary should be allowed to market teletex services. The public seems generally uninterested in the issues, and no one seems to know how to untangle them so that small incremental changes can be made which will have limited identifiable consequences.

Wedemeyer (1977) found these quite different types of policy issues when he attempted to identify trends in communication needs and rights for the state of Hawaii. One type of policy indicator he developed identified areas where there were strong disparities between needs and supplies. Persuasive one-way messages were an example where supply was far greater than the need, whereas access to governmental decision-making was needed far more than it was available. Projections of needs and supplies seemed to vary little over time. The other policy indicator he developed identified areas where changes in both supply and need were greatest over time. These areas tended to involve the new technologies. Supplies seemed to grow as fast as need and there seemed to be little feeling that everyone had a right to the technologies, so that these areas ranked very low using the first policy indicator. Wedemeyer's conclusion was that policymakers would monitor the rapid changes but not feel compelled to make new law.

The net result is that most policymakers shy away from the new technology issues. Responsibility devolves on a few farsighted individuals who have the breadth of understanding to see fundamental themes or emerging issues. In a real sense, these individuals act as educators of their colleagues, and are quite receptive to using research results if they make issues more comprehensible. One of the strategies that information and communication policy researchers have adopted is to try to identify these few policymakers who are willing to invest in learning and in educating their colleagues. The policymakers may be in Congress, in the executive branch, in international agencies, in regulatory agencies, in private business, in the judiciary, or in the media. Where the person is, or what the person's political persuasion is, is rarely important. What is important is that the person be willing to risk tackling issues which his or her colleagues and constituents do not yet understand. Using diffusion of innovation terms, the policymakers must be opinion leaders.

The stages of diffusion are also important in that responsiveness to research changes with time. Very often, researchers identify a problem long before policymakers are even aware of a need for change. The researchers feel that their work is falling on deaf ears. At other times, researchers are unaware that interest groups have formed and that policymakers are trying to get the groups to resolve their differences so that all parties can present a united front. The history of the copyright clearing center shows the influence of stages. When the concept of a clearinghouse was first introduced by the Committee to Investigate Copyright Problems Affecting Communication in Science and Education in 1966 (see Henry, 1980, Vol. 1), it was completely ignored. As revision of the copyright law dragged on over the years, the concept gradually was accepted by the publishers but not by librarians and educators. By the time that Congress established a commission to conduct research on new technological uses of copyrighted works, the educators received specific assurances that clearinghouses would not be considered. After the new copyright law was passed, the publishers set up a copyright clearinghouse on their own. One advantage that research has is that, once it is published, it remains accessible for many years. Even though the political or economic climate is not right at one time for the results, they may be resurrected at a later date.

IV. RESEARCHERS AS ADVOCATES

It is always important, in understanding the impact of policy research, to consider the role of the industries or bureaucracies involved. Through their everyday involvement or financial commitment, their influence far outweighs that of the researchers. From the policymaker's point of view, he or she is trying to make certain that all the interest groups who have a stake in the outcome are aware that a policy is being formulated, have articulated their interests, and have developed a negotiating position. One of the ways that the policymaker can insure this is to hold hearings where the interested parties are asked to come and state their views. Often the policymaker will circulate a draft of a proposed policy so that comments will be focused on the changes under consideration. Many times researchers have been viewed as one of the interested parties. Particularly when researchers take on the role of representatives of public attitudes, they tend to be cast as an interested party. For example, researchers concerned about violence on television or about the effects of advertising on children's programming have been viewed by policymakers as advocates.

The advocacy role tends not to work for researchers. Researchers are too few in number, have not been chosen as representatives of the public, are uncomfortable with making one-sided assertions, and often do not understand the need for negotiations. They often view their research as speaking for itself and unbiased. The other interest groups attempt to discredit the research by pointing out bias. Researchers tend to become outraged, and either withdraw or refuse to compromise. When the parties refuse to compromise, policymaking cannot proceed. Both the attempt to limit violence on television and advertising on children's programming (see Adler, 1980) have been stymied because the parties refused to negotiate.

One way that researchers have acted as interest groups has been through their demonstration projects. It may be possible in the early stages of a technology's development to make sure that it addresses some societal need. For example, researchers were concerned that communication satellites were not being used for low-cost delivery of public services to small isolated communities. Through federal funding, the ATS-F satellite was used to conduct a number of experiments in the delivery of a variety of social services. Based on the research results, some researchers have attempted to influence policymaking regarding satellites (see Parker, 1978).

During the 1970s, a large number of these demonstration projects were funded, and the proceedings of a recent NATO institute attempt to extract the essence of the experience (see Elton et al., 1978). When successful, the policy implications of these experiments can be significant, for they show where markets exist which otherwise might not be tapped.

A prime example is the field experiment conducted in Reading, Pennsylvania, where elderly citizens were able to use interactive cable television for community building. The National Science Foundation funded the project to allow these citizens in the community to develop interactive programming. Three sites were chosen, where the elderly congregated. Black and white camera facilities were installed. Also, facilities were placed in the city hall, the Social Security office, the county court house, and other community facilities. Not only could people carry on two-way dialogs from these sites, but viewers at home could get on the telephone and have their questions or comments patched into the broadcast. Not all programming had to be live, for videotapes of instructional information or prerecorded interviews could be inserted. This non-commercial, two-way, citizen-controlled programming captured the attention of the elderly, and, when the experiment was over, the community continued it without federal funding. (See Moss (1978) and Burns (1978) for more information.)

The Electronic Information Exchange System (see Hiltz and Turoff, 1979) is another example of a prototype system which has survived after funding has expired. Participants in a conference log onto the computer system and read messages submitted by others, send and receive private messages, and contribute their own comments. Like many forms of computer use, EIES is addictive and attracts a following who then counsel new users as they acquire experience. Participants are not deterred by lack of face-to-face contact, provided that there is a real need to communicate.

What is interesting about the Reading and the EIES experiences is that they involve community building. Most for-profit experiments take existing one-to-one or one-to-many markets and reduce the costs of messages. Community building creates a new market for few-to-few messages. A study by Dordick et al. (1981) suggests that the major potential benefit to society of the new information networks is that they create new markets. The cost of exchange are reduced, geographically dispersed groups can coalesce, and new information products can be created, promoted, and distributed.

There has been much debate over whether or not the government should have funded prototype studies like the remote community satellite services, two-way cable, or conferencing services. If such prototypes are successful, they are taken over or copied by private industry, and the government is accused of subsidizing business. If government does not turn them over to industry, government is accused of competing unfairly with private enterprise. If neither government nor industry continues the prototype, the accusation is either that there was no dissemination strategy or that government is wasting its money on liberal daydreams which do not make financial sense. Often the researchers get very involved in the prototype and are accused of selling the system or covering up its faults. If the researchers work at arm's length from the developers, then the developers accuse the researchers of being Luddites who would rather have the prototype fail for the sake of methodological purity than have the prototype changed in midstream so flaws can be corrected. If the researchers work closely with the designers, the researchers are accused of not getting results that indicate how design can be improved, and whatever results they do get are too equivocal or come too late. Shinn (1978) provides an excellent analysis of the utility of social experimentation in policy research. He suggests that it tends to be very expensive, gets mixed up with politics, takes a long time, is subject to many confounding external events which introduce noise into the results, raises ethical questions about manipulating people, often provides inconclusive results, tends to have little impact on policy making, and often suffers from poorly thought-out theory. He suggests that social experimentation not be used unless laboratory results show clearly that the theory behind the experiment is sound, and then used only when the issues are of long run importance to policymakers. For whatever reason, very little publicly funded prototype research is underway. Private industry continues to introduce new products and services, and is becoming more systematic about gathering evaluative data, but this data is very much proprietary.

V. RESEARCHERS AS STAFF MEMBERS

Researchers have been far more successful when they have avoided being typecast as interested parties or promotors. Usually this has happened when they have acted as staff for policymakers. Then ''research'' involves accumulating the opinions of the interest groups and finding the underlying dimensions. Borchardt (1975), from many years' experience as a Senate Committee staff member, felt that the essential job of the staff member was to find a way to represent the issue so that the parties would agree upon a small number of distinct dimensions which could then set the framework for bargaining. This corresponds very closely to Mitroff and Betz's (1972) dialectic decisionmaking model. There is no doubt but that the dimensions the interested parties feel are important often will not be theoretically interesting, or the interest groups may be unimpressed with the dimensions that are extremely important to researchers. In particular, when parties for some reason do not want new policy made, they may refuse to even cooperate in characterizing the problem. Occasionally, however, researchers will, through working with the interested parties, gain a far more accurate and fundamental understanding of policy issues which can contribute to other research in their discipline.

A. Privacy

Consider the case of privacy research. Westin and Baker (1972) carried out a major study for the National Academy of Sciences of computerized information systems, to assess how systems were evolving and how the evolution affected individual rights. The researchers gathered data from 55 managers of large information systems and found that information systems were not radically changing from manual practices but were automating the same types of records and carrying along the same types of sharing practices as existed before. The researchers felt that automation was still in a very early stage and that practices which both guaranteed individual liberties and also made good management sense could be introduced. The major policy recommendations were that (1) citizens have a right to see and contest their own records, (2) limitations be placed on the sharing by agencies of data, and (3) limitations be placed on the types of data that can be gathered.

The government responded by setting up an advisory committee to recommend privacy policy, and it came up with a number of "fair information practices," such as (1) there should be no secret databases, (2) individuals should be able to find out what records exist about them and how they are being used, (3) uses of information should be limited to those providers expressly consent to, (4) individuals should be able to challenge and correct inaccurate information, and (5) organizations should clearly identify who is responsible for their files (see U.S. Department of Health, Education, and Welfare, 1973). A number of the members of the advisory committee, including Willis Ware of the Rand Corporation, were researchers and were quite familiar with the Westin study. Congress took the recommendations of the advisory committee and incorporated them into the Privacy Act of 1974.

As part of the Privacy Act, a Privacy Protection Study Commission was set up to look further into the need for privacy protection. Ware was one of the Co-directors and he included a number of privacy researchers on the staff. The commissioners came from government, business, and academia. Through intensive hearings and analyses, the commission shifted from privacy to information management policy. In the U.S. Privacy Protection Study Commission's (1977) final report, they make clear that the fundamental nature of the problem is that advances in computer and telecommunication technology favor the large organization and its records over the individual and his or her personal rights. The need is for practices which restore the limits individuals in face-to-face transactions can impose on what they divulge and how it is used. The Commission broke the issues into many specific subissues and proposed specific policies for each of the areas. Many of the proposals have been enacted into law because they represented compromises interest groups would support. Legislators have commented that the work of the Commission is some of the most effective policy work researchers have done.

Some researchers feel the commission approach has given too much away. Marchand (1979) points out that current U.S. privacy relies too much on voluntary compliance with practices by business, relies too much on individuals for enforcement of their rights, and varies too much from state to state. In areas like computerized criminal records, Marchand (1980) argues that the affected individuals cannot effectively speak out or organize, and that government ceases to be the mediator and becomes the advocate of automated records. Researchers, along with civil liberties groups and the press, must act as advocates of the public interest and not compromise it away. Hoffman (1980) brought most of the privacy researchers together to try to come up with a research agenda for the next decade, and found a tension between people like Ware, who were committed to moderating the influence of our irreversible commitment to computers, and people like Rule (Rule et al., 1980), who argued that we should oppose computerization and move toward a more decentralized society.

B. Cable Television

Another instance where researchers have been effective as staff is the case of cable television. In the 1970s researchers became advocates of cable television (see Baer, 1973). The reason for this advocacy was two-fold. Cable television was going to permit two-way interaction, thereby allowing people to seek information they wanted, and, second, cable television through a plethora of channels would allow a greater amount of diversity. Advocacy of cable was pleasing to cable television owners but backfired in the sense that cable television was forced to support public access channels and provide for two-way services without proof of any cost/benefit. Research began to play a significant role as economic models began to be developed for television (see Noll et al., 1973; Owen et al., 1974). Particular studies were done using models to assess the economic impact of cable on broadcasters (Park, 1972). The issue shifted from whether or not people would use cable in a manner different from television to whether or not cable would have an economic impact on broadcasters. Since this was the dimension of greatest interest to broadcasters and cablecasters, the research became central to the policy debate. Park's (1973) analysis of the ways in which the different interest groups distorted the research for their own ends is very interesting. It is important to note that, unlike much economic research, the models were easy to understand and the implications of the models were made clear.

As the economists became familiar with the Federal Communications Commission (FCC) through cable regulation and through attempts to figure out the costs and accounts of telephone companies, the FCC became aware of how little economic expertise it had on its staff. It not only added economists to its staff, but it supported efforts to turn the Office of Telecommunications Policy (now the National Telecommunications and Information Agency (NTIA)) into a research and planning resource for the Commission. The record of both the FCC's second computer inquiry and the Congressional attempts to rewrite the Communications Act of 1934 are characterized by intense involvement by economists trying to determine where competition exists in aspects of the telephone market, where public good economics apply or do not apply, and to what extent arms'-length subsidiary proposals in fact ensure that cross-subsidization will be minimized. Leland Johnson, a Rand economist who shifted from cable television economics to telephone economics, took a leave to absence from Rand to work with the NTIA and has helped shape the framework for discussions of regulatory reform for the telephone industry. The issues discussed by the FCC or by Congress make sense economically and parallel his analysis of the issues (Johnson, 1978).

C. Copyright

The parallel from information policy analysis involves the long history of copyright legislation. The new industries which were emerging were what Henry (1975) called "neo-publishing", i.e., photoduplication or computerization. In the early stages of copyright revision efforts, researchers were funded to conduct studies establishing a basis in fact for copying practices. When researchers attempted to go beyond offering fact and proposed new policies, they were treated as meddlers who did not have an interest to represent. For a period of about six years, negotiations primarily involved the interest groups. Eventually, the parties and Congress agreed that issues involving the new technologies should be separated out so that policymakers could act on those issues where interests were clear-cut without affecting the new technologies. The Commission on New Technological Uses of Copyrighted Words (CONTU) was set up by Congress to consider them. Research was contracted for by the Commission, and researchers helped the staff better understand how the new technologies differed from the old ones. In particular, a study by Braunstein et al. (1977) is cited by Ploman and Hamilton (1980) as being influential in decisions made by CONTU as to the applicability of copyright for computer programs. In the CONTU, policymaking researchers had access without being viewed as interest groups.

VI. RESEARCHERS AS FACILITATORS

There are other effective roles for the researcher, but roles which do not involve working in support of a policymaking staff. One of the roles involves legitimating or publicizing trends. Over many years, Oettinger and his colleagues at Harvard have attempted to lay a foundation of data showing that computer and communication technology are converging in such a way that institutional regulation no longer is appropriate. They have worked closely with policymakers in business and government and circulate their reports among their funders for reactions before publishing them. While this may ensure blandness, it often increases the likelihood of accuracy. An example of their work is *High and Low Politics: Information Resources for the 80's* (Oettinger et al., 1977). In it, they consider a number of information policy arenas where the functional needs or proposed systems of information technology users cut across the product or regulatory lines of traditional carriers and product suppliers. In each case, statemanship backed up by inquiry was needed to balance the interests of the diverse interest groups. An indication of the Harvard group's impact has been the spread of the term ''compunications,'' which they use to describe the convergence of the technologies. Another example has been the work of Porat (1977) in using national income accounts to demonstrate the emergence of an ''information economy.'' Porat, when he directed the communication program at the Aspen Institute, worked extensively with policymakers to make clear to them where changes in the economy required new policy efforts. Porat not only sought to educate the decisionmakers, but has attempted to educate the public via a television special. Other researchers, for example Ithiel Pool and George Gerbner, have worked extensively over many years to keep policymakers informed of the impacts of technologies like television and the telephone. Groups, like the Aspen Institute, have funded telecommunication policy conferences each year near Washington, where researchers and policymakers can interact (see Dordick, 1979). Machlup (1980) has begun a series of books attempting to capture the economic totality of the knowledge industry that he began in his classic *The Production and Distribution of Knowledge in the U.S.* (Machlup, 1962). These nondirective attempts at clarifying the nature of modern trends are quite productive in legitimizing public and policymaking interest in the information society. They have led policymakers like Nora and Minc (1980) of France or Masuda (1981) of Japan to focus the directions of government planning. They have led to further popularization, like Toffler's *Third Wave* (1980). Twenty years ago, very few people had any personal experience with computerized information systems. Today it is not surprising to find popular magazines and newspapers proclaiming the presence of the information or communication or computer age. The establishment of buzz words like ''information economy,'' ''post-industrial society,'' ''compunications,'' or ''telematics'' make it possible for policymakers to justify their interest in the subject to their constituents or followers.

VII. FROM CLARIFICATION TO POLICY

When the researcher as facilitator is most effective is when he or she is able to conceptualize a problem in a manner which shows both interest groups and policymaking staff researchers what needs doing. An excellent example of this is the emergence of information resource management in response to the growth of bureaucracy. The problem is expressed as an information overload, declines in productivity, or excessive governmental regulation. Porat's (1977) information economy study clarified the nature of the problem by highlighting the secondary information sector—the internal information bureaucracy of organizations—and by showing how large it has become. One reason the secondary sector has mushroomed is that there never has been a good way to measure its productivity. A Presidential commission, the Commission of Federal Paperwork Reduction, was set up to see how government could reduce the internal bureaucracy. Forrest Horton, as head of the staff of the Commission, was able to draw both on his extensive experience as a governmental comptroller and his academic training in resource management and economics. He was able to introduce current management science thinking about information productivity and resource management (see Horton, 1979, and U.S. Commission on Federal Paperwork, 1977) to the problem. As staff director, he not only was able to gather data, testimony, and ideas, but suggested a comprehensive information resource management policy for paperwork reduction. With the combined pressure from business and government, his comprehensive policy has been enacted into law and has the potential for dramatically restructuring government practices. The Paperwork Reduction Act requires government to start calculating how much its reporting requirements are costing data preparers. Individuals are identified who are responsible for managing information resources. Accounting techniques are to be set in place which make it more likely that the costs and benefits of information gathering, processing, use, and storage can be assessed. Perhaps a major drawback of the scheme is that it is such a major change—introducing state of the art management concepts throughout the largest bureaucracy in the world—that ignorance and inertia may neutralize it. If ignorance and inertia do not do the job, perhaps the sheer pressure from business and government to deregulate and cut back government may destroy it. The Paperwork Reduction Act is being used to eliminate regulations indescriminately, whereas Horton's philosophy was to develop a systematic rationale for regulation. Under normal policy research circumstances, there would be a large number of fellow researchers who would work to educate the implementors and to publicize misuse of the concepts. In Horton's case, much of the academic world had been caught by surprise, and is only slowly learning how fast the ideas are being put into practice. By the time a policy research constituency has been developed, it may not be possible to separate the information resource management concepts from their implementation history.

It is interesting to note that Porat's work may have received too much publicity too fast. Followup work by Rubin and Taylor (1981) and from a variety of OECD countries (Organization for Economic Cooperation and Development, 1980) suggests that the information sector may actually be getting smaller. The reduction seems to be due to the fact that information and communication technologies do not increase in cost as fast as other goods, so the relative percentage going to information industries is decreasing. King and Kraemer (1981) point out that even though hardware costs may be decreasing, the impact of automation appears to be increasing indirect costs in terms of maintenance, scarcity of experts, and inflexibility of procedures, so that information work becomes less productive. While the new information industries are exciting and visible, they are very small compared to the vast educational, financial, and managerial portions of the information sector. When looking at the international aspects of information exports, both Rubin and Taylor (1981) and Leeson (1981) find that trade in information goods and products is far smaller than anticipated. Heavy export of computer equipment or rights to patents and copyrights is insignificant compared to agricultural or military exports. Perhaps what this means is that national accounts are very imprecise tools to measure what is happening in the portion of the economy which is experiencing the most change. Entire economies change very slowly. If the essence of the information economy is the need to better manage information resources, then policy changes in government and industry may result in this large sector gradually becoming smaller.

VIII. THE U.S. RESEARCHER INTERNATIONALLY

The reason that imports and exports are causing great concern is that many countries no longer believe in the free flow of information between nations. The problem has taken two forms: (1) the feeling by third world countries that the free flow of information results in one-way export of U.S. entertainment and news coverage, and (2) a feeling by many countries that free flow of information results in sensitive national data flowing from them to the United States. The concern is that the United States, possessing powerful information and communication technologies is perpetuating a form of colonialism. The essence of the problem revolves around the role of nations and their control over national culture. Entertainment and news in the United States act as a mirror to the society. While the image is often biased or distorted, the image is usually designed by Americans, selected for Americans, or intended for audiences similar to Americans. Many people in developing countries do not see themselves in the media, or see only the stereotypes that Americans would like to see. Countries who guard their data or information industries express a concern that information abroad creates dependency and that the rights of database subjects may not be protected abroad the way they are at home.

Researchers have worked hard to help clarify the nature of the dispute and the factors which underlie it. Harms (1977) has collected opinions from scholars around the world regarding the nature of the right to communicate, and has tried to suggest the dimensions of cultural integrity which international policymaking should address (Harms, 1980). Katz and Wedell (1977) have traveled around the world documenting the nature of mass media entertainment. Nordenstreng and Schiller (1979) have collected a number of research articles which reveal the extent of ownership and influence exerted by Western multinational advertisers, market researchers, and program distributors. In a recent discussion between Pool and Schiller (1981), who are often considered to be philosophically quite distinct, there is a strong sense of agreement over the nature of the dilemma posed to other countries by American information and communications. This consensus is *not* shared by many of the large organizations which are involved in the international information trade. An attempt in UNESCO to convert inflamed rhetoric into a balanced policy position resulted in the now-famous MacBride report (International Commission for the Study of Communication Problems, 1980) and what is often referred to as the new world information order. The American press was outraged at the report. A series of articles in the *Journal of Communication* (Autumn, 1981) document how the report was treated in the press as compared to how the American representatives felt about the results of the negotiations.

Research regarding international policy issues is extremely difficult, for no international research community yet exists. The interest groups who negotiate policy are governments, and researchers are expected to work for their governments. An interesting example of researchers acting as national representatives occurred during the World Administrative Radio Conference (WARC) of 1979, as described by Robinson (1980). WARCs have historically been conducted by engineers, and there was great fear that the third world would politicize the activities. While the 1979 WARC was far less political than anticipated, it was recognized that most countries came to bargain rather than allocate the spectrum based on sound economic principles. In a similar manner, the OECD allows researchers to present data about national information planning or privacy policies, but only as it aids in negotiating common positions. International organizations are not yet strong enough to have researchers act as significant factors through involvement on the staff. The researchers are also very limited in their ability to serve as educators of policymakers and the public, for it is hard to transcend national or regional identity. It is almost impossible for researchers to act as champions of those being adversely affected, unless those adversely affected come from one's own national interest group.

IX.SUMMING UP

From all of the studies, both national and international, it is clear that the role of the researcher is limited. Research works best when it frames the questions, rather than when it attempts to answer them. Data gathering can play a useful role in documenting that a problem exists, or in helping to organize those experiencing a common plight. Research seems to work best when it comes from a staff stance rather than from an advocacy stance. If one takes the immense impacts of the privacy commission or paperwork reduction commissions as examples, research reporting works best when the reports not merely state findings but specifically indicate what needs to be done. It certainly helps for the cause to be popular, so that interest group momentum is behind the recommendations. It would help policy researchers to spend some time working with policymakers to find out what issues are ripe, who to work with in order to get things enacted, and what representatives of interest groups should be included. Neustad's (1981) parting comments after having sheparded information policy issues through the Carter White House were that researchers had an obligation to actively inform the policymakers and become involved.

From an academic point of view, one needs to consider whether or not policy research has contributed to the disciplines. This is where the difference between information and communication policy research becomes sharp. Communication research is developing a firm basis in theory. The television violence research may not have had much impact on policymaking, but it has contributed to understanding of how information affects behavior. Interactive cable research and computer conferencing research have had some impact on the theory of group communication. The research on copyright, privacy, the information economy, and information resource management fit nicely at the policy level, but do not tie into a sound theoretical base in information science. The reason may be that what theoretical base there is in information science is not applied. Communication research is very interested in change—how attitudes change, how groups form, how innovations are disseminated. Information science is less concerned with change, focusing more on relevance and information structure. Those areas of information science that do focus on change—growth of new knowledge and user needs studies—are perhaps the link with communication research. The theoretical base that underlies the research into privacy, copyright, computer impacts, and information resource management is a theory of information practices. The economics of information is developing, but more in economics than in information science. The contributors to information policy research are coming from law, economics, management, communication, and political science. Very few of the significant policy contributions have come from people who call themselves information scientists. Information scientists would do well to embrace the work of the policy researchers and help force a theoretical base for the field that ties relevance to need, structure to growth, and that shows how information can be managed effectively to allow us to create the economic and information environments we desire.

The model of the policy process which has been used throughout this analysis emphasizes that policymaking is a process of reconciling the diverse interests of many interest groups. In the early stages of a problem, researchers may be most effective as documenters of the problem and clarifiers of the nature of the problem. If they get involved as advocates of some group or as promotors of some solution, they often do not fare very will. They tend to be more effective if they can find ways to work with an interest group or can work as staff of the policymaker. As staff, the smallness of their numbers does not count, but the danger is that the power of the interest groups will be so strong that attempts to establish the dimensions of the policy will not work. Researchers must retain their commitments to two worlds, and must be reminded by their academic colleagues when the excitement of power leads to theoretically unsound policymaking.

REFERENCES

Adler, R. P. (1980). ''The Effects of Television Advertising on Children.'' Lexington, Massachusetts: Lexington Books.

Baer, W. S. (1973). ''Cable Television: A Handbook for Decisionmaking.'' Santa Monica, California: Rand Corporation.

Borchardt, K. (1975). ''Legislative Compromise Techniques.'' Cambridge, Massachusetts: Harvard University, Program on Information Technologies and Public Policy.

Braunstein, Y. M., Fischer, D. M., Ordover, J. A., and Baumol, W. J. (1977). ''Economics of Property Rights as Applied to Computer Software and Data Bases.'' Springfield, Virginia: National Technical Information Service. (PB 268 787.)

Brimmer, K. W. (1982). U. S. telecommunications common carrier policy. *Annual Review of Information Science and Technology 17,*33–82.

Burns, R. (1978). Beyond statistics. *In* M. C. J. Elton, W. A. Lucas, and D. W. Conrath (Eds.), ''Evaluating New Telecommunications Services,'' pp. 215–226. New York: Plenum.

Caplan, N. (1977). A minimal set of conditions necessary for the utilization of social science knowledge in policy formulation at the national level. *In* C. H. Weiss (Ed.), ''Using Social Research in Public Policy Making,'' pp. 183–198. Lexington, Massachusetts: Lexington Books. (Policy Studies Organization Series, 11.)

Dordick, H. S. (Ed.). (1979). ''Proceedings of the Sixth Annual Telecommunications Policy Research Conference,'' (1978). Lexington, Massachusetts: Lexington Books.

Dordick, H. S., Bradley, H. G., and Nanus, B. (1981). ''The Emerging Network Marketplace.'' Norwood, New Jersey: Ablex.

Elton, M. C. J., Lucas, W. A., and Conrath, D. W. (Eds.). (1978). ''Evaluating New Telecommunications Services.'' New York: Plenum. (NATO Conference Series II Systems Science, Vol. 6.)

Harms, L. S. (Ed.). (1977). ''The Right to Communicate: Collected Papers.'' Honolulu, Hawaii: University Press of Hawaii.

Harms, L. S. (1980). An emergent communication policy science—context, rights, problems, and methods. *Communication 5,* 65–87.

Henry, N. L. (1975). ''Copyright, Information Technology, Public Policy: Public Policies— Information Technology'' New York: Marcel Dekker.

Henry, N. L. (Ed.). (1980). "Copyright, Congress and Technology: The Public Record," Vols. 1–5. Phoenix, Arizona: Oryx.

Hiltz, S. R., and Turoff, M. (1978). "The Network Nation: Human Communication via Computer." Reading, Massachusetts: Addison-Wesley.

Hoffman, L. J. (Ed.) (1980). "Computers and Privacy in the Next Decade." New York: Academic Press.

Horton, F. W., Jr. (1979). "Information Resources Management: Concept and Cases." Cleveland, Ohio: Association for Systems Management.

International Commission for the Study of Communication Problems. (1980). "Many Voices, One World." (MacBride Report.) Paris: UNESCO.

Johnson, L. L. (1978). Boundaries to monopoly and regulation in modern telecommunications. *In* G. O. Robinson, (Ed.), "Communications for Tomorrow," pp. 127–156. New York: Praeger.

Katz, E., and Wedell, G. (1977). "Broadcasting in the Third World: Promise and Performance." Cambridge, Massachusetts: Harvard University Press.

King, J. L., and Kraemer, K. L. (1981). Cost as a social impact of information technology. *In* M. L. Moss (Ed.), "Telecommunications and Productivity," pp. 93–130. Reading, Massachusetts: Addison-Wesley.

Leeson, K. (1981). "Trade Issues in Telecommunications and Information." Washington, D. C.: National Telecommunications and Information Administration.

Machlup, F. (1962). "The Production and Distribution of Knowledge in the U.S." Princteon, New Jersey: Princeton University Press.

Machlup, F. (1980). "Knowledge, Its Creation, Distribution, and Economic Significance." Vol. 1, Knowledge and knowledge production. Princeton, New Jersey: Princeton University Press.

Marchand, D. A. (1979). Privacy, confidentiality, and computers. *Telecommunications Policy 3*, 192–208.

Marchand, D. A. (1980). "The Politics of Privacy, Computers and Criminal Justice Records." Arlington, Virginia: Information Resources Press.

Masuda, Y. (1981). "The Information Society as Post-Industrial Society." Bethesda, Maryland: World Future Society.

McDonald, D. D. (1982). Public sector/private sector interaction in information services. *Annual Review of Information Science and Technology 17, 83–97.*

Mitroff, I. I., and Betz, F. (1972). Dialectical decision theory: A meta-theory of decision making. *Management Science 19,* 11–24.

Moss, M. L. (1978). The development of two-way cable television: Applications for the community *In* M. C. J. Elton, W. A. Lucas, and D. W. Conrath (Eds.), "Evaluating New Telecommunications Services," pp. 199–214. New York: Plenum.

National Research Council. Study Project on Social Research and Development. (1978-1979). [Reports] Vol. 1–6. Washington, D.C.: National Academy of Sciences.

Neustad, R. M. (1981). Information policy—what next? *Bulletin of the American Society for Information Science 7* (No. 3), 16–19.

Noll, R. G., Peck, M. J., and McGowan, J. J. (1973). "Economic Aspects of Television Regulation." Washington, D.C.: Brookings Institute.

Nora, S., and Minc, A. (1980). "The Computerization of Society: A Report to the President of France." Cambridge, Massachusetts: MIT Press.

Nordenstreng, K., and Schiller, H. I. (Eds.). (1979). "National Sovereignty and International Communication." Norwood, New Jersey: Ablex.

Oettinger, A. G., Berman, P. J., and Read, W. H. (1977). "High and Low Politics: Information Resources for the 80's." Cambridge, Massachusetts: Ballinger.

Organization for Economic Co-operation and Development. (1980). "Report on Economic Analysis of Information Activities and the Role of Electronic and Telecommunications Technology." Paris: Organization for Economic Cooperation and Development.

Owen, B. M., Beebe, J. H., and Manning, W. G., Jr. (1974). "Television Economics." Lexington, Massachusetts: Lexington Books.

Park, R. E. (1972). Cable television, UHF broadcasting, and FCC regulatory policy. *Journal of Law and Economics 15,* 207–232.

Park, R. E. (1973). "The Role of Analysis in Regulatory Decisionmaking: The Case of Cable Television." Lexington, Massachusetts: Lexington Books.

Parker, E. B. (1978). Communication satellites for rural development. *Telecommunications Policy 2,* 309–315.

Ploman, E. W. and Hamilton, L. C. (1980). "Copyright: Intellectual Property in the Information Age." London: Routledge & Kegan Paul.

Pool, I. de S., and Schiller, H. I. (1981). Perspectives on communication research: An exchange. *Journal of Communication 31* (No. 3). 15–23.

Porat, M. U. (1977). "The Information Economy: Definition and Measurement." Washington, D.C.: U.S. Department of Commerce, Office of Telecommunication.

The Press, the U.S. and UNESCO. (1981). *Journal of Communication 31* (No. 4), 102–187.

Robinson, G. O. (Ed.) (1978). "Communications for Tomorrow: Policy Perspectives for the 1980s." New York: Praeger.

Robinson, G. O. (1980). Regulating international airways: 1979 WARC. *Virginia Law Review 21,* 1–68.

Rubin, M. R., and Taylor, E. (1981). The U.S. information sector and GNP: An input-output study. *Information Processing and Management 17,* 163–194.

Rule, J. B., McAdam, D., Stearns, L., and Uglow, D. (1980). "The Politics of Privacy: Planning for Personal Data Systems as Powerful Technologies." New York: Elsevier.

Shinn, A. M. Jr. (1978). The utility of social experimentation in policy research. *In* M. C. J. Elton, W. A. Lucas, and D. W. Conrath (Eds.), "Evaluating New Telecommunications Services," pp. 681–700. New York: Plenum.

Sundquist, J. L. (1978). Research brokerage: The weak link. *In* National Research Council. Study Project on Social Research and Development, "Knowledge and Policy: The Uncertain Connection," pp. 126–144. Washington, D.C.: National Academy of Sciences.

Toffler, A. (1980). "The Third Wave." New York: William Morrow.

U.S. Commission on Federal Paperwork. (1977). "Information Resources Management in Federal Agencies." Washington, D.C.: Government Printing Office.

U.S. Congress. 97th Congress, House of Representatives, 1st Session. (1981a). "Information Science and Technology Act." (HR 3137.) Washington, D.C.: Government Printing Office.

U.S. Congress. 97th Congress, House of Representatives, 1st Session. (1981b). "To Reorganize the International Communications Activities of the Federal Government." (HR 1957.) Washington, D.C.: Government Printing Office.

U.S. Department of Health, Education, and Welfare, Secretary's Advisory Committee on Automated Personal Data Systems. (1973). "Records, Computers, and the Rights of Citizens." Cambridge, Massachusetts: MIT Press.

U.S. Domestic Council. Committee on the Right of Privacy. (1976). "National Information Policy: Report to the President of the United States." Washington, D.C.: National Commission on Libraries and Information Science.

U.S. National Telecommunications and Information Administration. (1981). "Issues in Information Policy." Washington, D.C.: Government Printing Office.

U.S. Office of Technology Assessment. (1981). "Computer-Based National Information Systems: Technology and Public Policy Issues." Washington, D.C.: Government Printing Office.

U.S. Privacy Protection Study Commission. (1977). "Personal Privacy in an Information Society." Washington, D.C.: Government Printing Office.

Wedemeyer, D. J. (1977). "Forecasting Communication Needs, Supplies and Rights for Policy Making and Planning in the State of Hawaii." Unpublished dissertation, Stanford University.

Weiss, C. H. (1980). Knowledge creep and decision accretion. *Knowledge 1*, 381–404.

Weiss, C. H., and Bucuvalas, M. J. (1977). The challenge of social research to decision making. *In* C. H. Weiss (Ed.), ''Using Social Research in Public Policy Making,'' pp. 213–234. Lexington, Massachusetts: Lexington Books. (Policy Studies Organization Series, 11.)

Westin, A. F., and Baker, M. A. (1972). ''Databanks in a Free Society: Computers, Record-Keeping and Privacy.'' New York: Quandrangle/New York Times.

Zimmerman, E. K., and Brimmer, K. W. (1981). National planning for data communications. *Annual Review of Information Science and Technology 16*, 3–52.

3

Comparative Communication Research: A Response to World Problems

Alex S. Edelstein*
School of Communications, DS-40
University of Washington
Seattle, Washington 98195

(*This review was written while the author was Aw Boon Haw professor of Communication Research at the Chinese University of Hong Kong.)

I. INTRODUCTION

During the past decade, an intensified debate about "intellectual imperialism" has incorporated such issues as the "imbalance of news flow" among nations, the Western controlled communication technologies, and ubiquitous communications media and content. Such metaphors as "intellectual imperialism" and "imbalances of news flow" have been provocative politically but, fortunately, they have been emerging as evocative intellectually as well. We are enjoying a great deal of communication about international communication.

To judge the efficacy of comparative communication research as a response to such world problems as news flow, we need to address two basic concerns: first, what kinds of international communication problems have been attacked by scholars, and second, what has been their productivity—substantive, conceptual, and methodological? What can comparative studies tell us that we need to know and can learn in no other way?

In a recent treatment of *Comparative Communication Research* (Edelstein, 1982), the author traced nine major themes, each reflecting the concerns of scholars of particular historical and "events" periods. They included comparative modernization, political development, news flow, values and culture, images, the journalist, systems, public opinion, and the new communication technologies. Because of their dominance as research concerns, and their interrelatedness in some instances, this study reviews the first six of these substantive areas and examines their relevance to world problems.

By comparative studies we mean the simultaneous (more or less) observation of two or more entities (nations or regions) that are judged to be equivalent on one variable so that concomitant variation on another variable may be observed. The purpose in looking for commonality along one set of variables is to determine commonality or variation among another set of related variables, so that generalization across cultures may be made. The comparativist is sensitive to the probability that there are more commonalities across (population groups) societies than within societies; i.e., there is more variance within than between. The comparativist does not seek to solve a problem in one nation, but one or more problems that affect many nations.

This has created the need to be attentive to the nuances of conceptualization and methodology. There need be equivalence of concepts, of methodologies, of languages/meanings, of sampling, of stimulus situations, and of data analysis and reporting to permit comparisons to be made. Whether or not comparative research is unique or even distinctive in its concerns is not the most important or even the most relevant question. What is important is the point of view—a world or perhaps regional perspective—that comparativists bring to their research.

This conceptual approach is distinctive in important respects from those adopted for cross-national, cross-cultural, or intercultural communication.

As a consequence, most scholars concentrate their efforts on only one approach. It is the unusual scholar—unusual in productivity as well as in interests—who diffuses his or her attention evenly across these concerns. One can think of Pool, Schramm, Gerbner, Osgood, Lerner, and a few others, perhaps, but generally we can identify comparativists, cross-culturalists, cross-national and intercultural scholars by the corpus of their research. Even those we have named have been more occupied with comparative than with any other approach.

Pool's major studies (Pool, 1970; Pool et al., 1952a,b) have taken up the comparative use of symbols. Only recently has he concerned himself with cross-cultural—the impact of one cultural vehicle (violence on television) upon another culture. Schramm has been more of a comparativist than a cross-culturalist. His flow studies (Schramm, 1959, 1980) and efforts to test educational technology are illustrative. Gerbner's (1961, 1966, 1969, 1973, 1977) research is predominantly comparative, while asserting a personal concern with the diffusion of values across cultures, i.e., cross-cultural.

While comparative analysis requires an extraordinary attention to functional equivalence, in cross-cultural research the purpose is only to determine the impact of message X from country A upon country B. The investigator assumes unique rather than common characteristics of countries A and B. The assumption is that the uniqueness of content will produce a substantial impact of one culture (dominant) upon another.

Intercultural communication research reflects yet another concern: How does person X of country A communicate with person Y of country B? This is a similar question to that which we asked about the impact of the mass media of country A on the audiences of country B, except that in intercultural communication we presume interpersonal interaction and exchange, e.g., reciprocal effects on persons A and B. In mass communication we have more of a one-way phenomenon.

To draw a final distinction, cross-national simply describes the amount and direction of flow—whether news, airline reservations, mail, or banking information—across national boundaries. Many cross-national studies are not concerned with the consequences of flow, although the data may be used for speculative purposes. All this adds up to a view of international communication as a field of study characterized by a number of foci: comparative, cross-cultural, intercultural, and cross-national. We will treat only comparative studies here.

In the preface to *Comparative Communication Research,* Schramm (1982) made these two important observations: first, many more comparative studies need be done, and second, a surprising number have been done. Those studies that we review express that profusion of comparative research and the imperative, as well, that more need be done. We will review only those studies of modernization, development, imbalances of news flows, values and cultures, images, and the journalist.

II. MODERNIZATION

Those of us who were in graduate school in the 1950s remember our considerable awe at the contemplation of Daniel Lerner's (1958) *The Passing of Traditional Society.* It has continued to be cited as the first if not the seminal work in communication and modernization. Lerner was a member of a distinguished research team which included Charles Y. Glock, Paul F. Lazarsfeld, Robert K. Merton, William J. Millard, Jr., and Robert O. Carlson. Lerner produced the critical piece of work that was to be published after almost 10 years of dedicated group effort. Lerner first had analyzed data from Turkey, and later was asked to undertake the reporting of the data from 6 countries; this led to his postulation of empathy, literacy, urbanization, and mass communication as the elixir of modernization.

Lerner's work has lost lustre and seeming validity over several decades under the impact of more sophisticated research conceptualization and expanding data bases. We now know (Lee, 1981) that traditional ways may also be modernizing ways, and that assumptions about political development that are based upon linear models often collapse of their own weight. Schramm and Ruggels (1967), among others, questioned the validity of Lerner's statistical projections. They conceded, however, that they could not command entirely comparable data and that the advent of new forms of mass communication actually had made replication impossible.

Lerner was aware of the limitations of his own analysis. He stated that his model existed only to be superceded by one that could produce a better fit of the data. And he was candid about his biases. He acknowledged that he had taken as a model the Western frontier—ever expanding, ever beckoning—which he conceded might be *historically* Western but was *sociologically* global. Numerous countries had modernized by following the path of urbanization, industrialization, and literacy that Lerner had specified.

Lerner anticipated remarkably the communication research renaissance that we are witnessing, which is based upon situational rather than transituational analyses, the use of less intrusive questionnaire methodologies, and a shift in perspective to the point of view of the respondent rather than that of the observer. Dervin (1980) has sketched these trends convincingly. Few of Lerner's critics have looked at his questionnaire to note its remarkable perseverance as a research approach that is again coming into vogue.

Lerner's questionnaire also suggested some of the properties of a problem-solving or decision-making process. Lerner focussed upon the needs and aspirations of his respondents—what problems they faced, problems facing the nation, whether or not problems were difficult to solve, and how those problems might be solved. Radio commanded attention; later, comparative studies were to discover that radio sets and use correlated more highly and systematically with development than did newspaper circulation. And questions about national images were asked—about people and about nations—similar to the studies to be done decades later.

The social scientists who followed Lerner were to take up his question of modernization in new contexts. McClelland (1961) posed personal needs for power, affiliation, and achievement as the great motivators of behavior. One intriguing finding was a negative correlation between achievement and affiliation; power and achievement, where correlated, were associated with development. McClelland did not so much defend his variables, or the findings themselves, as seek to advance the comparative method, for comparativeness, he said, lent strength to his findings. He had demonstrated the feasibility of comparing mass communication content (children's fiction) as a way of describing the common nature of societies and the values that they imposed.

The Lerner thesis also stimulated, in part, the work of Inkeles and Smith (1974). Their perspective of the individual-in-society accommodated Lerner's focus upon the individual and McClelland's social-psychological view as well. Inkeles and Smith believed that men were not "born modern" but were made so by life experience. The authors examined work in a factory, which they described as an institutional and bureaucratic structure in which individuals played roles. They discovered that this prepared many individuals in so-called "traditional" settings to be open to new experience, ready for change, and disposed to hold opinions that extended beyond the immediate environment. They acquired information, were future-oriented, and were engaged in decision-making. Mass communication was one of the forces that shaped this behavior, equivalent in its importance and functions to the school, the family, the factory, and the urban setting.

Pye (1963) and his colleagues agreed that mass communications could be a critical variable governing political development. Of methodological interest is the fact that the Pye group operated comparatively by *conceptual consensus*. Each study director in 10 countries was given a memorandum, suggestive but not prescriptive, which outlined subjects relevant to the analysis of political culture and communication. Each author provided an historical perspective for that nation. The group viewed the comparative approach as a way of transcending the compartmentalization of studies of political systems.

Almond and Verba (1963) sought to make studies of political modernization more comparable than the Pye approach. But Almond and Verba did not extend the concern for mass communication. They sought more to advance political modernization in disciplinary terms and to extend thinking about conceptualization and methodology. Reading, watching television, and radio usage were incorporated as indicators of civic competence, but these data were not analyzed as major aspects of the conceptualization.

It is understandable, therefore, that there has been no major comparative work on communication and political modernization since Almond-Verba. Part of this loss of interest might be attributed to the shift in attention to economic development. Political scientists such as Frederick Frey provided the linkage to this shift in focus and accompanying point of view.

III. ECONOMIC DEVELOPMENT AND COMMUNICATION

The scholars who were attracted to communication and economic development were more applied in their orientation than those who had dealt with modernization; they perceived economic development as a problem that was more amenable to research strategies. Civic competence was as remote as the urban cultures that the term reflected. Frey (1973) noted that most nations bore the underdeveloped label; they contained more than two-thirds of the world's populations, and, although there had been some progress in a few of these societies, there seemed little basis for confidence that major problems of development were being solved or that the gaps between the "have" and "have not" nations were being reduced.

Given this, it was paradoxical that the scholars who had shifted their attention to economic development were to suffer such severe criticism, most of it from fellow scholars. In part, this criticism was ideological and demanded that certain assumptions be made about the nature of societies. But much of the criticism demanded simply that there be improvement in the state of the art of communication research. Frey (1973) insisted that concepts had to be stated less ambiguously, conceptual and operational equivalence needed to be defined more explicitly, and data needed to be reported more contextually. There should be more theory-building based on data collection and analysis and less testing of assumptions that had no empirical bases. Generalizations should emerge from data rather than data being used to test preconceived ideas that were neither scientific nor empirical in origin. To compare nations with respect to communication resources or development, it was necessary to understand the bases of one's assumptions. The historical context of development in given cultures or regions needed to be taken more fully into account.

McAnany (1980) suggested that some studies of communication were not productive because of the absence of development, i.e., change. It was fixity, rather than change, that was characteristic of most underdeveloped societies. McAnany concurred that the most pressing world problems were economic, but he saw them located in rural rather than in urban settings. He urged that communication studies be shifted from efforts to bring about change to those examining the consequences of change.

In seeming contrast to the McAnany view, other scholars were concerned that efforts to heighten the impact of development by communication would result in gaps being widened between those who already had information and those who did not; the so-called "knowledge gap" would be widened by the efforts of change agents and communication practitioners and researchers (Tichenor et al., 1970). Comparative studies were needed to observe the conditions under which information campaigns met their objectives of improving the lot of the rural poor, not only in absolute terms but also in relation to those who were not as poor. Basic inequalities existed in communication skills, levels of knowledge, social contacts, relevant experience, and accessibility to media channels among segments of the rural populations.

Ettema and Kline (1977) suggested, however, that a "difference" gap was more conceptually productive than a "deficit" gap. There were actually situations in which the least equipped could become the most benefited by communication; as examples, in situations where they were more highly motivated to learn because of a sense of the potential usefulness of the information. The conceptualization better explained so called "ceiling effects," where less learning on the part of the most competent was attributed to the logic that they already had learned all that could be learned.

There were basic conceptual and methodological problems. Roy et al. (1969) wondered if what they measured as adoption in India was equivalent to adoption in Costa Rica. Was there equivalence in the research instruments? Was the language that described an innovation, such as a chemical fertilizer or a vaccination, equivalent in the two cultures? The obstacles to achieving equivalences in field settings were formidable. Conditions varied greatly for planning, for controlling stimulus situations, and for ensuring the participation of respondents in field experiments. Despite these constraints, Costa Rica-India comparisons were possible and inferences were made from the data. One important finding was that the modern-traditional dichotomy showed no effects in either country; this questioned the Lerner thesis and held open a basis for generalizing across societies.

The development communication researchers were emotionally committed to the idea of assisting host countries. Hursh-Cesar and Roy (1976) complained about scholars who had no commitments. They referred to them as "data exporters," "self-enhancing theory-builders," "research bankers" who financed projects but did not suffer them through, "itinerant grantsmen," and "instant research guns," for hire at a price. Yet most were dedicated and, in the professional context, it appears out of keeping for them to have suffered so much criticism.

The Rogers and Shoemaker (1969) three-nation study of agricultural innovations in Brazil, Nigeria, and India was one of the largest comparative efforts, and was one of several studies that was attentive to the conceptual and methodological problems noted by Frey (1973). A number of generalizations emerged. Among them was the encouraging finding that there were many more similarities than differences across the relevant aspects of the three cultures. The differences could be explained by country-relevant conditions such as rates of literacy, different rates of access to print or broadcasting, and broadly defined attributes of culture.

The development studies thus contributed useful knowledge that could be applied across cultures. This argued against the view that the assumptions that guided the nature of the research had limited the usefulness of that research. In many cases, the findings transcended local and regional differences and processes. The comparative approach had looked for commonalities and hence had discovered them; by contrast, the ideological thrust of criticism had emphasized differences, and consequently found them as well.

IV. THE NEW INTERNATIONAL INFORMATION ORDER

The criticism of communication research on modernization and economic development found resonance in demands for a New International Information Order. Modernization and economic development lacked the generality and ideological content that could be promised by a debate about news flow. Additionally, there was the precedent of the debate generated in UNESCO about a new international economic order.

Actually, world news flow and related ideological issues were not new problems; the United Nations in 1948 had debated freedom of information, and studies had been undertaken into patterns of international news flows and opinions. But there were no empirically derived criteria against which balance or quality of content could be judged adequately. The comparative method was adopted as a way of gaining perspective, however limited. If country A sent more information to country B than it received, that was an imbalance. If the content failed to meet idealized standards or values, it was "deficient" and a remedy might be proposed. Comparative methods became a surrogate for the acknowledged lack of standards about how much news flow, in what directions, was enough, and what content was acceptable.

As early as the 1950s, UNESCO sponsored a study by Kayser (1953) that found great "imbalances" in the play and content of foreign news carried by world newspapers. International Press Institute (1953, 1954a,b) studies came to similar conclusions. Pool et al. (1952a,b) carried out substantial studies of the transmission of symbols and values by prestige newspapers. Schramm (1959) reported how 14 elite newspapers reported two crisis situations in 1956, the workers revolution in Hungary and the Western intervention in Suez.

Schramm felt that elite newspapers were similar enough to be compared, yet variable enough to illustrate the diversity of cultures. Elite newspapers spoke for and to the elites of their own nations; they could speak, as well, to elites of other nations. As Pool had contended, a world polity was connected by the elite press.

Schramm observed, however, that elite newspapers differed in the sources of their power, if not in their functional roles. Each reflected national interests, but the sources of power determined how these interests would be expressed journalistically. Even among the Communist newspapers, there were substantial variations. Some were given more to analysis and commentary; others were characterized more by the ways in which they described events, sometimes in exhaustive detail—a kind of interpretation by exposition. Were elite newspapers, no matter how diverse the governments and societies that they represented, similar enough structurally to permit useful generalization?

In keeping with the special interests of government, Schramm found great variations in the proportion of news reported about each of the two crisis events and in the sources of that news. *Pravda* obtained 67 percent of its news from the Sino-Soviet area, and only 10 percent from Western Europe; by contrast, *Le Monde* obtained 50 percent of its news from Western Europe and 12 percent from the Sino-Soviet Bloc. East European countries depended upon Sino-Soviet sources for two thirds of their news, as did *The People's Daily*. Thus a generalization emerged; each newspaper relied on its geographic, economic, political, social, and ideological partners as its source of news. This was reflected also in the proportion of space devoted to the crises; East European sources gave substantial attention to Hungary, but *Pravda* almost ignored it, giving 45 times as much coverage to Suez, a staggering proportional variation. Thus another generalization emerged. Each elite newspaper reflected the "interests" of its political system.

This aspect of self-interest was reflected later in several comparative studies conducted in the Middle East. The changing relationships set in motion by the two wars (1967 and 1973) brought the attention of both Arab and Western scholars to questions relating to the balance and nature of news flow between the Middle East and the West, particularly the United States. Dajani and Donohue (1973) found that both the patterns of news flows and the nature of it (whether favorable or unfavorable) were highly situational and were explained by political, ideological, cultural, and economic ties. At the time, most political news coverage was given to the United States and to the Soviet Union. France was low in this category but high in cultural news (Abu-Lughod, 1962). But when France shifted its foreign policy so that it was more acceptable to the Arabs, attention to French foreign policy in the Arab press increased apace. Much of the total content, as might be expected, was explained by Arab attitudes toward Israel.

UNESCO again expressed its interest in the problems of international communication by stimulating a study of news flow among 13 countries (Sreberny-Mohammadi et al., 1980). A U.S. team added 16 nations to that array to permit more adequate generalization on both regional and global bases (Stevenson and Cole, 1979, 1980). The UNESCO study contained lessons for those who attempt large-scale comparative studies without adequate financial support and consultation among scholars. There were problems of getting information from countries, replicating sampling procedures, explicating content categories, and achieving reliability of coding. In many respects, conceptual equivalence was more hoped for than attained. Nonetheless, some improvisations occurred and some useful generalizations emerged.

The study mapped the "news world" of each region. Every country other than Yugoslavia and Poland reported more news that occurred within its own geopolitical region than in any other region. Generally, there were "balances" of news flow which incorporated also "reciprocities of ignorance," that is, certain nations and regions ignored one another. Certain types of news were present in virtually all media systems; regionalism was a strong predictor of news flow and content; and news personalities were similar as the foci of the news. Thus comparative analysis demonstrated that the problems of journalism and international communication were more common across cultures than they were different; there was a certain inescapable normativeness in journalism, and, as Schramm had demonstrated, the media served national interests as well.

Schramm (1980) also carried out a major study to determine the impact of wire services in Asia. He selected 16 of the most prestigeous dailies and examined their use of wire news for a one-week period. He found that with few exceptions the newspapers followed pretty much the pattern of what was distributed by the wire services. A somewhat dispiriting finding was the discovery that only a minute fraction of the foreign news that originally was distributed actually was read.

While these comparative studies answered some questions, that is, who communicated with whom, and why, they did not propose any threoretical formulations that would permit the testing of hypotheses. No single variable explained the problem of "imbalances." There was an evident need to develop concepts that would explain rather than merely describe news flows.

Actually, some early and pertinent theorizing was proposed by Galtung and Ruge (1965). They explained news content based upon 12 factors from which they derived three major hypotheses. The factors, in summary, included a media "time span" for events; the amplitude, singularity, familiarity, and predictability of the event; its appeal to elites; its personal and negative character; and combinations of these conditions. The results of a comparative content analysis generally confirmed the theory and suggested modifications to it. The significance of the work lay in its potential for generating more productive comparative studies.

Galtung (1971) also generated a theory of "structural imperialism" that explained the likelihood of news flow. This theory proposed that certain nations were central in terms of dominance and that "periphery" nations were dependent or interdependent in terms of prior colonial relationships, culture, and geography.

Nnaemeka and Richstad's (1980) Pacific Islands study supported a number of hypotheses but observed that regional cooperation was enervating colonial-structured patterns. This breakdown was facilitated by the advent of satellite communication technologies that permitted point-to-point communication. The NIIO research was also criticized for the inadequacy of data analysis.

Nnaemeka and Richstad (1980) met some of these demands, employing both extramedia and intermedia variables. They hypothesized that nations with similar characteristics would demonstrate similar patterns of news flow. This was generally confirmed, but the nature of the news exercised an influence as well.

What can the comparative method tell us about "imbalances" and the prospects for mitigating it? As Rosengren (1974, 1977) suggested, the answer does not rest so much with the methodology as with the theory and conceptualization that propose its application. The comparative method can not answer questions that are not asked, nor can it substitute for theory that is not provided.

Present patterns of flow appear to be explained in part by geographical proximity, colonial dependencies, trade and economic relations, human infrastructures, communication technologies, political ideologies, political structures, military and security relationships, diplomatic relations, race, culture, language, religion, and other factors. What are the constraints and potentialities existing in each of these variables? Which explain how much variance, alone or interdependent with other variables? These questions are amenable to research.

From a comparative perspective, it would be helpful if variables could explain variance across cultures or regions, for that would make the task of addressing imbalances that much easier to approach: one prescription for a common problem. But if comparative analysis is used merely to portray differences, as has been the purpose in many instances, then remedies will not be found, for remedies would not be sought.

V. VALUES AND CULTURE

The debate over "imbalances" in news flow demonstrated that research was needed that would ask questions that could be answered. The questions about "imbalances" were not themselves imponderable; what was confusing and even deceptive was the lack of relevant criteria that could be applied. What was balanced or imbalanced? How much more flow, in what direction, under what conditions, would meet defined standards of performance?

The debate over values portrayed in mass media—questions about the nature and "quality" of content—took on some of the same ambiguity of definitional standards as did the debate about "quantity." There was no ascertainable standard for "quality." Indeed, content was defined by such broadly stated terms as "symbolic functions," "collective consciousness" (Gerbner, 1969, 1973), "collective imagery," "collective influence" (Gerbner, 1966), and "communities of thought" (Gerbner, 1966). The society defined the media and the media defined "common consciousness" and, indeed, "cultivated it." (Gerbner, 1977). One could not speak of the individual except as expressing values of culture or community; one studied mass communication content but not the individuals who used or failed to use it. One could not accept a societal principle of "aggregates," for aggregates had meaning only in the generalized sense of membership in a community.

But Gerbner and colleagues did not provide empirical bases for defining these boundaries and parameters and attributing them to collective rather than to individual (often unconnected) behaviors. Individual behaviors which were aggregated at one moment in time were simply inferred as "collective" behavior. Nor did the companion thesis of media "cultivation" account for the production of media content to meet audience needs as suggested by Bauer's (1964) formulation of the "obstinate audience."

The work of another genre of scholars—Weaver et al. (1980), Murray and Kippax, (1978), Wilhoit and De Bock (1976), Edelstein (1974), Vidmar and Rokeach (1974), Katz, et al. (1973), among others—stands in seeming contrast as comparative analysis to this point of view. These scholars approached the study of comparative media effects by looking at the "uses" of mass communication by "aggregated" individuals. There were no assumptions as to context or community, and they engaged in audience rather than content studies.

The fundamental difference in point of view asserted that audiences select from what was available but use the content to satisfy their own needs, solve their own problems, engage in their own enjoyment, and create their own sense of well-being.

The "uses" and "gratifications" approach does not accept the implication that homogeniety is created by mass communication within national cultures. Rather, it tests the proposition that there are more individual *differences* than commonalities *within* cultures, and there are more *similarities* than differences *across* cultures. This would make mass communication more ubiquitous *across* cultures than *within* them; cross-culturally, those of similar economic and social status, and those with similar levels of education and intellectual interests, would use mass communication more similarly than did members of different economic, social, and intellectual classes, and hence are more able to communicate "across" than "within" national "boundaries."

Thus a "class" issue also was implied by the debate. The "uses" perspective saw cross cultural commonalities by social class, while the structuralists, despite being influenced by Marxist thought, eschewed that position in favor of all-powerful mass communication that transcended class. This would be explained by the Marxist view that capitalism controls the means of production and has *produced* content precisely *for individuals, aggregates,* and *classes,* rather than for *community* consumption. Comparative studies, therefore, that look at the content of East European and Soviet media and view them in apposition to Western media content must take into account the concept of community and see if, indeed, different conceptual approaches (the individual and the community) produce different mass communication or mass communication effects.

Gerbner was clearly working within the assumptions and "givens" of the "critical research" school, characterized more recently by Christians and Carey (1981) as within the realm of "qualitative research." Thus symbolic meaning is a matter of context; it permits more individual or naturalistic observation, and so-called sensitized concepts, where original meanings must be captured yet explicated. This combines a scientific need for precision with the necessity to represent complex culture accurately. Van Poecke (1980) is critical of Gerbner for failing to explicate and to make the linkages from the symbolic environment, or context, to the data at hand.

In examining two of the Gerbner studies—one of educators and the other of film heroes—a great many cross-cultural commonalities as well as differences were portrayed. Gerbner (1966) perceived differences to be more likely, for he concluded that it was difficult to compare "socialist morality" and "dedication to a revolution" with laissez faire liberalism. Gerbner (1966) reported comparisons of images of teachers focussed upon what he called general features of "collective imagery." His teams analyzed stories from Western and Eastern European/Soviet countries. He insisted that these stories be viewed in system terms rather than as aggregates of individual creative acts. They were shaped by collective influences that "cultivated" common assumptions of communities rather than of separate individuals. This was a product of historical continuity and the structures of media organizations that produced the content for mass consumption. What emerged was a set of findings in which the images of teachers were more similar than different across cultures. In the East, teachers were more favorably portrayed, but Gerbner conceded that teachers had been assigned different tasks in the capitalist and socialist cultures. Hence they were not comparable.

In his study of film heroes, Gerbner (1969) again reported commonalities as well as differences among East and Western European nations and the U.S. Film settings reflected the concerns of each nation; those of Yugoslavia and other East European nations were still focussed upon World War II. Western heroes were rich, carefree, and powerful, while Eastern Europeans glorified the intelligentsia, workers, and peasants. Eastern European heroes were primarily students, while in the U.S. and Yugoslavia they were military men. In Italy and Poland they were farmers, and in Poland and Czechoslovakia they were laborers. But all nations glorified heroes.

Gerbner achieved a commendable degree of international collaboration and was able to generate comparisons along dimensions of time, place, social, personal, value, and thematic characteristics, but he was able to do little other than code the "manifest" content of the films, being forced to put aside more explicit treatment of "symbolic meaning," "collective imagery," and "cultivation" which he had attributed to media. The gap remained between conceptualization and operationalization.

Yet Gerbner's work remains significant and, indeed, seductive. It has met the test of "maximizing comparisons" suggested by Glaser (1965) in the demonstration of equivalences across capitalist and socialist states. It is in keeping with the suggestions by Christians and Carey (1981) that we compare social wholes, and it has provided demonstrations of cultural differences as well as commonalities.

Gerbner's interest in comparing East and West is a broadly shared one. Robinson and Converse (1972) compared the uses of leisure time in 12 Western and European countries, the U.S.S.R., the U.S., and Peru. Again, the findings were more similar than different across political cultures. Television in all countries cut down on other media, but most people used more than one medium of communication in a given day. An interesting difference was that the highly educated in Eastern Europe spent more time with television content than their U.S. intellectual counterparts; this may have been a function of the differences in content of television.

Edelstein (1974) and Wiio and McCallister (1981)—who retested Edelstein's findings on sex discrepancies and mass communication uses— addressed commonalities across cultures, Edelstein in Yugoslavia and the U.S. and Wiio and McCallister in Finland. Both found the same sex differences, demonstrating similarities across social classes in three societies but differences within.

Edelstein's study innovated conceptual bases for comparison, allowing individuals to state their own problems, but comparing those problems that were the most salient for each individual. The equivalence was in salience, not in the nature of problems which often differed in substance.

The extent of variation *within* a national culture was illustrated by Murray and Kippax (1978). They "matched" three towns to compare children's media behavior where there was a lot of television, a little, and none at all. Children in low access towns spent as much time with the media, nevertheless, as those in high access towns; availability spelled use. Children who used television saw it as informative and placed it between the cinema as entertainment and the printed word as knowledge.

Weaver and DeBock (1980) tested the gratifications concept as knowledge, diversion, and personal identity, with Dutch and U.S. audiences. Their study also replicated the Katz et al. (1973) research in Israel, permitting a three-way perspective. Audiences in the U.S and Holland were more comparable than any other "pairs." This was attributed to more comparable media systems and population roles and characteristics. However, in Holland media were used more for personal needs, but in the U.S. media were used most to kill time.

Murray and Kippax (1978) replicated Katz's study with an Australian sample. There were many similarities along social characteristics of age, sex, and education; and television commonly was perceived as the most gratifying of the media. But Israelis emphasized the strengthening of knowledge and the understanding of society, while Australians were more self expressive in the context of family relations, friends, and self. In both societies, needs were best met by nonmedia sources.

DeBock (1980) and colleagues replicated the Berelson (1949) and Kimball (1959) studies on missing the newspaper in Holland, and their findings lent confirmation to the general proposition of media uses directed toward gathering information, personal enhancement, killing time, etc. The authors concluded that these findings had a great deal of cross-national validity. And Vidmar and Rokeach (1974) found that in comparing viewers of "All in the Family" in Canada and the U.S., the generality of prejudice obtaining across cultures was validated.

In the last analysis, it is difficult to compare the Gerbner collective thesis with the differentiated approach. Applicable standards are lacking. How much "variation within" is permitted by the thesis of societally defined boundaries and parameters? How much "commonality across" cultures and "variations within" would support an individual differences perspective? From the standpoint of the comparativist, the relevant question is how much commonality need be present to permit useful generalizations to emerge? As cloudy as was the NIIO debate, it permitted relevant observation and measurement. Scholars have not determined empirically the nature or extent of "collective imagery," "collective consciousness," and "cultivation" effects of the mass media.

VI. THE CONSTRUCTION OF IMAGES

The study of comparative images has attracted academic interest over several decades. But the term "image" has been underdefined and overly invoked. No one definition has been generally adopted. Scott (1965) came closest with a straightforward description of an image as a collection of attributes that defined an object; these were cognitive, affective, and communicative in the sense that images invoked responses from those who perceived them. We might add to that the concept of a mental structure of some kind that integrates the cognitive, affective, and communicative components. Boulding (1959, 1965) made the term relevant to international communication by asserting that images were the bases upon which nations communicated.

Isaacs (1958, 1962) called images "scratches on our minds" and compared the perceptions of China and India held by American elites. The methodology was personal—a selection and snowballing technique of interviewing knowledgeable and significant observers. One provocative finding was that Americans tended to like Indians less and Chinese more as they got to know them better, but they also learned to distrust Chinese. The bases for these perceptions were only vaguely defined by the observers, but Isaacs was able to conclude that certain values and behaviors were consistent for the Chinese and inconsistently held for the Indians. As one example, the Indians spoke of moral imperatives but were governed by constraining social laws and by personal rigidities.

Later scholars worked at defining the concept "image" and achieving more systematic bases for comparisons. Kelman and Ezekial (1970) looked at the cognitive components of knowledge and ability to differentiate. Edelstein and Hall (1979) asked respondents to describe attributes of modern and traditional Japan and China and showed that there were many more attributes for Japan (because of the hiatus of reporting of China) and a greater ability on the part of respondents to differentiate with respect to Japan than China. Earlier, Willis (1968) had shown that individuals discriminated between peoples and countries. He determined conditions under which people hated a people more than a nation and vice versa. In all of these studies, greater knowledge was associated with a greater ability to differentiate or discriminate.

These elements were expressed in an early study by Wolfe (1964), who saw images as collections of evaluative "statements" about nations and peoples. This might be thought of as a "public opinion" perspective. Thus Latin Americans portrayed the United States as a world leader, anti-Soviet, responsible for the relative obscurity of Latin America in the world press, both imperialist and generous, playful, sports-loving, but shallow in appreciation of the arts and the humanities.

Conrad (1955) found that newspapers in East and West Germany were means by which individuals formed images and maintained them, and that selectivity of content by newspapers narrowed the range of beliefs and images that individuals might hold.

Pisarek (1981) made the persuasive point that socialist and nonsocialist newspapers were much more alike than different in important ways and that differences merely were given more attention. This was because of the greater tendency to differentiate "political" images as contrasted with "social" or "cultural" images. Pisarek reported that although each culture had different heroes, the media portrayal was of actors who came from similar places in the social structures of the different cultures. This finding was consistent with those of Gerbner (1969).

Gerbner and Marvanyi (1977) explored the similarities and differences in images of the "outside world" that societies portrayed in their media systems. The study included 60 daily newspapers from 9 capitalist, socialist, and third world countries. The authors represented, visually, the misshapen worlds represented by each nation, so that one could observe that, while two-thirds of the U.S. world picture was made up of North America, Western Europe, and Asia, plus Israel and the Arab countries, in the Third World the Soviets loomed large, followed by Asia, Western Europe, North America, and South America. The principle was to suggest that international pictures represented the realities perceived by each culture at a particular time for a special set of reasons.

One of the more discerning "image" studies was that of Rachty (1979), who noted that elements dropped out, were added, replaced, or reformulated. She conceptualized image as subjective knowledge and identified factors that contributed to the maintenance of images. Some were relatively persisting. Belkaoui (1978) used an attributional approach to compare Arab and Israeli images in weekly magazines and demonstrated change over time based upon the perceptions of the two Arab-Israeli wars.

Gerbner (1961) looked at United Nations coverage of *The New York Times* and the Hungarian party newspaper and concluded that the Hungarian paper was agreement-oriented while *The Times* was procedural and conflict-oriented. The comparison was curious for its coding decisions; ideological appeals to peace and "battling" could be coded agreement-oriented for the Hungarian newspaper because the "battle" was for peace! It was curious, too, because there was no common basis for comparison; two different approaches to news gathering and portrayal based upon entirely opposite and conflicting points of view were presented. The study illustrated that things that are too alike, or too different, cannot be compared meaningfully.

Overall, these and other studies were informative, but they did not reflect a systematic and cumulative approach to the study of images. The variations in approaches, in topics, and in motivation (scholarly and political/ideological) made it difficult to abstract a set of principles to guide systematic inquiry.

VII. THE ROLE OF THE JOURNALIST

While the NIIO debate lacked standards of performance, comparative studies of the journalist foundered because of the application of inappropriate standards. First World concepts of professionalism were applied to journalists from Third World countries. Comparisons in some respects demonstrated the commonality of idealized journalistic practices, but actual practice fell short of what was idealized.

There was the problem again of comparing unlikes: African journalists whose traditons were those of storytellers with those of India, whose traditions were steeped in social criticism and philosophy; those of Latin America, whose problem was economic survival and whose milieu was conflict and uncertainty, those in the West who worked in relatively autonomous political environments, and those whose roles were incorporated into the governmental structure. How to compare all of these journalists meaningfully? How to abstract principles that might have common bases in all societies?

Passin (1963) pointed out that it was impossible to compare journalists in the new states without an understanding of traditions and specific historical experiences. He noted the linkages between literature, politics, and journalism as a part of the transitional process. To the extent that the individuals were essayists and responsible for their own ideas, they were writers; when they directed this to the political process and had a hand in it themselves, they were politicians; when they reported what politicians said, they were journalists.

Pye (1963) noted that journalists in the new states were too underpaid and too often coopted by the state to claim professionalism; this status required an independent force, an objective and analytical view, and nonpartisanship in the political process. But this view would rule out journalists who showed attributes of professionalism although in the service of the state. Hardt (1979) cited the ''messenger'' role of the journalist in moving between elites and masses; societies might be compared along this dimension.

Starck and Sudhaker (1979) questioned professionalism as not taking into account sufficiently the indigenous values, ideologies, personalities, and social and economic structures that might permit equivalence and degrees of comparison among nations.

Day (1968) used a formal measure of professionalism in assessing job satisfaction among journalists from Bolivia, Mexico, and Argentina; his sample was young, urban, educated, and of higher than average income. While Bolivians were pessimistic, Mexican journalists were optimistic about their professinal future. But nearly all journalists in the countries studied were required to hold part-time jobs in addition to working in journalism. There was a realization of the low status that was endemic in the field.

Menanteau-Horta (1967) and McLeod and Rush (1969) found instances of job satisfaction, but evidence of disaffection and occupational poverty as well. Very few could support themselves only as journalists. The authors concluded that professionalism was relatively unattainable in Latin America and hence comparison with American journalism was not fruitful.

There has been surprisingly little comparative analysis of the journalist in the First World setting. Boyd-Barrett (1970) did an ''inferential comparison'' of journalists in a discussion of journalism recruitment and training in Great Britain. He concluded that journalism was not a profession, although there were journalists who held professional values and functioned in a professional manner. He proposed that the issue was not whether journalism was a profession, but rather if journalism were susceptible to professionalization along given dimensions. Tunstall (1970) developed many of these concerns.

Donsbach (1981) suggested that it was not necessary to invoke the criterion of professionalism; rather, journalists should be compared on competence and legitimacy. The competence would relate to public communication, and the legitimacy would reflect the degree of institutional support (the willingness of the administrative structure, as suggested earlier) for journalistic activities. Donsbach compared a German sample of journalists with Latin Americans and Americans. A great many differences were noted in the practice of journalism and observation of a professional code of conduct, but there was a common core of attitudes toward journalism as a field. To contribute to a greater competence among journalists, Donsbach suggested that the journalist should be required to study media audiences and effects, to cope with a rational model of decision-making, and to devote himself or herself to public communication. Noelle-Neumann et al. (1980) compared German and British journalists on an array of variables and reported those same differences in practice but a common under-standing of what journalism was supposed to encompass.

Each of these studies helped point to some commonalities and differences in journalistic outlook and practice. But what is necessary is a conceptual frame-work for addressing journalists in all societies—similar to that proposed by Donsbach—but incorporating other journalistic roles and functions as well. "Profession" is a "borrowed" term which carries unnecessary conceptual baggage.

VIII. SUMMARY

This review has asserted the extent to which comparative communication re-search reflects the attributes of a disciplined field of study. There is some emerging theory, a variety of research traditions, a mounting body of literature, and distinctive conceptual and methodological concerns. "Comparative" may be distinguished from commonly used references to cross-cultural, transnational, and intercultural research. And "comparative" may be applied to an unique ar-ray of world problems—a number of which we have discussed.

The reader will be aware that one-nation studies were omitted that bore on substantive and theoretical considerations which we have addressed. These were omitted purposefully, to permit the distinctive character of comparative analysis to emerge.

As the reader also will observe, the traditions of comparative communica-tion research are rooted in other disciplines, notably political science, sociology, and psychology. Some of this extradisciplinary interest has waned, as can be seen in the relative loss of interest in political modernization. There the interest of political scientists shifted either to economic development as the handmaiden of political evolution or to theories about press freedom and the professionalization of journalists. We have touched upon the latter concern, but we have not discussed the corollaries of press freedom. Some of the conceptual problems of addressing that problem are analogous to those we observed with respect to studies of the professionalization of the journalist, namely, an absorp-tion with testing theories that were not derived from the setting that is to be ob-served. Professionalization as a journalistic concept has limited application to Third World and even to Second World countries, unless it is grounded in politi-cally or economically defined roles of the journalist. Similarly, theories of press freedom that are based on economic and social indices need to take account of political structures and historical traditions.

We have not been able in this brief essay to treat many other areas of comparative communication research. There are important concepts that are being brought to bear upon comparative public opinion, information systems, international cooperation, and conflict. Comparative methods are essential in those areas to note the extent to which behaviors are universal and/or based upon understood dynamics, or if they are largely unique to the political and social structures, e.g., the contemporary and derived cultures in which they are found. The challenge to comparative communication research is to identify the important world problems that can be addressed most meaningfully and effectively.

How much theory, how much literature, how much social importance need be attached to an intellectual area before it takes on the properties of a field within a discipline? Ironically, this is the question we asked about international news flow, about differences within and between societies, and about the extent to which professionalization was an apt conceptual approach to the study of the journalist. The answer must be a relative one: when there is enough theory to be of value, when there is enough literature to be of substance, and when there is enough application to make its utility evident. Add to this the importance of the distinctiveness of an approach, that is, point of view as well as scientific method. The comparativists are distinctive in their goals of describing commonalities across cultures as well as within them; they, therefore, are distinctive in their approach to conceptualization, looking for important commonalities that can be the bases for inferences to concomitant similarities and culturally determined differences. The comparativists are trying to make ever larger statements about nations, about regions, and about world communities. In this important sense, comparativists are engaged in the study of not just one nation or region, but in the study of individuals in all societies.

This is intended to be a critical essay; our criterion has been the availability of empirically tested and derived data. Thus, while a number of concepts employed by comparativists are attractive and propose substantial foci for research, the evidence itself is lacking. The critical researcher, particularly, has been ready to propose conclusions that depend upon empirical observation on the basis only of assumptions and "self-evident" realities. While perhaps unchallengeable as concepts, empirical observations must be made to afford the strength of evidence and validation. There are always questions as to the extent to which concepts may govern as well as interest in the contingencies that are attached to them that may be specified.

IX. REFERENCES

Abu-Lughod, I. (1962). International news in the Arabic press: A content analysis. *Public Opinion Quarterly 26*, 600–612.

Almond, G. A., and Verba S. (1963). "The Civic Culture," 2nd Ed. Boston, Massachusetts; Little, Brown.

Bauer, R. A. (1964). The obstinate audience: The influence process from the point of view of social communication. *American Psychologist 19*, 319–328.

Belkaoui, J. M. (1978). Images of Arabs and Israelis in the prestige press, 1966-1974. *Journalism Quarterly 55*, 732–738.

Berelson, B. (1949). What "missing the newspaper" means. *In* P. F. Lazarsfeld and F. N. Stanton (Eds.), "Communication Research, 1948-1949, pp. 111–129. New York: Duell, Sloan and Pearce.

Boulding, K. B. (1959). National images and international systems. *Journal of Conflict Resolution 3*, 120–131.

Boulding, K. B. (1965). "The Image." Ann Arbor, Michigan: University of Michigan Press.

Boyd-Barrett, O. (1970). Journalism recruitment and training: Problems in professionalization. *In* J. Tunstall (Ed.), "Media Sociology: A Reader," pp. 181–201. Urbana, Illinois: University of Illinois Press.

Christians, C. G., and Carey, J. (1981). The logic and aims of qualitative research. *In* G. Stempel and B. Westley (Eds.), "Research Methods in Mass Communication." Englewood Cliffs, New Jersey: Prentice-Hall.

Conrad, R. (1955). Social images in East and West Germany: A comparative study of matched newspapers in two social systems. *Social Forces 33*, 281–285.

Dajani, N., and Donohue, J. (1973). Foreign news in the Arab press: A content analysis of six area dailies. *Gazette 14*, 155–170.

Day, J. L. (1968). The Latin American journalist: A tentative profile. *Journalism Quarterly 45*, 509–515.

DeBock, H. (1980). Gratification frustration during a newspaper strike and a TV blackout. *Journalism Quarterly 57*, 61–66; 78.

Dervin, B. (1980). Communication gaps and inequities: Moving toward a reconceptualization. *Progress in Communication Sciences 2*, 73–112.

Donsbach, W. (1981). Legitimacy through competence rather than value judgments: The concept of journalistic professionalization reconsidered. *Gazette 27*, 47–67.

Edelstein, A. S. (1974). "The Uses of Communication in Decision-Making: A Comparative Study of Yugoslavia and the United States." New York: Praeger.

Edelstein, A. S. (1982). "Comparative Communication Research." Beverly Hills, California: Sage.

Edelstein, A. S., and Hall, E. P., Jr. (1979). Sources of images of modern and traditional Japan: Situational and cognitive perspectives. *Studies of Broadcasting 15*, 15–30.

Ettema, J. S., and Kline, F. G. (1977). Deficits, differences, and ceilings: Continent conditions for understanding the knowledge gap. *Communication Research 4*, 179–202.

Frey, F. W. (1973). Communication and development. *In* de S. Pool, F. W. Frey, W. Schramm, N. Maccoby, and E. B. Parker (Eds.), "Handbook of Communication," pp. 337–461. Chicago, Illinois: Rand McNally.

Galtung, J. (1971). A structural theory of imperialism. *Journal of Peace Research 8*, 81–118.

Galtung, J., and Ruge, M. H. (1965). The structure of foreign news. *Journal of Peace Research 2*, 64–91.

Gerbner, G. (1961). Press perspectives in world communication: A pilot study. *Journalism Quarterly 38*, 313–322.

Gerbner, G. (1966). Images across cultures: Teachers in mass media fiction and drama. *School Review 74*, 12–30.

Gerbner, G. (1969). The film hero: A cross-cultural study. *Journalism Monographs* (No. 13).

Gerbner, G. (1973). Teacher image in mass culture: Symbolic functions of the "hidden curriculum." In G. Gerbner, L. P. Gross, and W. H. Melody (Eds.), "Communications Technology and Social Policy: Understanding the New 'Cultural Revolution.' " New York: John Wiley & Sons.

Gerbner, G. (1977). Comparative cultural indicators. In G. Gerbner (Ed.), "Mass Media Policies in Changing Cultures," pp. 199–205, New York: John Wiley & Sons.

Gerbner, G., and Marvanyi, G. (1977). The many worlds of the world's press. *Journal of Communication 27* (No. 1), 52–66.

Glaser, B. (1965). The constant comparative method of qualitative analysis. *Social Problems 12*, 436–445.

Hardt, H. (1979). "Social Theories of the Press: Early German and American Perspectives." Beverly Hills, California: Sage.

Hursh-Cesar, G., and Roy, P. (1976). "Third World Surveys: Survey Research in Developing Nations." Columbia, Missouri: South Asia Books.

Inkeles, A., and Smith, D. H. (1974). "Becoming Modern: Individual Change in Six Developing Countries." Cambridge, Massachusetts: Harvard University Press.

International Press Institute (1953). "The Flow of the News." Zurich, Switzerland: International Press Institute.

International Press Institute (1954a). "As Others See Us." Zurich, Switzerland: International Press Institute.

International Press Institute (1954b). "The News From the Middle East." Zurich, Switzerland: International Press Institute.

Isaacs, H. R. (1958). "Scratches on Our Minds." New York: John Day.

Isaacs, H. R. (1962). "Images of Asia: American Views of China and India." New York: Capricorn Books.

Katz, E., Gurevitch, M., and Haas, H. (1973). On the use of the mass media for important things. *American Sociological Review 38,* 164–181.

Kayser, J. (1953). "One-Week's News: Comparative Study of 17 Major Dailies for a Seven-Day Period." Paris: UNESCO.

Kelman, H. C., and Ezekial, E. S. (1970). "Cross-National Encounters." San Francisco, California: Jossey-Bass.

Kimball, P. (1959). People without papers. *Public Opinion Quarterly 23,* 389–398.

Lee, C. C. (1981). "Media Images of America: Problems, Findings, and a Case Study." Unpublished, Southern Illinois University.

Lerner, D. (1958). "The Passing of Traditional Society: Modernizing the Middle East." New York: Free Press.

McAnany, E. G. (Ed.). (1980). "Communication in the Rural Third World: The Role of Information in Development." New York: Praeger.

McClelland, D. C. (1961). "The Achieving Society." Princeton, New Jersey: Van Nostrand.

McLeod, J. M., and Rush, R. (1969). Professionalization of Latin American and United States journalists. *Journalism Quarterly 46,* 583–590, 784–789.

Menanteau-Horta, D. (1967). Professionalization of journalists in Santiago de Chile. *Journalism Quarterly 44,* 715–724.

Murray, J. P., and Kippax, S. (1978). Children's social behavior in three towns with differing television experience. *Journal of Communication 28,* (No. 1), 19–29.

Nnaemeka, T., and Richstad, J. (1980). Structural relations and foreign news flow in the Pacific region. *Gazette 26,* 235–257.

Noelle-Neumann E., Kocher, R., and Elliot, P. (1980). "Professional Views of Journalists: A German-English Study." (Paper presented at the International Association for Mass Communication Research meeting, Caracas, Venezuela.)

Passin, H. (1963). Writer and journalist in the transitional society. *In* L. W. Pye (Ed.), "Communications and Political Development," pp. 82–123. Princeton, New Jersey: Princeton University Press.

Pisarek, W. (1981). Heroes of foreign news: A Polish perspective on newsmakers in socialist and nonsocialist newspapers. *Mass Communication Review Yearbook 2,* 759–768.

Pool, I. de S. (1970). "The Prestige Press: A Comparative Study of Political Symbols." Cambridge, Massachusetts: MIT Press.

Pool, I. de S., Lasswell, H. D., and Lerner, D. (1952a). "The 'Prestige Papers': A Survey of Their Editorials." Stanford, California: Stanford University Press. (Hoover Institute Studies, Series C: Symbols, No. 2).

Pool, I. de S., Lasswell, H. D., and Lerner, D. (1952b). "Symbols of Democracy." Stanford, California: Stanford University Press. (Hoover Institute Studies, Series C: Symbols, No. 4).

Pye, L. W. (Ed.). (1963). "Communications and Political Development." Princeton, New Jersey: Princeton University Press.

Rachty, G. (1979). "Foreign News in Nine Arab Countries." (Paper presented at Conference on International News Media, Cairo.)

Robinson, J. P., and Converse, R. E. (1972). The impact of television on mass media usage: A cross-national comparison. *In* A. Szalai (Ed.), "The Use of Time: Daily Activities of Urban and Suburban Population in Twelve Countries." Paris: Mouton.

Rogers, E. M., and Shoemaker, F. F. (1969). "Diffusions of Innovations in Brazil, Nigeria and India." East Lansing, Michigan: Department of Communications, Michigan State University. (Research Report No. 24.)

Rosengren, K. E. (1974). International news: Methods, data, and theory. *Journal of Peace Research 11*, 145–156.

Rosengren, K. E. (1977). International news: Four types of tables. *Journal of Communication 27* (No. 1), 67–75.

Roy, P., Waisanen, F. B., and Rogers, E. M. (1969). "The Impact of Communication on Rural Development: An Investigation in Costa Rica and India." Paris: UNESCO.

Schramm, W. (1959). "One Day in the World's Press: Fourteen Great Newspapers on a Day of Crisis." Stanford, California: Stanford University Press.

Schramm, W. (1980). Circulation of news in the Third World: A study of Asia. *Mass Communication Review Yearbook 1*, 589–619.

Schramm, W. (1982). Preface. *In* A. S. Edelstein, "Comparative Communication Research," pp. 7–12. Beverly Hills, California: Sage.

Schramm, W., and Ruggels, W. L. (1967). How mass media systems grow. *In* D. Lerner and W. Schramm (Eds.), "Communication and Change in the Developing Countries," pp. 57–75. Honolulu, Hawaii: East-West Center Press.

Scott, W. A. (1965). Psychological and social correlates of international images. *In* H. C. Kelman (Ed.), "International Behavior: A Social-Psychological Analysis," pp. 71–103. New York: Holt, Rinehart and Winston.

Sreberny-Mohammadi, A., Nordenstreng, K., Stevenson, R., and Ugboajah, F. (1980). "The World of the News: The News of the World." (Final Report of the Foreign Images Study Undertaken by the International Association for Mass Communication Research.) Paris: UNESCO.

Starck, K., and Sudhaker, A. (1979). Reconceptualziing the notion of journalistic professionalism across differing press systems. *Journal of Communication Inquiry 4*, 33–52.

Stevenson, R. L., and Cole R. R. (1979). "Foreign News Coverage in the Press of 13 Nations." (Paper presented at the USICA Seminar on Problems of International Communication and the Free Flow of Information, Washington, D.C.)

Stevenson, R. L., and Cole, R. R. (1980). "Patterns of World Coverage by the Major Western Agencies." (Paper presented at the International Communication Association meeting, Acapulco, Mexico.)

Tichenor, P., Donohue, G., and Olien, C. (1970). Mass media and differential growth in knowledge. *Public Opinion Quarterly 34*, 158–170.

Tunstall, J. (Ed.) (1970). "Media Sociology: A Reader." Urbana, Illinois: University of Illinois Press.

Van Poecke, L. (1980). Gerbner's cultural indicators: The system is the message. *Mass Communication Review Yearbook 1*, 423–431.

Vidmar, N., and Rokeach, M. (1974). Archie Bunker's bigotry: A study in selective perception and exposure. *Journal of Communication 24* (No. 1), 36–47.

Weaver, D., and DeBock, H. (1980). Personal needs and media use in the Netherlands and the United States. *Gazette 26*, 171–194.

Wiio, O. A., and McCallister, L. (1981). "Sex and Communication Uncertainty: A Comparison of American and European Organizations." Helsinki, Finland: Department of Communication, University of Helsinki.

Wilhoit, G. C., and DeBock, H. (1976). "All in the family" in Holland. *Journal of Communication 26* (No. 4), 75–84.

Willis, R. H. (1968). Ethnic and national images: People vs. nations. *Public Opinion Quarterly 32*, 186–201.

Wolfe, W. (1964). Images of the United States in the Latin American press. *Journalism Quarterly 41*, 79–86.

4

Critical Perspectives on the State of Intercultural Communication Research

Rita Atwood
Department of Radio-Television-Film
University of Texas, Austin
Austin, Texas 78712

I. INTRODUCTION

Interest in the area of intercultural communication research has expanded rapidly in recent years as academic institutions have developed courses, academic associations have created special divisions, and both public and private sector enterprises have originated training programs concerning intercultural communication. In addition, evidence of this expansion can be found in the proliferation of communication journal articles, as well as a number of contemporary books focusing on intercultural communication issues (Asante et al., 1979; Casmir, 1978; Condon and Yousef, 1975; Dodd, 1977; Fischer and Merrill, 1976; Harms, 1973; Prosser, 1973; Ruhly, 1976; Samovar and Porter, 1982; Samovar et al., 1981; Sarbaugh, 1979; Sitaram and Cogdell, 1976; Smith, 1966).

A. Diversity in Intercultural Communication Research

While a large portion of past research on intercultural communication has stemmed from scholars who have centered attention on interpersonal contact among individuals from diverse cultures, increasing attention is being given to the role of mass communication software and technology as vehicles of intercultural exchange. Prosser (1978, p. 340) describes the significance of mass media technology in the realm of intercultural communication by saying:

> Intracultural, intercultural, and cross-cultural communication almost literally cannot take place without the availability of channels and media, whether of a traditional form such as the drum or the technological form such as the transistor radio or satellite communication. Some writers have assumed that such communication takes place almost entirely in the interpersonal setting. This view misses the point that technology and the technological communication systems have the most profound effect on all human interaction.

Adler's (1976, p. 363) emphasis on the importance of mass communications in interpersonal and intercultural communication is similar. He argues that the network capacity of mass communication has made possible the potential for contact among people everywhere for the first time in history, and he suggests that the impact of such potential is enormous.

The beneficial or detrimental nature of such an impact is the subject of numerous debates regarding whether mass communication fosters or hampers intercultural understanding, and whether media and new information technology serve as tools of cultural hegemony and erosion, or as tools of productive modernization and development. Thus, a growing number of researchers are examining the ways in which cultural groups differ in their utilization of mass media, as well as how mass media influence cultural stability and change (Edelstein, 1974; Gerbner, 1977; Guback, 1969; Katz and Wedell, 1979; Lee, 1980; Lent, 1978, 1979; McAnany, 1980; McAnany et al., 1981; McPhail, 1981; Nordenstreng and Varis, 1974; Nordenstreng and Schiller, 1979; Pool, 1972; Rogers, 1976; Schiller, 1969, 1976, 1979; Smythe, 1981; Tunstall, 1977; Wells, 1972, 1974).

Although the augmentation of research literature regarding mass communication and culture is of great value to the field of intercultural communication inquiry, this literature only heightens the confusion surrounding the description of boundaries which encompass such inquiry. For example, Sarbaugh (1979, pp. 5–6) claims that intercultural communication is often equated with international communication because national boundaries are easier to identify than cultural boundaries. Condon and Yousef (1975, pp. 48–49) suggest that it is much more difficult to identify cultures than to identify nations, and cautions that "A nation is a political entity which may contain within it many quite different cultures; similarly, national borders may politically distinguish areas which are culturally identical." Maletzke (1976, p. 410) differentiates between intercultural and international communication research in this way:

Whereas intercultural communication is an exchange of meaning between cultures, international communication takes place on the level of countries or nations, which is to say across frontiers. This means, intercultural and international communication can, on occasion, be identical, but this is not always so. Very often people who belong to a common culture are separated by a state frontier, with the effect that international communication is taking place within a single culture. And, the contrary case, humans of quite differing cultures can be united in the same state, so that within this single state intercultural communication can take place. It is thus that one tends to use the word international when speaking of communication on the purely political level, whereas the concept of intercultural communication corresponds more to sociological and anthropological realities.

Numerous other types of distinctions flourish within the intercultural communication's literature. Harms (1973, p. 41) separates "intercultural" communication from "cross-cultural" communication by explaining that the former consists primarily of dyadic interchange in informal circumstances, whereas the latter consists of one-way communication in large formal group contexts. Samovar et al. (1981, p. 35), however, suggest that "cross-cultural" and "transcultural" communication are terms synonymous with "intercultural communication." Rogers and Burdge (1972, p. 31) distinguish between cultural groups and "subcultures" by arguing that "a subculture contains many elements of the broader culture of which it is a part, yet it can be characterized by particulars which set it apart from other parts of the culture." Other perspectives on cultural groups and communication have resulted in terms such as intracultural, interracial, interethnic, and transracial communication (Alcock et al., 1979; Dodd, 1977; Sitaram, 1982; Smith, 1966). Rich and Ogawa (1981, p. 46) have even suggested the notion of "contracultural" communication to represent the interaction between a dominant culture in a colonial relation to a subservient culture.

This range of divergent descriptions reflects the complexity of intercultural communication research—a complexity which is not without its drawbacks. Stewart (1978, p. 265) addresses several of these problems, and states:

> Intercultural communication is called a field for simplicity in writing. This area of communication is so loosely structured that some writers deny to it the status of a field in any formal sense. The ambiguous theoretical structure reflects the status of both major concepts, communication and culture, which have stoutly resisted formal definitions in the social sciences.

Saral (1980, p. 396) also discusses the ambiguity of boundaries in intercultural communication research, and says:

> . . . in spite of the wide recognition received by intercultural communication in the form of academic, business, and professional acceptance, the field is still somewhat at a crossroad and has not managed fully to define and/or delimit its scope.

However, Saral (1980, p. 397) calls for more than efforts toward definitional specificity, suggesting instead that the most "conspicuous inadequacy" of intercultural communication research is the lack of useful theories and research models.

B. Calls for Conceptual Shifts

A variety of scholars are expressing similar concerns and are calling for significant shifts in the conceptualization and operationalization of intercultural communication variables. Becker (1969, p. 4) contends that it is time to depart from intercultural communication research traditions which have addressed complex problems with "cookie-cutter" methods. Chu (1976) criticizes both the inadequate concepts and the lack of comparative research which have hampered intercultural communication studies. Casmir (1978, p. 4) claims that the bane of much of past research in both intercultural and international communication contexts is that "episodic, highly limited, but often interesting and informative reports of culture-specific ways of dealing with such matters as food, time, sex, family relations, and age have unfortunately done little to allow broader, generally applicable, or generalizable insights." Asante et al. (1979, p. 12) argue that certain basic notions about human behavior underlying past intercultural communication research are in need of a "revolutionary overhaul." Atwood and Dervin (1982) charge that the limited utility of past communication research incorporating socio-cultural predictors of communication behavior is related to a set of inappropriate assumptions regarding communication and culture. Yu (1977, p. 171) focuses attention on research related to communication policy and national development, but nevertheless articulates one of the central problems facing intercultural communication scholars when he says:

> It is all very easy—and fashionable these days, too—to say that we live in intimately interdependent world, that formulation of communication policies should go beyond the traditional rather piecemeal approach to individual communication

systems . . . . For this task to be completed, we need no less than a major conceptual breakthrough about communication and development, and about the "interdependence"—at national, regional, and global levels—between communication systems and political, economic, cultural, and social systems.

Yu (1977, p. 171) goes on to say that the need for sorting out the vast array of ideas existing in research literature on communication, culture, and national development would be "ridiculous, if it were not so imperative."

In a sense, any critical review of an area as complex as intercultural communicaton confronts the same kind of dilemma that Yu suggests. Although a number of scholars advocate the need for conceptual breakthroughs in intercultural communication research, some of the most basic tasks of sorting out, identifying, and assessing the concepts that have guided research to date have only been initiated in recent years. The paucity of this kind of critical analysis of the intercultural communication literature is due, in part, to the ambiguity problem that Saral (1980) and Stewart (1978) emphasize. The nature and scope of the field of intercultural communication widens and narrows somewhat like an accordion, depending on which scholar is calling the definitional tune. While this review and critique of several important conceptual issues is no exception to such scholarly selectivity, an effort is made to draw widely from both interpersonal communication and mass communication literature relating to intercultural communication issues. However, there are rich bodies of literature dealing with linguistics and nonverbal communication, among others, which are not treated in this article. Nevertheless, the debate concerning what most appropriately falls into the arena of intercultural communication serves as a starting point for examining several fundamental assumptions at the core of this debate. In addition, the calls for significant conceptual shifts in intercultural communication research require that these basic assumptions be assessed.

Therefore, the purpose of this review is to call attention to the complexity and confusion existing within intercultural communication research; to identify and describe several major sources of this complexity and confusion; and to offer several alternative concepts which may improve the utility and coherence of future inquiries. Consistent with these objectives, this review contains a brief description of several controversies emerging in intercultural communication literature, and an overview of the historical development of assumptions which underlie these controversies. In addition, several significant challenges to both the conceptualizations and operationalizations of cultural and communication variables evident in past research are presented.

II. HISTORICAL DEVELOPMENT OF CONCEPTS
RELATED TO CULTURE AND COMMUNICATION

Any discussion of major assumptions in past intercultural communication research should include a review of the definitions of culture which have guided such research. However, as Dodd (1977, p. 9) points out, "culture has been defined by theorists in many fields of inquiry so that nearly two hundred definitions of 'culture' exist.'' Actually, Dodd's estimation of the number of definitions regarding culture probably stems from work by Kroeber and Kluckhohn (1952), who attempted to describe the various types of cultural definitions in existence and cited almost 200 different versions. In spite of the fact that this estimate may be somewhat misleading (Michaels, 1982), intercultural communication scholars have availed themselves of the rich and diverse heritage of views on culture. While a comprehensive accounting of these myriad definitions of culture is beyond the scope of this article, a sample of various definitions will suffice to illustrate the range and scope.

A. Legacy of Views on Culture

Most scholars agree that the term ''culture,'' as it is used in most social science research, originated with the works of Tylor (1958) in the 1880s. Other anthropologists such as Boas, Malinowski, and Kluckhohn have been cited by intercultural communication scholars as being influential in shaping the concept of culture (Sarbaugh, 1979). However, this legacy reflects the assertion made by Hall (1977, p. 12) that ''few anthropologists are in agreement as to what to include under the general rubric of culture.'' One illustration is that, while Herskovits (1966, p. 305) argues that culture is the ''man-made part of the environment,'' Triandis et al. (1972, p. 4) suggest that researchers should focus on a ''cultural group's characteristic way of perceiving the man-made part of the environment.'' Other scholars adhere to the position that culture consists primarily of shared norms and values (Goodenough, 1956; Kluckhohn, 1951; Kluckhohn and Strodtbeck, 1961; Sitaram and Cogdell, 1976; Sitaram and Haapenen, 1979). Harms (1973, p. 32) says that culture ''consists of the learning acquired by the members of a group in the process of living as they live.'' Glenn (1966 p. 248–272) suggests that the ''culture of a population can be defined as the sum total of the meanings shared by that population.'' Rogers and Burdge (1972, p. 30) offer another broad view of culture when they describe culture as ''material and nonmaterial aspects of a way of life, which are shared and transmitted among the members of a society.'' Samovar and Porter (1982, p. 31) describe the complex heritage of views on culture in this way:

> Formally defined, culture is the deposit of knowledge, experiences, beliefs, values, attitudes, meanings, hierarchies, religion, timing, roles, spatial relations, concepts of universe, and material objects and possessions acquired by a large group of people in the course of generations through individual and group striving.

Given the multiplicity of meanings for culture utilized in intercultural communication research, then, it is not too surprising to find the variety of terms denoting specific approaches to intercultural communication research described in an earlier section of this article. It would not be difficult to expand the list of these types of distinctions by adding, for example, intersexual communication, interpolitical communication, intersocioeconomic communication, and interreligious communication. However unadvisable this may seem to some, it does seem to be a direction that the field of intercultural communication research is taking. This direction is related not only to ambiguity of the notion of culture, but also to the related ideas concerning cultural homogeneity and heterogeneity. In fact, the attempt to focus on more specific and narrow conceptions of cultural groups may be a response, in part, to the increasing number of scholars calling for clarification of cultural similarity and difference. Asante et al. (1979, p. 11) argue for the need to explicate the similarities and differences which foster or deter communication across cultures. Prosser (1978, p. 336) suggests that "central to the study of communication between members of different cultures is the importance of similarities and differences as they affect all intercultural and cross-cultural communication." Dodd (1977, p. 4) equates cultural homogeneity and heterogeneity in terms of "sociocultural experiences" and says:

> One can refer to cross-cultural communication as a process of interpersonal or media interaction between persons of differing sociocultural experiences. Just what constitutes the perimeters of "differing sociocultural experiences" is still a matter of scholarly discussion.

In addition to such scholarly discussion regarding the nature of similarities and differences in "sociocultural experiences," there exists a considerable range of perspectives regarding the ways in which cultural homogeneity and hetereogeneity are associated with similarities and differences in communication behavior and communication processes. In fact, some researchers treat culture and communication as synonymous or inseparable (Smith, 1966; Prosser, 1978). Condon and Yousef (1975, p. 4) state that "much of what is called 'patterns of communication' could be—and is, in other contexts—called cultural patterns." Samovar et al. (1981) suggest that culture and communication are viewed as identical by many cultural anthropologists, and these views have influenced communication researchers. Fitchen (1978, p. 131) argues that "culture may be regarded as a preference for certain patterns of communication."

Therefore, in order to more clearly identify some of the basic assumptions which have guided intercultural communication research, it will be useful to go beyond a brief description of the legacy of views on culture and provide a cursory review of the development of ideas regarding communication.

B. Legacy of Views on Communication

Many contemporary scholars in communication have adopted or adapted classical assumptions concerning persuasion and rhetoric as fundamental to theories of communication. Several of the main tenets of this historical tradition are that the power, skill, and intentions of the sender will determine the degree of message persuasibility and, subsequently, the effects of the message upon the receiver. Harper (1979, p. 262) examines the historical traditions of communication theory and concludes that "definitions of human communication throughout history exhibit a striking consistency." She identifies several of these consistent components as the notion that communication is usually an attempt to influence others, and that these attempts involve both the discovery and transmission of ideas. Harper (1979, p. 267) states:

> From the classical through the modern period, theorists agree that communication is ultimately a means of influencing others' beliefs and/or behaviors in "contingent" affairs. Thus, in their definitions, most theorists emphasize conviction, or instruction, and persuasion.

Current descriptions of communication theory and definitions of communication support the argument that certain ideas about communication have changed very little since Aristotle's time (Littlejohn, 1978; Mortensen, 1973). For example, Shannon and Weaver (1949, p. 95) conceive of communication as "all the procedures by which one mind can affect another." Miller (1966, p. 2) explains the nature of communication as situations in which "a source transmits a message to a receiver with the conscious intent to affect the latter's behaviors." Discussing intercultural communication, Smith (1966, p. 3) suggests that "through communication people control one another's behavior and unite themselves into groups." Samovar et al. (1981, pp. 10–16) state that the focus of communication resides in meanings assigned by the receiver; however, they go on to define communication as the process in which a source transmits a message to receivers with the intent of inducing a particular change in attitude or behavior.

While the previous examples have stemmed largely from researchers who focus on interpersonal communication, researchers interested in mass communication exchanges have also based their inquiries on similar ideas, incorporating the notion of channels for mediated communication (Lasswell, 1948; Westley and Maclean, 1957). Although scholars engaging in current critical approaches to intercultural mass communication have expanded the idea of sender to include institutions and international systems of message production and dissemination, they continue to emphasize the sender intentions, and the persuasive power of messages as crucial elements in the power struggle of cultural dominance (Guback, 1969; Hachten, 1981; Lent, 1978; McPhail, 1981; Nordenstreng and Schiller, 1979; Tunstall, 1977; Wells, 1972, 1974).

It should be noted that the role of the receiver in the communication process, and the function of receiver feedback to senders, has not gone unnoticed in communication and information theory. However, the attention paid to the role of the receiver has been tempered by the importance attributed to sender and message in the bulk of past research. This issue is discussed in more detail in a later section of this article.

Based on these summaries of the development of concepts relating to both culture and communication, two, somewhat circular, ideas about the links between culture and communication can be identified. The first of these ideas is that culture is deterministic of communication, and the second is that communication is a vehicle for the transmission of culture and, therefore, deterministic of such culture. A number of related assumptions have relevance for critical commentary on the state of intercultural communication research.

III. ASSUMPTIONS REGARDING THE RELATIONSHIP OF CULTURE AND COMMUNICATION

The notion that culture is a determinant of communication behavior, as well as of the institutions and technology associated with communication processes, is prevalent in intercultural communication research. In addition, a closely related notion of communication senders, messages, and channels influencing the stability and transformation of cultural systems is evident.

A. Culture as Deterministic of Communication

Numerous intercultural communication researchers have expressed the view that culture shapes and determines human communication behavior and the communication technology and institutions related to this behavior. Samovar and Porter (1982, p. 31) express such a perspective in this way:

> Culture is persistent, enduring and omnipresent; it includes all of the behavioral reinforcements received during the course of a lifetime . . . . Perhaps a way to understand cultural influence is by way of an analogy with electronic computers. As we program computers to do what they do, our culture to a great extent programs us to be what we are. Our culture affects us in a deterministic manner from conception to death—and even after death in terms of funeral rites.

Other scholars have made more direct reference to the influence of culture on human communication behavior. Hall and Whyte (1973) delineate a number of specific ways in which culture determines the kind of interpersonal interaction among people. Harms (1973, p. 30) states that "the cultural background of a communicator influences almost every detail and every pattern of his communication activities." Dodd (1977, p. 1) suggests that "socio-cultural communication involves cultural and social system variables as antecedent factors influencing intercultural or cross-cultural communication." Kim (1979, pp. 435-436) describes the impact of culture on communication behavior by saying:

> Culture is imprinted in the individual as a pattern of perceptions that is accepted and expected by others in a society. Since we are programmed by culture from the very

day we are born, we are rarely conscious of the "hidden grips" of culture that influence the way we think and move, and the way we express ourselves verbally and nonverbally . . . . we are deeply controlled by culture.

Thus, the notion of cultural determinism appears to lead to the conclusion that cultural homogeneity is associated with similarities in communication behavior, whereas cultural heterogeneity is related to differences in communication behavior.

Closely associated with this assumption is the belief that when people are from different cultural backgrounds, and are therefore thought to differ in their communication behaviors, they will have a much more difficult time understanding one another. This assumption is articulated by Smith (1966, p. 565) when he says that a message exchanged across cultural boundaries "greatly increases the possibility of misunderstanding and of unexpected reactions." Dodd (1977, p. 1) states that "cultural differences or similarities alone are potent enough to hinder or to heighten communication." Singer (1982, p. 55) argues that the degree of similarity of perception existing among individuals corresponds directly to their ease of communicating with each other, to the frequency of their interaction, and to their sense of common identity. Tyler (1978, p. 364) suggests that the greater the gap between cultural backgrounds, the greater the number of "gaps" that will be encountered in attempting communication. Harms (1973, p. 3) summarizes the ramifications of cultural distance in the communication process by saying:

Communication between communicators of similar cultural backgrounds is usually easier, more reliable, faster, safer, etc., than is communication between communicators of dissimilar cultural backgrounds.

Intercultural communication literature provides ample opportunity to witness the manifestations of these assumptions. For example, numerous studies of subcultures in the United States have attempted to offer evidence that people's communication behavior, particularly their information seeking and use behaviors, differ in accord with observable, invariant cultural characteristics. These cultural characteristics are often represented by demographic variables such as race (Comstock and Cobbey, 1979; Comstock et al., 1978; Dervin and Greenberg, 1972; Poindexter and Stromann, 1979); or socioeconomic status (Childers and Post, 1975; Ettema and Kline, 1977; Greenberg and Dervin, 1970.) As Dervin (1980, p. 78) points out:

When research is conducted using the traditional communication model, the results consistently show that those with less education and lower incomes are less likely to be information seekers, use expert information sources, be informed generally, have informed interpersonal contacts, . . . have information processing skills, have sufficient background information that would allow them to become aware of and understand informational messages, or trust establishment and organizational sources.

In addition, researchers have arqued that such subcultural distinctions have utility in predicting the ease with which people are able to communicate, (Blubaugh and Pennington, 1976; Browne, 1968; Cohen, 1968; Pennington, 1979; Smith, 1966).

More specifically on the level of mass communication, researchers have also viewed mass media content and technology as shaped by cultural forces. These research contexts include stereotyping of cultural minorities, as well as foreign peoples, and the creation of communication technologies and systems of message production and distribution. However, the focus of most of these research endeavors is on the cultural impact of communication, or the role of communication in the transfer of culture.

B. Communication as Deterministic of Culture

The distinctions between assumptions of culture influencing communication and communication influencing culture are often hazy in intercultural communication research, because the assumptions relate to two different phases in the same process. In other words, emphasis on communication as a vehicle for the transmission of culture implies that communication has been culturally determined. Nevertheless, it is useful for the purposes of this article to consider some of the major arguments concerning the deterministic nature of communication, particularly in regard to the maintenance and transformation of culture.

Communication has long been viewed as a mechanism by which people maintain, as well as express, their cultures (Hall, 1977). With the advent of mass communications and new information technology, there was initial optimism that people from less-developed "cultures" could benefit by exposure to information from the more developed "cultures." This was a view of communication, then, which involved the notion of cultural transformation, the modernization of societies (Lerner, 1958; Pool, 1963; Pye, 1963; Rogers, 1962; Rogers and Shoemaker, 1971; Schramm, 1964).

More recently, an increasing number of scholars have voiced concern that mass media content created in one cultural context and exported to another may have detrimental effects on the members of the recipient culture. As Bogart (1976, p. 66) says, not only do media create new life interest and mold tastes, but "the world of media no longer mirrors the world of real events. It helps create it." Nordenstreng and Schiller, (1979, xii) argue that "the cultural agencies of the world, a nation, and a local community are determined by the informational system . . ." which they claim is organized on the basis of the power and values hierarchy of the worldwide business system. Sauvant (1979, p. 13) summarizes the concerns of cultural dominance via mass media in this way:

Through television, therefore, an increasing number of persons is exposed, on a daily basis, to the way of life of the main developed countries, to their preconceptions and ideals. Together, all these mechanisms . . . disseminate the values and behavioral patterns of a few major developed countries, which thus keep— intentionally or not—the developing countries within the sociocultural orbit of these countries.

Thorough overviews and summaries of the proliferating body of literature dealing with mass media imperialism, cultural dependency, and mass media and national development can be found in works by Casmir (1978), Fischer and Merrill (1976), Hur (1982), Mattelart and Siegelaub (1979), Mattos (1982), McAnany (1980), McAnany et al. (1981), and Nordenstreng and Schiller (1979). In addition, studies which focus specifically on certain types of imported media content are illustrated by Beltran (1978), Breen (1975), Guerrero et al. (1976), Goldsen and Bibliowicz (1976), Marquez (1975), and Tsai (1970).

The notion of communication impacting culture is also evident in studies which investigate the ways in which media content developed by White males in the United States stereotype and affect ethnic minorities and women (Busby, 1974; Butler and Paisley, 1980; Poindexter and Stromann, 1979; United States Commission on Civil Rights, 1977, 1979). Examples of how ethnic minorities in other nations are affected by media content and technology can be found in Coldevin (1976), Granzberg et al. (1977), and Hudson (1977).

One avenue of response to these concerns about the negative influence of communication on culture has been pursued by researchers suggesting that forms of traditional communication or folk media be given more attention (Ascroft and Gleason, 1980; Ascroft and Brody, 1982; Hachten, 1971; McLean, 1982). Another avenue has been pursued by those who suggest various systems of alternative communication (Atwood and Mattos, 1982; Matta, 1981). What these different perspectives have in common is the desire to discover ways in which the current communication systems can be prevented from eroding important cultural components—components which may, in turn, be necessary for effective communication among members of divergent cultural and subcultural groups.

While a number of scholars agree in principle with the objectives of those researchers who wish to minimize the detrimental effects of culture on communication or communication on culture, they disagree with some of the assumptions which have guided such efforts. The following section presents several arguments regarding these basic assumptions.

IV. CHALLENGES TO TRADITIONAL ASSUMPTIONS IN INTERCULTURAL COMMUNICATION RESEARCH

The fundamental assumptions which have dominated intercultural research in both interpersonal and mass communication contexts involve the ways in which culture shapes communication, and the ways in which communication affects culture. Thus, cultural homogeneity and hetereogeneity have been seen as directly linked to similarities and differences in communication processes. However, there is a growing number of scholars who argue that past intercultural communication research based on these assumptions has failed to provide many of the insights needed for a clearer understanding of the relationship of culture and communication. In fact, there are a number of significant issues on which these scholars challenge the utility of past assumptions. Two of the most basic arenas of challenge can serve as the context in which several of these issues are discussed. The first of these is the challenge to the notion of culture as deterministic of communication, and the second is the challenge to the notion of communication as deterministic of culture. In the first case, arguments presented support the idea of subjective situational culture and, in the second, support the idea of subjective situational communication. Taken together, these arguments constitute a basis for suggesting that people situationally create, to varying extents, both their cultural identities and their communication behaviors, and that such creative activity must be taken into account in intercultural communication research.

A. Subjective Situational Culture

One of the main dilemmas underlying the notion of culture as deterministic of communication has been the diversity of ways in which cultural similarities and differences have been defined. Alternatives to the use of subcultural group criteria, such as race, and cultural criteria, such as national citizenship, have been offered. For example Samovar et al. (1981) and Sarbaugh (1979) recommend viewing cultural homogeneity and heterogeneity on a continuum. Thus, French and North American cultures would be seen as more similar than Asian and North American cultures. However, there are scholars who contend that a more radical shift in the conceptualization of cultural similarities and differences is needed.

Martin (1976, p. 431) says that thinking about culture on a geographic continuum assumes unrealistic distinctions. He states:

> To say that a person belonging to the Western culture and another to the Oriental culture is to suggest mutual exclusivity that certainly does not exist. Two individuals belonging to the so-called Western culture may be more different in many of their cultural traits than one of these individuals is from someone belonging to the so-called Oriental culture.

Tyler (1978, p. 365) reinforces this position by suggesting that researchers recognize that "the complexity between cultural differences is often greater within cultures." Tyler et al. (1979, p. 232) state that "often differences within any individual culture are as great as the difference between cultures."

These researchers are positing that past efforts at employing cultural distinctions as predictive of human communication behaviors have not paid adequate attention to variance which occurs within the boundaries of those distinctions. For example, Sarbaugh (1979, p. 3), points out that "even within the same family, there develop different norms, beliefs, social positions, etc. which complicate the transactions in which those persons engage." Prosser (1976, p. 422) argues that because no two persons are the same, each person is a "cultural communicator," and "each of us communicates interculturally all the time at many levels." This argument, however, poses a seemingly paradoxical problem: if researchers wish to understand the relationship of cultural and communication variables, then cultural similarities and differences must be identified in some way—yet the vast array of possibilities for conceptualizing and operationalizing cultural homogeneity and heterogeneity appear to make the task of any theoretical consensus impossible.

In response to such an apparent paradox, certain scholars are suggesting that the confusion over the multiplicity of cultural definitions arises from epistemological questions, not merely definitional ones. In other words, these researchers argue that the approach to classifying people into cultures or subcultures has been based largely on the estimations of the researcher/observer, rather than on the perception of the actor/subject under study. Thus, prior research in intercultural communication has aggregated people into cultural collectivities on the basis of observable characteristics, rather than on subjective reports of cultural affinity as perceived by the individuals under study. Casmir (1978, p. 261) discusses the problem of making accurate obsevations of cultural identity and states:

> Much of the problem results simply from the dynamic nature of man, the dynamic communication of human beings, the constantly changing nature of the total human process and the human communication process. This must be coupled with the fact that what we summarize as culture is always used, interpreted, or rejected by individual human beings in keeping with their personal survival needs. Cultural consistencies thus may be no more than statistical averages compiled by an observer, for which we may have difficulty finding specific examples in the daily lives of members of a given culture.

The issue Casmir raises is a very significant one for intercultural communication researchers—the issue of whether our delineations of cultural homogeneity and heterogeneity have a useful fit with the delineations that people make for themselves.

Other scholars concerned with basic assumptions in intercultural communication research have expressed similar perspectives. Adler (1976, p. 366) contends that the "center, or core, of cultural identity is an image of the self and culture intertwined in the individual's total conception of reality." Triandis (1972, p. 341) asserts that future research must examine the way in which individuals "cut the pie of experience" in terms of cultural similarities and differences. Hall (1977, p. 100) suggests that any understanding of cultural context in the communication process must take the message receiver's views into account. E. Stewart (1978, p. 296) states:

Although we may speak of culture as transcending the individual, the assumption does not detain us from defining all aspects of culture as they might be carried by the individual in his head, as internal cognitive form . . . .

Nicassio and Saral (1978, pp. 346–347) describe the need for a shift in orientation away from causal inferences derived solely from the researcher perspective. They say:

It is always problematic to ascribe causal significance to culture for differences in individual behavior patterns because culture is a subject variable, and as such, does not lend itself to being studied independently of the individuals who are emitting the behavior.

Therefore, one of the important points of disagreement between those who adhere to traditional approaches in intercultural communication research and those who are suggesting new directions for future research consists of whether to rely on researcher-observer or subject-actor constructs of cultural identity. These new directions do not exclude the possibility of valuable contributions stemming from researcher-observer inference—from ethnographic and participant observation techniques, for example. However, several scholars who challenge traditional approaches argue that many of the socio-cultural variables used have not proven very useful because they reveal more about the way researchers see the world than the way their subjects of inquiry do (Atwood, 1980; Atwood and Dervin, 1982).

In addition, a number of researchers have posited that not only is it important to elicit subject-actor perspectives, but that such perspectives are productively studied in situational contexts, including the time and space bound conditions related to cultural identity. For example, Hall (1977, p. 140) says that ''situational frames are the building blocks of both individual lives and institutions.'' Cherry (1973, p. 583) suggests that self-concept, including cultural affinity, varies on different occasions. Saral (1981, p. 400) describes the situational nature of cultural heterogeneity and communication in this way:

Cultural differences seem to be more apparent in some contexts than in others, and what seem to be cultural differences in communication are sometimes better accounted for by situational differences than by cultural variation.

Situational similarities and differences from the subject-actor perspective, then, may offer an alternative context for intercultural communication research, a context which places the idea of culture closer to ideas of cognitive processing than to ideas of observable characteristics or artifacts (Prosser, 1976). The same kind of shift may be necessary for the concepts associated with communication processes if the goal of a theoretically consistent approach to intercultural communication is to be achieved.

B. Subjective Situational Communication

The concept of communication as deterministic of culture has also been the subject of numerous debates. For example, Sarti (1981, p. 319) criticizes literature dealing with communication and cultural dependency by arguing that it contains inferences regarding cultural erosion that are only partially supported by evidence. She suggests that the reactions of peoples in underdeveloped nations need to be explored before we can understand "what types of changes occurred effectively in their daily lives, their knowledge, their consciousness." Halloran (1981, pp. 50-52) urges a move towards concepts of communication which involve individuals, not merely structures, in the study of intercultural and international communication. Salinas and Paldán (1979, p. 93) argue for subjective understanding of culture and communication by stating:

> . . . although the development of the media has decisive importance for the cultural homogenization and ideological control of the population, it cannot be assumed to have an all-powerful and homogenous effect . . . . cultures and subcultures are the expression of men's and women's lived experience of their conditions of existence. Accordingly, the constant invasion of meanings that do not express this reality will often generate some limits to its assimilation. It is important, therefore, to study the conditions affecting the reception of the messages, as well as to examine the possible distance between the models of interpretation provided by the media and the real level of assimilation by the "audience" to them.

Thus, corresponding to the arguments that intercultural communication inquiries need to take subjective perceptions of cultural identity into account, there are scholars who support the need to take subjective perceptions of communication more seriously. J. Stewart (1978), suggests that the maxim "meanings are in people" is widely voiced in communication research, but seldom operationalized. He argues that researchers need to pay more than hollow lip service to such an important tenet.

Most intercultural communication researchers discuss, in one form or another, the idea that communication involves the meanings people assign to messages. Condon and Yousef (1975, p. 2) say the communication occurs when behavior is "perceived and interpreted by another, whether or not it is spoken or intended or even with person's conscious awareness." Samovar et al. (1981, p. 12) define communication as "that which happens whenever meaning is attributed to behavior or the residue of behavior." Sarbough (1979, p. 2) claims that an act of communication has taken place when "one person assigns meaning to a verbal or nonverbal act of another." Samovar and Porter (1982, p. 6) state that "communication is a receiver phenomenon."

However, most of these researchers and many others involved in intercultural communication research continue to utilize approaches associated with persuasion theories of communication. These approaches focus on source-constructed messages rather than on receiver-constructed messages. Atwood and Dervin (1981, p. 549) say that "this view treats information as some sort of concrete substance which sources put into messages and transmit to receivers," and Dervin et al. (1980, p. 592) have labeled this view "the absolute information assumption." Research approaches which are based on this assumption usually treat receivers as passive, empty receptacles who are at the mercy of sender intent and persuasive power (Atwood, 1980; Atwood and Dervin, 1982; Atwood and Mattos, 1982; Atwood et al., 1982; Dervin, 1979, 1980; Dervin et al., 1980, 1982).

This discrepancy between what intercultural communication researchers say about the role of receivers, and what they actually study in terms of source-constructed messages, can be explained partly by the pervasive influence of "neo-Aristotelian logic" (Asante et al., 1979, p. 18). Casmir (1978) describes the impact of Aristotelian thought in this way:

> More recently, we began to stress that "meaning" has to be sought in the mind and experience of the receiver, while still attempting to structure rather simplistic circular-feedback, mechanistic-interaction, or cause-effect models of human communication . . . . Meanwhile a number of views, still fragmented, atomistic, some built upon mechanical mental models or applying traditional approaches, continue to appear in our publications. They are often strongly influenced by the old, well-established approaches to the study of communication, based on centuries of Aristotelian and mechanistic thinking.

Several researchers charge that it is such "mechanistic" thinking about communication that has prevented communication scholars from treating message receivers as the unique creative entities they are. In order to tap into this uniqueness and creativity, these same researchers suggest investigating communication processes in the situational contexts in which they occur (Atwood and Dervin, 1982; Atwood et al., 1983; Carter, 1975, 1977; Dervin, 1980; Dervin et al., 1980, 1982; Edelstein, 1974; Grunig, 1979; Grunig and Disbrow, 1977; Mischel, 1973).

Concerned primarily with intercultural communication, Howell (1978, pp. 23-24) explains that "every communication act is localized in time and space," and that "events are meaningful in context, bound by time and space." Nicassio and Saral (1978, p. 346) discuss the need for situational approaches to intercultural communication research by calling for "an integrated perspective which recognizes the importance of both individual uniqueness and environmental setting" and which "allows the behavioral scientist to take into account the variability in the behavior within individuals across situations and variability between individuals to identical environmental settings." Casmir (1978, p. 249) suggests moving toward "a model which focuses on the situational, interactional, communication processes between individuals from various nations or cultures." This kind of a model, Casmir (1978, p. 250) argues, would force us, "in each instance, to start with a basically new, situational, systems-model for what may be significantly different situation, created by the interaction of all contributing parts."

Taken together, the preceding arguments support the need to examine both cultural and communication variables from the actor-subject frame of reference in situational contexts. Such a shift in our approach to intercultural communication research, as well as intercultural communication training, could have far reaching ramifications involving not only the utility of future research efforts, but our capacity for communicating interculturally as well.

V. SUMMARY AND CONCLUSIONS

This review has attempted to trace the historical development of the concepts of culture and communication which have guided research in intercultural communication, and to describe some of the contexts in which such concepts have been applied. In addition, it has presented several significant challenges to traditional approaches in the area of intercultural communication research. More specifically, these challenges contain suggestions for placing more emphasis on the subjective reports of individuals regarding both their cultural identity and their communication behavior in constantly changing situations.

These challenges, in essence, constitute a call for a move away from deterministic, mechanistic ideas about the relationships among cultural and communication variables toward a more phenomenological approach which places the individual's creative cognitive capabilties at the center of attention. Therefore, rather than relying on notions of culture determining communication or communication determining culture, researchers may be able to gain greater insight into the ways in which people utilize their cultural and communication environments, as well as the ways in which such environments are perceived as constraining.

The type of insight being referred to here might have relevance for intercultural communication training and policy, in addition to intercultural communication research. For example, alterations might be implemented which sensitize people first to their own situational use of cultural repertoire and construction of communication behaviors, including the encoding and decoding of messages, and then sensitizes them to similar processes taking places for others. Further, the implications of exploring situational intercultural communication may have relevance for those institutions, organizations, and systems charged with communicating to diverse cultural groups.

In sum, researchers concerned with intercultural communications have a formidable, yet exciting, task before them. On one hand, they must recognize and evaluate the cultural and communication structures within which people learn to interact. On the other hand, they must acknowledge that the individual uniqueness and creativity of people often transcends the boundaries of such structures. The literature reviewed in this article provides evidence that intercultural communication scholars have begun to seek innovative means for integrating these seemingly paradoxical tasks.

VI. REFERENCES

Adler, P. S. (1976). Beyond cultural identity: Reflections on cultural and multicultural man. *In* L. A. Samovar and R. E. Porter, (Eds.), ''Intercultural Communication: A Reader,'' 2nd ed., pp. 362–380. Belmont California: Wadsworth.

Alcock, A., Taylor B., and Wilton, J. (1979). ''The Future of Cultural Minorities.'' New York: St. Martin's Press.

Asante, M. K., Newmark, E., and Blake, C. A. (1979). ''Handbook of Intercultural Communication.'' Beverly Hills, California: Sage.

Ascroft J., and Gleason, G. (1980). ''Communication Support and Integrated Rural Development in Ghana.'' (Paper presented at the International Communication Association, Acapulco, Mexico.)

Ascroft J., and Brody A. (1982). ''Do the Modern Mass Media Cause Poverty: A Return to Traditional Media.'' (Paper presented at the International Communication Association, Boston, Massachusetts.)

Atwood, R. (1980). ''Communication Research in Latin America: Cultural and Conceptual Dilemmas.'' (Paper presented at the International Communication Association Convention, Acapulco, Mexico.)

Atwood, R., and Dervin, B. (1982). Challenges to sociocultural predictors of information seeking: A test of race versus situation movement state. *Communication Yearbook 5*, 549–579.

Atwood R., and Mattos, S. (1982). Mass media reform and social change: The Peruvian experience. *Journal of Communication 32* (No. 2), 33–45.

Atwood, R., Allen R., Bardgett R., Proudlove, S., and Rich, R. (1982). Children's realities in television viewing: Exploring situational information seeking. *Communication Yearbook 6*, 605–626.

Becker, S. (1969). Directions for intercultural communication research. *Central States Speech Journal 20*, 3–13. (Also published *In* L. A. Samover and R. E. Porter (Eds.). (1976). ''Intercultural Communication: A Reader,'' 2nd ed., pp. 346–356. Belmont, California: Wadsworth.

Beltrán, L. R. (1978). TV etchings in the minds of Latin Americans: Conservatism, materialism, and conformism. *Gazette 24* (No. 11), 61–81.

Blubaugh, J. A., and Pennington, D. L (1976). ''Crossings Differences in Interracial Communication.'' Columbus, Ohio: Bobbs-Merrill.

Breen, M. P. (1975). Severing the American connection: Down under. *Journal of Communication 25* (No. 2) 183–186.

Browne, S. (1968). Dialogue between the races: A top priority. *Today's Speech 16*, 5–8.

Busby, L. J. (1974). Defining the sex-role standard in network children's programs. *Journalism Quarterly 51*, 690–696.

Butler M., and Paisley W. J. (1980). ''Women and the Mass Media: A Sourcebook for Research and Action.'' New York: Human Sciences Press.

Carter, R. F. (1975). ''Elementary Ideas of Systems Applied to Problem Solving Strategies.'' (Paper presented at the Annual Meeting of the Far West Region of The Society for General Systems Research, San Jose, California.)

Carter, R. F. (1977). ''Theory for Researchers.'' (Paper presented to the Association for Education in Journalism, Carbondale, Illinois.)

Casmir, F. L. (1978). A multicultural perspective of human communication. *In* F. L. Casmir (Ed.), ''Intercultural and International Communication,'' pp. 241–260. Washington, D.C.: University Press of America.

Cherry, C. (1973). Thoughts on the relevance of the communication explosion to the future of world order. *In* M. H. Prosser (Ed.), "Intercommunication Among Nations and Peoples," pp. 576–587. New York: Harper and Row.

Childers T., and Post J. (1975). "The Information Poor in America." Metuchen, New Jersey: Scarecrow Press.

Chu, G. C. (1976). Problems of cross-cultural research. *In* H. Fischer and J. Merrill (Eds.), "International and Intercultural Communication," pp. 435–445. New York: Hastings House.

Cohen, R. A. (1968). Language of the hard-core poor: Implications for cultural conflict. *Social Quarterly 9*, 19–28.

Coldevin, G. O. (1976). Some effects of frontier television in a Canadian Eskimo community. *Journalism Quarterly 53*, 34–39.

Comstock, G., and Cobbey, R. E. (1979). Television and the children of ethnic minorities. *Journal of Communication 29* (No. 1), 104–115.

Comstock, G., Chaffee, S., Katzman, N., McCombs, M., and Roberts, D. (1978). "Television and Human Behavior." New York: Columbia University Press.

Condon, J. C., and Yousef, F. (1975). "An Introduction to Intercultural Communication." New York: Bobbs Merrill.

Dervin, B. (1979). "Sense Making as a Prerequisite for Information Equality." (Paper presented at the 7th Annual Telecommunication Policy Research Conference, Skytop, Pennsylvania.)

Dervin, B. (1980). Communication gaps and inequities: Moving toward a reconceptualization. *Progress in Communication Sciences 2*, 73–112.

Dervin B., and Greenberg, B. S. (1972). The communication environment of the urban poor. *In* F. G. Cline and P. Tichenor (Eds.), "Current Perspectives in Mass Communication," pp. 195–234. Beverly Hills, California: Sage.

Dervin, B., Harlock S., Atwood, R., and Garzona, C. (1980). The human side of information: An exploration in a health communication context. *Communication Yearbook 4*, 591–608.

Dervin, B., Nilan M. S., and Jacobsen, T. L. (1982). Improving predictions of information use: A comparison of predictor types in a health communication setting. *Communication Yearbook 5*, 807–830.

Dodd, C. H. (1977). "Cross Cultural Communication." Dubuque, Iowa: Kendall-Hunt.

Edelstein, A. (1974). "The Uses of Communication in Decision-Making: A Comparative Study of Yugoslavia and the United States." New York: Praeger.

Ettema J., and Kline, J. G. (1977). Deficits, differences, and ceilings: Contingent conditions for understanding the knowledge gap. *Communication Research 4*, 179–202.

Fischer, H., and Merrill, J. (1976). "International and Intercultural Communication." New York: Hastings House.

Fitchen, R. (1978)., Transactional analysis of intercultural communication. *In* F. L. Casmir (Ed.), "Intercultural and International Communication," p. 131. Washington, D.C.: University Press of America.

Gerbner, G. (1977). "Mass Media Policies in Changing Cultures." New York: John Wiley and Sons.

Glenn, E. S. (1966). Meaning and behavior: Communication and culture. *Journal of Communication 16*, 248–272. (Also published *In* L. Samover and R. E. Porter (Eds.). (1976). "Intercultural Communication: A Reader," 2nd ed., pp. 170–188. Belmont, California: Wadsworth.)

Goldsen R., and Bibliowicz J. (1976). Plaza Sésamo: "Neutral" language or "Cultural Assault." *Journal of Communication 26* (No. 2), 124–126.

Goodenough, W. H. (1956). Residence rules. *Southwestern Journal of Anthropology 12*, 22–37.

Granzberg, G., Steinbring, J., and Hamer, J. (1977). New magic for old: TV in Cree culture. *Journal of Communication 27* (No. 4), 154–157.

Greenberg, B. S., and Dervin, B. (1970). "The Uses of the Mass Media by the Urban Poor." New York: Praeger.

Grunig, J. E. (1979). Time budgets, level of involvement, and use of mass media. *Journalism Quarterly 56*, 248–262.

Grunig, J. E., and Disbrow, J. B. (1977). Developing a probablistic model for communications decision making. *Communication Research 4*, 145–168.

Guback, T. (1969). "The International Film Industry." Bloomington, Indiana: Indiana University Press.

Guerrero, R. D., Reyes—Lagunes, I., Witzke, D. B., and Holtzman, W. H. (1976). Plaza Sésamo in Mexico: An evaluation. *Journal of Communication 26* (No. 2), 145–245.

Hachten, W. A. (1971). "Muffled Drums: The New Media in Africa." Ames, Iowa: Iowa State Unviersity Press.

Hachten, W. A. (1981). "The World News Prism." Ames, Iowa: Iowa State University Press.

Hall, E. T. (1977). "Beyond Culture." New York: Anchor Press, Doubleday.

Hall, E. T., and Whyte, W. F. (1973). Intercultural communication. *In* C. D. Mortensen (Ed.), "Basic Readings in Communication Theory." New York: Harper and Row.

Halloran, J. D. (1981). The context of mass communication research. *In* E. G. McAnany, J. Schnitman, and N. Janus (Eds.), "Communication and Social Structure," pp. 21–58. New York: Praeger.

Harms, L. S. (1973). "International Communication." New York: Harper and Row.

Harper, N. (1979). "Human Communication Theory: The History of a Paradigm." Rochelle Park, New Jersey: Hayden.

Herskovits, M. J. (1966). "Cultural Dynamics." New York: Alfred A. Knopf.

Howell, W. S. (1979). Theoretical directions for intercultural communication research. *In* M. K. Asante, E. Newmark, and C. A. Blake (Eds.), "Handbook of Intercultural Communication," pp. 23–43. Beverly Hills, California: Sage.

Hudson, H. E. (1977). The role of radio in Northern Canada. *Journal of Communication 27* (No. 4), 130–139.

Hur, K., (1982). International mass communication research: A critical review of theory and methods. *Communication Yearbook 6*, 531–554.

Katz, E., and Wedell, G. (1979). "Broadcasting in the Third World." Cambridge, Massachusetts: Harvard University Press.

Kim, Y. Y. (1979). Toward an interactive theory of communication-acculturation *Communication Yearbook 3*, 435–453.

Kluckhohn, C. (1951). Values and value orientations in the theory of action. *In* T. Parsons and E. A. Shils (Eds.), "Toward a General Theory of Action." Cambridge, Massachusetts: Harvard University Press.

Kluckhohn F. R., and Strodtbeck, F. L. (1961). "Variations in Value Orientations." Evanston, Illinois: Row and Peterson.

Kroeber, A. L., and Kluckhohn, C. (1952). Culture: A critical review of concepts and definitions. *Papers of the Peabody Museum of American Archaeology and Ethnology 47*, 1–223.

Lasswell, H. D. (1948). The structure and function of communication in society. *In* L. Bryson (Ed.), "The Communication of Ideas," pp. 37–51. New York: Institute for Religious and Social Studies.

Lee, C. C. (1980). "Media Imperialism Reconsidered: The Homogenizing of Television Culture." Beverly Hills, California: Sage.

Lent, J. A. (1978). Media worldwide: An overview of mass communication. *In* F. L. Casmir (Ed.), "Intercultural and International Communication," pp. 656–684. Washington, D. C. University Press of America.

Lent, J. A. (1979). "Third World Mass Media: Issues in Theory and Research." Philadelphia, Pennsylvania: Temple University Press. (Studies in Third World Societies, No. 9.)

Lerner, D. (1958). "The Passing of a Traditional Society." New York: Collier-Macmillan.

Littlejohn, S. W. (1978). "Theories of Human Communication." Columbus, Ohio: Charles Merrill.

Maletzke, G. (1976). Intercultural and international communication. *In* H. Fischer and J. Merrill (Eds.), "International and Intercultural Communication," pp. 409–417. New York: Hastings House.

Marquez, F. (1975). The relationship of advertising and culture in the Phillipines. *Journalism Quarterly 52*, 436–442.

Martin, L. J. (1976). The cultural communicator. *In* H. Fischer and J. Merrill (Eds.), "International and Intercultural Communication," pp. 417–424. New York: Hastings House.

Matta, F. R. (1981). "A Model for Democratic Communication." (Development Dialogue.) Uppsala, Sweden: Dag Hammarskjold Foundation.

Mattelart A., and Siegelaub, S. (Eds.). (1979). "Communication and Class Struggle." New York: International General.

Mattos, S. (1982). "Domestic and Foreign Advertising in Television and Mass Media Growth: A Case Study of Brazil." Unpublished dissertation, University of Texas, Austin.

McAnany, E. G. (1980). "Communications in the Rural Third World: The Role of Information in Development." New York: Praeger.

McAnany, E. G., Schnitman, J., and Janus, N. (Eds.). (1981). "Communication and the Social Structure." New York: Praeger.

McLean, P. F. (1982). "Traditional Forms of Communication: Creative Vehicle for Solving Development Needs." (Paper presented at the International Communications Association, Boston, Massachusetts.)

McPhail, T. (1981). "Electronic Colonialism." Beverly Hills, California: Sage.

Michaels, E. (1982). "TV Tribes." Unpublished dissertation, University of Texas, Austin.

Miller, G. (1966). On defining communication: Another stab. *Journal of Communication 16*, 88–98.

Mischel, W. (1973). Toward a cognitive social learning reconceptualization of personality. *Psychological Review 80*, 253–283.

Mortensen, C. D. (1973). "Basic Readings in Communication Theory." New York: Harper and Row.

Nicassio, P. M., and Saral, T. B. (1978). The role of personality in intercultural communication. *Communication Yearbook 2*, 345–350.

Nordenstreng K., and Varis, T. (1974). "Television Traffic: A One Way Street?" Paris: UNESCO. (Reports and Papers on Mass Communication, No. 70.)

Nordenstreng K., and Schiller, H. I. (Eds.). (1979). "National Sovereignty and International Communication." Norwood, New Jersey: Ablex.

Pennington, D. (1979). Black and white communication: An assessment of research. *In* M. K. Asante, E. Newmark, and E. A. Blake (Eds.), "Handbook of Intercultural Communication," pp. 383–403. Bevery Hills, California: Sage.

Poindexter, P. M., and Stromann, C. A. (1979). "Minorities and the Mass Media: A Review of the Literature: 1948-1978." (Paper presented to the Minorities and Communication Division, Association for Education in Journalism, Houston, Texas.)

Pool, I. de S. (1963). The mass media and politics in the modernizing process. *In* L. W. Pye (Ed.), "Communication and Political Development." Princeton, New Jersey: Princeton University Press.

Pool, I. de S. (1972). Communication in totalitarian societies. *In* I. de S. Pool, F. W. Frey, W. Schramm, N. Maccoby, and E. B. Parker (Eds.), "Handbook of Communication," pp. 462–511. Chicago, Illinois: Rand McNally.

Prosser, M. H. (1973). Communication, communications, and intercommunications. *In* M. H. Prosser (Ed.), "Intercommunication Among Nations and People," pp. 1–23. New York: Harper and Row.

Prosser, M. H. (1976). Intercultural and international communication. *In* H. D. Fischer and J. C. Merrill (Eds.), "International and Intercultural Communication," pp. 409–417. New York: Hastings House.

Prosser, M. H. (1978). "The Cultural Dialogue: An Introduction to Intercultural Communication." Boston, Massachusetts: Houghton-Mifflin.

Pye, L. W. (1963). "Communication and Political Development." Princeton, New Jersey: Princeton University Press.

Rich A. L., and Ogawa, D. M. (1981). Intercultural and interracial communication: An analytical approach. *In* L. A. Samovar and R. E. Porter (Eds.), "Intercultural Communication: A Reader," 2nd ed., pp. 43–48. Belmont, California: Wadsworth.

Rogers, E. M. (1962). "Diffusion of Innovations." New York: Free Press.

Rogers, E. M. (1976). "Communication and Development: Critical Perspectives." Beverly Hills, California: Sage.

Rogers, E. M., and Burdge, R. J. (1972). "Social Change in Rural Societies," 2nd ed. Englewood Cliffs, New Jersey: Prentice-Hall.

Rogers, E. M., and Shoemaker, F. (1971). "Communication of Innovations." New York: Free Press.

Ruhly, S. (1976). "Orientations to Intercultural Communication." Chicago, Illinois: Science Research Associates.

Salinas, R., and Paldán, L. (1979). Culture in the process of dependent development: Theoretical perspectives. In K. Nordenstreng and H. I. Schiller (Eds.), "National Sovereignty and International Communication," pp. 82–98. Norwood, New Jersey: Ablex.

Samovar, L. A., and Porter, R. E. (1982). "Intercultural Communication: A Reader," 3rd ed. Belmont, California: Wadsworth.

Samovar, L. A., Porter, R. E., and Jain, N. C. (1981). "Understanding Intercultural Communication." Belmont, California: Wadsworth.

Saral, T. B. (1980). Intercultural communication theory and research: An overview of challenges and opportunities. Communication Yearbook 3, 395–405.

Saral, T. B. (1981). "Intercultural Communication: Some Philosophical Issues." (Paper presented at the Annual Meeting of Society for Intercultural Education, Training, and Research.)

Sarbaugh, L. E. (1979). "Intercultural Communication." Rochelle Park, New Jersey: Hayden.

Sarti, I. (1981). Communication and cultural dependency: A misconception. In E. G. McAnany, J. Schnitman, and N. Janus (Eds.), "Communication and Social Structure," pp. 317–335. New York: Praeger.

Sauvant, K. P. (1979). Sociocultural emancipation. In K. Nordenstreng and H. I. Schiller (Eds.), "National Sovereignty and International Communication," pp. 9–20. Norwood, New Jersey: Ablex.

Schiller, H. I. (1969). "Mass Communications and American Empire." New York: A. M. Kelley.

Schiller, H. I. (1976). "Communication and Cultural Domination." White Plains, New York: International Arts and Sciences Press.

Schiller, H. I. (1979). Transnational media and national development. In K. Nordenstreng and H. I. Schiller (Eds.), "National Sovereignty and International Communication," pp. 21–32. Norwood, New Jersey, Ablex.

Schramm, W. (1964). "Mass Media and National Development." Stanford, California: Stanford University Press.

Shannon, C. E., and Weaver, W. (1949). "The Mathematical Theory of Communication." Urbana, Illinois: University of Illinois Press.

Singer, M. R. (1982). Culture: A perceptual approach. In L. A. Samovar and R. E. Porter (Eds.), "Intercultural Communication: A Reader," 3rd ed., pp. 54–61. Belmont, California: Wadsworth.

Sitaram, K. S. (1982). A model of human communication. In S. B. Day (Ed.), "Companion to Life Sciences." New York: Van Nostrand.

Sitaram, K. S., and Cogdell, R. (1976). "Foundations of Intercultural Communication." Columbus, Ohio: Charles E. Merrill.

Sitaram, K. S., and Haapenen, L. (1979). The role of values in intercultural communication. In M. K. Asante, E. Newmark, and C. A. Blake (Eds.), "Handbook of Intercultural Communication," pp. 145–147. Beverly Hills, California: Sage.

Smith, A. G. (Ed.) (1966). "Communication and Culture." New York: Holt, Rinehart and Winston.

Smythe, D. W. (1981). "Dependency Road: Communications, Capitalism, Consciousness, and Canada." Norwood, New Jersey: Ablex.

Stewart, E. (1978). "Intercultural Communication. In F. Casmir (Ed.), "Intercultural and International Communication," pp. 260–265. Washington D.C.: University Press of America.

Stewart, J. (1978). Foundations of dialogic communication. Quarterly Journal of Speech 64, 183–201.

Triandis, H. C., and Associates. (1972). "The Analysis of Subjective Culture." New York: Wiley.

Tsai, M. K. (1970). Some effects of American TV programs on children in Formosa. *Journal of Broadcasting 14,* 229–238.

Tunstall, J. (1977). "The Media are American: Anglo American Media in the World." New York: Columbia University Press.

Tyler, V. L. (1978). Intercultural communication indicators. *Communication Yearbook 2,* 363–371.

Tyler, V. L., Hall, P., and Taylor, J. S. (1979). Intercultural communication data acquisition. *In* M. K. Asante, E. Newmark, and C. A. Blake (Eds.), "Handbook of Intercultural Communication," pp. 231–253. Beverly Hills, California: Sage

Tylor, E. B. (1958). "Primitive Culture." 2 vols. New York: Harper.

U.S. Commission on Civil Rights (1977). "Window Dressing on the Set, Women and Minorities in TV." Washington D.C.: U.S. Government Printing Office.

U.S. Commission on Civil Rights. (1979). "Window Dressing on the Set: An Update." Washington, D.C.: U.S. Government Printing Office.

Wells, A. (1972). "Picture Tube Imperialism: The Impact of U.S. Television in Latin America." Maryknoll, New York: Orbis.

Wells, A. (1974). "Mass Communications: A World View." Palo Alto, California: Mayfield.

Westley, B. H., and MacClean, M. S. (1957). A conceptual model for communication research. *Journalism Quarterly 34,* 31–58.

Yu, F. T. C. (1977). Communication policy and planning for development: Some notes on research. *In* D. Lerner and L. Nelson (Eds.), "Communication Research—a Half Century Appraisal." Honolulu, Hawaii: Union Press of Hawaii.

5 Semiotics and Communications Studies: Points of Contact

Gertrude J. Robinson
and
William O. Straw
Graduate Program in Communications
McGill University, Montreal, Quebec
Canada H3A 2K6

I. INTRODUCTION

A. Objectives of the Review

In an insightful article, James Carey makes a distinction between two approaches to communication studies: the "transmission" and the "ritual" (Carey, 1977, pp. 412–413). He goes on to say that the transmission view underlies American studies and arises from a 19th century preoccupation with the extension of transportation across a huge continent. This view focuses on communications as a process of transmitting messages at a distance for the purposes of control. In contrast, the preponderant European view, historically grounded in distinct national cultures, is ritualistically oriented. It is concerned with communication as a process through which shared culture is created, modified, and transformed. Both of these views have important consequences for the ways in which communications questions are posed and problematics raised.

At the risk of oversimplifying, he suggests that U.S. communications studies have been preoccupied with effects and functions and have elaborated the conditions under which persuasion occurs. This research, both mass and interpersonal, has focused on the precise sociological and psychological conditions under which attitudes are changed, formed, stabilized, or redirected. The problematic of British studies, in contrast, has been wider. It has explored the relationship between culture and society, between expressive forms and the social order. Communications studies, from the "ritual" point of view, are interested in the ways in which communities of people, living in a particular place and time, make "sense" out of their existence and surroundings.

These distinctions, though rough and approximate, are important because they signal the entry point and relevance of semiotics (the study of signs or signification) to communication studies, which is the focus of this article. To begin with, it appears that semiotics has its initial contact point with European rather than North American communications researchers, because they view the analysis of meaning creation or signification as fundamental to explaining culture and human activity. The argument goes something like this. The uniqueness of human beings lies in their capacity to produce symbols; and language, the preeminent symbolic form, is the symbol of that capacity. The goal of communication studies as cultural science is consequently to understand man's symbolizing behavior, to elaborate on "the webs of significance he himself has spun" (Geertz, 1973, p. 5). All forms of communication, according to this view, are texts for which the researcher must construct a "reading." In contrast to the American behavioral science orientation, Geertz suggests that the communication scholars' reading task is like that of the literary critic: to interpret the interpretations.

One way of doing this, and this is the second point of contact between semiotics and communication studies, is by viewing culture with its artifacts, institutional rituals, and the full range of human communication patterns as a set of meaning producing practices. These practices are structured and patterned by constraints. Hence the search for a grammar, for the identification of codes, for the determination of levels within the act, and for the system of communications which determine the act. The movement from the study of language to the study of systems of signs that might be like languages is a movement speculated on by Ferdinand de Saussure and Emile Durkheim. It brings with it a concern with the full range of human communication and, with that concern, an assumption of culture's systematic nature.

The range of objects of study and theoretical frameworks encompassed by semiotic research makes an exhaustive description of the field impossible. (For evidence of this diversity, see the anthologies edited by Sebeok, 1975b, 1978.) The first section of this paper, therefore, explores only one major current of semiotic research which has had the widest impact on communication studies. This is the tradition growing out of the work of Ferdinand de Saussure. We begin by situating Saussurean semiotics in relation to the North American tendency of Locke-Peirce-Morris. Following this, the relationship of semiotics to structuralism, and the importance of notions such as "code," "text," and "intertexuality" to an analysis of meaning are examined.

In the second section we demonstrate the contributions of semiotics to an understanding of television news. Much of the initial work reviewed here was done in Great Britain, at the Centre for Cultural Studies in Birmingham and the British Film Institute in London. All of these studies are inscribed with a cultural science approach to communications, though their political and epistemological bases and their types of semiotic inquiry vary. In conclusion, we assess how this style of work has weathered the "sea change" and whether it has had an impact on Canadian and U.S. communications investigations. Such an assessment includes an examination of the relationship of the cultural science approach to the emerging "critical" stance within North American communication studies (Slack and Allor, 1981).

B. Semiotics and the Sciences

Two principal traditions of semiotic inquiry may be discerned: the European tradition originating in the work of a Swiss linguist, Ferdinand de Saussure (1966), and subsequently developed primarily in France in the 1960s; and the Anglo-American or "Locke-Peirce-Morris tradition" (Sebeok, 1975a, p. 12). Both currents share a view of semiotics according to which it possesses a trans-disciplinary vocation. Insofar as semiotics studies the phenomena of signification and meaning-production in all its manifestations, it is a master discipline which includes within it specialized sub-disciplines such as linguistics, information theory, and cultural anthropology (Saussure, 1966; Morris, 1938).

In practice, however, the domains of scientific inquiry envisioned as falling under the umbrella of semiotics have remained for the most part untouched by it. Nevertheless, one can distinguish between the Anglo-American and European research traditions on the basis of their relationships to existing disciplines and objects of study. Anglo-American semiotics, whose roots lie in the program set out by Morris (1955), is characterized by a denial of fundamental discontinuities between human and non-human communication, and thus encompasses the study of animal communication (zoosemiotics) as well as human meaning-production (Sebeok, 1975a, p. 4). Within this tradition, a number of previously isolated communicational sub-disciplines (such as proxemics, kinesics, and zoosemiotics) have been retroactively integrated within semiotics, and semiotic theory at a higher level of generality seeks to establish links between such research (see Eco, 1975). Much of this convergence has taken place within the institutional and theoretical contexts established by Thomas Sebeok, and has mainly affected disciplines within the social and natural sciences.

The second major current within semiotic research is that rooted in the linguistics of Roman Jakobson and the structural anthropology of Claude Lévi-Strauss, whose conceptions of language and linguistic structure are derived, ultimately, from those of Saussure. Saussure (1966, p. 16) proposed linguistics as that science "that studies the life of signs within society," and, indeed, many of the early schools of semiotic research were characterized in practice by a close relationship to cultural and humanistic studies, and by what its detractors see as its "anthropocentrism" (Sebeok, 1975a, p. 4). The work of the so-called "Prague School," in analysing such cultural forms as theatre and poetry, affirmed this link early in the development of semiotics (see Garvin, 1964).

This article deals only with the latter of these research traditions. While the "American" school is ultimately no less pertinent to communications studies understood in their most inclusive sense, we suggest that work within it has not provided a coherent interdisciplinary attempt to reshape the study of culture. Furthermore, English-language studies of the media in which the influence of semiotics has been felt have drawn primarily on semiotics growing out of the Saussurean, or European, tradition. Finally, recent developments in "critical" communications theory, or in those research currents which draw upon variants of Marxism, have found Saussurean semiotics of greater relevance than work within the American tradition.

II. SEMIOTICS AND THE TEXT

The key to the innovations brought by Saussurean semiotics to communications studies lies in the notion of "text." In replacing the concept of "message" with that of "text," semiotics seeks to revise the manner in which communicative acts are theorized. Central to these innovations is an implicit dissatisfaction with the concept of "information" as an analyzable entity which passes from a sender to a receiver, through a channel, in the form of a coded message. The manner in which these terms within the communication process have been reconceptualized is the subject of this section. We shall see that while Saussurean semiotics is initially characterized by an almost exclusive emphasis on the intrinsic properties of the text (or message), this analysis ultimately results in new insights about the interrelationships between senders, receivers, channels, and contexts.

A. Semiotics and Structuralism

Saussurean semiotics is founded on the proposition that non-linguistic communication or signification is based on systems of signs whose structures are analogous to those of verbal or written language. Saussure's major contribution to linguistic theory is his argument that languages consist, not of inventories of words which designate extra-linguistic entities or concepts, but of a system, within which each unit (such as a word or morpheme) is meaningful only in its *difference* from other such units (Saussure, 1966). A given unit of meaning, therefore, depends upon the entire linguistic system to be meaningful, insofar as it possesses no intrinsic meaning of its own. Nothing in the concept of /dog/, for example, suggests the word "dog" or its acoustic representation. There is thus no intrinsic relationship of a word (or signifier) to the idea or concept associated mentally with it (its signified). The linguistic sign (the combination of signifier and signified) is founded upon an arbitrary relationship established by social convention and usage.

In later writings by Roman Jakobson and Morris Halle, these principles of structure are extended to units of language such as the phoneme (meaningful units in a word's acoustic make-up). Whereas for Saussure words are meaningful in their difference from each other, Jakobson and Halle see this relationship in the more restricted sense of a binary opposition. A phoneme can be described in terms of the presence or absence within it of significant features, such as whether or not it is voiced. The qualities of "voiced" and "unvoiced" are in binary opposition, and meaningful only in relation to each other (Jakobson and Halle, 1956).

In short, then, linguistic statements are inconceivable without an underlying language system, and this system is itself based upon a number of binary, oppositional relationships. While structural linguistic theory had thus far been concerned primarily with the formal properties of language (its phonology and syntax), semiotics seeks to apply these principles to the study of meaning, and, subsequently, to other communication practices making up whole cultures.

An early application of principles of linguistic segmentation to cultural artifacts was undertaken by Propp (1975), in a study of folk-tales published in the early 1920s. By suggesting that folk narratives were constructed through the selection and combination of a number of invariant formal functions, Propp pointed to a morphological analysis of linguistic statements which would operate at a level higher than that of the phrase or sentence. Three decades later, the structural anthropology of Claude Lévi-Strauss (1966) represented the first major attempt to apply the tools of structural linguistics to the study of cultural groups.

Thus, for example, within a mythic account of a quest, the various characters, events, and attributes depicted can be seen as surface manifestations of an opposition underlying a given culture's worldview, such as that between man's earthly origin and his divine creation. A myth thus becomes a "text," in the sense that it contains a structure intrinsic to it. The internal relationships between its parts (the oppositions between its underlying themes), for instance, determine its function within the culture. As a text, a myth's meaning is reducible neither to information which the sender wishes to transmit (the cultural worldview underlying a myth escapes consciousness), nor to the events and entities to which it refers literally (its referential level). Although mythology can be viewed as the process by which a culture communicates with itself (Barthes, 1968, p. 32), this is obviously communication of a different order than that schematized in sender-receiver models.

B. Semiotics of the Text

For Lévi-Strauss, myths are based on a system analogous in the strict sense to that of language: a unit of myth, or "mytheme" (i.e., a thematic element of the myth's underlying structure) is meaningful only in its opposition to other mythemes. (See, for an illustration, Lévi-Strauss, 1970.) Ultimately, insofar as it presupposes a cultural unconscious within which these systems of meaning reside, this perspective requires a philosophical conception of knowledge which is itself organized according to the principles of binary opposition (cf., Pettit, 1977). Later semioticians differ in the degree to which they accept the innateness of oppositional structure to meaning in general. What almost all share, however, is the project of linking the systematic or structured nature of signification to the cultural context of communication. Thus, while Morris (1955, p. 7), for example, identifies signification as "goal seeking behaviour," Saussurean semiotics views it as an act based upon a language-like system of signs and possessing the characteristics of a text.

The early work of Roland Barthes seeks to link the formal, systemic aspects of texts to their cultural contexts through the concept of "connotation," which was first proposed in the work of Louis Hjelmslev (Barthes, 1957, 1964, 1968; Hjelmslev, 1966). Briefly stated, if the linking of signified (the mental image of concept) to signifier (expression) constitutes the semiotic sign, one can, following Hjelmslev, see the sign itself as the signifier within another sign relationship of a higher order. In Barthes' (1964) analysis of an advertisement for Italian foods, for example, the first or denotative level of meaning consists in the relationship between the objects depicted photographically and the mental image associated with them. These various denotative elements interact to produce the connotation of "Italianity," the cultural resonances surrounding Italian food and cuisine. Both the denotative signifier (the images of Italian food) and their signifieds (the mental representations of these foods) become the signifier within another sign which has as its signified these connotative senses. The study of connotative meanings will, Barthes (1968, p. 91) claims, be "very close to a real historical anthropology," in that it uncovers the ideological significance of semiotic texts within their wider cultural context.

In communicational terms, analyses such as these represent an orientation towards messages and their contexts, rather than towards the encoding and decoding processes associated with senders and receivers (or what later theorists would call "speaking" and "reading" subjects; see D. Morley, 1980). While arguing for the groundedness of meanings (particularly connotative levels of meaning) in culturally-determined ways of understanding the world was a necessary theoretical step away from perspectives which emphasized the intentionality of senders or receivers, this approach could not account for those differences in decoding which might result from different positions occupied by receivers within the socio-economic order.

The principal heritage of this work has been the development of a variety of elaborate methods for studying narrative structures, building upon the earlier work of the Russian, Vladimir Propp (Propp, 1975; see also Genette, 1972; Greimas, 1966; Scholes, 1978; Silverstone, 1981).

The narrative conventions underlying a particular literary genre were frequently seen to constitute a "code." In early works of textual semiotics, the term "code" is frequently synonymous with that of "language;" both designate the system necessary for an act of signification. A "message" is to a "code" as speech is to the language in which it is expressed (Barthes, 1968, pp. 18-19). Nevertheless, even in the early writing of Barthes, codes exist on a variety of levels—the personal, social, cultural, and ideological—and in varying degrees of fixity. In more technical terms, a code is that principle which "apportions the elements of a conveying system to the elements of a conveyed system" (Eco, 1976, p. 48).

Clearly, however, a literary text has as its principal code the language in which it is written. If its narrative structure is likewise a code, then the definition of a code as a particular language is difficult to sustain. Increasingly, therefore, a text is viewed as drawing upon a variety of codes, which originate outside of it but which are necessary for its intelligibility (Eco, 1979; Metz, 1974b). A Hollywood western film, for example, invokes the narrative conventions of its genre, the ideological resonances associated with representations of the American frontier, the editing patterns of classical Hollywood cinema, the place of its stars within cinematic mythology, etc. These are all codes—but not, in any rigorous sense, part of languages—and the nature of a viewer's response to the text becomes a function of his or her familiarity or competence with the range of codes which participate in the text's construction.

C. Text and Intertext

This rethinking of the concept of "text" results in a major conceptual shift within textual semiotics. While in its early, structuralist versions, Saussurean semiotics had regarded a text as closed, and structured by the internal relationships between its parts, it is now seen to open onto its cultural context at all points, and to comprise a plurality of culturally-based principles of meaning. Importantly, the new meaning of a text is conceived as fluid and variable. It depends upon its reader and the context in which it is received. In addition, the structuralist notion of surface and underlying levels of meaning are replaced by the spatial metaphor of the text as a field upon which codes cross each other and are interwoven. (Barthes, 1974).

While the retention of the term "code," even in this sense, suggests systematicity and structure, theorists associated with the literary journal *Tel Quel* conceptualize the open nature of the text in somewhat different terms. According to Julia Kristeva, for instance, texts are always situated within larger networks of other texts (or discourses). The individuality of a given text, therefore, results from the specific ways in which it brings together and interweaves elements (meanings, semantic resonances, conventions of form, etc.) from other texts. This necessary opening of a text onto wider bodies of discourse is termed "intertextuality" (Kristeva, 1969, p. 146).

Such an interpretation amounts to a redefinition of the relationship of texts to the social surroundings in which they are produced and received. Rather than opposing a text to its non-semiotic context (seen in political, social, or economic terms) and viewing the latter as a causal determinant of the former, Kristeva and ohers seek to situate given instances of discourse within broad networks of cultural forms and representations. In one sense, then, after a detour through literary studies, semiotics rediscovered the links with the study of popular culture which had marked its beginnings—with Propp's analysis of folk tales, Bakhtin's examination of the oral tradition and carnivalesque in Renaissance culture (Bakhtin, 1965), and, at the beginnings of French semiology, with Lévi-Strauss's anthropology and Barthes' studies of popular myth. However, these aspects of meaning-production were not explored more fully until the cross-fertilization of French semiology and British cultural studies, the focus of the next section, had occurred.

D. Conclusions

We have characterized Saussurean semiotics as that tradition which attempts to link the formal, structural aspects of communicational messages to their cultural contexts. The notion of "text," it is argued, allows for an exploration of this relationship more than does that of "message," which carries with it a connotation of intentionality and unmediated transmission. Texts as open systems raise questions about the reading ability of the receiver as well as the cultural context within which the text is read. It thus directs attention to the complex participatory efforts made by the receiver in any interpretive situation and the ways in which historicity affects the encoding and the decoding of a particular text.

In addition, we show that the role and nature of context within signifying practices is conceived in different ways within the development of Saussurean semiotics. Writers such as Lévi-Strauss and the early Barthes interpret it very broadly as ''culture in general.'' With the introduction of the notion of ''code,'' however, it becomes possible to distinguish between the interpretative practices of different groups which are distinguishable by their social position, their educational level, and their gender. Blumler's uses and gratification analysis of varying audience responses to political communication would have gained interpretative strength by correlating the audience responses, not only with their social status, but with an analysis of the codes utilized in election coverage (Blumler, 1973). The concept of ''intertextuality'' further extends this orientation by drawing attention to the importance of the presentation modes of other media in audience interpretations. It helps us recognize that the knowledge acquired from deciphering a Western novel, for instance, is carried over as a strategy into making sense out of a Western film. Such familiarity, it appears, is also used to make sense out of news clips of the Vietnam war, where U.S. combat solidiers were filmed representing the ''good guys'' so familiar from encounters on the range (Gans, 1979, ch. 6).

In part because of the literary orientation of Saussurean semiotics, the role of institutions and the relationships of power within society in the production of meaning is generally neglected. Since these are more evident as determinants in the electronic and journalistic media, it is to be expected that many of the concepts will be revised in their applicaton to these domains. The following section, therefore, examines examples of British television analyses which draw upon Saussurean semiotics, with particular attention to the manner in which semiotic concepts and methodological tools are rendered compatible with political theories of society.

III. SEMIOTICS AND MEDIA STUDIES: THE CASE OF TELEVISION ANALYSIS

A. The British Context: Communication Studies as Cultural Science

The previous section suggests that Saussurean semiotics developed primarily within literary studies, and was thus initially associated with humanistic, rather than social-scientific, disciplines. With its emphasis, at least in its early stages, on the intrinsic structure of texts, and its refusal to equate the latter with ideas or messages, Saussurean semiotics did not address the role of institutions and the relationship of power in society which are central to media effects studies or to investigations of information flow. Even those examples of French semiotic research which analyze the reading of a text do so by examining how the formal properties of texts work to construct ideal readers, rather than by concerning themselves with the responses of actual audiences. In addition, when, as in the case of the *Tel Quel* group, French theorists use Marxist theories of society and ideology, the Marxist variant employed (that of Louis Althusser) is anti-sociological and rarely concerned with such factors as socio-economic position or ideological predisposition (see Coward, 1977).

The most important cross-over of semiotic analysis from the humanities to communication studies occurs within British cultural studies, beginning in the early 1970s. Two factors account for this development. First, British media studies, in contrast to American communication research, have their roots in the study of literature, and in the reconceptualization of culture associated with such writers as Raymond Williams, Richard Hoggart, and E. P. Thompson (for an account, see Hall, 1981, pp. 21–22). The work of Hoggart demonstrates that culture is not static but dynamic. Williams' analyses explore how art is only one of many kinds of social communication, while Thompson illustrates the historical specificity of culture as a plurality of practices linked to class.

The interest in the historic specificity of cultural practices provided the second impetus for the receptivity of British researchers to semiotics. Though the "New Left" had introduced the Marxist concept of ideology, there was as yet no way of analyzing it. Semiotics seemed to offer the methodological and conceptual tools for examining the formation of ideology and the media's role in its creation and reinforcement. The realization that material conditions are centrally involved in the development of all expressive forms resulted in a downgrading of the privileged status texts enjoyed in French semiotics. For British cultural studies, consequently, texts require interpretation along with economic, political, and ideological practices.

In this section, we examine the transfer of Saussurian semiotics to British cultural studies using television analysis as the particular focus of interest. This choice is made both because television analysis poses particular problems for behaviorally oriented content analysis approaches, and because we are engaged in a television news analysis ourselves. After this, Stuart Hall's work is discussed in detail, because it provides the impetus for the Birmingham school's endeavor to come to terms with both its literary and sociological antecedents and to develop a holistic account of cultural and communication practices. In conclusion, other ways of conceiving the relationship between meanings and culture, based on previously outlined semiotic frameworks, are examined, and their usefulness for television studies assessed.

B. Semiotics and Ideology: Marxist Studies

Within British cultural studies of the 1970s, the dominance of two schools is generaly acknowledged (e.g., Coward, 1977, pp. 75–76). The first of these emerged in connection with the film journal *Screen,* which is published by the Society for Education in Film and Television. In 1973, *Screen* began to introduce the work of French film semioticians such as Metz to its English readers. In subsequent years, *Screen* has drawn on the work of the *Tel Quel* group, particularly its attempts to converge semiotics with Althusserian Marxism and the psychoanalysis of Jacques Lacan (for an account, see Coward and Ellis, 1977). This work explains how filmic presentation modes are related to the institutions which produce them, why films are so compelling, and how audiences learn to read filmic messages.

The second current, which is more directly relevant to this review, is the work of the Birmingham Centre for Contemporary Cultural Studies (CCCS) and its former director, Stuart Hall. In contrast to *Screen,* this group's attempts to link the structure of TV messages to their producing institutions and to audiences rely more heavily on the Marxism of Antonio Gramsci, and on theories of cultural signification which focus on the role of communication. Hall's (1973) important initial paper on television uses a sociological framework to conceptualize a circuit of communication, each step of which is subsequently defined and analyzed. Rather than regarding that which this circuit carries, however, as a pre-existing idea or behavioral impulse, Hall, in the light of the Centre's anthropological definition of "culture," is concerned with how ideas are formed and how opinions and representations develop.

One of Hall's principal points of departure is a statement by Umberto Eco: "Semiology shows us the universe of ideologies arranged in codes and sub-codes within the universe of signs" (quoted in Hall, 1973, p. 11). This perspective enables him to link an anlysis of the role of ideas or ideologies within society with an interest in how, through coding, messages are sent, received, and interpreted within communicational circuits. Gramscian Marxism is likewise better suited to an inquiry into the dominance of ideas within society than Althusserian Marxism, which views ideology as a localized institution-subject relationship (see Hall, 1977). In addition, the extreme stratification of British society has encouraged the CCCS to seek to account for subcultural formations among minorities and the oppressed. Althusser's highly determinist perspective cannot account for the differential reading practices used by working class sub-groups, teenagers, and women (see Hall et al., 1976b).

Hall's initial paper on television seeks answers to the following communicational questions. First, how does one acknowledge television's social role without adopting a strictly causal model according to which television provokes pre-given responses or behaviors? Second, if television news does not immediately produce certain types of behavior or impose certain ideas, how can this fact be conceptualized without accepting the extreme relativism of subjective reading? Finally, how does one account theoretically for the observation that, on the one hand, television is a powerful institution within society, yet on the other, it is also part of that society? It employs people socialized within it and produces messages which are, generally, accepted by audience members with varying political-ideological positions and points-of-view.

Hall's solution is to regard the news production and reception processes as an ongoing interplay between cognitive frames (or "meaning structures") and linguistic or formal coding structures. At the moment of production, organizational and technical constraints, professional ideologies (journalists' conceptions of newsworthiness, etc.), and other determinants operate to create a "meaning structure" which, in addition, draws ideological elements, such as ways of conceiving political events, from outside the broadcasting instituion. This is the "encoding" stage of television's communication.

At the moment of reception, viewers also actively "decode." In this process, they draw upon their familiarity with the structural or formal elements of television news, as well as upon ideas, opinions, and world-views resulting from their socialization and position within the socio-economic order:

> It is this set of de-coded meanings which "have an effect," influence, entertain, instruct or persuade, with very complex perceptual, cognitive, emotional or behavioural consequences (Hall, 1973, p. 3).

In describing the process by which viewers decode the television message, Hall invokes what Morley has called the "structured polysemy" of the message (P. Morley, 1980, p. 10). While a signifying element (such as a filmed report) may be read or received in a variety of ways, such readings are constrained by the textual context in which they appear, by their place within what Raymond Williams calls the "flow" of television (Williams, 1974, p. 95). The interpretation given to a visual image, for example, will be shaped in part by the voice-over description which accompanies it. This contextualization tends to favor a reading consistent with a socially-determined "preferred meaning" (Hall, 1973, p. 9).

This notion of "preferred meaning" is not as simple or deterministic as it seems on the surface. According to Hall, it contains two notions, both of which have to do with the receiver's active decoding capacities. The first is linked to Gramsci's concept of hegemony, which refers to the interpretive ascendancy which certain social groups have over others, and thus their ability to make their own understandings of social phenomena accepted as valid (Gramsci, 1971, p. 12; see Hall, 1973, 1977). Each culture exhibits a hierarchy of "preferred meanings" which provide the foundations for its ideological horizons. These hierarchies of "preferred meanings" are not fixed and immutable for all time, nor are they the same for all kinds of social phenomena. Active decoding implies, second, that certain audience segments to not accept these hierarchies. Such rejection is partially dependent on social class, education, and gender (Hall, 1973, p. 13).

"Preferred meanings" contained within media messages are also not necessarily adopted passively by the audience. Research repeatedly demonstrates that audience interpretations are extremely difficult to predict. One must therefore view audience interpretations as an ongoing interaction between those elements of the de-coding process which result from the viewer's interests and response to his or her experience, and those which segments of society, by virtue of their domination, succeed in disseminating as unquestioned means of understanding reality. Hall, following Parkin (1972), proposes several categories of readings, of which the most important, for demonstrative purposes, is the negotiated reading:

> Decoding within the *negotiated version* contains a mixture of adaptive and oppositional elements: it acknowledges the legitimacy of the hegemonic definitions to make the grand significations, while, at a more restricted, situational level, it makes its own ground rules, it operates with "exceptions" to the rule. It accords the privileged position to the dominant definition of events, whilst preserving the right to make a more negotiated application to "local conditions" to its own *corporate* positions (Hall, 1973, p. 17).

In Hall's perspective, however, categories of reading are offered more as ideal points on a spectrum than as predictive descriptions immediately assignable to audience groups classified according to class, sex, race, etc. D. Morley (1980) is almost alone in having attempted to extend a similar theoretical framework to empirical audience research. Groups of viewers were selected on the basis of similar backgrounds and social standing, and their responses to specific public affairs broadcasts in a group situation were recorded. Morley's attempt to find consistencies within each group, despite its interest, is problematic. He himself acknowledges the risk inherent in assuming that decoding occurring in a group context approximates that which would transpire were the viewer alone, or within a familial context (D. Morley, 1980, pp. 25–26). In addition, Morley transcribes each response rather than reducing it to a number of shared variables. While this retains the richness of individual readings, research along similar lines which seeks to reach conclusions with statistical validity may prove laborious.

C. Structuralism and Communication Studies

Structuralism, as indicated in the previous section, deploys models of structural linguistics as a paradigm for the scientific study of culture. It assumes that language, which is the medium for the production of meaning, is both an "ordered" system and a means of "expression." Systems of signs can therefore be systematically and rigorously studied, but not within a framework of simple determinancies. For Birmingham, structuralism's emphasis on the irreducibility of culture helped avoid the Marxian tendency to reduce all cultural phenomena to society and history.

Structuralism's contribution to understanding signifying practices lies in its emphasis on the forms of arrangement, the *how* of cultural systems. According to Hall, structuralism decenters cultural processes from their authorial center. It shows that culture is not a product of consciousness but can be better understood as the inventories, the folk taxonomies, through which social life is "classified out" in different societies. This brings the concept closer to an expanded definition of "ideology," but without the connotations of "false consciousness" associated with it in some Marxist writing (Hall, 1981, pp. 30–31).

Structuralist analysis, of the type proposed by Lévi-Strauss, has been applied to films, advertisements, as well as television. It reduces the relativism of infinite meanings by searching for unvarying thematic oppositions underlying the text's manifest content. Peter Wollen has argued that a structuralist analysis of films made by a single director may reveal consistent thematic patterns which run throughout his or her work and establish that director's status as a creative artist within the film industry (Wollen, 1969). More frequently, the thematic structures discovered within media texts are seen as originating within the larger culture in which these texts are produced. Thus, in her structuralist analysis of advertising, Leymore regards television commercials as manifestations of widespread cultural "myths," organized around fundamental oppositions such as that between "happiness" and "misery" (Leymore, 1975, p. 154). Similarly, the analysis by Fiske and Hartley of a British television drama reveals that it is "a conscious enactment of the values of an ordered, stable, liberal-conservative society" (Fiske and Hartley, 1978, p. 171).

Two other semiotic concepts, "connotation" and "intertextuality," provide means for linking the semantic structure of a text to the individual or organizational world view which underlies it. As previously noted, Hjelmslev's important distinction between denotation and connotation draws attention to significations which rely on extra-textual sources. The relevance of this idea is demonstrated in two recent books which analyze how connotation works to sustain a particular nationalistic ideology associated with the British army and how the concept can be used to clarify television's unique narrative style.

Fiske and Hartley's "Reading Television" provides an example of how the image of British soldiers in Belfast within a newscast refers, at a primary, denotative level to the actual situation photographed. Yet, at higher levels of meaning, significancies of a more generalized nature emerge. Among these are such cultural resonances as professional competence and paternal concern for "our lads," which participate in the semiotic effects the British military images may produce. These connotative effects in turn may coalesce into a nationalistic ideology vis-à-vis the Irish Catholics (Fiske and Hartley, 1978, p. 42).

Silverstone's "The Message of Television" uses connotation to distinguish between the expressive and formal aspects of television communication. He notes that in its expressive dimension, television is like film; it unwinds, presenting us with a succession of sounds and images. Formally however, television is a public language of implicit meaning, where the immediate, the visual, the expressive symbolism all stress the common set of experiences uniting diverse audiences. Part of this common set of experiences is a notion of the mythic. How the mythic is conveyed in television discourse is the major focus of this work (Silverstone, 1981, pp. 37–38).

A final semiotic insight from which television analysis has benefited is Julia Kristeva's expanded notion of "intertextuality." This refers to the ways in which the construction of a given text, its meanings, semantic resonances, and conventions of form result from its relationship to other texts. In contrast to mythic explanations, analyses of this kind provide insight about shared conventions of representation. The coverage by British television of the seizure of Iran's embassy in London, according to Bazalgette and Paterson (1980/81), illustrates how intertextuality works. Journalistic accounts of this event drew upon the conventions of the spy or thriller novel. Clearly the links proposed by such studies are never of an immediately causal nature. An assertion that the reading of thriller fiction caused British journalists to cover an embassy siege in this fashion would be difficult to sustain. Nevertheless, such analyses may fruitfully point to cases where certain means of recounting events and rendering them intelligible are shared by a variety of otherwise unrelated representational genres.

None of the analytic frameworks summarized here—the structuralist, connotative, or intertextual perspectives—in themselves offer a coherent framework for linking the structure of television messages to the media institutions which produce them. Nor, in themselves, do they enable the researcher to analyze the variety of readings which a given television message may encounter. Their usefulness is mainly suggestive, in that they propose frameworks by which the semantic structuring of messages or texts may be linked to the individual or cultural world-view which underlies them.

D. The Rhetorics of Television News

Thus far, we have examined uses of semiotic theory concerned with the nature of the meanings produced by television messages, and with the place of such meanings within ideologies and cultural mythologies. However, semiotics also offers a variety of methodological tools for analyzing what might be called the "rhetorics" of television, and particularly of television news. The emphasis in such work is on the stylistic or formal devices through which television messages are constructed. While such analyses may not in themselves contain a comprehensive conceptualization of the social effectivity of television, they may be integrated within existing social theories as one level within a larger analytic framework.

One way of viewing these approaches would be to see them as relating the semiotic notion of ''text'' to Raymond Williams' concept of ''flow'' within television programming. In this work, attention is directed on the program as a whole, in terms of the manner in which it strives for formal and ideological coherence and binds disparate sounds and images together into an ongoing discourse or message. For Williams (1974), television differs from the printed media primarily in that it unfolds in controlled sequence through time, rather than across space. To this technological feature of television is added the tendency of television programmers to ensure that television unfolds without interruption (such interruption bringing with it the risk that viewers will change stations). This flow is sought, not only between programs, but within them as well.

Thus, the presentation of most news programming is structured so as to avoid obtrusive breaks which result from the juxtaposition of apparently unrelated news items, or between different forms of representation (anchor person in studio and actuality film, for example). Devices by which announcers signal the beginning of film sequences, or call upon correspondents to report, have been analyzed as syntactical links which maintain the news program's flow (Brunsdon and Morley, 1978; Glasgow Media Group, 1976, 1980; Hall et al., 1976a). Likewise, the various relations of categories of images to classes of sounds have been numerated, and their function within the structuring of the news program analyzed (Connell, 1980).

British researchers have been influential in linking formal or stylistic studies of the news program to an analysis of how news defines and constructs social issues and events. In a sense, such work can be seen as building upon the ''agenda-setting'' current within Anglo-American news research (McCombs and Shaw, 1972), insofar as it is concerned with the processes by which political and social phenomena are rendered meaningful within news accounts.

However, while ''agenda-setting'' studies investigate news in terms of its selection criteria and their effects on the public discussion agenda, the semiotics-based work discussed here is concerned with ways of knowing the interaction of cognitive frames and representational styles or structures. In an influential article, Hall et al. (1976a) show in detail how the format and manner of presentation of a British public affairs program works to define the public sphere as that social sector which is occupied by politicians and parliamentary activity, to the exclusion of other social actors or arenas of political struggle. The Glasgow Media Group, (1976, 1980) in turn, has demonstrated that British television news regularly establishes textual links between phenomena in such a way as to create the impression that labor strife is the principal cause of economic hardship. The division of labor within journalistic teams, the use of graphics and statistics, and the ordering of news items within a broadcast, all combine to produce a representation of political and economic affairs in which the phenomena of strikes and inflation are causally linked.

Another presupposition of such analysis is that the relationships between image and sound function to ground television news in a structure which produces the impression of credibility. Connell (1980, p. 145) has demonstrated the mutual reinforcement of the visual and the aural within television news; images serve as proof of the truth of the spoken descriptions, and the latter serve to fix and bind the significance of the image within a desired range of interpretations. These levels together work to integrate represented events within what Tuchman has called the "web of facticity" of television news (Tuchman, 1978). An important element in creating this "web of facticity" is the illusion of reality which is created at all levels. "Real" time and "real" space are scrupulously maintained in news interviews and in announcer relations with the unseen audience (Robinson, 1980). The sense of "reality" is further reinforced by the visual components of television news, which not only illustrate what is being talked about, but are inserted in such a way as to transport the audience to the very place where the action is (Brunsdon and Morley, 1978).

It should be evident from this account that semiotic analysis does not allow for a distinction between message and channel, or between the manner of presentation of a news program and the information conveyed. In addition, its insistence that news coverage of social phenomena always takes the form of constructed representations of such phenomena has meant that it is not concerned with questions of "bias," i.e., with judging the fidelity of such representations to a pre-existent reality. While the existence of such "reality" is itself never questioned, the implication is that television news is a manner of "knowing" reality, and thus inevitably bears the marks of the forms and contexts in which this "knowing" occurs.

IV. CONCLUSIONS AND IMPLICATIONS FOR AMERICAN COMMUNICATIONS RESEARCH

North American communication research, it was suggested in the Introduction, differs in philosophical assumptions, questions raised, and methods used from one of the major communications traditions in Great Britain. While U.S. researchers have been preoccupied with effects and functions, as well as the analysis of institutions responsible for producing messages, the cultural studies approach has been concerned with intellectual formations, the relationship between culture and society. Williams (1976) ponders the absence of a sociology of "systems of signs" and notes that it will have to become part of future research enterprises related to communications.

> A genuine sociology of systems of signs would be necessarily concerned, in historical and materialist ways, with the specific technologies which are now dominant forms, but with these technologies as *systems of signs* and not at an abstracted technical level (Williams, 1976, p. 505; emphasis in original).

Such a sociology of the system of signs and their formation in historical context has been growing in the Centre for Cultural Studies at Birmingham and is now exportable. The reasons for this, it seems to us, are three-fold. First, North Americans are becoming increasingly aware of the limitations of behaviorally oriented research methodologies. In addition, a small group of "critical" communication theorists are providing home grown examples of phenomenological and Marxist communications studies. Finally, there is a Canadian variant of the cultural studies approach which is appearing in North American journals. All of these are beginning to ameliorate the methodological limitations encountered in news research. Among these are: the inability of gatekeeper, organizational production, and cybernetic studies to conceive of newsmaking as more than a complex selection process. There is also the difficulty of relating selection processes to audience responses, and problems encountered in linking communication practices to other social practices, such as elite power, media concentration, and media use in electioneering. A few researchers are beginning to make the connection between organizational constraints, professional practices, and the signifying features of the news product. Their work, however, is still sketchy and would benefit from semiotic approaches. Among these are Tuchman (1978) and Newcomb (1979).

The growing work of U.S. "critical" communication theorists reviewed by Slack and Allor (1982), which places communication studies into a social and historical context, is also preparing the way for the adoption of the British cultural studies approach in that it stresses the important connection between theories of communication and theories of society. This link is made through the realization that monopolies of knowledge confer social power to particular groups. These groups utilize multiple means for guarding access to their special knowledge and also have the power to determine the timing of its distribution. Communication patterns and their resultant knowledge structures have been explored in the psychological literature on stereotyping and rumor production, in political research on election coverage, in organization research on decision-making, and in information theoretic studies of center-periphery exchanges of communication technologies between the First and Third Worlds. American critical research thus shares with its European counterpart a common understanding that communications studies are historically grounded and cannot be adequately explored within a purely functionalist framework. The reason for this is that functionalist explanations are unable to pose epistemological questions about the ways in which groups of people "come to know" socially relevant matters. Slack and Allor, (1982) conclude, therefore, that though incohesive, critical approaches do more than "focus on the broader social context" in a neutral manner, as Rogers asserts (Rogers, 1982); all critical approaches recognize that the choice of a theory to explain society is itself a politico-ideological choice. It delimits the way in which the role of communication in the political context is conceptualized and how research questions are posed (Slack and Allor, 1982, p. 12).

The third reason for the increased relevance of the cultural studies approach and its heightened visibility on the North American continent is the existence of a Canadian variant of this work. More integrated than U.S. critical work, these studies are either grounded in French structuralist traditions or in the Birmingham approach. Two Montreal universities, the Université de Montréal and McGill University, as well as Simon Fraser University, are the principal seats of this work. Researchers utilizing French semiotic approaches to clarify the narrative structures of the Québec téléroman and political reporting are Méar (1980), Hamad (1981), and Repentigny (1981). Robinson (1980) and Tremblay et al. (1981) use a cultural approach to investigate the differences in signification practices of the press and television news for English and French audiences. Crowley (1981) and Melody and Salter (1981) study technological biases, while Theall (1978) and Leiss and Kline (1978) use semiotic variants to investigate advertising. The same is true of Jackson (1981), who is documenting the intertextuality between CBC radio drama and other modes of popular expression. All of these researchers draw on Innis and McLuhan, who developed such notions as "monopolies of knowledge," "center" and "periphery," and "empire and hinterland," in exploring the development of Canadian culture (Innis, 1972; Robinson and Theall, 1975).

We believe that semiotic analyses of media as language systems, though incomplete, contribute a number of insights for communication studies of which only the four most important will be mentioned here. To begin with, semiotic theory, with its insistence that texts are irreducible to messages and the latter irreducible to the effects they produce, provides a wider explanatory framework for understanding significatory processes than purely behaviorally based theories. Analyzing the complex cultural "baggage" involved in signification requires much more than a simple reflection or correspondence theory between events and interpretations. Even cognitive effects studies do not provide an adequate conceptualization of the fundamental distinction between signifier and signified. Semiological studies suggest that an understanding of how people make sense out of texts requires a distinction between form, substance, and purport. The complexity of investigating these distinctions is suggested by Silverstone:

> I might tell a story (form) of Red Riding Hood (substance) and my telling will draw on all manner of information from the world at large (purport). This will be incorporated into the tale and thereby given substance. The same stories (contents) however, can be presented in different media; they can be told in different modes of expression. At this level (too) the distinction between form and substance holds (Silverstone, 1981, p. 27).

Semiotics also provides methodological tools for resolving problems in television content research. Quantitative studies of news coverage, for example, regularly encounter major barriers in quantifying recurrences in descriptions of different types of events or news-makers, because of ambiguities connected with minimal quantifiable units. The easiest course, that of simply transcribing the spoken presentation and applying principles of linguistic segmentation, ignores the potentially crucial dimension of visual imagery. Even if a means for segmenting the visual level of television discourse could be developed, the question of the relationship between the aural and visual levels of television's signification remains to be accounted for. Here, semiotic researches into the cinema (Metz, 1974a,b) and visual signification (Schefer, 1969) possess a potential relevance to television studies. Silverstone, for instance, makes extensive use of Metz to understand the denotative dimension of a television series, while he uses Propp to get at the connotative dimension of television narrative. Propp identifies not only a set of functional units at the base of the narrative, but a principle of linguistic analysis, commutation, which helps to explain how a narrative unfolds (Propp, 1975). Two basic units, the sequence (significant diachronically) and the segment (significant synchronically) can thus be isolated, and serve as the beginning point for a systematic analysis of how the narrative style works in television drama (Silverstone, 1981, pp. 147–148).

Semiotics additionally offer a more comprehensive base for understanding audience behaviors. Audience decodings, it is suggested, are not isolated facts, but integrated patterns. These patterns are related to a person's familiarity with codes, repertoires, and such extra textual factors as gender and social position. Like uses and gratifications research, semiotics suggests that the audience is active. It is not a "tabula rasa" on which sensory data are inscribed, but actively interprets already at the level of sense impressions. Semiotics clarifies these interpretative competencies. Contrary to certain sociological theories, it suggests that there is no one to one correspondence between social structure and discourse, and language is not reducible to class position. There is also no automatic way of deducing which codes a reader will mobilize in relation to a particular text, because decoding strategies intervene between classes and languages. Yet, following Bernstein and Bourdieu, position in the social structure, education, and gender surely have a structuring and limiting effect on the *range* and repertory of decoding strategies available to different audiences segments.

Semiotics clarify, moreover, how different readings of a text are possible. Clearly this is not only a result of differences in psychological make-up, as suggested by learning theory, but also a result of the characteristic features of the text itself. Work by both Hall (1973) and D. Morley (1980) has indicated that the theory of the polysemic nature of the text precludes a necessary correspondence between the encoding and decoding circuits. Yet, a text does *prefer* a certain reading through utilizing certain narrative conventions, ideological resonances, and editing practices, which seem "natural" and "credible" to certain audience segments. The concept of "preferred reading" is useful in that it indicates that the various codes involved in the structuring of a text do foster intersubjectivity. Yet this intersubjectivity does not necessarily imply that the reader subscribes to the ideological problematic of the text. An example of this distinction is the fact that a statement about the economy made by a Republican politician is perfectly intelligible to a Democrat, though that person need not subscribe to "REAGANOMICS." In sum, semiotics asserts that systems of codes affect the interpretative repertoires and strategies available to audience members in making sense of their surroundings.

Semiotics, finally, extends and explains the findings of uses and gratifications research that the media satisfy fantasy drives. Yet in contrast to functionalist theory, semiotics regards audience gratifications as derivative from textual, structural, and cultural forces, which provide the context in which the individual orients himself/herself (McQuail and Gurevitch, 1974). The determinants for the fantasy drive can be explained in a variety of ways. Mills and Marcuse invoke a macro-level conflict theory to make the point that in industrial society, people need relief from the monotony of work. The media are therefore organized and programmed in such a way as to provide diversion and relaxation. Silverstone provides a more semiotic explanation of this enjoyment, basing it on the narrative form and framing conventions of television texts. The mythic part of television, according to Silverstone (1981, p. 76), lies in its form of expression which is both similar to and different from the world of everyday experience. Moving from one to the other involves a transformation which is partially accomplished by the narrative structure and partially by framing.

Though the ambitious objectives set out by its founders for semiotic theory have remained unfulfilled, its potential for understanding human communication practices are extensive. We have argued that, in spite of the fact that semiotic theory has neither unified scientific research, nor elaborated a comprehensive framework for the study of signification, it has highlighted the "how" of communication. It provides a foundation for relating rule governed texts to a theory of culture or ideology, in which these texts, whatever they are, make sense. Within television studies, semiotics has furthermore produced a new interest in the narrative strategies and formats in which social phenomena are represented and in the ways in which we come to know public events.

REFERENCES

Bakhtin, M. (1965). "Rabelais and His World." Trans. by H. Iswolsky. Cambridge, Massachusetts: MIT Press.
Barthes, R. (1957). "Mythologies." Paris: Editions du Seuil.
Barthes, R. (1964). Rhétorique de l'image. *Communications* (No. 4), 40–51.
Barthes, R. (1968). "Elements of Semiology." Trans. by A. Lavers and C. Smith. New York: Hill and Wang.
Barthes, R. (1974). "S/Z." Trans. by R. Miller New York: Hill and Wang.
Bazalgette, C., and Paterson, R. (1980/1981). Real entertainment: The Iranian Embassy siege. *Screen Education* (No. 37), 55–67.
Blumler, J. G. (1973). "Audience Roles in Political Communication: Some Reflections on their Structure, Antecedents and Consequences." (Paper presented at the Ninth World Congress of the International Political Science Association, Montreal, Canada.)
Brunsdon, C., and Morley, D. (1978). "Everyday Television: 'Nationwide.' " London: British Film Institute.

Carey, J. (1977). Mass communication research and cultural studies: An American view. *In* J. Curran, M. Gurevitch, and J. Woolacott (Eds.), "Mass Communication and Research," pp. 409–426. London: Edward Arnold.

Connell, I. (1980). Television news and the social contract. *In* S. Hall, D. Hobson, A. Lowe, and P. Willis (Eds.), "Culture, Media. Language," pp. 139–156. London: Hutchinson.

Coward, R. (1977). Class, "culture" and the social formation. *Screen, 18* (No. 1), 75–105.

Coward, R., and Ellis, J. (1977). "Language and Materialism." London: Routledge and Kegan Paul.

Crowley, D. (1981). The communication of bias and the bias of communication. *In* L. Salter (Ed.), "Communication Studies in Canada," pp. 199–211. Toronto, Ontario: Butterworths.

Eco, U. (1975). "Looking for a Logic of Culture." Lisse, The Netherlands: Peter De Ridder Press.

Eco, U. (1976). "A Theory of Semiotics." Bloomington, Indiana: Indiana University Press.

Eco, U. (1979). Can television teach? *Screen Education* (No. 31), 15–24.

Fiske, J., and Hartley, J. (1978). "Reading Television." London: Methuen.

Gans, H. J. (1979). "Deciding What's News." New York: Pantheon Books.

Garvin, P. L. (Ed.) (1964). "A Prague School Reader on Esthetics, Literary Structure, and Style." Washington, D.C.: Georgetown University Press.

Geertz, C. (1973). "The Interpretation of Cultures." New York: Basic Books.

Genette, G. (1972). "Figures III." Paris: Editions du Seuil.

Glasgow University Media Group. (1976). "Bad News." London: Routledge and Kegan Paul.

Glasgow University Media Group. (1980). "More Bad News." London: Routledge and Kegan Paul.

Gramsci, A. (1971). "Selections from the Prison Notebooks." Ed. and trans. by Q. Hoare and G. Nowell-Smith. New York: International Publishers.

Greimas, A. (1966). "Sémantique Structurale." Paris: Larousse.

Hall, S. (1973). "Encoding and Decoding in the Television Discourse." (Occasional Paper, Birmingham Center for Contemporary Cultural Studies.)

Hall, S. (1977). "Culture, the media and the "Ideological effect." *In* J. Curran, M. Gurevitch, and J. Wollacott (Eds.), "Mass Communications and Society," pp. 315–348. London: Arnold.

Hall, S. (1981). Cultural studies and the centre: Some problematics and problems. *In* D. Hobson, A. Lowe, and P. Willis (Eds.), "Culture, Media and Language," pp. 15–47. London: Hutchison.

Hall, S., Connell, I., and Curti, L. (1976a). The "unity" of current affairs television. *Cultural Studies* (No. 9), 51–93.

Hall, S., Clarke, J., Jefferson, T., and Roberts, B. (Eds.). (1976b). "Resistance Through Rituals." London: Hutchison.

Hamad, M. (1981). Le contenue comme miroir de la communication: L'école europenne de sémiotique. *In* L. Salter (Ed.), "Etudes Canadiennes en Communication," pp. 276–286, Toronto, Ontario: Butterworths.

Hjelmslev, L. (1966). "Prolegomena to a Theory of Language." Madison, Wisconsin: University of Wisconsin Press.

Innis, H. (1972). "Empire and Communication." Toronto, Ontario: University of Toronto Press.

Jackson, J. (1981). On the implications of content and structural analyses. *In* L. Salter (Ed.), "Communication Studies in Canada." Toronto, Ontario: Butterworths.

Jakobson, R., and Halle, M. (1956). "Fundamentals of Language." The Hague, Netherlands: Mouton.

Kristeva, J. (1969). Le mot, le dialogue et le roman. *In* "Recherches Pour Une Semanalyse," pp. 143–175. Paris: Editions du Seuil.

Leiss, W., and Kline, S. (1978). Advertising needs and commodity fetishism. *Canadian Journal of Political and Social Theory* (No. 2), 5–30.

Lévi-Strauss, C. (1966). "The Savage Mind." Chicago, Illinois: University of Chicago Press.

Lévi-Strauss, C. (1970). "The Raw and the Cooked." Trans. by J. and D. Weightman. New York: Harper and Row.

Leymore, V. L. (1975). "Hidden Myth." New York: Basic Books.

McCombs, M. E., and Shaw, D. L. (1972). The agenda-setting function of mass media. *Public Opinion Quarterly, 36,* 176–187.

McQuail, D., and Gurevitch, M. (1974). Explaining audience behavior: Three approaches considered. *In* J. Blumler and E. Katz (Eds.), ''The Uses of Mass Communications, Current Perspectives in Gratifications Research,'' pp. 287–302. Beverly Hills, California: Sage.

Méar, A. (1980). Recherches Québécoises sur la télévision. Laval, Quebéc: Les Editions Cooperatives Albert Saint-Martin.

Melody, W., Salter, L., and Heyer, P. (Eds.) (1981). ''Culture, Communication, and Dependency. The Tradition of H. A. Innis.'' Norwood, New Jersey: Ablex.

Metz, C. (1974a). ''Film Language: A Semiotics of the Cinema.'' Trans. by M. Taylor. New York: Oxford University Press.

Metz, C. (1974b). ''Language and Cinema.'' The Hague, Netherlands: Mouton.

Morley, D. (1980). Texts, readers, subjects. *In* S. Hall, D. Hobson, A. Cowe, and P. Willis (Eds.), ''Culture, Media, Language,'' pp. 163–173. London: Hutchinson.

Morley, P. (1980). ''The 'Nationwide' Audience.'' London: British Film Institute.

Morris, C. (1938). ''Foundations of the Theory of Signs.'' Chicago, Illinois: University of Chicago Press.

Morris, C. (1955). ''Signs, Language and Behavior.'' New York: George Braziller.

Newcombe, H. (Ed.). (1979). ''Television, the Critical View!'' New York: Oxford University Press.

Parkin, F. (1972). ''Class Inequality and Political Order.'' London: Paladin Books.

Pettit, P. (1977). ''The Concept of Structuralism: A Critical Analysis.'' Berkeley, California: University of California Press.

Propp, V. (1975). ''Morphology of the Folktale.'' Trans. by L. Scott. Austin, Texas: University of Texas Press.

Repentigny, M. (1981). L'election du Parti Québécois en Novembre 1976: Axiologie du discours de press. *In* L. Salter (Ed.), ''Etudes Canadiennes en Communication,'' pp. 250–275, Toronto, Ontario: Butterworths.

Robinson, G. (1980). ''The Referendum on Quebec Television: A Semiotic Approach to Television News Analysis.'' Association for the Study of Canadian Radio and Television (ASCRT) Congress, Ottawa, Ontario. (Unpublished.)

Robinson, G., and Theall, D. (1975). ''Studies in Canadian Communications.'' Montreal, Québec: McGill University, Graduate Program in Communication.

Rogers, E. M. (1982). The empirical and the critical schools of communication. *Communication Yearbook 5,* 125–144.

Saussure, F. de (1966). ''Course in General Linguistics.'' Trans. by W. Baskin. Toronto, Ontario: McGraw Hill.

Schefer, J. L. (1969). ''Scénographie d'un Tableau.'' Paris: Editions du Seuil.

Scholes, R. (1978). ''Structuralism in Literature.'' New Haven, Connecticut: Yale University Press.

Sebeok, T. (1975a). ''Zoosemiotics: At the Intersection of Nature and Culture.'' Lisse, The Netherlands: Peter De Ridder Press.

Sebeok, T. (Ed.). (1975b). ''The Tell-Tale Sign: A Survey of Semiotics.'' Lisse, The Netherlands: Peter De Ridder Press.

Sebeok, T. (Ed.). (1978). ''Sight, Sound and Sense.'' Bloomington, Indiana: Indiana University Press.

Silverstone, R. (1981). ''The Message of Television: Myth and Narrative in Contemporary Culture.'' London: Heineman Educational Books.

Slack, J. D., and Allor, M. (1982). ''The Political and Epistemological Constituents of Critical Communications Research.'' (Paper presented at the 1982 Conference of the International Communications Association, Boston, Massachusetts.)

Theall, D. (1975). Communication theory and the marginal culture: The socio-aesthetic dimensions of communication study. *In* G. Robinson and D. Theall (Eds.), ''Studies in Canadian Communications.'' Montreal, Québec: Graduate Program in Communications, McGill University.

Theall, D. (1978). ''Models of Interpretative and Structural Analysis to Study the Cultural Effects of Television Advertising on TV Viewers in the Montreal Area.'' Québec, Québec: Le Service de la Recherche, Le Ministère des Communications.

Tremblay, G., Charron, C. Y., Lizotte, P., Lavoi, R., and Bau, J. F. (1981). ''Le Livre Blanc et la presse Francophone à Montréal.'' Canadian Communication Association Congress, Halifax, Nova Scotia. (unpublished.)

Tuchman, G. (1978). ''Making News: A Study in the Construction of Reality.'' New York: Free Press.

Williams, R. (1974). ''Television: Technology and Cultural Form.'' London: Fontana.

Williams, R. (1976). Developments in the sociology of culture. *Sociology 10*, 497–506.

Wollen, P. (1969). ''Signs and Meaning in the Cinema.'' London: Secker and Warburg.

6

Coding Social Interaction

Joseph P. Folger*
Department of Communication
University of Michigan
Ann Arbor, Michigan 48109

Dean E. Hewes
Department of Speech Communication
University of Illinois
Urbana, Illinois 61801

Marshall Scott Poole
Department of Speech Communication
University of Illinois
Urbana, Illinois 61801

---

*Authors are listed alphabetically.

One of the great ironies of the field of communication is that we so seldom study our namesake. Our journals are replete with studies of the relationships among self-reports of communicative behaviors or structural relationships linking communicants—viewing-time, communication networks, and the like—but all too seldom do we explore the content and function of the actual messages. Fortunately, this ironic state of affairs has begun to have an impact on researchers within and without our field. We are now finding that social interaction has a profound impact on such diverse phenomena as language and cognitive development (Bruner, 1975; Perret-Clermont, 1980), affective bonding (Ainsworth, 1969; Bowlby, 1969), relational definition and development (Altman and Taylor, 1973; Watzlawick et al., 1967), and the structuring of the social order (Giddens, 1976; McPhee and Poole, 1980), to name but a few.

Why was this irony permitted to become so telling? The problem was that, despite early theoretical accounts highlighting the importance of social interaction (for instance Bales, 1950; Watzlawick et al., 1967), only in recent years has the needed technology been developed to make the quantitative study of social interaction feasible. After all, social interaction is damnably complex. And despite the keen insights into the methods for its study provided us by such pioneers as Robert Bales (1950, 1970) and Edgar Borgatta (1962), we are only now coming to understand how the complexities of social interaction might be tamed methodologically.

This chapter contains a summary and extension of work begun at the University of Wisconsin-Madison eight years ago to address the methodological problems inherent in studying social interaction empirically. We have also drawn freely, and with gratitude, on the storehouse of insights provided us by the pioneers in this area, as well as like-minded contemporaries in sociology, communication, and social psychology who have pursued independent, though parallel lines of research. Here we address the most basic question in the analysis of social interaction: *How do we identify appropriate, reproducible units for the study of social interaction and assign those units empirically valid meanings?*

I. WHAT IS "CODING"?

We begin by drawing an analogy between "coding" and "interpretation." When people read or see a text, or participate in social interaction, they must make sense of what they experience—they must make an interpretation of that experience. At minimum this involves a), identifying the units of a text amenable to interpretation (for example, Bales', 1950, discussion of the "social act" or Miller and Kintsch, 1981, on "parsing"); b), employing the configuration of these units, the setting and social knowledge as the context for the interpretation (cf. Bateson, 1978; Bochner and Krueger, 1979; Goffman, 1981); and c), utilizing this context, plus a set of interpretive rules, to make some plausible, and hopefully accurate, interpretaton (cf., Hewes and Planalp, in press). Standards of *consistency* and *accuracy* are key to this process. Without the consistent identification of interpretable units, relevant contextual factors, and use of interpretive rules, interpretations would be random. Communication would be impossible. Without standards of accuracy, be they empirical, idiosyncratic, or socially sanctioned, interpretations would be arbitrary. Were there no socially shared standards for labeling and explaining actions, for example, the resulting arbitrary interpretations would make communication impossible.

The process of coding social interaction manifests strong parallels to the process of interpretation. Coders must identify units of texts amenable to theoretically meaningful interpretation (Gottman, 1979). Coders must utilize contextual cues—the configuration of the text, setting, as well as thoretical principles—in assigning meanings both to the units and the text as a whole (Bales, 1950; Cappella and Hewes, in progress). And, just as social actors must exploit standards of consistency and accuracy to communicate their interpretations to others, so too must scientists exploit their quantitative analogs to those standards—*reliability* and *validity*.

Although these two scientific standards are certainly better understood than their interpretive counterparts, this understanding is by no means universally reflected in research. For example, during the last decade roughly 30 percent of the articles employing coding in national communication journals either reported no reliability estimates or seriously underreported them. In virtually every case, the procedures employed were inadequate. During the same period, less than 10 percent of the studies reported any empirical evidence for the validity of their coding schemes. In fact the very nature and necessity of validity data has itself been a source of controversy (Fisher, 1980a; Folger and Poole, 1980, 1982; Rogers and Millar, 1981).

In Section II we examine standards of consistency applicable to both unitizing and categorizing discourse. Our primary focus is on the kinds of reliability data needed to support claims of reproducibility made in typical studies of social interaction. We are particularly interested in those studies employing sequential techniques—lagged-sequential analysis, Markov processes, and the like (cf., Capella and Hewes, in progress; Gottman, 1979; Hewes, 1980; Sackett, 1979). In Section III we explore the nature of accuracy in coding social interaction, making what we feel to be some unique conceptual and methodological contributions to this currently murky issue. Finally, in Section IV we identify questions, as yet unanswered, that are central to the development of interaction analysis as a scientific enterprise. Through these three sections we have tried to provide empirical illustrations of both the problems found in coding and their potential solutions.

II. CONSISTENCY IN CODING

Reproducibility of findings is a hallmark of science. Applied to interaction analysis, reproducibility requires consistency in the identification of units to be categorized or rated, as well as consistency in the labels or rating assigned to those units. The former kind of consistency we label "unitizing reliability" after Guetzkow (1950), while the latter we have creatively labeled "interpretative reliability." As we noted in our discussion of interpretation, those two interrelated forms of consistency are necessary but not sufficient to guarantee a useful, nonarbitrary, communicable interpretation. Unitizing reliability provides us with quantitative verification that we are identifying consistently phenomena in a text across time and/or coders. Once we have established this kind of consistency, we need quantitative assurance that common labels, attributes, functions, etc. are attached consistently to the units (interpretive reliability). Thus if unitizing reliability fails, interpretative reliability must also fail; the reverse is not necessarily the case.

A. Unitizing Reliability

1. Possible Units.

Social interaction can be unitized into a variety of segments. In some cases these units may be as small as 300 milliseconds (Capella and Streibel, 1979) or as large as the whole "theme" of an interaction (Gottman, 1979, p. 49). For instance, Bales (1950, p. 39) employed the "act" as his unit of analysis, defining it as "the smallest discriminable segment of verbal or nonverbal behavior to which the observer, using the present set of categories after appropriate training, can assign a classification under conditions of continuous serial scoring." The "speech," "turn," or "turn at talk" has also been employed as the unit of analysis of many researchers (cf., Hewes et al., 1980; Riskin and Faunce, 1972; Rogers and Farace, 1975), and includes all actions and/or statements made by a single speaker while s/he holds the floor. The former unit—the act—enjoys the advantage of permitting a more microscopic representation of interaction, particularly within-turn patterns (for instance, Bales 1953). Unlike the act, the latter—the turn—can be identified without reference to the content of a particular coding scheme. What is said does not affect a coder's ability to demark a turn. In addition, by eliminating the complexities of within-turn patterns, the use of the turn as a unit of analysis engenders simpler techniques for data analysis (Hewes, 1979). Of course, it buys this simplicity at the cost of more complex interpretive coding. If more than one codable act occurs within a turn, which interpretation is to be assigned to the whole turn?

We cannot make any flat statements concerning the relative utility of time units, acts, turns, themes, and so on as units for coding social interaction. Each has its advantages. With proper training, all can probably be used reliably, although arbitrary choices of time units may not prove appropriate for particular coding schemes (Hatfield and Weider-Hatfield, 1978). Our point is simply that unit choices cannot be made independent of the research question, coding scheme, and data analytic tools to be employed. Efforts by some researchers to establish the "correct" unit irrespective of such concerns (Geller et al., 1942; Hatfield and Weider-Hatfield, 1978) are probably doomed to failure.[1] In fact, on-going research of the segmentation of behavior (Bower et al., 1979; Ebbesen, 1981; Newtson, 1976) suggests that unitization in natural settings is probably strongly influenced by the goals of social actor. We suspect that this would be as true for the empirical researcher. Certainly radically different pictures of social interaction result from the use of different units with the same coding schemes (Hatfield and Weider-Hatfield, 1978).

2. Measuring Unitizing Reliability.

As our discussion indicates, unitizing reliability is a basic requirement for interpretive reliability. If an index of interpretive reliability is too low, the fault may lie with the coding rules, with unitizing, or both. Thus assessing the degree of unitizing reliability is a necessary pre-condition for a well-documented quantitative study of social interaction. It becomes particularly crucial under three conditions: if the index of interpretative reliability is low and one needs to locate the source of the problem; if the units of analysis are conceptually independent of the coding system ("turns", for instance); if the units themselves are interesting phenomena in their own right, as in the study of segmentation of the stream of behavior (Barker, 1963; Bower et al., 1979; Ebbesen, 1981; Newtson, 1976) or research on turn durations, speaker latencies, etc. (cf., Cappella and Joseph, 1981; Hewes, 1979; Hewes et al., 1980).

Harold Guetzkow wrote a classic, and neglected, article on the assessment of unitizing reliability in 1950. Guetzkow's index is based on the premises that two independent, equally skilled coders unitize a text each into same specifiable number of units (O_1 for coder 1 and O_2 for coder 2). The sample value of the index of unitizing reliability is label U, and computed as

$$U = (O_1 - O_2)/(O_1 + O_2)$$

Thus if coder 1 identifies 58 units and coder 2 identifies 85, U = .189 ((85–58)/(85+58)). In other words, there is a discrepancy of 18.9 percent between either coder and the best estimate of the "true" number of codes (the average of the two coders' estimates). (Note: U is thus an estimate of *disagreement*,

---

[1]It is certainly likely that there are some levels of segmentation too fine to detect specific categories. If one were looking for "statements of agreement," for instance, 0.03 second increments would be too fine. Nevertheless, even in this example, judgments of the "correct" unit depend on the coding scheme being used. Units are neither too fine nor too coarse except in reference to the goals of the researcher as reflected in a coding system.

rather than an estimate agreement as are most indices of reliability). With U in hand, Guetzkow provides us with a method of estimating associated confidence intervals.[2]

Although Guetzkow's index is certainly useful, it falls short of being ideal. To be ideal, an index of unitizing reliability should estimate the degree of agreement between two or more coders in identifying specific segments of text. That is, an ideal index should quantify the *unit-by-unit agreement* between two or more coders. Neither U or his more sophisticated index based on U does this. Guetzkow's indices only show the degree to which two coders identify the *same number of units* in a text of fixed length, not whether those units were in fact the same units. Figure 1 may take this point clearer. As you can see, in both (a) and (b) each coder has identified ten units. In both (a) and (b) Guetzkow's indices point to perfect unitizing reliability; however, unit-by-unit reliability in (b) is certainly less than perfect.

In order to generate an alternative index of unitizing reliability, we need to unitize the text two ways—first, using whatever units are of theoretical interest to us (hereafter, the "actual" units) and, second, using the same objective fixed standard (hereafter, the "objective" units). For example, if we were coding "acts," we might pick time units (seconds), some number of words, and so on, as the objective units. The only requirements are that objective units a) be convenient to use, and b) be smaller than the average length of the actual units. If, for instance, the average length of an "act" in our text was 2.0 seconds, we might make our objective units one second in length—half the length of the average act (cf., Arundale, 1977). By segmenting more finely than the majority of our actual units, we are trying to avoid having two or more actual units encompassed within an objective unit. Figure 1 (a) and (b) contain these objective units in the form of hash marks along the time line.

Once we have segmented the text objectively, we look objective segment by objective segment to see if our coders agreed or disagreed on the occurrence of an actual unit within that objective unit.[3] If both agree that a unit has occurred or that a unit has *not* occurred, this constitutes agreement. We can then compute an index of agreement or disagreement from this information. Examples of this procedure or ones with comparable intent are found in Hewes et al. (1980), Newtson and Engquist (1976), Newtson et al. (1977), and Ebbesen and Allen (1979).

---

[2]Guetzkow provides a Figure for the translation of U and n into an estimate of the lower bound of theoretical accuracy (σ/h) at the 99 and 95 percent confidence levels (see his Figure 3 and pp. 55–57).

[3]This is a little trickier than it sounds. Do you count an actual unit that overlaps two or more objective units as falling into all of them, one in which most of the actual unit appears, or some other option? The first of these criteria is more stringent than the second. The choice is arbitrary, probably, for most practical purpose. The most crucial decision is not which standard to apply but, rather, to choose some standard and to apply it consistently throughout.

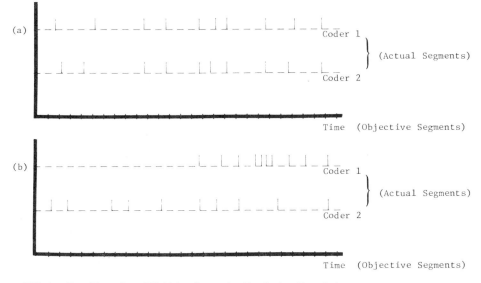

FIG. 1.   Two Examples of Unitizing Interaction Employing Two Coders.
Note: The solid line represents clock time; the dashed line represents the time line used by each coder. The vertical hash marks (I) represent units, either objective or actual.

Is it always necessary to go to so much work to provide evidence of unitizing reliability? Probably not in all cases. If one is using an exhaustive coding system, i.e., a coding system in which each and every act is coded, and Guetzkow's U is quite low, perhaps .10 or below, it *may* prove unnecessary to perform a unit-by-unit analysis. Similarly, if the actual unit is relatively objective and easily coded, Guetzkow's indices may suffice. On the other hand, if the units are subjective, the coding scheme is not exhaustive or the data are to be used for sequential analysis (lagged-sequential analysis, Markov process, etc.), unit-by-unit analysis is essential (more on this in Section II. B.2). In any event *some* measure of unitizing reliability should be reported in any quantitative study of social interact.

B. Interpretive Reliability

1. Coding Systems.

A coding system is defined by three attributes. First, it specifies, either explicitly or implicitly, the units of social interaction to be interpreted. Second, a coding system establishes the complete domain of interpretations that are to be made of any unit of a text. That is, the coding system contains a list of all descriptions, functions, ascribed goals, or intentions that could be assigned to any unit of the text, given the theoretical viewpoint of the researcher.[4] Finally, a coding system contains a set of rules for applying one or more interpretations to any given unit of discourse. Of course, these interpretive rules may be more or less explicit, ranging from the purely mechanical (for instance, Jaffe and Feldstein, 1970) to the largely intuitive (for instance, McCroskey and Wright, 1971).

Unlike early treatments of coding (Larzarsfeld and Barton, 1969), our definition does not require that coding schemes be composed of mutually exclusive categories or scales. Instead, we grant that coders may be required to code individual units multifunctionally, i.e., to code a unit in more than one category or along more than one dimension, in order to accurately characterize the text. In fact, the assumption of exclusivity can be positively harmful to the validity of coding systems (Hewes, 1979). In addition, our definition does not require that *every* unit be coded in some category; that is, it does not require that the coding system be exhaustive. As Guetzkow (1950, p. 48) pointed out years ago, many coding tasks require only that a subset of all possible units be coded. As an illustration, Folger and Puck's (1976) coding system, which codes relational dominance only in terms of the forms of questions in dyadic exchanges, is one example of what Guetzkow labeled "sieve" coding. At any rate, whether a coding system has explicit or implicit interpretative rules, whether or not it assumes exhaustiveness and/or exclusiveness, it must be applied consistently in order to guarantee the reproducibility of results.

2. Measuring Interpretive Reliability.

a. Global measures.   Given our definition of interpretative reliability, it should be clear that an index of interpretive reliability quantifies the extent to which interpretive rules are used consistently across coders, texts, and time. However, consistency can be characterized at a variety of levels. At the *global* level, consistency refers to the extent to which two or more coders (or a single coder at two or more points in time) can utilize the whole coding system consistently. Consequently, an index of global interpretive reliability usually summarizes the consistency with which coders are able to employ the system across all categories or dimensions. Two illustrative indices used on categorical data may make this point clear.

Guetzkow's (1950) P, and its associated indices, is among the most commonly used in the field of communication. P is a measure of the theoretically specified portion of n units that two (or more) coders will agree upon for a coding system of k categories. It is based on the assumptions that observed percentage

---

[4]Note: Interpretations of the text of a communicative exchange may be *derived* from the patterns of units observed (cf., Rogers and Farace, 1975). Thus, the interpretations of a text are not exhausted by the interpretations placed on its individual units even within a given theoretical framework.

agreement between coders (P')[5] is derived from independent judgments of each unit and that the probability of any unit being correctly categorized is equal for all units. In other words, no differences are assumed in the ease with which all categories can be employed. Finally P'—the observed proportion of agreement—is assumed to be based on data drawn from equally skilled coders (Guetzkow, 1950, p. 51). If these assumptions are met, P' can be used to estimate P.

As you might expect, the computation of P, and P's confidence intervals, is based on three parameters: P', n, and a t-statistic. The range of P for a given P' is expressed as

$$P = (t^2 + 2nP')/2(t^2 + n) \pm \sqrt{\frac{(t^2 + 2nP') - 4(t^2 + n)n(P')^2}{2(t^2 + n)}}$$

If $n = 200$, a small figure for most interaction analyses, the degrees of freedom associated with the t-statistic are effectively infinite (df = $^\infty$). Thus for an $\alpha = 0.01$, $t = 2.58$. If $P' = 0.70$, using the equation above, the range of P with a 99 percent confidence interval is approximately 0.619 to 0.769. Guetzkow (1950) also provides a figure for translating the lower limit of P (i.e., .619 in our example) into an estimate of the lower limit of the odds that any given unit will be classified incorrectly in a category system with k categories (see Figure 1, p. 52, and discussion on p. 53).

Recently, coders in other disciplines have begun to employ a useful alternative to Guetzkow's P. This index, Cohen's kappa (1960), has one distinct advantage over Guetzkow's P. P is based principally on the percentage agreement between two or more coders across categories, i.e., P is based on P'. P', however, does not remove what Gottman (1979, p. 97) calls "the base rate problem." That is, P' is inflated by the fact that coders may agree on some classifications by chance alone. For example if we are using a two-category system ($k = 2$), the odds are 0.5 *by chance alone* that a given unit would be classified accurately. Thus, the theoretical proportion of agreement between two coders (P) would be 0.50 by chance (Guetzkow, 1950, p. 51). This property of P, and of all other estimates of interpretative reliability based on percentage agreement figures alone, is not optimal *if* we are interested in assessing the skill of our coders. An

---

[5]P' is computed by counting the number of units on which both coders agree on its interpretation, and dividing that number by the total number of units on which the coders could either agree or disagree. Thus, if both coders each code the same 200 units and agree on their classifications in 150 cases, $P' = 0.75$. When more than two coders are employed, different standards of agreement are possible. For example, when four coders are employed, "agreement" could mean "unanimity" or "three-of-four." Some decision rule must be utilized to resolve disputes among coders, no matter how many coders are employed. Whatever that decision rule is, it should be the basis for the definition of "agreement" used to compute P'.

assessment of skill requires that we remove inflated base rates. On the other hand, P and similar measures are fine if we only want to assess the accuracy of categorization produced by skill and chance combined.

Cohen's kappa corrects for this baseline problem in a very simple way:

$$\text{Kappa} = (P' - P_c)/(1 - P_c)$$

where P' = the observed percentage agreement among coders (as in Guetzkow) and P_c is the proportion of chance agreement. If we assume, as did Guetzkow, that the probability of accurate classification is equal for all units, then $P_c = 1/k$, where k = the number of categories in the coding scheme. As an illustration, if $P' = .70$ and there are twelve categories, Kappa = .6727 (that is, $(.70-.0833)/(1-.0833)$). Kappa is always lower than P'; how much lower depends on the number of categories in the coding system. Extensions of kappa for more than two coders, estimates of kappa's variance, statistical tests, etc. are available in Fleiss (1971). Gottman (1979, ch. 5) provides a useful illustration of the kappa applied to interaction analysis.

Global indices such as Guetzkow's P and Cohen's kappa, as we have discussed them,[6] are the single most common variety reported in analyses of social interaction (cf., Bochner and Bochner, 1972; Courtright, 1978; Ellis, 1979; Fisher, 1970; Hawes, 1972; Mabry, 1975a, b, c; Stech, 1979). Although the specific indices employed may vary (Pearson's r, percentage agreement, intraclass correlation, as well as Guetzkow's P and Cohen's kappa), the typical interaction study reports only some global assessment of interpretive consistency (but cf., Donohue, 1981; Gottman, 1979; Hewes et al., 1980). As we shall see in II. B. 2.b. (immediately below), global indices can mask serious problems in data analysis.

b. Category-by-category-measures. Category-by-category measures of interpretive reliability go global measures one better. Rather than simply indicating the overall level of category consistency, category-by-category indices provide separate figures for consistency for each and every category, as their name implies. Whereas global indices, such as Guetzkow's P and Cohen's kappa (as we have discussed them), assume that the likelihood of accurate classification of any unit is equal for all units, category-by-category indices allow for the possibility that certain categories may be harder to use than others, thus possessing lower reliabilities. And, in fact, this is often the case. As an illustration, Donohue's (1981) coding scheme for dyadic negotiation possesses reliabilities ranging from .49 to 1.0, with an average global reliability of .74. Hewes et al. (1980) found a

---

[6]Note: Cohen's kappa can be used in estimating category-by-category interpretive reliabilities (see Gottman, 1979, p. 98), as can Guetzkow's P (see Donohue, 1981). Unfortunately, *typical* applications are only to estimates of global interpretive reliability.

similar range of reliabilities for a group decision-making coding system. On the other hand, Gottman's (1979) affect codes for his Couples Interaction Scoring System had much more homogeneous reliabilities (.871 to 1.0, based on Cronbach's α; see Gottman's Table 5.4). Our point here is that, although homogeneity in reliabilities across categories is certainly possible, it is by no means always the case.

Reporting only global interpretive reliabilities obscures the existence of potential nonhomogeneity; not only does this nonhomogeneity violate the assumptions of most global reliability indices, but it may also seriously undermine data analysis. On the simplest level, global measures do not warn either researchers or research consumers of potential problems with a coding system. Categories with low reliabilities are obviously in need of further refinement. These categories may be defined either ambiguously or inappropriately for the interaction to which they are applied (for instance, Hewes et al., 1980, on multifunctional coding of categories (6) and (8), p. 132). More seriously, however, are the consequences to hypothesis-testing. *When researchers wish to test hypotheses concerning either the distribution of coded units across categories or temporal dependencies between (or among) categories, category-by-category interpretive reliability estimates are essential.* They are essential because they permit researchers to detect potential sources of systematic bias in distributional and/or temporal dependency data.

In order to make this claim clear, let us define what we mean by "distributional" and "temporal dependency" data. Distributional data refers to those data where the relative frequency or probability of occurrence among categories is central to the hypotheses or research questions under investigation. As an example, Baird (1974) anticipated that groups with either cooperative or competitive orientations to the same discussion topic would (and did) manifest substantially different frequencies of certain functional aspects of communication ("initiates and develops themes," "expresses disagreement," "gives information"). Gottman (1979) also hypothesized distributional differences, this time between distressed and nondistressed couples in both the content and affect category systems (see also Gottman et al., 1977; see Riskin and Faunce, 1972, for related analyses).

"Temporal dependency" is a bit more complicated to define without some additional background. We noted in the introduction that much current research on social interaction employs sequential analytic techniques such as trend analysis (as in Poole, 1981), Markov chain analysis (Hewes, 1980), lag-sequential analysis (Sacket, 1979), and semi-Markov models (Hewes et al., 1980; Howard, 1971). Each of these techniques utilizes the temporal ordering of coded acts as part of the analysis. The last three techniques (Markov chains, lag-sequential, semi-Markov models) require "temporal dependency" data of the following form: If *A, B,* and *C* represent categories for units coded along a time-line left-to-right, then the sequence *A-B-C-A-B-C-A-B-C* manifests a strong temporal dependency. That is, B always follows A, C always follows B, and A always follows C. In other words, temporal dependency between or among categories means that the occurrence of some category I at some later time $t + K$ allows us to predict the occurrence of some category J at some later time $t + k + n$ ($n > 0$). This temporal dependency may be between adjacents acts (i.e., $n=1$), as in our example with categories A, B, and C, or it may be over some greater time lag ($n > 1$). At any rate, knowing the occurrence of some antecedent event I allows us to predict some subsequent event J beyond chance:

$$\text{Prob}(J \text{ at } t + k + n/I \text{ at } t + k) \neq \text{Prob}(J)$$

In English, the probability of J, knowing that I occurred previously, is not equal to the probability of J occurring without knowing the previous event. Another way of saying this is that knowing that I has occurred *reduces our uncertainty* about J's subsequent occurrence (Gottman and Bakeman, 1979). Uncertainty may be reduced completely (perfect prediction), as in our example with categories A, B, and C, or to some lesser extent—thus the use of the probability terminology in the mathematical expression above. Thus, temporal dependency data are data in which the temporal ordering of codes is used, hopefully, to reduce uncertainty concerning the occurrence of specific codes. The greater the temporal dependency between codes the more adequately we can describe and predict a string of coded interaction data.

Now suppose that we had a set of data that we wished to analyze either distributionally or temporally. For simplicity, let us assume that we have a two category coding system (A and B) and that the temporal dependency occurs only between temporally contigous events ($n=1$). These dependencies can be represented in the abstract in matrix form to which we have set hypothetical values.

$$t + k + 1$$

$$
\begin{array}{cc}
A & B
\end{array}
$$

$$
t + k \quad
\begin{array}{c}
A \\
B
\end{array}
\begin{pmatrix}
m_{AA} & m_{AB} \\
m_{BA} & m_{BB}
\end{pmatrix}
\begin{array}{c}
f_{A.} \\
f_{B.}
\end{array}
=
\begin{pmatrix}
0.70 & 0.30 \\
0.60 & 0.40
\end{pmatrix}
\begin{array}{c}
100 \\
200
\end{array}
$$

Where m_{AB} (.3) is the observed odds that a B will occur at $t + k + 1$, given that A occurs at $t + k + 1$; m_{BA} (.6) is the observed odds that an A will occur at $t + k + 1$, given that a B occurs at $t + k + 1$; and so on. The symbols $f_{A.}$ and $f_{B.}$ refer to the observed frequency of units coded as As and Bs repectively. Thus they reflect distributional information. These matrix entries (m_{AA}, etc.) are called "transition probabilities," since they describe the probability of a transition occurring between instances of categorized units. The matrix itself is called a "transition matrix" (cf., Hewes, 1980).

Let us further suppose that there is some differential source of reliability in categorizing units. For example, the odds of a unit categorized as an A actually being an A might be .90. The odds of a unit categorizing a B actually being a B might be .60. Note: These figures are not percentage agreement estimates (Guetzkow's P'). They are, instead, more closely related to Guetzkow's p, which we have not discussed previously (see Guetzkow, 1950, pp. 51–53 for the relationship between P' and p). Again, we can represent this kind of data in matrix form. This appears below with both symbols and hypothetical data:

$$
\begin{array}{cc}
 & A_a \quad\quad B_a \\
\begin{array}{c} A \\ B \end{array} &
\begin{pmatrix} \text{Prob}(A_a|A \text{ Prob }(B_a|A) \\ \text{Prob}(A_a|B \text{ Prob }(B_a|B) \end{pmatrix}
= \begin{pmatrix} .9 & .1 \\ .4 & .6 \end{pmatrix}
\end{array}
$$

Where $\text{Prob}(A_a/A)$ is the probability (.9) of a unit coded as A actually being an A, $\text{Prob}(A_a/B)$ is the probability (.4) of a unit being coded a B actually being an A, and so forth.   Thus the matrices above describe sources of both accurate classification and confusion between categories. In our hypothetical case, category B is more easily confused with category A than the reverse (.4 *vs* .1).

How would these sources of misclassification affect our actual distribution of As and Bs as well as the actual pattern of temporal dependencies? Although we will not present the complete formal treatment here (see Cappella and Hewes, in preparation; Hewes, in preparation), there are some observations we can make. The simplest is that distributional information is potentially biased by two factors—the unequal observed frequencies of A and B (i.e., $f_A \neq f_B$) and the unequal odds of misclassification between A and B (i.e., $\text{Prob}(A_a/B) \neq \text{Prob}(B_a/A)$). In our example, the odds are that 10 observed As are actually Bs (f_A (Prob $(B_a/A)) = 100 \times .1$), while 80 observed Bs are actually As (f_B (Prob$(A_a/B)) = 200 \times .4$). Thus, in truth, there are 170 As ($100-10+80$), though we only observed 100. In effect we erred by 70 percent in establishing f_A. And, since the total number of observed units is a constant (i.e., $f_A + f_B$ doesn't change as we correct the errors), f_B is really 130, although we observed 200 Bs ($100+200-170=130$)—we erred by 35 percent in estimating f_B. From this example, it should be clear that category-by-category estimates of interpretive reliability are crucial if we are to have some warning about potential sources of systematic biases in distributional information.[7]

---

[7]We may have biased distributional information even if the category-by-category reliability estimates are uniform. Low but uniform category-by-category reliabilities, coupled with an unequal marginal distribution of units across categories, can also produce biases. For example, if Prob $(A_a|A) = \text{Prob}(B_a|B) = 0.70$ in our example above, f_A would really be 130, though it was observed to be 100, and f_B would really be 170, though it was observed to be 200.

The same justification for reporting category-by-category reliability applies to the testing of temporal dependency hypotheses. Here the reasoning is more complex, although the reader can get some intuitive sense of it in Figure 2. Figure 2 describes potential sources of systematic bias in transition probabilities associated with low and/or nonhomogeneous category-by-category reliabilities. Since transition probabilities are estimated under the assumption that units have been coded reliably, they are vulnerable to category unreliability. For instance, if we were to estimate the odds that an A follows a B (m_{AB}) from observed pairs of As and Bs, and we know that we may be mistaken in labeling a unit as an A ($\text{Prob}(B_a/A) \neq 0$) or as a B ($\text{Prob}(A_a/B) \neq 0$), then our transition probability estimate could be wrong. Figure 2 reflects this fact for m_{AB} by noting that some number of observed A-B transitions may really be A-A transitions if the second member of the observed pair was coded incorrectly. Some observed A-B transitions may really have been B-B transitions if the first member of the pair was coded incorrectly, and some A-B transitions may have truly been B-A's if both units in the pair were coded incorrectly. On the other hand, some observed A-A transitions may really have been A-Bs if the second member was coded incorrectly, and so on for the other possible transitions.

If we had estimates of the probabilities of accurate and inaccurate classification (i.e., $\text{Prob}(A_a/B)$, $\text{Prob}(A_a/A)$, and so on) and we assumed that both coding judgments and their associated errors were independent, it is possible to estimate the amount of systematic bias that might have resulted from three sources—*unequal distributions of coded units* (see note 7), *unequal probabilities of classification and misclassification* (as in our previous example), and *the de-*

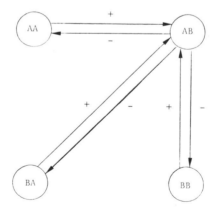

FIG. 2.   Sources of Misclassification Error for Transition AB.
Note: Circles indicate the occurrence of transitional events defined by the cooccurrence of two units. For example, AB represents the occurrence first of a unit classified as an A followed immediately by a B. Plus ($+$) and minus ($-$) indicate that erroneous classifications of one or both events could add or substract from the total number of transitional events observed, in this case the number of ABs.

gree of temporal structure observed in the data. The complete mathematical treatment of these issues is too cumbersome to present here (cf., Cappella and Hewes, in preparation; Hewes, in preparation), but the gist can be obtained from an example. If we again use the hypothetical data introduced earlier in an illustration, the following results are obtained: m_{AA} was observed to be .7, but the actual value is .68; m_{AB} was observed to be .3, but the true value is .32; m_{BA} was observed to be .4, but in actuality it is .61; and for m_{BB} the observed value was .6, but the true value is .39. The last two transition probabilities changed by 53 and 35 percent, respectively, from their observed values. This represents a serious source of bias, bias originating in the conjoint impact of the three factors noted previously.

What are researchers to do about these sources of bias? Researchers must determine if the conditions that promote such biases obtain in their data. This involves four steps.

a. Assess the category-by-category reliabilities of the coded date using percentage agreement, versions of Guetzkow's P, or Cohen's kappa, or Cronbach's alpha adapted to that purpose. If reliabilities are reasonably uniform and high (.9 or higher), it is very unlikely that there is a serious problem with bias for either distributional or temporal dependency hypothesis testing.

b. Assess the equality of the distribution of frequencies across categories. If the distribution is reasonably uniform (approximately equal frequencies across categories) and condition a is met, the likelihood of bias is even less than if a is met alone. Bias is quite likely if unequal distributions of frequencies occur in categories with widely varying levels of reliability, or if there are uniform but low probabilities of classification accuracy (less than .9).

c. Determine if coders are systematically confusing categories. Systematic confusion results in assymetric misclassification of units (i.e., Prob(A_a/B) $\neq$ Prob(B_a/A) in our example). This is almost guaranteed in coding systems with low numbers of categories (Ellis, 1979, RELCOM; Gottman's, 1979, affect codes; Rogers and Farace's, 1975, control codes) which have nonhomogeneous category-by-category reliabilities, although it may occur in more elaborate coding systems. Funkhouser and Parker (1968) developed an index of systematic unreliability at a category-by-category level that does not require direct estimates of classification accuracy (Prob(A_a/A, etc.). A more sophisticated version could be derived from Bishop et al.'s (1975) discussion of the analysis of incomplete contingency tables. Whichever technique is employed to test for systematic confusion among coders, if it is present the effects of unequal frequency distributions and nonhomogeneous category-by-category reliabilities will be more on transition probability estimates than if it is absent. If systematic confusion is present, it represents a potentially major source of bias even if category-by-category reliabilities and frequency distributions are approximately equal.

d. Test the degree of temporal dependency present in the data. Although this will not affect biases in distributional hypotheses, it will in temporal dependency hypotheses. *Ceterus paribus,* the stronger the temporal dependency the greater the bias produced by low, nonhomogeneous, and systematic sources of classification error discussed above. Tests for temporal dependency are to be found in Anderson and Goodman (1957) and Kullback et al. (1962), among others.

Studies hypothesizing differences in the distributions of units across categories under different antecedent conditions should routinely report the results of *a - c*; studies hypothesizing temporal dependencies of any sort should report the results of *a-d*. Only with such information can the researcher or consumer of quantitative analyses of social interaction anticipate the existence of biases in the data. Although steps *a-d* do not provide direct estimates of the magnitudes of these biases, they do provide a rough guide to their assessment. Work is currently underway to provide methodologies that will yield magnitude estimates and correct for biases if present (Cappella and Hewes, in preparation; Hewes, in preparation).

3. Miscellanea.

In the preceding discussion, we have touched on the nature of consistency in the interpretative act of scientific coding. Our focus has been on issues that have received far too little attention in the extant literature. But, by focusing on these issues, we have been forced to ignore other, perhaps more mundane, but equally important issues. In this section, we comment briefly on two important issues not discussed in earlier sections. Our purpose here is simply to alert researchers to these issues and point to relevant literature.

Our discussion to this point has emphasized the problems in assessing the reliabilities associated with categorical coding systems to the exclusion of continuous systems. Fortunately, most of the problems of continuous systems (usually called rating systems), are widely and thoroughly discussed in the standard psychometric literature (Nunnally, 1967; Lord and Novick, 1968; Torgerson, 1958; and especially Cronbach et al., 1972). The interested reader should consult these sources on all but one novel problem. That problem arises when one constructs continuous indices of some aspect of social interaction by summing across occurrences of different types of behavior. Argyle and Dean's (1965) (also Argyle and Cook, 1976) equilibrium theory of affiliative behavior warrants the creation of this kind of index out of such diverse behaviors as eye-contact, proximity, and body lean (see Cappella and Joseph, 1981, pp. 105-114). If these behaviors are expected to covary positively, no problem arises. Standard psychometric theory applies. If, however, these behaviors are substitutable one for the other—that is, they each signify the existence of some psychological or relational state, or they covary negatively as in equilibrium theory—the researcher is faced with a problem. The problem is this: If there is supposed to be no covariation or negative covariation among these elements of an index, then standard measures of internal consistency for continuous measures (such as Cronbach's *a*) do not apply. This creates something of a sticky problem is assessing the reliability and validity of these indices—a problem also found in the so-called multi-act criteria used in studies of personality/behavior and attitude/behavior relationships. Relevant discussions of multi-act criteria and their methodological requirements by Fishbein and Ajzen (1974), Hewes and Haight (1980), and Jaccard and Daly (1980), as well as Epstein (1979), should prove suggestive of ways to cope with this problem in the coding of social interaction (also see Cappella and Hewes, in preparation, for a more detailed discussion of this issue).

The second and final issue we discuss in this section stems from several negative analogies between coders and interactants in social settings. At least in most communicative exchanges we would expect social actors to be more involved in the exchange than coders, to be engaged in the task of interpretation for a shorter period of time, and to be more likely to obtain feedback on the accuracy of their interpretations. These negative analogies imply that coders' consistency and accuracy may suffer from fatigue and "drift" due to lack of feedback—and, in fact, they do (Johnson and Bolstad, 1973). Interobserver agreement tends to decline over time (Romanczyk et al., 1973) unless coders believe they are being randomly spot-checked (Taplin and Reid, 1973). In addition, without continued reference to a written coding manual, or retraining, subsets of coders may drift away from one another in their interpretations of the data, though each subgroup may be consistent within itself. Thus, drift represents a potential source of systematic bias in coding. Few if any researchers publishing in communication journals demonstrate an awareness of these potentially serious sources of coding error. Fortunately, Gottman (1979, ch. 5) provides an exemplary model of both the training strategies and quantitative data that should be evinced to rule out these twin threats to coding consistency and accuracy—decay and drift.

We have come to the end of our discussion of reliability. Throughout, we have maintained that there are similarities between the natural and scientific tasks of interpreting social interaction. Both involve the minimal requirements of consistency and accuracy of interpretation. Unitizing and interpretive reliability are the scientific counterparts of the consistency requirement. We discuss the scientific counterparts of accuracy in the section to follow. In our discussion of reliability, we have tried to emphasize the need for improvements in the quality of data provided to support claims of the consistency of a coding system when applied to a particular text. Although our position could be labeled as too restrictive, we hope to have demonstrated some compelling and relatively novel reasons for our methodological Puritanism. In the section to follow, we play out a similar line on the methodological requirement of validity.

III. THE ACCURACY OF INTERPRETATIONS

As we noted in the introduction, both coders and social actors are responsible not only for the consistency with which they interpret similar events but also for the accuracy of those interpretations. To be accurate, an interpretation of some coded event must be compared to some standard. For example, social actors, if they are to be understood, have as their standard the conventionalized meanings of particular events assigned by the listener. In many cases, those same standards will be shared by many listeners who form a "speech community;" in other cases, those meanings may be idiosyncratic to a particular person, relationship, family, etc. For coders the standard of accuracy may be the conventionalized usages of a speech community and/or the empirical criteria of a scientific theory. Unless coders and social actors make interpretations that are judged accurate against *some* set of standards, they both may be generating nonsense.

A. Accuracy and the Validity of Coding Systems

The scientific equivalent of interpretive accuracy is "validity" (Kerlinger, 1973, ch. 23). To say that the interpretation of a set of events is valid is to say two things: a), the events have been labeled or categorized consistently (reliably); b), the coding system used to make the interpretation can accurately discriminate between those events that are and are not consonant with preferred or "correct" interpretations (Carlsmith et al., 1976). In other words, an interpretive scheme, including a scientific coding system, must be reliable as a minimal requirement for validity and must identify true variability in interpretations judged against some standard.

This sketch of the nature of validation is not controversial when applied to self-report instruments (personality measures, attitude scales, etc.); it becomes so, at least operationally, when applied to coding schemes for social interaction. Although we can point to some recent examples of the validation of coding schemes (Folger and Sillars, 1980; Gottman, 1979; Poole and Folger, 1981b; Stiles, 1980; Wish et al., 1980), and even a few classic examples (Bales, 1970; Borgatta, 1962), the vast majority of interaction coding schemes have been employed without any recourse to evidence for their validity (Cappella and Hewes, in preparation; Folger and Poole, 1980). This state of affairs has arisen, in part, because early discussions of coding gave short shrift to the issue of validity (cf., Holsti, 1969; Lazarsfeld and Barton, 1969). Further, the effort involved in validating a coding scheme can be great—nor are all theorists convinced that it is effort well spent (for instance, Fisher, 1977b, 1980a). Finally, there is a disturbuing difference between the nature of validity in self-reports and coding schemes—a difference that may have obstructed the development of validational procedures in the latter case.

In validating a measure of an attitude, for example, we know who "has" the attitude, and we can ask those people to supply us with various indicators of the presence or degree of the attitude they possess. They may respond to sets of Likert-type belief statements theoretically associated with the attitude; they can react to evaluative semantic differential items; they can even be observed performing attitude-relevant behaviors. In other words, those that supposedly possess the attribute supply us with the data to validate that fact. In contrast, coding systems are intended to reflect *someone's* description/interpretation of social interaction, but whose description/interpretation is not as obvious as in the case of self-report measures. Should these schemes reflect only a particular theorist's interests? Should the communicator's perspective be given special attention, or the listener's or some third party's, or all four? And what if there are differences of opinion among the four? In validating coding schemes, it is not immediately obvious who is the appropriate source of validity data. Fortunately, now we can begin to provide guidelines for choosing among sources of validity data, an issue to which we return after a more thorough discussion of the conceptual bases of validity.

Although there is a long history of coding scheme use in the study of face-to-face interaction, there is little agreement about the type of evidence needed to establish the validity of interaction coding instruments. The validity issue was raised, however, as far back as 1962, when Borgatta argued for revisions in Bales' IPA scheme. Borgatta's revisions were an attempt to account for differences in the intensity of acts that were not acknowledged by the IPA system. His concern was that one act could count for more in an exchange than others that fall in the same category (e.g., one act coded as "tension release" could do far more to relieve tension than other comments placed in this category.) Borgatta argued that the coding scheme should be sensitive to these differences or it could seriously misrepresent interaction. Terrill and Terrill's (1965) revisions of Leary's Interpersonal Behavior Categories (1957), and Ellis's modifications in the Rogers and Farace (1975) relational coding scheme, stemmed from a similar concern about possible differences between acts falling within the same category. These attempts at revision were prompted by a concern for possible inaccuracies in claims drawn about interaction coded with the schemes. In advancing their changes, the authors argued that researchers could make mistaken observational and explanatory claims if their instruments did not incorporate the revised categories. The revisions were premised either explicitly or implicitly on an argument about the validity of the coding scheme in question.

As coding schemes were constructed and revised, however, a key validity question remained largely unaddressed: On what evidence should one rely in claiming that a coding instrument offers an accurate interpretation of messages exchanged in an interaction? This question is central because its answer determines the grounds on which one assigns codes to a message or makes revisions in categories. Few strides can be made in determining what constitutes appropriate procedures for validating interaction coding schemes until the theoretical issues involved in validity are sufficiently clarified. Consequently, our focus in this discussion is on the various types of validity that are needed to establish the accuracy of interaction-coding schemes and on the forms of evidence that can be invoked in support of a scheme's interpretations.

B. Types of Validity

Any discussion of validation must start with the classic trichotomy of face, predictive, and construct validities. Here we accept this trichotomy, amending it somewhat for application to coding systems, while relegating special classes of validity ("convergent," "discriminant," Campbell and Fiske, 1959; "representative," Folger and Poole, 1982; Poole and Folger, 1981a; "semantic," Krippendorff, 1980) to the status of sources of evidence with which to support validity claims. Since our definitions of the classic types of validity are affected somewhat by the special problems in coding, we begin with a general discussion of terminology.

Figure 3 presents our conception of the various forms of validity. X and Y signify *theoretical constructs,* i.e., variables that can be instantiated in various ways, all of/or which are consistent with a given theoretical definition and none of which exhausts the meaning of the construct. For instance, the "control" dimension of communication (Millar and Rogers, 1976; Watzlawick et al., 1967) could be labeled a construct because its general, theoretical definition has led to the construction of a variety of coding systems (Courtright et al., 1980; Ellis, 1979; Folger and Puck, 1976; Mark, 1971; Rogers and Farace, 1975), all seemingly conceptually consistent with the theoretical definition (cf., Cappella and

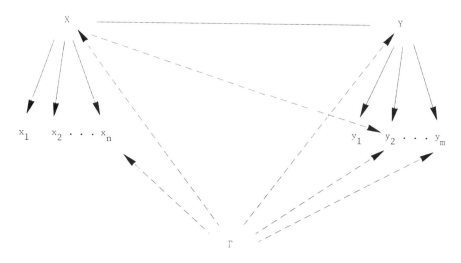

FIG. 3.   Factors Affecting the Construct Validation of a Coding System.
Note: X and Y are constructs standing in some theoretical relationship to one another (solid line). Each construct has multiple operationalizations ($x_1, x_2, \ldots, x_n; y_1, y_2, \ldots, y_m$) linked to it by solid arrows. Finally, confounding "third variables (Γ) may enhance or suppress relationships between operationalizations of the constructs (dashed arrows).

Hewes, in preparation; O'Donnell-Trujillo, 1981).[8] Thus, in general terms, our constructs X and Y have operational linkages to various instantiations $(x_1, x_2, \ldots, x_n; y_1, y_2, \ldots, y_m)$, operational linkages that should provide the basis of some validational test. Figure 3 represents these purportedly empirical relationships in terms of solid arrows connecting the constructs with their operationalizations. In addition, the solid arrow linking X with Y indicates that these constructs are associated theoretically in some manner. In this case we will assume that link is causal.

Of course, empirical relationships between construct and operationalization or between operationalizations may be biased by theoretically irrelevant factors. Two such factors are represented in Figure 3 by dashed lines. The first of these biasing relationships is captured by the dashed lines linking construct x with operationalization y_2. This source of bias arises when one or more operationalizations of one construct are "impure"—that is, they contain aspects of another, theoretically relevant construct. As a consequence, any empirical test linking the two constructs will be confounded by this impurity (Costner and Schoenberg, 1973). For instance, we have already argued that many units of social interaction are multifunctional; they serve more than one function simultaneously (Hewes, 1979). If so, efforts to study the empirical relationships between these functions may face this sort of bias. As an illustration, although global judgments of control and affiliation in relational settings often lead to the conclusion that they are orthogonal (Bochner et al., 1977), one might well find some empirical relationship between them, were coding systems used to operationalize both constructs. The reason? Folger and Poole (1982) have argued persuasively that the control codes used in several popular coding systems may also reflect affiliation. (We will detail this argument later in this analysis.) If this is true, the possibility exists that control moves also simultaneously signal affiliation or its opposite (hostility). Thus the multifunctional nature of control moves would lead to a biased empirical relationship between the two constructs, affiliation and control, because the operationalizations of each contained the other *by definition*. Affiliation and control may be perceptually distinct and still be functionally interrelated. Whether this is true remains to be seen, but it does suggest the potential importance of one source of bias represented in Figure 3.

Another source of bias that might arise in the validation of coding systems is signified in Figure 3 by the construct Γ and the dashed arrows linking it to

---

[8]Interpretively-based coding procedures can offer insights of the type that Watzlawick et al. (1967) provide in their analysis of punctuation. Individuals' perceptions have to be examined in order to see that the interaction patterns are premised on different assumptions about whose behavior is the stimulus and whose is the response. The second-order insights about punctuation are premised on subjects' perceptions but step beyond those interpretations to point to characteristics of the interaction which can only be seen from an observer's standpoint.

several operationalizations of both X and Y. Γ is simply a stand-in for any theoretically irrelevant variable that might link operationalizations *within* a construct or *between* constructs. If the former, then the interrelationships among a set of operationalizations of a given construct will be biased positively or negatively. For instance, if several categories of a communication anxiety coding system (Mulac and Sherman, 1974) also reflect general fluency, regardless of anxiety level, then the internal consistency of these categories might reflect both their common relationship to anxiety and the mistaken assumption that differences in fluency solely reflect differences in manifest anxiety. In other words, a theoretically irrelevant variable, general fluency (Γ), might bias the empirical relationships among categories of communication anxiety ($x_1, x_2, \ldots, x_n$).

Similar problems can arise in assessing the relationships between constructs X and Y. This case is the classic "third variable" problem encountered in making causal inferences of any sort. Is there some excluded variable that causes both variables or stands in some causal chain relating them such that excluding the third variable from statistical analysis will bias the results? If the third variable (in our case Γ) causes both X and Y, for instance, then we might observe an apparent correlation between X and Y but mistakenly impute a causal relationship between them. As an illustration of this possibility, consider the results of a study by Courtright et al. (1980) linking relational satisfaction to patterns of dyadic control coded using the Rogers and Farace (1975) system. If, as we noted earlier, control codes may equally well be construed as codes of affiliation/hostility (Folger and Poole, 1982), then the observed relationship between control interaction patterns and relational satisfaction may be due, in part, to the influence of affiliation/hostility (Γ) on satisfaction. In other words, we might speculate that there is a correlation between control and affiliation/hostility produced by the fact that the Rogers and Farace system confounds the two constructs. If it is affiliation/hostility that produces relational satisfaction, but affiliation/hostility is not examined explicitly (as it was not in Courtright et al.), then we might conclude erroneously that control affects relational satisfaction. Thus the classic problem of the excluded "third variable" plays as important a role in the validation constructs as it does in other tests of empirical relationships.

1. Face Validity.

With the contents of Figure 3 firmly in mind, we now consider each of the three basic types of validity as applied to coding systems, beginning with face validity. Establishing the face validity of some coding system x_i entails an assessment only of the coding categories that have been chosen to represent the construct (X or Y). The researcher, and others familiar with the theoretical construct, assess the degree to which the coding system embodies that construct, the degree to which the coding system is logically consistent and the categories clearly defined (Holsti, 1969; Lazarsfeld and Barton, 1969). Obviously, much of this analysis involves the subjective, qualitative assessment of the solid arrow linking x to x_i, although, as we noted earlier, low interpretive reliabilities could indicate conceptual or definitional problems in a coding system.

Beyond these minimal assurances of face validity, a careful examination of coding errors may be informative. Seibold et al. (1981, pp. 668-669) proposed four types of coding failures that might signify a problem with the validity of a coding system. Two of these are related directly to the notion of face validity.

1. *Categorization failures:* "Theoretically significant statements or speech acts that fall into no categories or which straddle the boundary between categories."
2. *Production anomaly:* "Acts which clearly fall into a theoretical category, but which are atypical members of that category by virtue of their production. For instance, an act might be stretched over an unusually long time, or include seemingly irrelevant parts, or be produced jointly by several speakers, or be understood and interrupted by another speaker while only partially produced. [Persistent] findings like these can lead us to doubt that a category is capturing the essence of such instances; or to conclude that the category is too broad."

Thus the notions *categorization failure* and *production anomaly* invite us to examine the specific nature of inconsistently coded categories or units difficult to code. Therein may lie sources of face invalidity, as Seibold et al. (1981) demonstrated in their test of three coding schemes based on different theories of argument. Clearly, these two notions cannot be applied effectively without recourse to some theoretical framework; however, if coupled with the subjective and logical rules of face validity referenced earlier, they form canons of face validity for coding systems more useful and strenuous than the "catch-as-catch-can" procedures that characterize most current efforts.

But even with these more elaborate procedures, face validity is not without its weaknesses. Face validity, by itself, includes no direct empirical checks on the validity of the coding system. Only indirect empirical asessment is made through reliability estimates. While careful construction of a system clearly enhances its claims to validity, there is also a need to verify the scheme's accuracy independent of the process of its construction. As Tudor (1976) notes, the interpretations embodied in social constructs may be artifacts of the observer's particular perspective. Whether or not this situation arises in the construction of a coding system can only be determined by independent verification tests. Logical consistency, the subjective impressions of the constructor, and ease-of-use are at best necessary but not sufficient conditions to ensure the accuracy of interpretations made through application of a coding system.

2. Predictive Validity.

Since face validity has as its major weakness a lack of empirical evidence, it is little wonder that some researchers have turned to a procedure that does rely on data to support validational claims. One such procedure is predictive validity. The predictive validity of a coding system is assessed by using a purported relationship between constructs to generate plausible hypotheses. These may be derived from theory, hunches, or previous research. For instance, the predictive validity of a coding scheme of verbal intimacy (x_i) might be assessed through an anticipated relationship with perceived uncertainty about a relational partner, as operationalized by a self-report instrument (y_j), since theoretically the greater the intimacy (X) between members of a dyad, the less the uncertainty each member has concerning the other (Y) (Berger and Calabrese, 1975). Should the relationship between the two operationalizations prove acceptably large and in the direction predicted by theory, a researcher might claim the verbal intimacy coding system is predictively valid.

In terms of Figure 3, tests of predictive validity involve at least three sets of empirical linkages, two posited by theory (or hunch or previous literature), and one source of bias assumed not to exist. In our example, this means that the theoretical linkage between X and Y is presumed to be true as is the operational link between the criterion variable (y_j) and the construct Y. Further, we must assume the absence of links between some, perhaps unknown, variable Γ and the two operationalizations (x_i and y_j). If any of these presumed links is in error, the association between x_i and y_j is not an adequate test of predictive validity. If X and Y are not truly associated or y_1 is not a valid measure of Y the test for predictive validity could fail even if the coding system (x_i) is valid; if Γ operates in linking x_i and y_j other than through X and Y, the test of predictive validity could prove positive even if the coding scheme was invalid. In short, tests of predictive validity are risky because they can fail in so many ways. Furthermore, if a researcher relies on the apparent truth of some relationship between constructs X and Y to establish the predictive validity of a coding system x_i, then that relationship cannot be tested substantively using x_i at some point in the future. Since the X-Y relationship is used to define x_i, x_j cannot be used later to prove that X is related to Y.

3. Construct Validity.

Limitations and shortcomings of face and predictive validity suggest that construct validity is an essential condition for coding scheme validity. Construct validity is defined as the degree to which an operationalization measures the theoretical construct it is supposed to measure (Cronbach and Meehl, 1955). In terms of Figure 3, this implies that an operationalization x_i must be linked to its theoretically defined construct X and not linked directly to other constructs (Y and/or Γ) or opeationalizations of those constructs (y_1, $y_{.2}$, . . . , y_m) that would confound tests of the target construct (X) within the theoretical system that defines it. The process of construct validation, then, must involve a theoretical framework. Without a conceptual definition of X, one could not generate x_i, let alone a number of theoretically related x's that might be expected to correlate with x_i ("convergent validity," Campbell and Fiske, 1959). Without a theory, one would have no basis for identifying those other constructs (Y and Γ) and operationalizations that should be conceptually distinct from X and related to it empirically only in specifiable ways ("discriminant validity," Campbell and Fiske, 1959).

The necessity of assessing the convergent construct validity of coding system is brought home nicely in a recent article by O'Donnell-Trujillo (1981). O'Donnell-Trujillo compared the distributional information generated by Ellis' (1979) five-category RELCOM coding system with Rogers and Farace's (1975) three-category control coding system on the same set of transcripts taken from 18 marital dyads. Both coding systems are grounded in the same theoretical tradition; both systems conceptually define relational control identically, although there are some operational differences (O'Donnell-Trujillo, 1981, pp. 100–101); both coding systems manifest moderate and relatively homogeneous global interpretive reliabilities among pairs of coders (.71 to .89 for Ellis'; .91 to 1. for Rogers and Farace's).

Given these similarities, one might argue that these two coding systems represent comparable operationalizations (x_i and x_l) of the underlying construct, relational control (X). As such they should reveal comparable patterns in the coded dialogue—in other words the patterns they reveal should converge—if they are good operationalizations of the construct. Unfortunately, they do not converge on an act-by-act basis. When Ellis' scheme is collapsed to a three-category system, the act-by-act similarity of the two systems is .27 using Cohen's kappa. Even when Ellis' scheme is not collapsed, marked discrepancies are revealed in the two coding systems (see O'Donnell-Trujillo, 1981, pp. 99–100). Remarks coded as relationally neutral by one coding system (Rogers and Farace) were coded as mildly dominant by the other (Ellis). Similarly, some remarks coded as relationally neutral by Ellis' system were coded as dominant by Rogers and Farace's. These act-by-act differences are particularly telling, since both Ellis and Rogers and Farace subscribe to a theoretical system in which temporal dependencies in acts are of central importance. As you may recall in our discussion of act-by-act interpretive reliability (Section II.B.3), unless strong and homogeneous consistencies exist in act-by-act categorization, estimates of temporal dependencies may be seriously biased. The same can be said of the act-by-act accuracy of categorization. As serious as the disjuncture between the Ellis and the Rogers and Farace systems is for distributional information, the implications may be far more severe for the temporal dependencies revealed by the two systems. Unfortunately, O'Donnell-Trujillo did not provide a direct demonstration of this problem.

O'Donnell-Trujillo's research has served researchers in relational communication well by highlighting a serious problem in convergent validity faced by either Ellis' system, Rogers and Farace's, or both. It also demonstrates the general importance of assessing convergent construct validity on any coding system, as does a study by Burleson et al. (1981) for the issue of discriminant validity. More important, however, O'Donnell-Trujillo concludes his study by emphasizing the importance of a question raised by Poole and Folger (1978) some years before: From whose perspective—theorist, participant, or outside observer—are we to seek validational evidence?

In adapting construct validity theory to interaction coding systems, we must also take the unique nature of the coding process into account. Coding schemes are, in essence, translation devices. They translate interactors' utterances or behaviors into a smaller set of "meaningful" categories and thereby provide the researcher with an abstraction or simplified account of what occurs in the exchange. The central issue in validating coding schemes is the *type* of meaning they assign to utterances. Part of the function of coding rules is to specify the evidence that can be used to recognize when an instance of a category has occurred in interaction. Depending on the evidence one employs to claim that an utterance falls into a category, coding categories are "meaningful" in very different senses (Poole and Folger, 1981b). The level of meaning a coding system is designed to discover has important theoretical implications, because it determines the sorts of explanations the researcher can advance about the interaction. As we will see below, it also dictates the appropriate strategy for construct validation of the coding system (Folger and Poole, 1980; Poole and Folger, 1981a).

Mabry's (1975a) recent coding of the category "particularism" provides a good illustration of the researcher's choice concerning the type of evidence used to classify utterances. Mabry's scheme is based on Parson's theory of social action, and it encodes eight types of symbolic action, one of which is particularism. When he defined this category, Mabry specified that particularistic themes are those in which members take "direct account of one another's presence in the situation." He included "direct supportive or non-supportive statements, eye and body contact shifts that single out each member from the other, and talking about individual contributions" as acts which signify the particularism construct (Mabry, 1975a, p. 293).

In applying this category to interaction, Mabry relied on an outside observer's perspective to conclude that an interactor has taken direct account of another's presence. He provided a dictionary of behaviors that the observer could use as evidence to conclude that an act evidences "particularism;" the observer's judgment is the final arbiter of occurrence. Another researcher interested in coding particularism might have used different types of evidence; for example, the interpretations of the interactors themselves that certain behaviors "took direct account of the other's presence." However, in employing the categories as he did, Mabry has chosen a mode of observation that limits the type of information he will accept as evidence for the occurrence of the categories. This limitation is, of course, useful because it permits careful operationalizations. But

Mabry has also limited the types of claims he can make about groups studied with his coding scheme. His data reflect an outside observer's perspective and he can make no claims about the interpretations of behavior made by the group members themselves.

There are three distinct modes of observation a researcher could use in coding interaction (Poole and Folger, 1978, 1981b). Each source focuses on a different aspect of social experience. Interaction may be observed and meanings may be assigned to messages (1) from an outsider's theoretical view of what is experienc*ed,* as in Mabry's scheme, or (2) in terms of the social process of experienc*ing* (where the theorist's objective is to identify the culturally-shared or standardized meanings that participants are experiencing as they interact), or (3) from the viewpoint of the experienc*er* (where the idiosyncratic interpretations shared only by the participants in the interaction under investigation are the theorist's object). In choosing one of these approaches, the interaction researcher becomes committed to a particular way of viewing interaction, and, most important for our purposes, to a particular set of requirements for establishing the construct validity of the system. As we will see, choice of a mode of observation involves choice of a particular type of theoretical construct (X), as well as choice of a type of measurement (x_i), and therefore sets the frame of reference for any construct validational study.

a. Validation in the Experienced Mode.   The investigator working within the experienc*ed* mode studies social interaction solely from the viewpoint of the theorist. The theorist is assumed to have direct access to the categories which are important in explaining and understanding interaction. In identifying an act as an instance of a category, the researcher makes no claim to participants' culturally-shared or idiosyncratic interpretations; the categories are theoretically-defined distinctions that make no assumptions about how participants perceive the behaviors in the scheme's classifications. The categories explain interaction solely in terms of the observer's theory, and the theory itself is not founded on interpretations participants share or negotiate.

Fisher et al.'s (1979) Social Information Processing Analysis scheme and his work in relational communication (Fisher, 1977a, b, 1980b) are both founded explicitly on the assumptions of the experienc*ed* approach. Fisher takes and instrumentalist stance toward coding interaction in small groups or dyadic settings. He claims that

> [B]ehaviors are not necessarily the manifestation of some internal motivation, such as belief, need, drive, etc. A behavior may be judged meaningful regardless or even despite its internal stimulation. To go beyond the behavior is superfluous and may even confuse the issue. In this sense, the communicative phenomena of interest are externalized and accessible to other interactants and observers. (Fisher, 1980a, p. 3)

Fisher designs and revises coding schemes so that the ability of the observer to discriminate among theoretically interesting interaction behaviors is facilitated.

Similarly, Rogers and Millar have developed and employed coding schemes that track relational control in dyadic interaction from an experienc*ed* perspective. The relational coding schemes draw distinctions among one-up, one-down, and neutral categories (Mark, 1971; Millar and Rogers, 1976; Rogers and Farace, 1975; Rogers-Millar and Millar, 1979) and have specified additional measures of relational intensity that attempt to capture the weight various control codes carry in interaction (Rogers et al., 1980). These researchers view the relational functions of messages (i.e., the one-up, one-down, or one-across codes assigned to message types like question-extension and disagreements) strictly as observer-defined variables or as arbitrary constructions of the investigator. Their theoretical position is that "interpretive processes are neither necessary for communication research nor directly observable" (Rogers and Millar, 1981).

In the experienc*ed* perspective, the theoretical adequacy and empirical workability of the system are the only important frame of reference for evaluating the coding scheme. For this reason, construct validation of an experienc*ed* coding scheme entails the same requirements outlined in psychometric theory. The measure must be supported by the nomological network, and the coding system's categories must have convergent and discriminant validity with other measures of the same theoretically-defined constructs. This view must be compared with that of Fisher (1980b), who argues that high interpretive reliability establishes coding system validity by demonstrating the existence of a community standard shared by raters. In our view, high reliability is a necessary condition for experienc*ed* construct validity, but it is not sufficient, because the system must also be shown to "work" within the nomological net of its theoretical framework (Cronbach and Meehl, 1955). This requires going beyond the bounds of internal logic, and therefore beyond interpretive reliability to theoretical assessment of the system. Our previous discussion of discriminant construct validity gives ample evidence for this claim.

It is important to assess construct validity in the experienc*ed* mode because validation grounds the meaning to the observer's categories. The study by O'Donnell-Trujillo (1981) illustrated this point and at the same time provided an excellent example of convergent construct validation. In the face of such findings, relational researchers cannot proceed with confidence until (1) they have fathomed the conceptual reasons behind the differences, or (2) the construct validity of one of the systems has been shown to be superior to that of the other in terms of performance in relevant nomological networks.

A critical precondition for the construct validity of experienc*ed* coding systems is that the theoretical construct reflected in the system's categories measure must be cast at the experienc*ed* level. If the scheme's theoretical constructs involve or make claims to culturally-shared or idiographic interpretations—that is, if the categories of the system do not match the theory it operationalizes—at least two types of problems are possible.

First, there may be a lack of convergence among different schemes designed to code the same constructs. Folger and Poole (1982) have argued that this problem occurs in relational research. On the one hand, most relational theories assume relational messages (e.g., dominant control messages) have shared meanings for participants; that is, they are best studied from the experienc*ing* perspective (Bateson, 1936; Leary, 1957, Wish and Kaplan, 1977). On the other hand, as we have noted, relational coding systems are defined only from the external observer's point of view and do not explicitly take culturally-defined meanings into account. Hence, theory and operationalizations are cast at different levels in relational research and researchers have overlooked an important baseline for establishing coding validity (subjects' shared interpretations). As a result, the various coding schemes designed to code the one-up, one-down, and one-across control functions would be likely to yield different interpretations of the same interaction, due to the theorists' restricted and unvalidated grasp of cultural conventions. As Folger and Puck (1976) and Folger and Sillars (1980) argue, the lack of convergent validity found by O'Donnell-Trujillo could be due to this problem. As long as the researchers conception of coding remains in the experienc*ed* perspective, there is no criterion that can be invoked to arbitrate these differences; the only way out is to recognize that experienc*ing*-level theoretical constructs require an experienc*ing*-level coding system.

Folger and Poole (1982) have pointed to a second interpretive problem that emerges when coding schemes treat constructs that are part of interactants' shared meanings as observer-defined categories in a coding instrument. If experienc*ing* constructs are coded with observer-defined categories and there is no verification that the researchers' claims are consistent with shared interpretations, any relationship in which the categories are used as independent variables is overdetermined—several equally-defensible explanations are possible for the same coded results. They illustrate this point by examining interpretative problems with relational coding schemes.

In studies of interaction between married couples, for example, researchers using the relational coding schemes are specifically interested in patterns of symmetrical ($\uparrow\uparrow$, $\downarrow\downarrow$, $\rightarrow\rightarrow$) or complementry ($\uparrow\downarrow$, $\downarrow\uparrow$) interacts. The explanation offered for high proportions of symmetrical interaction is that these exchanges "reflect spouses' attempts to clarify vague or ambiguous role definitions" (Parks and Dindia-Webb, 1979:23). The couples are resolving the relational definition issue; they are each vying for similar relational stances. This account is clearly a possible explanation for high rates of symmetrical exchange in an interaction. It is the most plausible explanation, however, only if the assumptions about what acts are one-up, one-down or one-across reflect interactants' interpretations.

If there is no assurance that the relational codes assigned to various message types are consistent with interactants' interpretations, then other theoretical explanations may account equally well for the occurrence of symmetrical exchange. Assume, for example, that at least some of the thirty-five acts that are coded as one-up by the

Rogers and Farace scheme are seen by interactants not (or not only) as attempts at control but as hostile or unfriendly statements. (This is not an entirely unlikely possibility, since one-up categories include non-supportive statements, orders, disagreements, etc.) Further, assume that some of the eight acts coded as one-down are not recognized as indicants of submissiveness but of affiliation. Leary (1957) contends that a complementary response on the horizontal (affiliation-hostility) dimension of the interpersonal behavior circle is one which matches the behavior just offered. That is, affiliative statements are likely to be met with affiliative responses and hostile statements are likely to evoke hostile responses (Peabody, 1970). From Leary's theoretical standpoint, if what is coded as one-down is seen culturally as affiliative behavior by the interactants, and what is coded as one-up is seen as hostile behavior, then high rates of symmetrical exchange would occur not because the relationship was ill-defined or because the interactants were vying for the same control position but because the interactants were responding, quite predictably, to a strong reciprocity norm governing affiliative and hostile behavior (Folger and Poole, 1982, pp. 239–240).[9]

The interpretive problems outlined above can only be avoided if researchers recognize that the theoretical constructs they are coding are part of interactors' shared interpretations. Coding schemes developed and used in the experienc*ed* perspective only allow the identification of constructs that make no claim about participants' interpretations; they cannot be used to operationalize constructs which are culturally-shared. This may represent a serious limitation in view of Folger and Poole's (1980) argument that nearly every coding system is essentially grounded in culturally-standardized usage, whether its creators explicitly recognize this or not. In addition, most theories in communication assume people are active subjects whose activities are premised on the meanings they assign to events and to other's communicative behaviors. These considerations imply that the experienc*ing* mode of observation, which focuses on culturally-defined meanings, is particularly important for communication research.

b. Validation in the Experiencing Mode.   The investigator working within the experienc*ing* mode views the categories in a coding scheme as representations of culturally shared interpretations. The researcher is concerned with interactors' perceptions because the theoretical constructs the scheme encodes are recognized as culturally-shared meanings and are grounded in shared interpretive rules. In the experienc*ing* mode, the researcher makes claims not only that his or her categories are useful or meaningful, but also that the categories actually represent shared interpretations of interactors. Hence, for the experienc*ing* perspective, the validity of a coding system depends not only upon

---

[9]Reprinted from *Communication Yearbook 5* with permission of the International Communication Association.

the correspondence between the coding categories and the researcher's theoretical domain, but also upon the corresopndence between the meanings ascribed to utterances by the coding scheme and the meanings which are commonly ascribed to the utterances in the population of language users to which the interactors belong (Folger and Poole, 1982).

It is instructive to translate these validity conditions in terms of Figure 3. Because of the interpretive status of the constructs that lie behind the scheme, both the theoretical constructs (X in Figure 3) and their measures (x_1, x_2, . . . , x_n) are cast at a different level than the corresponding variables for the experienc*ed* mode. The theoretical construct X represents a culturally-defined concept, and the measures (x_1, etc.) are chosen by interpretive rules that link them to X. As with experienc*ed* systems, correspondence between the coding categories and theoretical domain is demonstrated primarily by showing support for the X-x_i relationship. However, convergent validity and discriminant validity are different in experienc*ed* and experienc*ing* modes. Because the theoretical domain of the experienc*ing* mode is shared interpretations, comparable measures must be designed to tap cultural-level constructs: categories that are supposed to encode shared interpretations can only be assessed vis-a-vis other categories or measures that also tap shared interpretations. Hence, entirely different types of measures are compared in the validation of experienc*ing* than in experienc*ed* coding systems. Because experienc*ing* coding systems are designed to measure shared meanings, convergent validity is particularly important. The researcher must show that the categories are consistent with other measures of shared interpretations. In other words, convergent construct validity in the experienc*ing* mode is an indication of the degree of consensus shared by members of a community in the interpretation of given types of communication behavior. Poole and Folger (1981a) have termed this last form of validity *representational validity,* because it demonstrates that the coding system represents shared interpretations. Representational validity is the *sine qua non* of coding systems in the experienc*ing* mode.

There have been several cases in which coding scheme authors have sought evidence which, at least in part, helped to establish the validity of coding schemes. Borgatta (1962) relied upon peer ratings to make revisions in Bales' IPA system. Hawes (1972) constructed a coding scheme for analyzing medical interviews through a stimulated recall method. Subjects were asked to watch videotapes of their own interaction and to describe their thoughts and feelings during various sequences of the exchange. Based upon the subjects' comments, Hawes then defined a set of thirteen categories to code how "messages facilitated, maintained or impeded information processing in medical interviews." Thus, Hawes used the information obtained from the stimulated recall sessions to derive functional categories that were based on common interpretations of what was important in the medical inverviews. The categories were not derived from a set of theoretical distinctions (i.e., they were not cast in the experienc*ed* mode),nor were the classifications made on the basis of how the participants themselves saw the function of each message (i.e., the categories were not applied in the experienc*er* mode). Similarly, Folger and Sillars (1980) offered an empirical assessment of the coding assumptions made in the relational coding schemes. They tested whether messages marked as ''one-up,'' ''one-down,'' or ''one-across'' by the Rogers and Farace coding scheme were consistent with interactors' common understanding of the control significance of these messages.

Folger and Poole (1980; Poole and Folger, 1981a) have attempted to outline and demonstrate procedural options for establishing the representational validity of interaction coding schemes. They suggest that any method aimed at verifying the assumptions a coding scheme makes about subjects' culturally-shared interpretations entails three general requirements. The researcher must (1), determine what representation or interpretation of interaction the subjects' interpretation of interaction yield; (2), determine what representation the coding scheme yields to the same interaction; and (3), draw an empirical comparison of the two representations.

Folger and Poole caution that this three-step procedure appears deceptively simple, and they point to three major concerns that emerge in meeting those objectives of representational validity:

1) *Comparisons*. Comparison of the two representations is only possible if they are drawn in similar formats, preferably forms that allow statistical comparison, since this provides a more objective means of assessing similarity. For this reason, procedures for deriving subject and coding system representations of interaction usually utilize some method of assigning numerical values to interpretations, either directly (e.g., by having subjects rate qualities of interaction passages on semantic differentials), or indirectly (e.g., by using subject's Q-sorts to assign dissimilarity values to pairs of passages which are then scaled with multidimensional scaling procedures to derive a pictorial representation of subjects' common interpretations). Because these numerical indices are only mappings of interpretive outcomes, care must be taken that they do not overly distort or bias the interpretive process.

2) *Design*. There are a number of possible designs for representational validity studies, depending on the theory behind the coding scheme and the nature of the intersubjective construct in question. The researcher must make three key methodological choices in designing a study.

First the researcher must decide how much he or she can assume about the structure of the representation provided by the coding scheme and the structure of subjects' interpretive scheme. This decision is governed by two contingencies: (1), are the dimensions or constructs underlying the subjects' common interpretive scheme known to the researcher; and (2), has the coding system been designed to explicitly identify these dimensions? If the common dimensions underlying subjects' interpretive schemes are known, and if the coding scheme is explicitly designed to code statements in terms of these dimensions, then commonality assessment is relatively straightforward. The investigator need only code relevant segments of interaction and ask the participants in the interaction (or language users from the same population) to rate the interaction segments in terms of the known dimensions of their interpretive schemes. The results of the coded segments can then be compared to the participants' ratings, and the degree of overlap provides an index of commonality.

However, if either of the two questions cannot be answered in the affirmative, additional difficulties arise. When the dimensions of participants' interpretive schemes are unknown, some means of mapping the culturally-shared scheme must be found. If the coding scheme has not been designed so that it explicitly identifies dimensions of the subjects' common interpretive scheme (which is also usually the case if question (1) is answered "no"), then there is no straightforward way of comparing subject and coding system representations. In this case, some method must be found for deriving a coding system representation that can be meaningfully compared with the subject representation.

Studies by Folger and Sillars (1980), Stiles (1980), and Poole and Folger (1981a) exemplify various responses to the contingencies just enumerated. Folger and Sillars evaluated the representational validity of the Rogers and Farace relational coding system. In this case, the dimension underlying subjects' interpretive schemes (dominance-submissiveness) was known and the coding scheme was explicitly designed to identify this dimension (i.e., both questions could be answered "yes"). Folger and Sillars had subjects rate the dominance of actors in a number of interaction segments and used the Rogers-Farace scheme to code the segments, calculating an overall index of dominance for each actor from the coded data. They then compared the subjects' dominance ratings with those of the coding system by correlating the two indices.

Stiles (1980) developed a coding system that was designed to tap certain well-defined dimensions (which he presumed were common to subjects), but he was not sure that he knew the common dimensions of the subjects' interpretive schemes (in this case then, question (1) was answered "no," while question (2) was answered "yes"). He had subjects rate a set of passages on a number of scales and derived common dimensions with a multidimensional scaling (MDS) procedure. The MDS procedure provided loadings of each passage on the dimensions which could be used as indicants of subjects' common perceptions of the passages. The coding system representation of the passages was compared to the subject representation by regressing the dimensions identified by the coding system (i.e., the number of acts in each passage that could be classified in a given dimension) onto the dimensions of the subject space (the loading of the passage on each of the subject dimensions).

Poole and Folger (1981a) answered both questions negatively—they did not assume knowledge of the subjects' interpretive scheme or of the dimensions identified by the coding systems they validated. They mapped the subjects' representation of interaction by the multidimensional scaling (MDS) of complete paired comparisons of the passages. This procedure makes no assumptions about the dimensions underlying the subjects' shared interpretive scheme, since it relies only on subjects' judgments of similarity of passages. A similar method was used to derive an MDS representation of the passages by the coding systems. Since both representations were derived with MDS procedures, they could be compared by regressing dimensions of one space onto the other.

The second methodological decision centers on whether the subject and coding system representations of the passages should be based on judgments of the interaction itself (direct judgments) or on judgments about the actors (outcome judgments). In the first case, commonalities in subjects' interpretation of the interaction itself would be compared to some representation of the interaction by the coding scheme. In the latter case, subjects' common perceptions of the parties to the interaction would be compared to some "interaction profile" of the parties derived from the codings of the passages. The use of direct judgment is exemplified by Poole and Folger (1981a), that of outcome judgment by Stiles (1980) and Wish et al. (1980). The choice of approach should, in part, be based on the use to which the coding system is put. If the researchers will use the scheme to identify interaction patterns (phases of group decision-making, for example) then the direct judgment approach is preferable. If, on the other hand, the coding scheme will be used to characterize individual behavior or to identify types of individuals (as Bales (1970) does), then the outcome judgment approach is preferable.

A third methodological decision revolves around the length or complexity of the passages used in the validity study. Should the stimulus passages be such that each passage is a single coding unit (or utterance), or should the passages be episodes, consisting of a number of coding units? Several factors must be considered in deciding which approach to take: (1), Realism: It seems somewhat more realistic to have subjects judge episodes than single units, because most of their everyday judgments about interaction are probably based on the give-and-take between people rather than on single statements out of context. In an informal study, Poole found that most people reported it easier to make judgments about six- or seven-statement passages than about one- or two-statement passages. Subjects uniformly said that the longer passages gave them helpful context. (2), Complexity: Derivation of coding scheme representations is more complicated for episodes than for single units. If we have several consecutive units, how do we derive a summary index of a passage that can be compared to the subjects' representation? Such an index (either qualitative or quantitative) should take into account how subjects process interactive information. Some studies (Folger and Sillars, 1980; Stiles, 1980; Wish et al., 1980) have indexed codings of episodes by simply counting the number of times each category occurs in the episode. This profile is then used to relate the passage to other passages (e.g., by correlating them) and the passage relationships (or some transformation of them, e.g., via MDS) are then compared to the subjects' representation. Poole and

Folger (1981a) report an index which takes the ordering of statements in the passage into account. The latter procedure may be more realistic than the former, given the evidence of serial information processing in human judgment (Anderson, 1974), although no formal comparison of the two procedures has been attempted. (3), Efficiency: Use of single units makes category-by-category correction of the coding system much easier than does episodic analysis, because if the coding system and subject representations do not match, the locus of error in the system is immediately evident. If codings of episodes do not match common interpretations, it is quite difficult to determine which aspects of the coding system are responsible. This point implies that, where possible, both episodic and single unit approaches should be applied. The episodic approach demonstrates that the coding scheme can deal with discourse as normally encountered by subjects, while the single-unit approach permits category-by-category analysis and improvement of the coding structure.

3) *Properties of a valid subject representation.* The subject representation is a mapping of the outcomes of common interpretive processes. As such, it must be able to pass at least two tests to qualify as a valid criterion for the coding scheme representation.

First, evidence must be provided that the subject representation is common to subjects. Several studies, Folger and Sillars (1980), Planalp and Tracy (1980), Poole and Folger (1979), and Rosenberg (1976) try to produce evidence on this point. In other studies, subjects' responses are averaged (Stiles, 1980), or combined using data reduction techniques such as MDS (Wish et al., 1980), but no evidence that the representation is shared is supplied. While this omission does not necessarily invalidate these studies, it does leave an important objection open to potential critics.

It is clear that each member of a culture will have a different instantiation of the shared interpretive scheme. Therefore, any index of the shared interpretive scheme will be a "triangulation" of the scheme (which transcends any single instantiation) using subject responses as points of reference. The method of deriving a common subject representation should try to preserve the flavor of individual responses. However, complications introduced by the research design, other sources of error in the data, and the "mysteries" of multivariate analytic procedures, may distort the subject representation so that the responses of significant groups of subjects are not included in the final index. Further, in some cases we may be searchng for a shared construction that is not even there, forcing subjects to make an "unnatural" response along dimensions of our own creation. Taylor (1971) has argued that this is the case in the study of political attitudes and their relation to the legitimacy of social institutions. These possibilities make it imperative that we evaluate the degree to which the subject representation is held in common by subjects. There is simply no way of knowing whether any method—no matter how rigorous or conceptually strong it might be—will generate a subject representation that indexes shared interpretive schemes. We can only make such a determination a posteriori, for specific shared constructs and specific cultures, and we must collect and analyze our data in such a way that determination of commonality is possible.

A method to determine the degree to which the subjects share the derived representation must provide some measure of how subjects use the dimensions or typical constructs in the representation and assess similarity among measures. If subjects' use of the representational dimensions is similar within statistically-acceptable limits, then the hypothesis that the subjects share the representation cannot be rejected. Planalp and Tracy (1980) used ANOVA procedures to assess whether subjects shared a common set of rules. They were interested in shared rules governing topic changes in conversation and had generated a set of rules and predictions about subjects' reactions to hearing topic shifts that corresponded to various rules. To determine whether there were differences in subjects' usages of rules, they tested for a subject-by-type interaction (where type was a fixed-effect reflecting applications of different topic-change rules). Provided there are multiple responses per subject per cell, this test is a good means of determining convergence.

In a similar vein, Poole and Folger (1979) used INDSCAL, an individual-difference MDS procedure (Carroll and Chang, 1970), to derive a subject representation which depicted the relationships among passages in a multidimensional space. The INDSCAL procedure provides "subject weights" for each dimension. These subject weights indicate how heavily each individual depends on the dimension in evaluating the passages. If the representation is shared by subjects, then there should be considerable similarity in subjects' weightings of the dimensions. Poole and Folger detail a test for differences in subjects' dimensional weights, based on an ANOVA procedure for calculating the Spearman-Brown reliability coefficient. It yields a coefficient of intersubject reliability for each dimension of the INDSCAL solution that indicates how consistent the subject weightings of the dimension are. With a large number of subjects, discriminant analysis of subject weights can also be used to test for homogeneity of weightings. Generally, if MDS or factor analytical methods are used to derive the subject representation, it is preferable to use a three-way procedure such as the INDSCAL or ALSCAL MDS procedures (Kruskal and Wish, 1978) or three mode factor analysis (Tucker, 1972), since these also provide subject weights and thus allow testing of the commonality hypothesis. Borg and Lingoes (1978) have also reported an MDS procedure called PRINDIS that allows formal testing of subject weight commonalities.

A second property of a valid subject representation is congruence of observer-interactor interpretations. Schutz (1967) has argued that parties to an interaction have different "projects" than do observers from the same culture. Thus, the interactants in the stimulus passages may have quite different interpretations than do observers of the interaction (i.e., subjects who judge stimulus passages). Yet, although an interactant's perspective may differ from that of observers, if they belong to the same culture and share, in part, the same interpretive schemes, then there may be some interpretive congruence. Gouran and Whitehead (1971) compared participants' and observers' ratings of discussion statements and found high correlations between them (corrected for attenuation, five of eight correlations were not significantly different from $r = 1.0$). Schneider (1970) found correlations of similar magnitude for leader and follower judgments of the leader. On the other hand, Montgomery (1981) found strong differences between observers' ratings of the ''openness'' of an interaction between marital dyads and the ratings of each member of the dyad. Similarly, Gottman et al. (1976; also Gottman, 1979) found important discrepancies between the *intent* of a message (coded by the sender) and the *impact* of that same message (coded by the receiver), especially for distressed couples in interacting on highly conflict-laden topics. These results suggest that observer-interactor judgments may be congruent, but it is not a foregone conclusion in all instances. In particular, we would expect observer-actor representations to be congruent if one is tapping a common interpretive scheme. Of course, finding divergence is interesting in its own right, since it suggests the need to explore the nature, sources, and consequences of divergent interpretive schemes (Planalp and Hewes, 1981).

Representational validity is, then, an important requirement for establishing construct validity of a coding scheme in the experienc*ing* perspective. The need to provide evidence for coding claims in this perspective may have been ignored because coding scheme authors could argue that these procedures do little more than reify common sense. Coding scheme authors are often members of the body of language users whose shared interpretations are being mapped. As a result, researchers do have some access to the interpretations that are being incorporated in their scheme, and they rely upon their understandings in assigning interpretations. As we have noted, however, problems arise when researchers rely solely on their own assumptions about what the culturally-shared functions of messages are. Different researchers have made different coding claims about the same theoretical constructs, and the assumption that there is a common interpretation for some behavior may not always hold true. Establishing representational validity can insure that the claims made with the coded data are consistent with the researcher's major thoretical premise in the experienc*ing* mode, namely, that culturally shared interpretations are important for understanding social interaction.

Folger and Poole (1980) have argued that any coding scheme that attempts to code human *action* (as opposed to simple behavior) operates within the realm of shared interpretations and must therefore be shown to be representationally valid. To code language in its social context is to code within the context of commonly held interpretive schemes; it is to interpret (either explicitly or implicitly) the intersubjective meanings that are ''constitutive of the social matrix in which the individuals find themselves and act'' and that ''are not the property of a single person because they are rooted in social practice'' (Taylor, 1971, p. 48). One can attempt to develop and use a coding system to code *behavior* apart from any substratum of culturally shared interpretations held by the participants. Many fine research programs are based on just such behavioral coding systems (cf., Birdwhistle; 1970; Capella, 1979, 1980). The only features in interaction that can be identified and tracked by such a system, however, are those which remain invariant over all possible *interpretations* of the behavior (Wilson, 1970). The clearest examples of these experienced coding schemes are the ethologists' instruments for studying patterns of behavior where codes are made of touching, eye-gaze, length of response (see, for example, Blurton-Jones and Woodson, 1979). The ethological approach does not permit judgments about the motives of behaviors. This constraint makes it impossible to assign utterances to many seemingly objective categories such as Bales' ''gives opinion'' or Mabry's ''neutrality'' functions. Without judging that either the speaker or the hearer imputes the motive of opinion-giving to a statement, we cannot, for example, decide whether a comment is an opinion statement, a repetition of a conversation the speaker had with someone else, or story-telling (which would be coded as ''tension release'' or ''dramatizes'' in Bales' system). Thus the coding schemes employed in the experienc*ed* approach distill any imputation of meaning or motive from the participants' behavior, and in consequence, these schemes are legitimately exempt from any concern with representational validity. Most schemes that have been designed to study human communication, however, do not take this restricted focus and are, therefore, in need of validation under the experienc*ing* mode.

c. Validation in the Experiencer Mode.   Researchers working in the third perspective, the experienc*er* mode, are committed to coding interpretations idiosyncratic to the participants in the interaction sequence under investigation. In the experienc*er* mode the investigator is still guided by a set of theoretical constructs. However, the coding categories (x_i) which represent any particular construct (X) are applied only when the researcher has evidence that the participants *in the interaction being studied* would assign the coded function to the messages in the exchange. Unlike experienc*ing* research, the investigator in this mode does not assume, for example, that all disagreements carry a one-up control function for all participants. An act which could ''accurately'' be coded as a disagreement from an experienc*ing* perspective may, in the context of a particular relationship, be a submissive move. Presuppositions specific to the interactors' relationship may signal this submissive interpretation and as a result discount the culturally-shared meaning of the act. In the experienc*ing* perspective, these idiosyncratic meanings are of no central importance except insofar as they are a methodological foil to claims that there exists a shared interpretation for a particular behavior. In the experienc*er* perspective, an act is not identified as an instance of a category unless evidence is provided that the interactants under investigation see the function of the utterance as the category specifies.

Clearly, establishing construct validity in the experienc*er* mode is an ambitious and difficult task. The only systematic procedures for coding interaction in this perspective with which we are familiar are those developed by Labov and Fanshel (1977) in their rigorous analysis of one psychiatric interview. These authors have developed a set of guidelines and procedures (Comprehensive Discourse Analysis) aimed at identifying the idiosyncratic meanings exchanged in interaction. Labov and Fanshel (1977, pp. 58–59) contend that "the crucial actions in establishing coherence of sequencing in conversation are not such speech acts as requests and assertions, but rather challenges, defenses, and retreats which have to do with the status of the participants, their rights and obligations, and their changing relationships in terms of social organization."

Labov and Fanshel demonstrate that differences in rights and obligations in a relationship provide important evidence for interpreting messages that are exchanged during the psychiatric interview. They are interested in making claims about the idiosyncratic interpretations of messages because these claims are crucial for understanding the clients' development and the role of the doctor-patient interaction in that development. To verify their claims, these researchers draw upon discussions with the participants, responses to messages which clarify the idiosyncratic meanings the participants share, and a wide variety of contextual and background information that comes from medical histories or prior interview sessions.

Any analysis of interaction from the experienc*er* perspective relies more heavily on researchers' interpretive skills than analyses done in either of the first two modes. The sheer quantity of evidence Labov and Fanshel provide to support each interpretive claim is most intimidating. Nonetheless, it would be difficult to arbitrate differences among investigators who employ the comprehensive discourse analysis method but offer conflicting interpretations of the same interaction. Greater effort needs to be devoted toward delineating criteria for the validity of experienc*er* interpretations.

IV. CONCLUSIONS AND UNANSWERED QUESTIONS

We began this review by drawing an analogy between coders employing some coding system and social actors engaged in interpreting communicative acts. Both classes of people are engaged in making sense of a communicative exchange; both employ the text itself, contextual information, and interpretive rules in an attempt to produce relatively consistent and accurate interpretations. Our discussion has centered on methods for making the empirical study of social interaction maximally accountable to these standards of consistency and accuracy.

In Sections II A and B we underscored the importance of rigorous procedures for assessing the degree of unitizing and interpretive reliability. Throughout those sections, we pointed out that the bulk of empirical work on the analysis of social interaction has failed to live up to the standards we espouse. In one sense, this is not so much a criticism of this research as a plea for improvement in the future. Any new and burgeoning area of research is bound to be plagued by inadequate methodological standards and debates over correct standards. In another sense, however, our remarks concerning extant research on social interaction are intended to be quite pointed. With a few happy exceptions, the majority of this research has reached conclusions of questionable veracity, conclusions that are questionable because standards of reliability have been so lax as to permit us little confidence in their reproducibility. This state of affairs is nowhere better illustrated than in the failure of the vast majority of studies to report category-by-category interpretive reliability estimates. The degree of potential systematic bias induced by nonhomogeneous category-by-category reliabilities (and other factors discussed previously) is so great that conclusions concerning the relative distributions of coded units across categories and/or the sequential dependencies among categories could be entirely incorrect. It remains to be seen if this potential problem is an actual problem. At present there is good reason for concern. When available, category-by-category reliability estimates are often severely nonhomogeneous. Such data is desperately needed if we are to determine the degree of confidence to be placed in previous research on relational communication, group decision-making, and the like.

In Section III we looked at the thorny issue of validating coding systems. We were forced to address this issue since the most common bases of validity claims—evidence of reliability and the subjective impressions of face validity—are insufficient to establish the validity of a coding system. Reliability establishes only that units are being coded consistently. And, as we noted in our discussion of coding "drift" (Section II. B. 3), it is quite possible for subsets of coders to be consistent among themselves but inconsistent with those in other subsets. Subjective impressions of face validity add little evidentiary weight to a claim of validity, beyond establishing that the claim is plausible. If that claim is in dispute, neither face validity nor reliability are sufficient to permit ajudication.

But if we are to adjudicate this kind of dispute, there must be some standard against which the accuracy of the coding scheme can be judged. We have put forth the surprisingly controversial claim that two forms of construct validity—convergent and discriminant—offer particularly useful forms of evidence when assessing the validity of coding systems. Furthermore, we have offered a general typology of perspectives that one might adopt in validation. Although the distinctions among experienc*ed,* experienc*ing,* and experienc*er* modes for construct validation are relatively crude, they may help sensitize researchers to the difficulties of squaring data with interpretation in interaction analysis research. In the best of worlds, they may prompt more insight into the processes of interpretation underlying social interaction.

In constructing interaction coding schemes, researchers make implicit choices about the interpretive status of their coding categories. Some coding systems have been employed to code the shared meanings messages carry across a large body of language users; others attempt to code idiosyncratic interpretations that are only shared by the participants under investigation. Although some schemes have been offered strictly as observer-defined instruments, there are relatively few coding procedures that stand entirely outside the realm of subjects' interpretations. The distinctions among experienc*ed,* experienc*ing,* and experienc*er* modes of validation are meant to encourage researchers to acknowledge the interpretive objectives of their coding instruments and to stand as guidelines for the development of procedures that assess whether schemes reach their stated objectives.

In pointing to the sources of evidence for validating coding instruments, these modes raise the issue of when researchers should rely on subjects' interpretations to assign messages to coding classifications. The decision to anchor a coding scheme in subjects' interpretations falls directly from the theoretical assumptions that motivate the development or use of a scheme. A researcher's interpretive objective is grounded in some set of assumptions about what is most useful for studying social interaction. If a theory is built on an assumption that any exchange of behaviors is best understood by examining the culturally-shared or idiosyncratic interpretations interactants assign to their behaviors, then the theory can only be tested by employing procedures that gain access to these perceptions. Interpretive theories of behavior require interpretively-based coding procedures.

Using experienc*ing* or experienc*er* coding schemes does not, however, mean that researchers are limited to drawing claims about social interaction that are known to the participants being studied; all coding procedures are employed to provide insights that step beyond subjects' knowledge. Interpretively-based schemes are analytical tools for providing data that lead to claims about predictable patterns of interaction or the relationship between features of interaction and other exogenous variables. The shared or idiosyncratic interpretations embodied in the scheme are seen, from the standpoint of the researcher's theory, as the best source of evidence to discover useful theoretical claims that surpass subjects' understanding of their own behaviors.

The reliability and validity issues we have discussed inevitably add further requirements to the demanding task of coding social interaction. But any coding analysis is a worthwhile endeavor only if we can be confident that the data offer a reliable and accurate account of how messages are exchanged or interpreted in face-to-face encounters. Meeting these reliability and validity requirements can instill greater confidence in coding data and can result in the development of coding procedures that are true to the theoretical assumptions that prompted their construction.

V. REFERENCES

Ainsworth, M. D. S. (1969). Object relations dependency, and attachment: A theoretical review of the mother-infant relationship. *Child Development 40,* 969–1025.

Altman, I., and Taylor, D. A. (1973). "Social Penetration: The Development of Interpersonal Relationships." New York: Holt, Rinehart & Winston.

Anderson, N. H. (1974). Looking for configurality in clinical judgment. *Pyschological Bulletin 78,* 93–102.

Anderson, T. W., and Goodman, L. A. (1957). Statistical inferences about Markov chains. *Annals of Mathematical Statistics 28,* 89–110.

Argyle, M., and Cook, M. (1976). "Gaze and Mutualgaze." London: Cambridge University Press.

Argyle M., and Dean, J. (1965). Eye contact, distance and affiliation. *Sociometry 28,* 289–304.

Arundale, R. B. (1977). Sampling across time for communication research: A simulation. *In* P. M. Hirsch, P. V. Miller, and F. G. Kline (Eds.), "Strategies for Communication Research," pp. 257–285. Beverly Hills, California: Sage.

Baird, J. E., Jr. (1974). A comparison of distributional and sequential structure in cooperative and competitive group discussions. *Speech Monographs 41,* 226–232.

Bales, R. F. (1950). "Interaction Process Analysis." Chicago, Illinois: University of Chicago Press.

Bales, R. F. (1953). The equilibrium problem in small groups. *In* T. Parsons, R. F. Bales, and E. A. Shils (Eds.), "Working Papers in the Theory of Action," pp. 111–161. Glencoe, Illinois: Free Press.

Bales R. F. (1970). "Personality and Interpersonal Behavior." New York: Holt, Rinehart and Winston.

Barker, R. G. (1963). "The Stream of Behavior." New York: Appleton, Century and Crofts.

Bateson, G. (1936). "Naven." London: Cambridge University Press.

Bateson, G. (1978). The pattern which connects. *Co-Evolution Quarterly* (No. 18), 4–15.

Berger, C. R., and Calabrese, R. J. (1975). Some explorations in initial interaction and beyond: Toward a developmental theory of interpersonal communication. *Human Communication Research 1,* 99–112.

Birdwhistle, R. L. (1970). "Kinesics and Context." Philadelphia, Pennsylvania: University of Pennsylvania Press.

Bishop, Y. M. M., Flenberg, S. E., and Holland, P. M. (1975). "Discrete Multivariate Analysis: Theory and Practice." Cambridge, Massachusetts: MIT Press.

Blurton-Jones, N. G., and Woodson, R. H. (1979). Describing behavior: The ethologists' perspectus. *In* M. E. Lamb, S. J. Suomi, and G. R. Stephenson (Eds.), "Social Interaction Analysis: Methodological Issues," pp. 97–118. Madison, Wisconsin: University of Wisconsin Press.

Bochner, A. P., and Bochner, B. (1972). A multivariate investigation of Machiavellianism and task structure in four-man groups. *Speech Monographs 39,* 277–285.

Bochner, A. P., Kaminski, E. P., and Fitzpatrick, M. A. (1977). The conceptual domain of interpersonal communication behavior: A factor-analytic study. *Human Communication Research 3,* 291–302.

Bochner, A. P., and Krueger, D. L. (1979). Interpersonal communication theory and research: An overview of inscrutable epistomologies and muddled concepts. *Communication Yearbook 3,* 197–211.

Borg, I., and Lingoes, J. (1978). What weight should weights have in individual differences scaling? *Quality and Quantity 12,* 223–237.

Borgatta, E. F. (1962). A systematic study of interaction process scores, peer and self-assessments, personality and other variables. *Genetic Psychology Monographs 65*, 219–291.

Bower, G. H., Black, J. B., and Turner, T. J. (1979). Scripts in memory for text. *Cognitive Psychology 11*, 177–220.

Bowlby, J. (1969). "Attachment and Loss," Vol. 1. New York: Basic Books.

Bruner, J. S. (1975). From communication to language—a psychological perspective. *Cognition 3*, 255–287.

Burleson, B. R., Applegate, J. L., and Neuwirth, C. M. (1981). Is cognitive complexity loquacity? A reply to Powers, Jordan, and Street. *Human Communication Research 7*, 212–225.

Campbell, D. T., and Fiske, D. N. (1959). Convergent and discriminant validation by the multitract-multimethod matrix. *Psychological Bulletin 56*, 81–105.

Cappella, J. N. (1979). Talk-silence sequences in informal conversations I. *Human Communication Research 6*, 3–17.

Cappella, J. N. (1980). Talk-silence sequences in informal conversations II. *Human Communication Research 6*, 130–145.

Cappella, J. N., and Hewes, D. E. (In preparation). "Analyzing Social Interaction: Adaptation and Interspecter Influence." Hillsdale, New Jersey: Erlbaum.

Cappella, J. N., and Joseph, N. (1981). Mutual influence in expressive behavior: Adult-adult and infant-adult dyadic interaction. *Psychological Bulletin 89*, 101–132.

Cappella, J. N., and Streibel, M. J. (1979). Computer analysis of talk-silence sequences: The FIASSCO system. *Behavior Research Methods and Instrumentation 11*, 384–392.

Carlsmith, J. M., Ellsworth, P. C., and Aronson, E. (1976). "Methods of Research in Social Psychology." Reading, Massachusetts: Addison-Wesley.

Carroll, J. D., and Chang, J.-J. (1970). Analysis of individual differences in multidimensional scaling via N-way generalization of "Eckart-Young" decomposition. *Psychometrika 35*, 283–319.

Cohen, J. A. (1960). A coefficient of agreement for nominal scales. *Education and Psychological Measurement 20*, 37–46.

Costner, H. L., and Schoenberg, R. (1973). Diagnosing indicator ills in multiple indicator models. *In* A. S. Goldberg and O. D. Duncan (Eds.), "Structural Equation Models in the Social Sciences," pp. 167–199. New York: Seminar Press.

Courtright, J. A. (1978). A laboratory investigation of groupthink. *Communication Monographs 45*, 229–246.

Courtright, J. A., Millar, R. E., and Rogers, L. E. (1980). Message control intensity as a predictor of transactional redundancy. *Communication Yearbook 4*, 199–216.

Cronbach, L. J., and Meehl, P. E. (1955). Construct validity in psychological tests. *Psychological Bulletin 52*, 281–302.

Cronbach, L. J., Gleser, G. C., Nanda, H., and Rajaratnam, N. (1972). "The Dependability of Behavioral Measurements." New York: Wiley.

Donohue, W. R. (1981). Development of a model of rule use in negotiation interaction. *Communication Monographs 48*, 106–120.

Ebbesen, E. B. (1981). Cognitive processes in inferences abut a person's personality. *In* E. T. Higgins, C. P. Herman, and M. P. Zanna (Eds.), "Social Cognition: The Ontario Symposium," Vol. 1, pp. 179–225. Hillsdale, New Jersey: Erlbaum.

Ebbesen, E. B., and Allen, R. B. (1979). Cognitive processes in implicit personality trait inferences. *Journal of Personality and Social Psychology 37*, 471–488.

Ellis, D. G. (1979). Relational control in two group systems. *Communication Monographs 46*, 153–166.

Epstein, S. (1979). The stability of behavior I: On predicting most of the people much of the time. *Journal of Personality and Social Psychology 37*, 1097–1126.

Fishbein, M., and Ajzen, I. (1974). Attitudes toward objects as predictors of single and multiple behavioral criteria. *Psychological Review 81*, 59–74.

Fisher, B. A. (1970). Decision emergence: Phases in group decision-making. *Speech Monographs 31*, 53–66.

Fisher, B. A. (1977a). "Interaction Analysis: An Under-Utilized Methodology in Communication." (Paper presented to Western Speech Communication Association, Phoenix, Arizona.)

Fisher, B. A. (1977b). "Functions of Category Systems in Interaction Analysis." (Paper presented to the Speech Communication Association, Washington, D.C.)

Fisher, B. A. (1980a). "Relational Communication Research: A Critique and a Synthesis." (Paper presented to Western Speech Communication Association, Portland, Oregon.)

Fisher, B. A. (1980b). "RELCOM Research: Rationale and Results." (Paper presented to the International Communication Association Convention, Acapulco, Mexico.)

Fisher, B. A., Drecksel, G. L., and Werbal, W. S. (1979). Social information processing analysis: Coding ongoing human communication. *Small Group Behavior 10*, 3–21.

Fleiss, J. L. (1971). Measuring nominal scale agreement among many raters. *Psychological Bulletin 76*, 378–382.

Folger, J. P., and Poole, M. S. (1980). "On Validating Interaction Coding Schemes." (Paper presented at the International Communication Association Convention, Acapulco, Mexico.)

Folger, J. P., and Poole, M. S. (1982). Relational coding schemes: The question of validity. *Communication Yearbook 5*, 235–247.

Folger, J. P., and Puck, S. (1976). "Coding Relational Communication: A Question Approach." (Paper presented to the International Communication Association Convention, Portland, Oregon.)

Folger, J. P., and Sillars, A. L. (1980). Relational coding and perceptions of dominance. *In* B. W. Morse and L. A. Phelps (Eds.), "Interpersonal Communication: A Relational Perspective," pp. 322–333. Minneapolis: Burgess.

Funkhouser, G. R., and Parker, E. B. (1968). Analyzing coding reliability: The random-systematic-error coefficient. *Public Opinion Quarterly 23*, 122–128.

Geller, A., Kaplan, D., and Lasswell, H. D. (1942). An experimental comparison of four ways of coding editorial content. *Journalism Quarterly 19*, 362–370.

Giddens, A. (1976). "New Rules of Sociological Method." New York: Basic Books.

Goffman, E. (1981). "Forms of Talk." Philadelphia, Pennsylvania: University of Pennsylvania Press.

Gottman, J. M. (1979). "Marital Interaction: Experimental Investigations." New York: Academic Press.

Gottman, J. M., and Bakeman, R. (1979). The sequential analysis of observational data. *In* M. E. Lamb, S. J. Suomi, and G. R. Stephenson (Eds.), "Social Interaction Analysis," pp. 185–206. Madison, Wisconsin: University of Wisconsin Press.

Gottman, J. M., Notarius, C., Markman, H., Bank, S., Yoppi, B., and Rubin, M. E. (1976). Behavior exchange theory and marital decision making. *Journal of Personality and Social Psychology 34* 14–23.

Gottman, J. M., Markman, H., and Notarius, C. (1977). The topography of marital conflict: A sequential analysis of verbal and nonverbal behavior. *Journal of Marriage and the Family 39*, 461–477.

Gouran, D. S., and Whitehead, J. (1971). An investigation of ratings of discussion statements by participants and observers. *Central States Speech Journal 21*, 263–268.

Guetzkow, H. (1950). Unitizing and categorizing problems in coding qualitative data. *Journal of Clinical Psychology 6*, 47–58.

Hatfield, J. D., and Hatfield, D. W. (1978). The comparative utility of three types of behavioral units for interaction analysis. *Communication Monographs 45*, 44–50.

Hawes, L. C. (1972). Development and application at an interview coding system. *Central States Speech Journal 23*, 92–99.

Hewes, D. E. (1979). The sequential analysis of social interaction. *Quarterly Journal of Speech 65*, 56–73.

Hewes D. E. (1980). Stochastic modeling of communication processes. *In* P. R. Monge and J. N. Cappella (Eds.), "Multivariate Techniques in Human Communication Research," pp. 393–427. New York: Academic Press.

Hewes, D. E. (In preparation). "The Effects of Differential Category-By-Category Unreliability of the Sequential Struction of Coded Social Interaction Data." (Manuscript in preparation, University of Illinois, Champaign-Urbana.)

Hewes, D. E., and Haight, L. R. (1980). Multiple act criteria in the validation of communication traits: What do we gain and what do we lose? *Human Communication Research 6*, 352–366.

Hewes, D. E., and Planalp, S. K. (In press). "There is nothing as useful as a good theory . . . :" The influence of social knowledge on interpersonal communication. *In* C. Berger and M. Roloff (Eds.), "Communication and Social Cognition." Beverly Hills, California: Sage.

Hewes, D. E. Planalp, S. K., and Streibel, M. (1980). Analyzing social interaction: Some excruciating models and exhilarating results. *Communication Yearbook 4*, 123–144.

Holsti, O. R. (1969). "Content Analysis for the Social Sciences and the Humanities." Reading Massachusetts: Addison-Wesley.

Howard, R. A. (1971). "Dynamic Probabilistic Systems," Vol. 2. New York: Wiley.

Jaccard, J. J., and Daly, J. (1980). Personality traits and multipe-act criteria. *Human Communication Research 6*, 367–377.

Jaffe, J. J., and Feldstein, S. (1970). "Rhythms of Dialogue." New York: Academic Press.

Johnson, S. M., and Bolstad, O. D. (1973). Methodological issues in naturalistic observation: Some problems and solutions for field research. *In* L. A. Hamerlynck, L. C. Handy, and E. J. Mash (Eds.), "Behavior Change: Methodology, Concepts, and Practice," pp. 7–67. Champaign, Illinois: Research Press.

Kerlinger, F. N., (1973). "Foundations of Behavioral Research," 2nd ed. New York: Holt, Rinehart & Winston.

Krippendorff, K. (1980). "Content Analysis." Beverly Hills, California: Sage.

Kruskal, J. B., and Wish, M. (1978). "Multidimensional Scaling." Beverly Hills, California: Sage.

Kullback, S., Kupperman, M., and Ku, H. (1962). Tests for contingency tables and Markov chains. *Technometrics 4*, 573–608.

Labov, W., and Fanshel, D. (1977). "Therapeutic Discourse: Psychotherapy as Conversation." New York: Academic Press.

Lazarsfeld, P. F., and Barton, A. H. (1969). Quantitative measurement: A codificiation of techniques unique to social science. *In* L. I. Krimerman (Ed.), "The Nature and Scope of Social Science," pp. 514–549. New York: Appleton-Century-Crofts. (Published originally *In* D. Lerner and H. D. Lasswell (Eds.), "The Policy Sciences," pp. 155–192. Stanford, California: Stanford Univesity Press, 1951.)

Leary, T. F. (1957). "Interpersonal Diagnosis of Personality." New York: Ronald Press.

Lord, F. M., and Novick, M. R. (1968). "Statistical Theories of Mental Test Scores." Reading, Massachusetts: Addison-Wesley.

Mabry, E. A. (1975a). An instrument for assessing content themes in a group interaction. *Speech Monographs 42*, 291–297.

Mabry E. A. (1975b). The sequential structure of interaction in encounter groups. *Human Communication Research 1*, 302–307.

Mabry E. A. (1975c). Exploratory analysis of a developmental model for task-oriented groups. *Human Communication Research 2*, 66–74.

Mark, R. A. (1971). Coding communication at the relationship level. *Journal of Communication 21*, 221–232.

McCroskey, J. C., and Wright, D. W. (1971). The development of an instrument for measuring interaction behavior in small groups. *Speech Monographs 38*, 335–340.

McPhee, R. D., and Poole, M. S. (1980). "A Theory of Structuration: The Perspective of Anthony Giddens and Its Relevance for Contemporay Communication Research." (Paper presented at the Speech Communication Association Convention, New York.)

Millar, F. E., and Rogers, L. E. (1976). A relational approach to interpersonal communication. *In* G. R. Miller (Ed.), ''Explorations in Interpersonal Communication,'' pp. 87–103. Beverly Hills, California: Sage

Miller, J. R., and Kintsch, W. (1981). Knowledge-based aspects of prose comprehension and readability. *Text 1*, 215–232.

Montgomery, B. M. (1981). ''What You See is not Necessarily What You Get: A Comparison of Behavioral Observation and Self-Report Measures of Open Communication.'' (Paper presented at the International Communication Association Convention, Minneapolis, Minnesota.)

Mulac, A., and Sherman, A. R. (1974). Behavioral assessment of speech anxiety. *Quarterly Journal of Speech 60*, 134–143.

Newtson, D. (1976). Foundations of attribution: The perception of ongoing behavior. *New Directions in Attribution Research 1*, 223–248.

Newtson, D., and Engquist, G. (1976). The perceptual organization of ongoing behavior. *Journal of Experimental Social Psychology 12*, 436–450.

Newtson, D. Engquist, G., and Bois, J. (1977). The objective basis of behavior units. *Journal of Personality and Social Psychology 35*, 847–862.

Nunnally, J. C. (1967).''Psychometric Theory.'' New York: McGraw-Hill.

O'Donnell-Trujillo, N. (1981). Relational communication: A comparison of coding systems. *Communication Monographs 48*, 91–105.

Parks, M. R., and Dindia-Webb, K. (1979). ''Recent Development in Relational Communication Research.'' (Paper presented to the International Communication Association, Philadelphia, Pennsylvania.)

Peabody, D. (1970). Symmetry and asymmetry in interpersonal relations—with implications for the concept of projection. *Journal of Personality 38*, 426–434.

Perret-Clermont, A.-N. (1980). ''Social Interaction and Cognitive Development in Children.'' New York: Academic Press.

Planalp, S. K., and Hewes, D. E. (1981). A cognitive approach to communication theory: *Cogito Ergo Dico? Communication Yearbook 5*, 49–77.

Planalp, S. K. and Tracy, K. (1980). ''Not to Change the Topic But . . . : A Cognitive Approach to the Management of Conversation.'' (Paper delivered at the Internatinal Communication Association Convention, Acapulco, Mexico.)

Poole, M. S. (1981). Decision development in small groups I: A comparison of two modes. *Communication Monographs 48*, 1–24.

Poole, M. S., and Folger, J. P. (1978). ''Overture to Interaction Research: A Theory of Validation for Interaction Coding Schemes.'' (Paper presented at the Speech Communication Association Convention, Minneapolis, Minnesota.)

Poole, M. S., and Folger, J. P. (1979). ''A Method for Establishing the Representational Validity of Interaction Coding Schemes.'' (Paper presented at the Speech Communication Association Convention, San Antonio, Texas.)

Poole, M. S., and Folger, J. P. (1981a). A method for establishing the representational validity of interaction coding schemes: Do we see what they see? *Human Communication Research 8*, 26–42.

Poole, M. S., and Folger, J. P. (1981b). Modes of observation and the validation of interaction coding schemes. *Small Group Behavior 12*, 477–493.

Riskin, J., and Faunce, E. E. (1972). An evaluative review of family interaction research. *Family Process 11*, 365–455.

Rogers, L. E., and Farace, R. V. (1975). An analysis of relational communication in dyads: New measurement procedures. *Human Communication Research 1*, 222–239.

Rogers, L. E., and Millar, F. E. (1981). The question of validity: A response to Folger and Poole. *Communication Yearbook 5*, 249–257.

Rogers, L. E., Courtright, J. A., and Millar, F. E. (1980). Message control intensity: Rationale and preliminary findings. *Communication Monographs 47*, 201–219.

Rogers-Millar, L. E., and Millar, F. E. (1979). Domineeringness and dominance: A transactional view. *Human Communication Research 5*, 238–246.

Romanczyk, R. G., Kent, R. N., Diament, C., and O'Leary, K. D. (1973). Measuring the reliability of observational data: A reactive process. *Journal of Applied Behavior Analysis 6*, 175–184.

Rosenberg, S. (1976). New approaches to the analysis of personal constructs in person perception. *Nebraska Symposium on Motivation 24*, 149–272.

Sackett, G. P. (1979). The lag sequential analysis of contingency and cyclicity in behavioral interaction research. *In* J. D. Osofsky (Ed.), ''Handbook of Infancy Development,'' pp. 623–649. New York: Wiley.

Schneider, B. (1970). Relationships between various criteria, leadership in small groups. *Journal of Social Psychology 82*, 253–261.

Schutz, A. (1967). ''The Phenomenology of the Social World.'' Evanston, Illinois: Northwestern University Press.

Seibold, D. R., McPhee, R. D., Poole, M. S., Tanita, N. E., and Canary, D. J. (1981). Argument, group influence, and decision outcomes. *In* G. Ziegelmueller and J. Rhodes (Eds.), ''Dimensions of Argument: Proceedings of the Second SCA Summer Conference on Argumentation,'' pp. 663–692. Annandale, Virginia: Speech Communication Association.

Stech, E. L. (1979). A grammar of conversation with a quantitative empirical test. *Human Communication Research 5*, 158–170.

Stiles, W. B. (1980). Comparisons of dimensions derived from rating versus coding of dialogue. *Journal of Personality and Social Psychology 38*, 359–374.

Taplin, P. S., and Reid, J. B. (1973). Effects of instructional set and experimenter influence on observer reliability. *Child Development 44*, 547–554.

Taylor, C. (1971). Interpretation and the sciences of man. *Review of Metaphysics 25*, 3–51.

Terrill, J. M., and Terrill, R. E. (1965). A method for studying family communication. *Family Progress 4*, 259–290.

Torgerson, W. S. (1958). ''Methods of Scaling.'' New York: Wiley.

Tucker, L. R. (1972). Relations between multidimensional scaling and three-mode factor analysis. *Psychometrika 37*, 3–27.

Tudor, A. (1976). Misunderstandng everyday life. *Sociological Review 24*, 479–503.

Watzlawick, P., Beavin, J. H., and Jackson, D. D. (1967). ''Pragmatics of Human Communication.'' New York: Norton.

Wilson, T. P. (1970). Conceptions of interaction and forms of sociological explanation. *American Sociological Review 35*, 697–710.

Wish, M., D'Andrade, R. G., and Goodnow, J. E. (1980). Dimensions of interpersonal communication: Correspondences between structures for speech acts and bipolar scales. *Journal of Personality and Social Psychology 39*, 848–860.

Wish, M., and Kaplan, S. J. (1977). Towards an implicit theory of interpersonal communication. *Sociometry 40*, 234–246.

7

The Introduction and Diffusion of Technological Innovation in Industry: An Information Research Perspective

Carmel Maguire and Robin Kench
School of Librarianship
University of New South Wales
Kensington, New South Wales 2033
Australia

I. INTRODUCTION

A. The Field of Study

Literature on the diffusion of innovations is abundant, as many extensive bibliographies attest (Havelock, 1969; Kelly and Kranzberg, 1975; Project SAPPHO, 1972; Rogers et al., 1977). Yet as Rosenberg (1972, p.3) pointed out, serious study of the diffusion of new techniques in industry was, in 1972, an activity no more than 15 years old. In the ensuing 10 years, moreover, relatively little of the literature has been focused directly on the part played by information in technological innovation and diffusion. This review sets out to analyze the contribution, not only of those who would regard themselves as information researchers, but of all who recognize the nature of information and its transfer as factors in the diffusion of technological innovation, regardless of whether they work from bases in economics, psychology, sociology, philosophy, or the theory of organizations and their management. That research on the diffusion of technological innovations issues from so many different disciplinary wombs is natural. Such innovations are, after all, conceived and their live or still births take place in organizations where operations and interrelationships are shaped by economic, technical, political, social, cultural, and even architectural considerations. There is no way in which the field of study can be fenced off by any particular discipline or by the adherents of any particular approach or creed. It is argued here, however, that while diversity of background and approach is natural, the effects on the accumulation of a body of knowledge in the field have been harmful. Lack of integration has allowed unconscious reiteration of ideas and resuscitation of outmoded concepts. The tendency of different writers to give like phenomena different names and unlike phenomena the same names has also discouraged attempts to achieve integration by critical comparison and analysis of different studies. In short, the literature on diffusion of technological innovations exhibits all the features which blight the accumulation of knowledge in the social sciences. Despite this, it is possible, albeit demanding, to identify common preoccupations in the literature and to work towards a synthesis of the findings from the diverse research traditions. As preface to any such attempts, attention must be paid to definition of at least some of the most commonly and variously used terms.

B. Definitions

The definitions used in this review are those on which there appears to be most agreement in the literature. The term *invention* implies novelty in a product, a process, or a technique. *Innovation* is used to refer to the first application of a new idea or an invention in a product or process. The term *diffusion of innova-*

tions is used to refer to the process by which innovations are adopted by others, following the first application.

Technology transfer is the process by which knowledge developed by or in one group or institution is embodied in a way of doing things by other groups or institutions. A number of writers use this term synonymously with *diffusion of innovations,* but there is useful distinction to be made in reserving *technology transfer* to describe the special type of diffusion in which the technology has to be modified for application in a new environment. For this process the terms *adaptation* and *reinvention* are also used in the literature.

Technology may be regarded as any means which may be specified of doing anything. This review has chosen to focus on the technology which may be applied in secondary industry. Innovation and its diffusion in agriculture are mentioned only where the lessons learned have some particular relevance to innovation in secondary industry.

Information is at once the concept of which definition is most challenging and most avoided. The consequences of varied assumptions in the literature about the nature of *information* are explored in some depth in Section VI. In terms of general understanding, the most appealing definitions may well be the cosmic and the active, in which *information* may be regarded as what is contained in any exchange of meaning. More colorfully, Stafford Beer (1970, p.43) has maintained that "Data are a whole lot of meaningful patterns" whereas "Information is what changes us." In the context of inquiry into technological innovation, however, such definitions are of little help. In them the concepts of information and communication tend to coalesce, and they fail to account for and may even lead to under-valuing of passive stores of knowledge such as the formal literature. Comprehensive and precise definition of a phenomenon so pervasive and invisible in human systems as information may well be impossible. In consideration of the process by which technological innovations are achieved in industry, however, understanding of the term *information* has at least to comprehend knowledge, facts, ideas, opinions, judgments, and even feelings, relevant and irrelevent, available from any source, through formal or informal channels. To all these have to be added appreciation that information may be important in reducing or in increasing *uncertainty,* a condition which surrounds technological innovation. As Schon (1967, p.24) has noticed in his attempt to dispel the rational myths of invention and innovation, "of the various sources of novelty capable of throwing an organization into a state of uncertainty, none is more effective than technical innovation."

The bias of the literature is towards information as a commodity rather than a process, and the inadequacy of this conceptualization emerges from the review. Adoption of an information research perspective has guided the authors to choose to review those items from the vast and amorphous literature on technological innovation in which any aspect of the creation, accumulation, dissemination, and use of information has been recognized as an important variable in the diffusion process.

C. A Framework for the Literature

The literature on technological innovations seems to divide fairly readily into categories. There are studies carried out from different disciplinary bases using concepts and methodologies accepted in the different disciplines. Among these, most numerous are the contributions of economists (for example, Davies, 1979; Freeman, 1974; Mansfield, 1968) and management theorists (for example, Rubenstein, 1964; Sayles, 1974; Zaltman et al., 1973). There have also been large empirical studies (for example, Battelle, 1973; Langrish et al., 1972; Myers and Marquis, 1969; Project HINDSIGHT, 1969; Project SAPPHO, 1972; TRACES, 1968) carried out by teams which were multi-disciplinary and usually included scientists and engineers. In a third category are the studies of the use of information by engineers and scientists, of their information seeking behavior, and of patterns of information flow (for example, Marquis and Allen, 1966; Menzel, 1967; Pelz and Andrews, 1966; Rosenberg, 1967; Rosenbloom and Wolek, 1970; Rubenstein et al., 1970; Wolek, 1970).

Problems soon appear in this categorization, however. It is neither comprehensive nor sufficiently discriminatory. It does not admit accounts of the experience of inventive technologists in research or industrial environments, or of R & D managers in the diffusion of innovations and technology transfer. Admittedly, such writing is occasional and more likely to appear in technical publications or in reports of research policy discussions which may not be widely disseminated. (For example, Evans et al., 1972; Kolm, 1978, 1979). Yet, its exclusion may serve to perpetuate the myth of the indifference of inventors, especially in universities, to whether or not their innovative ideas find application.

More seriously, since the same writers tend to appear in different categories in the proposed classification, its discriminatory power is low. Other problems also appear. To try to categorize the literature by the discipline to which its authors belong can only emphasize differences and fail to identify overlaps in the substance of their work. There are, moreover, difficulties in assigning many writers on technological innovation to any one discipline. Researchers in management schools and policy research institutes, in particular, have reached those environments through many different disciplinary routes. Several are psychologists or sociologists by initial education. Several began their professional careers as engineers or scientists. Some have extended their interest in the problems of managing organizations so far and so deeply into the problems of the whole of human society that they may be more properly classified as philosophers. Warner (1974) surmounted this problem by, apart from vague references to political scientists, regarding as sociologists almost all of those who research the diffusion of innovations and who are not economists. Warner (1974, pp.439–440) made the just claim that ''the divergent perspectives and variables and the virtual isolation of the disciplines from one another have thus far failed to produce meaningful assimilation of the ideas of the one into the thinking of the other.'' The lack of communication, however, spreads well beyond the territories of economists, sociologists, and policy advisers.

In the proposed classification of the literature, it soon becomes obvious that the large empirical studies of technological innovation differ in scale rather than in essence from the myriad of smaller empirical studies which dot the literature. There are trends in the literature which show that certain types of studies were more likely to have been made in certain periods. The large empirical studies of the origins and transfer of notable innovations were carried out in the late 1960s and early 1970s. Publication dates for larger studies of the behavior of engineers and scientists as creators and users of information cluster in the late 1960s and in 1970. Yet the appearance and disappearance of these genres can be fully explained by neither the bandwagon effect of fashion nor the availability in that period of substantial research funds for social science research, the aims of which were not required to be much more specific than to increase understanding of complex modern society. A claim may be made, at least for tacit consensus among noteworthy researchers, that such approaches had yielded as much understanding as they were capable of providing. Thus when a study is pursued out of sequence, so to speak, such as the study of information transfer among engineers carried out by Schuchman (1981), the findings immediately seem out-of-date.

In the contemporary literature there tends to be strong emphasis on the relationship of technological innovations to productivity and on investment in creation of knowledge generally. This again may be attributed to conditions of worldwide economic malaise in which distributors of research funds, public and private, look kindly at proposals which appear to address directly problems whose solution promises economic benefits. It may be remarked, however, both that at least some economists have long been aware of the connection between productivity and innovation (Freeman, 1974; Mansfield, 1968) and that the work of Machlup (1962) and Porat (1977) in identifying and delineating modern Western society as information-based has led to much wider interest in the economics of information. Their work has opened new lines of inquiry in information research which include all aspects of investment in an information economy, one of which is, of course, investment in technological innovations.

While interesting and informative, the trends discernible in the literature do not readily provide a structure in which the major features, findings, insights, inconsistencies, and inadequacies can be collocated. The ideal structure would presumably be based on a reliable model of the innovation process, but the search for such a model has not so far yielded satisfactory results. Attempts to impose a linear model on the innovation process cannot encompass either the number of variables involved or the complexity of their interactions. Yet, in discussing the literature, the linear approach seems inevitable if contributions from different disciplines are to be brought together. It is therefore proposed in this review to take the linear communication model to which a large part of previous writing seems to fit and to supplement it with other generalizations about stages and phases in the innovative process. It will be necessary at the same time to report criticisms and to abandon linearity where it tends to impede or distort analysis.

Rogers (1962) was one of the first to emphasize communication in the process of diffusion of innovations. In his view:

> . . . at its most elemental level of conceptualization, the diffusion process consists of (1) a new idea, (2) individual A who knows about the innovation, and (3) individual B who does not yet know about the innovation. (Rogers, 1962, p.13)

In the later edition of this work, Rogers and Shoemaker (1971, p.11) developed this idea and fitted it into the S-M-C-R model wherein "A *source* sends a *message* via certain *channels* to the *receiving* individual."

Rogers (1962) also suggested that the process by which innovation is adopted could be divided into five stages: awareness, interest, evaluation, trial, and adoption. He also postulated that information sources and channels would differ in these different stages. Rogers based this conceptualization of diffusion of innovation largely on the traditions of rural sociology, but Ozanne and Churchill (1971) applied it in studying the adoption of a machine-tool innovation in industry. Other work on the role of information in the process of technological innovation and its diffusion has often made use of the five stages identified by Rogers (1962), adapting and sometimes renaming them (for example, Ettlie, 1976; Maguire and Kench, 1981c).

Another approach of information-focused research has been to attempt to distinguish the information that initiates innovation from information that assists in problem solving during the process, and from information that aids in the diffusion of the innovation to others (Myers and Marquis, 1969; Utterback, 1971). This is of course a highly artificial procedure. Like the five stages proposed by Rogers (1962), the three phases of information need are not clearcut. At any time different individuals or groups may be at different stages or phases on the same innovation. Decisions at any stage, influenced by any variable, may terminate, accelerate, or put back to an earlier stage consideration of the innovation and change the information requirements. As tools of analysis, it is obvious that linear models must be used cautiously. Yet, they at least offer guidelines for the building of this review and seem more likely than other approaches to allow an analysis of the substance of the literature.

Accordingly, the structure of the review is as follows: the sources of information for technological innovation are examined in Section II; Section III examines the channels through which information about technological innovation flows; Section IV concentrates on the barriers which may obstruct the acceptance of innovative messages; Section V analyzes the effects of government actions which by design or accident affect application and diffusion of innovative technology; Section VI attempts to isolate the differences in crucial concepts and assumptions which have shaped inquiry into the process of technological innovation, and to summarize the state of present knowledge.

II. SOURCES OF INFORMATION

A. Clearing Some Ground

One of the problems of terminology in the literature is that the distinctions made between sources of information and channels of information are not consistent. Rationally, a source may be regarded as a person or place in which the information resides, while the channel is the means by which it is carried to another person or place. But the rational view is hard to sustain in any natural way and, inevitably, arbitrary distinctions have to be made. In this review, for example, the choice has been made to regard the formal literature as a channel rather than a source of information. As such, discussion of the formal literature and its use in technological innovation is deferred until Section III.

Before this Section on the sources of information for technological innovation can proceed, another pervasive cause of confusion in discussion of the origins of innovations must be addressed. This confusion arises from the nature of information as a phenomenon. It is essentially boundless and indivisible in the general as well as the economic sense. Myers and Marquis (1969, p.74) remarked: "Theoretically the technical information comprising an innovation is infinite and can be analyzed in almost unlimited detail." In the context of the report of an empirical study, it seems reasonable to define arbitrary boundaries. Johnston and Gibbons (1975, p.29), for example, gave clear warning that: "It should be noted that the general source is that from which the problem-solver directly obtained the information, and not the original producer of the information. This avoids the difficulties of attempting to trace all the information to an ultimate source." In confronting the wider reality, however, other sources, intermediate and ultimate, cannot be dismissed so readily. An associated problem is the tendency of many writers to ascribe innovative ideas to the knowledge and experience of individuals or groups. This may easily obscure the contribution of the sources and the channels of information which have shaped knowledge and constituted experience.

The findings of Maguire and Kench (1981c) suggest that pursuit to some depth of the origins of innovative research ideas can yield interesting data on some of the events and circumstances which interact with the minds of individuals to spark such ideas. On the other hand, any delving into the remote past of innovative projects becomes hazardous. Among the severe methodological criticisms made by Mowery and Rosenberg (1979, p.118), in particular of Project HINDSIGHT (1969), and in general of the other large empirical studies of the origins of technological innovations, is the stricture that "a linear model of innovation is imposed retrospectively upon a very complex interactive process.'' In the difficulties which surround the achievement of practicable yet adequate research designs, it is no wonder that the implications of the results of many studies are by no means clear in themselves, let alone comparable with those of other studies.

With those caveats, this review proceeds to examine the studies which bear on the sources of information for technological innovation. First discussed is the contribution of sources inside and outside the organization in which innovation is being considered. Then consideration is given to whether any consensus has been achieved on the relative importance of the various external sources which have been identified. Some consideration is also given to the dilemmas of which the present state of knowledge about sources of information for innovation is part.

B. Internal and External Sources

Interest in investigating internal and external sources of information was stimulated by the inclusion by Carter and Williams (1957, pp.178–179) among the characteristics of the ''technically progressive firms'' which they identified in their study of British industry, of ''high quality of incoming information'' and ''a readiness to look outside the firm.'' Subsequent writers have tried to identify and compare the importance of internal and external sources of information at different stages of the innovative process.

1. Sources stimulating innovation

Several studies have attempted to discover the proportionate contribution of internal and external sources to the stimulation of innovation.

Langrish et al. (1972, p.134) came upon ''the problems associated with attempts to define 'origins' of innovation,'' even though they had tried to simplify the problems by setting the boundary at the source which had stirred to action the commercially successful innovations which had won the Queen's Award for British firms in 1966 and 1967. Langrish et al. judged that, of 158 ideas important in stimulating 51 innovations, 102 came from sources external to the firms. Battelle Memorial Institute (1973) tried, in lengthy chronological case studies, to trace significant innovations to the original scientific ideas at their source. Three of the innovations were expanded from the earlier TRACES (1968) study. Battelle reported that eight of the ten innovations had originated outside the environment in which they were eventually developed. This finding is hardly surprising in view of the orientation of the study.

Both Myers and Marquis (1969) and Utterback (1971) reported interviews with people in firms about the sources of information which had stimulated innovations. It could be complained that neither of the readily available reports is sufficiently explicit about who was interviewed in each firm and whether different versions of the events which led up to the innovations were obtained. Schon has referred to "the historical revisionism common to the field of innovation." Whether tainted by revisionism or not, in both studies most of the sources were external to the firms. Utterback (1971, p.130) reported 66.1 percent of the 59 stimulating "inputs" of ideas for new scientific instruments were from outside sources. Myers and Marquis (1969, p.46) reported that in 567 cases of innovation by railroad companies and their suppliers, computer companies and their suppliers, and housing industry suppliers, 51 percent of the 153 "major information inputs" which "evoked the basic idea" rather than "expedited the solution" came from external sources, or "external channels" in their terminology. The source of other than "major information inputs" to each innovation Myers and Marquis left to the imagination, since they confined the firms to one "major information input" for each innovation—a decision surely both arbitrary and distorting.

In a later study by Utterback et al. (1976, p.8) of 164 R & D projects in five different process industries in Europe and Japan, a different picture emerged. In the 59 firms, 65.6 percent of the ideas for 164 R & D projects, including successful, unsuccessful, and ongoing projects, were from sources within the firm.

2. Sources supporting the innovation process

Regardless of where innovative ideas originate, all but the most minor changes in industrial processes require further research and development within the firm to solve the problems which arise during the innovation process. Myers and Marquis (1969, p.46) and Utterback (1971, p.130) reported increased use of internal sources of information during this phase. The former gave a figure of 60 percent of 414 "major information inputs" and the latter 64.4 percent of 143 "inputs." It should be noticed, however, that methodological differences between the two studies make direct comparison hazardous.

A comparative study of successes and failures in innovations in the British chemical and scientific instrument industries, Project SAPPHO (1972, p.78), reported that "good external communications" appeared important to success in innovation. Included under this umbrella were "coupling with the scientific and technological community regarding the *specific* innovation project and the efficient use of outside technology where appropriate."

Another British study (Gibbons and Johnston, 1974) investigated 30 product innovations, including some small scale incremental innovations. Of a total of 887 "units of technical information" contributing to the resolution of technical problems arising in the development phase, 34 percent were categorized as from external sources, 30 percent from internal sources, and 36 percent from the problem-solver's experience and education. To have made the last-mentioned category seems sensible in view of the difficulty discussed above of putting internal or external tags on the knowledge and experience of individuals. Reporting the results of their study in another place, Gibbons and Johnston (1972, p.vi) also noted that, in particular innovations, one source was used more than another, and that large-scale innovations were produced by problem-solvers who relied more on information obtained outside the company.

The same writers (Johnston and Gibbons, 1975, p.32) also found that the frequency of use of a source of information did not correlate with the degree of impact the information "units" had on the innovation process. They remarked that "this provides confirmation that examining information in terms of source only does not provide a very sound basis for assessing its role in the innovation process." Broadening the implications of their findings, they added that the fact that information of high impact in the problem-solving stage of the innovation process is as likely as not to come from an infrequently used source, could not be taken to indicate that the source of the high impact information was being used insufficiently.

In the monograph which consolidates his several inquiries into the flow of information in R & D laboratories, Allen (1977, p.130) concluded from analysis of data gathered from 17 R & D projects that:

> a greater number of ideas for solution were suggested by sources outside the laboratory than by all other sources combined. . . . If messages from the customer were included in the count of messages from outside, then these sources were responsible for two-thirds of all idea-generating messages received by the project engineers.

3. Sources for the diffusion of innovations

Economists have largely focussed their attention on this phase of the innovation process. At first they sought to explain diffusion of innovations in terms of their profitability to the adopting firms. More recently, economists have come to recognize the complexity of organizational variables and the vulnerability to error of ex post facto judgments about the judgments of profitability and other market factors which preceded decisions about adoption of innovations. Useful analyses of these trends have been provided by Feller (1979, pp.297–299) and Ganz (1980, pp.598–600).

The sources of information used in the diffusion process are among the factors considered in debate about the influence of market factors on innovative behavior in organizations. That debate, concerned essentially with differing views of the effects of supply of and demand for new technology, is often referred to as the "science push versus market pull" debate. Since, however, the debate is referred not only to sources of information used in the diffusion of innovations, but to all phases of the innovative process, further discussion of the literature on market factors in innovation is presented in Part C.3. The effects of demand for and supply of innovation are also important in consideration of the necessity and feasibility of using public policy to stimulate industrial innovation. For that reason, the topic is also addressed in Section V, on the role of government.

Studies undertaken from the sociological viewpoint have, like Rogers (1962), sought to explain diffusion as a communication process. Referring to his five stage model of the innovation process, Rogers (1962, p.102) argued that "cosmopolite information sources are most important at the awareness stage, and localite information sources are most important at the evaluation stage." He defined "cosmopolite" as the degree to which an individual's orientation is external to a particular social system. Ozanne and Churchill (1971) used the concept in studying groups in firms making adoption decisions. They measured the "cosmopolite" variable in terms of the amount of travel undertaken by group members—a measure they derived from Carter and Williams (1957, p.179). Ozanne and Churchill reported that the groups with cosmopolite members used many more information sources and a greater variety of sources than groups lacking such members. Ozanne and Churchill, however, could not distinguish differences in behavior according to the stages in the adoption decision-making processes.

The cosmopolites soon begin to look like close relatives of the gatekeepers discussed in Section III. Again the difficulties of separating the sources of information from the channels become obvious.

Other studies, however, contribute more directly to sorting out the role of internal and external sources of information in the diffusion phase of innovation. Ettlie (1976) examined the diffusion of new numerically controlled machine tools in ten adopting organizations. He found that external sources were more important in the awareness stage, but that internal sources became more important in later stages. Allen (1975), in a study of diffusion of innovations in 10 Irish industries, found that, in 76 percent of the 63 cases, awareness of the innovation came to the firm from external sources, but he also found that 67 percent of the 102 messages used in the later problem-solving stages also came from outside the firm.

4. Summary

This examination of empirical data on the sources of information important in different phases of the innovation process has to be inconclusive; but some major ideas have been established. Good internal communications have been accepted as important in innovating organizations, and so has extensive use of external information sources. That innovators and adopters of innovations need to call upon many and diverse sources of information is also established. As Freeman (1977, p.251) remarked:

> To introduce a new product or process the firm must often obtain knowledge from many different sources; from customers, suppliers, universities, public laboratories, competitors, licensers and so forth.

Many doubts about the sources of innovation remain. But it is also doubtful whether more probing based on a linear communication model can serve to resolve them. It is obvious that the present state of knowledge about the sources of information important in the innovative process leaves several dilemmas which merit comment in this review.

C. Dilemmas about Sources

The problems which arise from imperfect understanding of the relationships between innovation and sources of information are part of three much larger dilemmas which are also strongly interrelated. They are: whether and how information contributes to the resolution of uncertainty in the innovation process; whether and what contribution basic scientific knowledge makes to innovative technology; and whether technological innovation and its diffusion are influenced more by "market pull" or "science push."

1. The uncertainty dilemma

Schon (1967) has been quoted in Section I.B. on the uncertainty into which technological innovation plunges industrial firms. Ten years later, Freeman (1977, p.256) remarked that "the bureaucratization of innovation, new management techniques and the concentration of R & D activities in large firms have not necessarily reduced the uncertainty associated with innovation in capitalist markets." A little light has been shed on this topic by research on the sources of information for innovation. Blandin and Brown (1977), in their study of managers in two industries, reported significant positive correlations between the level of uncertainty perceived by managers and their reliance on external information sources. Utterback (1974, p.623), in a general article on technological innovation and diffusion, suggested that information flow from the external environment is more critical for firms in industries when technologies are changing rapidly than for firms in more stable fields. (These findings link well with the economic argument by Newman (1976) discussed in Section IV.C.)

Writers on sources of information for technological innovation seem, by and large, to imply that the more use of external sources by an organization the better for the innovation process. This seems to ignore the insight from management theorists that an organization also has to protect its stability by not accepting too much information from the external environment. While recognition of this factor is implicit in some of the innovations literature, it does not, however, seem to have been used to explain phenomena like the non-use of apparently highly relevant sources. Take-up by other researchers of "the selection environment concept" developed by Nelson and Winter (1977) could add depth to their analysis.

Uncertainty is a concept which recurs throughout this review, especially in Section V on the role of government, since, as Nelson and Winter (1977, p.47) have pointed out: "Explicit recognition of uncertainty is important in thinking about policy."

2. Science, invention, and innovation

Much of the discussion on external sources used in innovation has centered on the contribution of basic science to technological innovation. What empirical studies have found on this topic seems to have been very much a function of what they set out to find, and the degree to which the formalized knowledge of science and technology has emerged as important seems to have depended particularly on the time-scale adopted in the studies.

Langrish et al. (1972) concentrated on the immediate sources of information which had stirred firms to initiate innovations. That they reached the following conclusion (Langrish et al., p.41) is therefore not surprising: "We fail to find much direct input by basic science into innovation but believe that there is a substantial contribution in various latent forms." In contrast, TRACES (1968) set out to track to its original source the knowledge upon which the innovations were founded. The technique was to identify "research events" which had made the innovations possible. Again, in view of the orientation of the study, the finding that 70 percent of the events were those of basic scientific research is not surprising. Neither is the finding by Project HINDSIGHT (1969) that there was little relation to basic science in the development of certain weapons systems. HINDSIGHT after all did not trace events further back than 20 years.

Gibbons and Johnston (1974) identified a range of "information units," some of which they classified as scientific, which had assisted in the resolution of technical problems arising in the course of innovations. Their conclusions were (Gibbons and Johnston 1974, p.230):

In this study, 36 percent of the information which contributed to the development of an innovation and which was obtained from outside the company during the innovation had its origins in basic scientific research. Of *all* information obtained by "problem-solvers" during an innovation, approximately one fifth could be similarly classified.

Associated with these studies has been a tendency to comment on apparently under-used sources of information. Thus Langrish et al. (1972), having categorized sources according to the type of organization from which the information came, reported that only 10 of the 102 ideas important in stimulating the innovations came from universities. An even less favorable picture emerged for universities and government research institutes in the study of the diffusion of innovations in Irish industry by Allen (1975). At the same time, with all phases of the innovation process in mind, Langrish et al. (1972), together with other British writers (Gibbons and Johnston, 1974; Pavitt and Walker, 1976) have indicated their belief that government funded laboratories and institutes are important as sources of information in the United Kingdom. There are differences in the way research is structured in different countries, and apparent contradiction in the data relating to public institutions as sources of information may be at least partly resolved by the insight from Roberts and Peters (1981, p.123), relating to universities, that "the 'idea bank' concept, though tempting, is unfortunately not especially helpful because it ignores the need to focus upon the process of transfer of ideas from inventor to potential user."

Much of the discussion about the importance of scientific knowledge to innovation has been merely a rehearsal in a different theater of the pure versus applied science debate. Not only is any dichotomy hard to sustain logically; in the context of innovation, it is clearly based on an inadequate linear model in which basic research leads to applied rsearch, which leads on to development, production, and utilization. That the debate persists is evidence of the strength of human need to simplify the complexity of reality.

3. Science push and market pull

Possibly as a reaction to older assumptions that if useful technology existed it would be used, many writers have rejected the ''science push'' in favor of the ''market pull'' model to account for successful innovation. This dilemma is also referred to in the literature as the ''needs/means'' debate. Mowery and Rosenberg (1979) have demonstrated that arguments for the pre-eminence of needs in several of the large empirical studies of innovations cannot be validly based on the evidence adduced. They noted that, apart from crucial differences among the studies, arguments in favor of ''market pull'' have tended to concentrate on the stimulation of innovation phase, whereas this model could be more relevant to the diffusion phase.

The findings of Von Hippel (1976, 1977), on the dominant role of users in stimulating innovations in the scientific instrument industry and in the manufacture of semi-conductors and electronic subassemblies, could be seen to favor the ''market pull'' theory. These innovations, however, occur in high technology industries with large R & D capacity which lead the field in the areas of their research and which employ both scientists and engineers with highly specialized expertise. It is hardly surprising then that the information needed by the machine tool industry to manufacture machines to the specifications of these innovative customers is provided by the customers. An interesting and rare sidelight on needs/means in relation to sources of innovative ideas within the firm is shed by Holt (1978). In an in-depth study of a large engineering firm in Scandinavia, he discovered that suggestions for minor improvements and variations in existing products usually came from the marketing departments, whereas those for radical changes came from the engineering side.

Innovations research does not yet seem to have explored inter-industry differences in use of information sources sufficiently, and what have emerged are little more than intriguing hints that such differences exist. Project SAPPHO (1972) found notable differences between the chemical industry, where the innovations were all process innovations, and the scientific instrument industry, where they were product innovations. Pavitt and Walker (1976, p.42) offered another angle on the needs/means debate in pointing out that, whereas users of innovations in industry and utilities can tell innovating firms what they want, this is not necessarily true in consumer markets or in those for public services. Both public services and individual consumers may lack the information and the technical competence necessary either to specify their wants or to evaluate proffered innovations.

Consideration of markets returns us rapidly to uncertainty, the dilemma with which we began. The needs/means debate in relation to innovation suggests a tangent. There are affinities, not only with market research for consumer products, but in the debates about needs, wants, and demands in the studies of information use which have been attempted by designers and managers of information services. Some of these affinities will be pursued in Section VI. This review now examines the literature relating to the channels through which information affecting the innovation process flows.

III. CHANNELS OF INFORMATION

A. Formal and Informal Channels

Great attention has been paid in the literature on technological innovations to the relative importance of formal and informal channels of information, or, as the literature more frequently terms them, to personal and impersonal channels. The terms "personal" and "informal" are used to refer to the channels by which information is obtained from people. "Formal" and "impersonal" are terms used to refer to the use of formalized stores of information, whether through consulting the literature, libraries, or other professional information services. It will be remembered that in this review the formal literature has been classified as channel rather than source, partly because this distinction fits better with the orientation of the innovations literature, but mostly because to regard published matter as source and consultation of it as channel is a distinction too unnatural to be sustained.

Many writers have stressed the frequency of use of personal channels in the communication of information to and in industrial settings. Among them are Allen (1966, 1975, 1977), Czepiel (1974), Myers and Marquis (1969), Maguire and Kench (1974), Pavitt and Walker (1976), Rogers (1962), Rothwell and Robertson (1973), and Utterback (1971). As with the discussion of sources of information in Section II, the substance of the literature may most readily be revealed by examining findings in relation to the three different phases commonly identified in the innovation process.

1. Channels stimulating innovation

Some researchers have attempted to assign proportions to the information stimulating innovation carried by different channels. The numbers have to be viewed with some scepticism and certainly cannot be aggregated, but they give some basis for appreciation of apparent similarities and differences in the findings. Personal channels, variously described as "conversations," "discussions," "contacts," "meetings," and even "sources," have emerged as the means by which most exchanges of information take place in the earliest phase of the innovation process. Utterback (1971) reported that 57.6 percent of the inputs stimulating innovation came from discussions inside and outside the firm, whereas 15.2 percent came from the literature. Myers and Marquis (1969) reported communication of 34 percent of the "major information inputs" which evoked the basic idea for the innovations came through personal contacts, in contrast to 7 percent from the literature.

Langrish et al. (1972), in investigating the "method of transfer" of 102 important ideas derived from external sources by innovative British firms, attributed only 8 percent to personal contacts in the United Kingdom. Other instances of personal contact would have been hidden in their use also of "collaboration with supplier/customer" (12%) and "visit overseas" (6%) as "methods of transfer."

Despite the discrepancies in the figures, the studies quoted at least strongly suggest that informal channels play a more important role than formal channels in the means by which innovative technological ideas reach industrial firms.

2. Channels used during the innovation process

A different pattern in the usage of information channels has been reported in this phase of innovation. Utterback (1971, pp.130–131) deduced from his study of new scientific instruments that "search for information proceeds in a more definitely structured pattern during problem-solving than in the earlier idea generation phase." He reported that discussion inside and outside the firm accounted for 31.5 percent of channels used during the problem-solving phase, compared with 57.6 percent in the idea generation phase. Use of the literature also dropped from 15.2 to 8.4 percent, while the firms' own analysis and experiment provided 51.8 percent of the means by which information was obtained. Myers and Marquis (1969) also reported a fall-off in personal contacts in this phase from 30 to 17 percent, while personal contacts in the firm and use of the literature remained constant at each around 6 percent.

The British study by Johnston and Gibbons (1975) which focussed only on this phase of the innovative process reported that 29 percent of the information inputs came from the literature, 37 percent from the personal contacts, and 34 percent from the firms' own R & D activity. From these results, Johnston and Gibbons (1975, p.30) drew the implication that "this finding suggests that the conventional wisdom of the critical role of personal contact in information transfer may be over-emphasized." They immediately conceded, however, that "contact with individuals in both university and industry did contribute significantly to the innovation process."

Johnston and Gibbons might have been provoked to over-statement by a tendency in some other writing, notably in Rothwell and Robertson (1973), to denigrate the importance of formal channels. There is difficulty also, however, in reconciling the results reported by Johnston and Gibbons (1975) with Allen (1977). Allen did not specifically investigate the innovative process, but he analyzed the information seeking behavior of engineers in R & D laboratories engaged on problem-solving projects, many of which were projects related to innovations. Allen argued that engineers engaged in technological projects differ

markedly from scientists engaged in research projects who use the research literature as their major information channel, whereas engineers use informal channels of communication and read trade journals. Allen (1977, p.73) commented
that "most professional engineering journals are utterly incomprehensible to the
average engineer." Allen also reported frequent use of personal contact with
vendors, again at odds with Johnston and Gibbons (1975), who reported low use
of this channel. One can suppose that there were either marked differences in the
populations sampled in these two studies or in the tasks on which they were
engaged.

3. Channels used in the diffusion of innovations

It could at first be assumed that there would be less uncertainty about the
process by which an organization adopts a technological innovation already
proven elsewhere. On closer consideration, however, it becomes obvious that in
this stage the adopting firm has to some extent to work through the earlier
phases.

At the same time, some very interesting insights have emerged from studies of this phase of innovation. Among these are those of Czepiel (1974), who
recognized that previous studies of adoption decisions requiring very large investment had concentrated on economic factors. He sought instead to discover
whether diffusion of innovation in industrial societies could be studied as a
behavioral process.

He selected for study the diffusion of the continuous casting process in the
steel industry and reported (Czepiel 1974, p.176) that:

> Direct informal interpersonal contacts among decision-makers in different firms
> occurred about 5 times a month, on the average. . . . With respect to the innova-
> tion adoption decision itself, measured separately, respondents reported contacts
> with an average of 5.5 other firms. Some of these other firms were contacted on
> many occasions for this particular purpose.

Czepiel concluded that word-of-mouth communications in the diffusion of
innovations in industrial settings operated at a level of frequency sufficient to
indicate the existence of personal communications networks even among industry competitors. He also noted that the steel industry is a mature industry, that
firms in it have similar problems, and that findings may be different in new technology and highly competitive industries such as electronics. Czepiel made no
attempt to compare the importance of the personal communications network with
formal information channels.

Allen (1975), in his study of the adoption of new technology by Irish industry, found that information about the technology was nearly all obtained
through direct personal contacts, and that only about 8 percent of the "messages" received came through documentation. Allen also found that the supplier

or vendor was the most important channel for information needed to solve problems in the introduction of new technology, providing 31 percent of the "messages" used. Myers and Marquis (1969) also reported that firms adopting already existing innovations were more likely to obtain their information through personal contact—that contact was with vendors in 11 percent of the cases. Somewhat at odds with these findings are those of Ettlie (1976), who reported from his study of the adoption by 10 organizations of numerically controlled machine tools, that impersonal channels of information were most likely to account for awareness of a new production technology. Ettlie (1976, p.63) listed trade journals as contributing 25 percent, machine tool shows 20 percent, and distributors 20 percent. Ettlie (1976, pp.63–64) also made the interesting observation from his data that "organizations are not likely to access a wide variety of information sources during the awareness stage, and it appears that for this sample it would have been very difficult to predict eventual utilization of this innovation based on the knowledge of the variety of information sources used in the early stages of the adoption process."

4. Summary

It would be as easy as it is erroneous to gather from some of the innovations literature that formal and informal channels of communication are in competition and that the formal channels are losing. Happily, there has also been much clear thinking on the subject. Menzel (1967) argued that formal and informal channels had to be seen as complementary and not as alternatives. He pointed out that, while continual innovations in technology enable more communication services to be offered through formal channels, limits are set to the extent of their effectiveness by certain social and cultural characteristics of information users. He also pointed to some of the obvious advantages of informal communication.

One of the major advantages is the flexibility which personal communication offers in allowing refinement and redefinition of questions and the adaptation of answers to the level of the inquirer's interest and understanding. Rothwell and Robertson (1973) claimed, on the other hand, that libraries and selective dissemination of information services based on the formal literature will generally be of help only when the inquirer can define his or her information requirement closely. Rosenbloom and Wolek (1970, p.104) referred to the simple economics of turning round and "asking the next guy." This strategy may work very well in large organizations where the next guy is likely to know. One of the few *choses jugées* of information and communication research is that accessibility is a more powerful determinant of the use of an information channel than any other factor, including the quality of the information the channel carries.

Accessibility explains why all of us prefer to "ask the next guy," but Price (1967, pp.10–11) has suggested that technologists have another reason for using informal channels in that the information they want is often not published at all.

Often this is information about the use of techniques or about adaptations of apparatus. Menzel (1967, p.59) has noted that "information of this sort may be difficult to put into words briefly, and may be much more easily 'shown' than told." Collins (1974, p.176) reported that "to date, no-one to whom I have spoken has succeeded in building a TEA laser using written sources (including preprints and internal reports) as the sole source of information . . . though there is now a considerable literature on the subject." He added that "the transmission of skills is not done through the medium of the written word."

In the United States, the National Aeronautics and Space Administration (NASA) implemented an ambitious program in the 1960s based on information retrieval and document dissemination systems, designed to enhance the transfer of technology developed in the space program to the non-aerospace sectors of the economy. This program has generally been deemed a failure. Sayles (1974) recorded that few of the innovations had been utilized. He argued that this and much of the other official effort to encourage innovation had failed to realize how difficult the process of innovation is and how much skilled human intervention is required in its accomplishment. This touches on a topic which will be pursued somewhat further in Section V.

Matching their findings regarding use of internal and external sources of information, Blandin and Brown (1977) also suggested that the less predictable and more dynamic the organization's environmental setting, the more salient the role played by informal channels such as conversations and meetings (which they also call "sources") in the process of coping with uncertainty. Allen (1975) contended that document retrieval and reprint services were not effective, but that with advances in information processing technology they were relatively easy to produce. But to leap, as Rothwell and Robertson (1973, p.223) did, to the conclusion that "informal information retrieval is inherently more efficient than formal communication systems" is to overlook important limitations in the informal systems.

One of these limitations has been identified by Wolek and Griffith (1974). The information carried by informal channels is to a certain extent fortuitous, and Wolek and Griffith (1974, p.414) made the point that "there is no assurance that subsequent action is based upon the correct, complete, and best available information." It may be also difficult for an individual or an organization entering a new field, or for an innovator in a small company, immediately to make the wide range of personal contacts necessary to supply the information required. Allen (1977) and Pelz and Andrews (1966) are among writers who mentioned the beneficial effects of a diversity of contacts. Wolek and Griffith (1974) have pointed out that information received through any given channel might be valueless without information received through other channels. Like Menzel (1967), they have also argued strongly the interdependence of formal and informal information channels.

On more precise aspects of the role of formal and informal information channels in the technological innovation process, the literature leaves us, not only with partial answers, but with the suspicion that they are not always answers to comparable questions. More help is needed if we are to be able to examine critically such a proposition as that made by Langrish et al. (1972, p.46):

> It is not often that technology is transferred through personal contacts, but opportunities may be presented in these ways which subsequently alter the technological base of the company.

Identifications have been made of people, relationships among people, and of circumstances and events whose effects seem, at least, to influence application and diffusion of technological innovation strongly. The most interesting of these phenomena, the people who seem especially able to facilitate the communication of information important in innovation and the effects of the movement of people from one environment to another, are discussed in the remainder of this Section.

B. The Technological Gatekeeper and His Relatives

In studies of information flow in R & D laboratories, Allen (1967) identified a small minority of individuals to whom others turned for technical advice and assistance—the "stars" in the communication network. Allen termed them "technological gatekeepers." They differed from their colleagues in that they were better acquainted with the scientific and technological literature, and they maintained a greater degree of informal contact with members of the scientific and technological community outside their laboratories. In a later description, Allen (1977, p.166) wrote of the gatekeeper that "his principal contribution comes by way of the translation that he can perform. He converts documentary information or information gained through personal contacts into terms that are both relevant to and understandable by the members of his organization." In the earlier work, Allen (1967) saw the gatekeepers as elements in a two-step information flow process, and he compared their function to that of the "opinion leaders" identified by Lazarsfeld et al. (1944) in early communications research. Gatekeepers are informal channels in the terms adopted in this review, and Allen (1977, p.180), while recognizing that their role cannot be formalized, has offered some recommendations on how their presence may be exploited.

Allen's concept has been criticized on the strength of its theoretical basis, the effectiveness of the gatekeepers' role, and the generalizability of their existence to all environments. Rogers and Shoemaker (1971, pp. 204–208) have criticized the two-step flow model as an oversimplification of the communication process. Persson (1981) has argued that the two-step flow, whereby the content of formal channels is translated into informal communication, can lead to increased information gaps. Citing the "gatekeeper network" identified by Allen (1977, p.155), Persson (1981, pp.39–40) pointed out that the two-step hypothesis has to be a three-step process if those with fewer information sources are to be reached.

In the report of their study of mostly small scale product innovations, Johnston and Gibbons (1975, p.33) reported:

> No support was found for Allen's claims for the key role played by the "technological gatekeeper," each individual associated with a project appeared to have at least some contacts or sources of information which he regarded as his own. In the data relating to use of internal sources no "star" type of information network was detected in any innovation.

On the other hand, Maguire and Kench (1981b) identified a gatekeeper in a government R & D laboratory in New Zealand, and Holland (1972) has reported on a closely related species whom he called "special communicators." Having identified the focal individuals within informal communication networks, Holland (1972, p.38) suggested that "to affect the efficiency of informal information flow, the research manager's best hope for positively influencing informal networks lies in the identification and motivation of the special communicators in his organization." Creighton and Jolly (1981, p.4) have warned, however, that to make formal recognition of gatekeepers often causes their informal information role to change or to disappear.

Tushman and Katz (1980) have also reported on the role of gatekeepers in an R & D environment. While gatekeepers did not play an important role in information transfer in the more universally oriented tasks, Tushman and Katz found that, in the more locally oriented tasks, gatekeepers were active. Moreover, as well as mediating external information, they also appeared to facilitate the external communication of their more local project colleagues. Echoes arise here of the identification by Rogers (1962) of cosmopolite and localite members of organizations, which has been mentioned in Section II.B.3.

The product or process champion is another agent who has been identified as a positive contributor to the process of technological innovation (Langrish, 1972; SAPPHO, 1972; Schon, 1963). The influence of such individuals, whether they are the inventors or entrepreneurs, of course cannot cause adoption of the innovation. At least, however, the champion provides a channel likely to maximize the chances of widespread awareness of the existence of the innovation in environments where it could be applied.

There is also some evidence from Jervis (1975) that involvement of the innovator or inventor has been important to firms developing products based on the new technology. But much more evidence suggests that people who move into new environments more permanently can be important channels for the diffusion of innovations.

C. Movement of People

Several writers (Baker et al., 1967; Johnston and Gibbons, 1975; Myers and Marquis, 1969; Utterback, 1971) have found that the education and experience of the people on hand in the organization considering innovation will have important bearing on the outcome. Langrish et al. (1972, p.79) found that "transfer via person joining the firm" accounted for 20½ of the 102 important ideas from outside the award-winning firms, and commented that:

> the movement of individuals from one job to another appears to be a more efficient mechanism of transfer than pushing ideas through communication networks of the kind traditionally recognized.

In his analysis of 12 links between laboratories building early TEA lasers, Collins (1974) reported that 4 were forged by the long-term involvement of persons on visiting fellowships, on student placements, and other periods of work at the source laboratory.

Shimshoni (1970) found in the instrument industry, in electrical and mechanical engineering, and in electronics, that a very large proportion of innovations were associated with the mobility of technical leaders. He suggested that such movement allows a major reduction in the costs of gaining and using knowledge; that the information carried by the individual may be so constituted as to be readily applicable, in contrast to the form of information in the literature; and that personal interaction adds a dimension of stimulation over and above information transfer. He noted, however, that mobility and entrepreneurship seem to be of small importance where research organization, large-scale teamwork, and costly facilities are important, as in the chemical industry.

That a good deal of movement is likely to take place is suggested by Allen (1977), who noted the high turnover among engineers, which partly negated the effects of proprietary protectionism in industry.

Roberts and Wainer (1968) and Cooper (1971) have described another movement of individuals leading to the introduction of new technology. Many entrepreneurial individuals, having gained knowledge and expertise in a university laboratory or large industrial organization, usually in a field of high technology, have moved out to establish new firms to exploit their ideas.

Schon (1971) coined the term "cultural travellers" to describe the people who move from one sub-system to another, carrying with them technologies which will bring about change. That there has been some recognition at public policy level of the importance of mobility of people in the process of technological innovation is brought out in Section V.

There has, however, been a somewhat surprising lack of emphasis on the rather more obvious importance in the innovation process of the ability of receivers to understand the information in messages reaching them through any channel. This idea, of course, underlines much of the explanation of human preference for informal channels of communication. In the innovations literature, however, lack of ability to understand information is usually discussed as one of the barriers to information flow, and it is the first topic covered in the discussion of those barriers with which this review proceeds.

IV. BARRIERS TO INFORMATION FLOW

Many writers (Allen, 1977; Bierfelder, 1976; Rogers and Shoemaker, 1971; Rubenstein and Ettlie, 1979; Rubenstein et al., 1974; Schon, 1963; Tushman, 1977) have inquired into the gap between existing knowledge and the technology which has been applied, and have attempted to analyze the barriers or impediments to information flow. Some of the barriers, such as understanding, relate to the people involved in innovations and their distance, psychological as well as physical, from each other; others relate to the bureaucratic structures within which people work in organizations; others again relate to the nature of the technology and, in particular, to whether or not adequate economic gain can be derived from its application. Examples of the literature's examination of all three types of barrier are given below.

A. Understanding

In an experimental study, Churchman and Ratoosh (1961) gave groups a problem to solve and also gave them a report containing information on a fairly simple method of making the optimal decisions. Most groups ignored this solution message, and one group which accepted it did not understand it and later veered from it. On this result, Churchman and Ratoosh (1961, p.127) remarked that "the most subtle aspect of implementation lies in the concept of understanding."

Hayward et al. (1976), in a diffusion study focused on potential users' perceptions of an innovation, found that if it is easy to understand it will diffuse more rapidly. Rice and Rogers (1980) have pointed out that potential adopters are active participants in the innovation and diffusion process and that they are struggling to give meaning to the new information as the innovation is applied to the local context.

Appropriate knowledge and skills are obviously important factors in understanding and being able to apply new technology. So are opportunities for informal contact with those most knowledgeable about the technology. But Bierfelder (1976, p.185) has pointed out that the flow of information via interpersonal relationships can be obstructed if the transmitter and receiver have no common language. In this sense, of course, a common language implies much more than speaking the same tongue. Allen (1977) reported that an evaluation of the contribution of external sources of information to high-performing and low-performing R & D teams revealed, surprisingly, an inverse relationship between performance and use of external sources. Further inquiry revealed that there had been frequent use of consultants for very brief periods. Allen explained that the short-term consultants did not share a common viewpoint with the R & D engineers and were, therefore, prone to interpret the problems in different ways.

The findings of studies such as Myers and Marquis (1969) and Gibbons and Johnston (1974) have agreed that much of the information used in resolving other hand, that other likely environments were not susceptible to the innovations because they needed more help in appreciating the relevance of available information. Sayles (1974, p.198) noted that the NASA dissemination of information program, designed to stimulate technological innovation in the non-aerospace sectors of industry, became much more successful when NASA became willing to enter into "more intimate ties" with potential adopters, to assume advisory roles, and to work more closely with other government agencies.

B. Organizational Barriers

Organizations are by their very nature separate from the environments in which they operate. Burns (1969, p.20) has expressed this idea and its consequences for information flow very succinctly:

> it is the institutional framework essential for the development of science, technology and manufacturing industry which interposes immaterial but effective constraints on the transposition of ideas and methods between them.

The boundaries between organizations can hinder the flow of new ideas, and conditions in organizations can create resistance to them. Katz and Allen (1980) have noted that, where the membership of a group of R & D engineers has been relatively stable for several years, the group may begin to develop the attitude that it possesses a monopoly on knowledge in its area of specialization. Its members may tend to separate themselves from external sources of information by communicating with them less frequently. Consequently, new ideas are likely to meet the type of resistance which has been dubbed the "Not Invented Here" syndrome. Langrish et al. (1972) also reported instances of resistance to new ideas and exaggerated attachment to old ideas in the assessment of new technology in firms.

Schon (1971, p.90) has described "the dynamically conservative plenum into which information moves" in modern complex societies. Thus, the process of adoption and diffusion of new technology does not operate independently of the processes of bureaucratic change, with study of which the management literature is replete.

At the very least, anyone seeking to understand technological innovation needs to recognize that, as Schon (1963, p.82) pointed out:

> Resistance to change is not only normal but in some ways even desirable. An organization totally devoid of resistance to change would fly apart at the seams. It *must* be ambivalent about radical technical innovation. It *must* both seek it out and resist it. Because of commitments to existing technology and to forms of social organization associated with it, management *must* act against the eager acceptance of new technical ideas, even good ones. Otherwise the technical organization would be perpetually and fruitlessly shifting gears.

These truths, of course, are inevitably in conflict with the almost universal belief of economists and others that without innovation there can be no prosperity. A positive relationship between innovation and economic development and productivity is widely assumed, and Rogers (1976, p.229) has noticed the "pro-innovation bias" in the literature in relation to technology transfer programs in developing countries. Such bias is also obvious in the innovations literature referring to developed countries, where the fact that the benefits of many technological innovations are not available to all firms in an industry regardless of the information resources at their command is often overlooked.

A few of the studies concerned with innovations have recognized and tried to explore organizational as well as personal variables in the process of innovation. The accessibility of information to organizations, as to individuals, can be analyzed according to the cost of its acquisition to the inquirer. Allen (1977, p.130) described difficulties of communication within an organization where the psychological cost to the inquirer outweighed the advantages of using an internal personal contact for information. Differences in status can be very effective barriers to communication within organizations. Allen (1977) has also conducted experimental studies which demonstrated that access to personal information channels was susceptible to architectural constraints and physical distances within an organization. On the other hand, Collins (1974) found that physical distances between organizations need not constitute a barrier. In investigation of information seeking behavior and communication among laboratories, Collins found that it was the existence or lack of friendship among members in different laboratories, and not national boundaries, which affected whether communication took place.

In general, however, it could be concluded that the innovations literature has not yet achieved adequate assimilation of, or interaction with, the knowledge created by the students of organizational change.

C. Non-Appropriability of Information

As well as difficulties which arise from the interaction of new technology with personal and organizational variables, there is another combination of difficulties which can impede the introduction of new technology. These difficulties arise from the nature of information. Some economists have acknowledged what Newman (1976, p.472) has described as "the traditional problem that the information market must imperfectly allocate resources because information has unconventional properties as a commodity: non-appropriability, increasing returns in use, indivisibility." All these properties of information impinge on technological innovation, but non-appropriability, and the strategies designed to create and preserve property rights in information, are especially relevant to this discussion of barriers.

Let us first, however, take Newman's point (Newman 1976, p.489) that "the analysis of informational phenomena cannot be separated from the analysis of institutional phenomena." Institutions (or "organizations" in the terminology of this review) themselves supply information which Newman (1976, p.477) argued is perceived by them to be of high value for decision-making if the institutional structure is stable, and of low value if the institutional structure is unstable. This economic argument seems to fit nicely with the evidence of empirical studies that use of external sources and channels of information is likely to be greater in industries characterized by rapid technological change. (Cf., Blandin and Brown (1977) and Utterback (1974), discussed in Sections II.C and III.A.)

Newman (1976, p.472) has also pointed out that:

> If individuals are in a position to supply information but are faced with unsatisfactory supply conditions, they will—depending on the costs and benefits of institutional reform—attempt to modify these conditions. They will attempt through the legal system to redefine and extend the conditions pertaining to the ownership and use of information.

Attempts to achieve the latter aim can be seen in the efforts in all large Western countries by publishers and authors of printed and electronic media in recent years to have legislation adjusted and extended to protect their copyrights, in the face of ever more accessible and effective technology for copying information. Such efforts have met resistance from the users of information and their agents, including teachers and librarians, and from firms benefitting from widespread sales of new copying products such as videotape recorders. The interaction between innovative technology and structural change is probably nowhere more readily to be seen than in the publishing and printing industries, and especially in the media conglomerates capable of manufacturing information products in any and every physical format. Their activities form part of what has come to be known as the information sector of the economy.

Studies in the manufacturing sector have included useful insights into the techniques which industrial firms employ in attempts to appropriate information benefits. Von Hippel (1979) studied certain categories of process machinery innovations and produced interesting evidence of the types of innovation likely to be made by suppliers and users of such machinery. He showed the influence in this of "the appropriability of output-embodied innovation benefit" to the different types of firm and suggested that this variable could also be useful in determining the locus of innovation in other environments.

No attempt is made here to review comprehensively the plentiful literature on property rights in information to which Ganz (1980) has offered useful entrée. It is necessary, however, to mention briefly the main ways in which firms seek to appropriate benefits from information. Patents and the associated licenses are the most obvious mechanisms which can be used by inventors, whether individuals or organizations, to gain financial benefit from their innovations. Patents are meant to serve a dual purpose, bestowing rights in return for the disclosure of information about new technology. Potential users, unwilling to pay for the privilege, are in theory restrained by law rather than by lack of knowledge. Where reverse engineering is possible, as the study by Von Hippel (1979) made clear, legal restraint is not necessarily effective. The language of patents has always been notable for its obscurity, and this, coupled with deliberate omissions in description of techniques, can in some processes and products be effective barriers to unlicensed imitation. Bowman (1978, p.82) has noted that reproduction of the innovations described in chemical and pharmaceutical patents can be very difficult.

Patent legislation differs from country to country, for example, in the conditions under which the protection of the patent may be withdrawn if it is not used within a stipulated period. The implications of the law can have effects from the beginning of the innovation process. Maguire and Kench (1981a, p.69) have reported a case in which university researchers refrained from publication of their findings lest any disclosure could jeopardize the granting of a patent. Their lack of disclosure seemed to have increased the climate of scepticism which made later diffusion of the innovation difficult for the patent licensee.

Financial arrangements are also used by firms in the sharing of trade secrets outside the patent system. Langrish et al. (1972) reported that, in 10 percent of the cases where important ideas for later prize-winning innovations came from outside the firm, they came by way of commercial agreements. These included take-overs, sales of know-how, and licensing.

Newman (1976, p.490) has pointed out that institutions have to be reformed in order to alter the appropriability of information benefits, and he has sought to increase "appreciation of the complex links between information, rationality and dynamics" involved in such alterations. The approach adopted by Von Hippel (1979) seems capable of increasing understanding of the process and of the factors which influence decisions by individual companies and particular industries. Legislation and administration of a patent system can be seen as one of several ways in which governments have intervened to affect technological innovation in society generally. Other government policies and practices affecting innovation are discussed in the next Section of this review.

V. THE ROLE OF GOVERNMENT

A. Categories of Intervention

Governments of many countries have endeavored to encourage technological innovation which they consider vital to economic growth. Allen et al. (1978) offer a useful classification of the mechanisms by which government action can influence technological innovation. They suggest that government intervention can be divided into initiating, sustaining, and restructuring mechanisms.

1. Initiating mechanisms

Governments have offered a variety of incentives to firms to encourage innovation, through R & D investment subsidies, taxation rebates, technical and marketing advisory services, and sharing of patent rights. Roberts and Frohman

(1978, p.37) have remarked of the programs of four large United States Federal government agencies that:

> all these governmental programs start to encourage utilization of research only after the research and development results have been generated. Yet the most effective industrial approaches to increased research utilization begin much earlier in the innovation process—as far back as when ideas are generated and selected for development.

In reports by both Allen et al. (1978) and Rubenstein et al. (1977) of studies in European countries and Japan, the conclusion was reached that government action to initiate innovation was perceived by industrial managers as comparatively irrelevant.

Johnston (1976, p.163) has suggested that government policy is typically one of "backing losers." Johnston's remarks were made in the framework of United Kingdom government policy, but this criticism has also been made more generally. Johnston (1976, p.163) has argued that instead of "attempting to augment the low level of research in an industry, or offering incentives for rationalization," governments might better "offer specific support for 'winners,' i.e. industries with a record of effective technological growth, to diversify their capabilities where possible into traditional and ailing market areas."

2. Sustaining mechanisms

Allen et al. (1978) classified the sustaining mechanisms used by governments as those influencing the availability, utilization, and mobility of managerial and technical manpower; those assisting institutions with regard to the generation and utilization of technical knowledge; and those increasing the transfer of technical knowledge between institutions.

Allen et al. (1978) identified attempts to increase the transfer of technical knowledge as the predominant sustaining activity of governments. With this end in view, governments maintain systems for the examination and awarding of patents. But governments also concern themselves with some of the other mechanisms which affect innovative capabilities of industry. National inquiries have been held into engineering education (such as that which resulted in the Finniston Report for the United Kingdom) and into the mobility of people among the different environments on which technological innovation impinges (such as in the inquiry into interaction between government, academic, and industrial research and development activities, held by the Australian Science and Technology Council at the behest of the Federal government). These activities could suggest that some of the advice from the innovations literature, discussed in Section III, has been followed. At least, recognition seems to have increased at policy level that education is an important factor in applying new technology and that much of its spread is influenced by the movement of people.

Some governments have extended information services to include the provision of consultants to go to individual firms to help solve problems. The Technical Information Service of the Canadian National Research Council is one such service. Other governments, however, have shown marked tendency not to sustain such active and intimate involvement of their personnel. The history of both the Industrial Liaison Service in the United Kingdom and some of the schemes once funded under the U.S. Technical Services Act 1965 bear this out. As Hill (1980) has pointed out, passive systems are much cheaper to operate and maintain than active systems with high labor costs.

Both theory and practice support the contention that effective communication systems are those in which both the senders and receivers of information are active participants in the process. The program usually held up as a model for the achievement of technology transfer is that of the Extension Service of the United States Department of Agriculture (which is now part of the Department's Science and Education Administration). Farmers become users of the technology communicated to them by county agents and extension specialists. It also seems necessary to note that, according to Feller's sources (Feller, 1979, p.306), the U.S.D.A. spent $200m on this program in FY 1975 whereas the technology transfer programs of all other U.S. Federal agencies in that year commanded $31m.

Section IV.A has noted the report by Sayles (1974) that the effectiveness of NASA's program had been enhanced by that agency's willingness to assume "more intimate ties" with industry and with other government agencies. Roberts and Frohman (1978, pp. 36–37) also listed NASA, along with the U.S. Atomic Energy Commission, in reporting that "at least two Federal agencies have realized that effective industrial diffusion of their research results requires a strong coupling activity that attempts to match available technology to the prospective user's needs." That governments have a role in affecting such coupling of all technological information with the needs of all users has been suggested by Johnston (1976) and by Nelson and Winter (1977), whose arguments seem more appropriate to the general discussion of policy making in Part B of this Section. Let it suffice here to note that the costs involved in ventures like the U.S.D.A. program make it inevitable that policy thinking should turn towards the creation of mechanisms likely to create conditions in industry conducive to effective communication of information needed for innovation, rather than have government agencies provide active information and advisory services directly to clients in industry.

3. Restructuring mechanisms

Into the restructuring category come government regulatory activities, such as the promulgation of standards and changes in legislation or in the bases for calculation of taxation. They may affect, whether by design or accident, the necessity for, and capacity of, industry to adopt innovative technology. In the traditional distrust of government which prevails in industry, it is not surprising that firms usually perceive government influence on innovation as negative rather than positive. Some evidence in the literature suggests that this is not necessarily so. Allen et al. (1978) found that government regulatory constraints were more likely than not to be found in association with successful projects. Rubenstein and Ettlie (1979) reported in their study of innovation among suppliers to automobile manufacturers that a law or regulation concerning safety, the environment, or energy conservation was acknowledged as a stimulus to development or adoption of an innovation in 14 cases and seen as a barrier to innovation in 15 cases. Rubenstein and Ettlie (1979), as well as Tobin (1978) and Grabowski and Vernon (1979), have noted that, if the information reaching a firm reveals a regulatory agency's inconsistencies or the likelihood of introduction of new regulations, the uncertainty so generated will adversely affect innovations. It seems then that government regulation need constitute a barrier to innovation only when communication with industry is poor and regulations appear to be made without cognizance of likely effects in industry. Here again, though, we meet the uncertainty which surrounds judgments about the likely effects of technological innovations.

B. Bases for Policy

Nelson and Winter (1977, p.47) have pointed out that "explicit recognition of uncertainty is important in thinking about policy." Evidence has been quoted above to indicate that at least some government agencies have forsaken the certainty that new technology will be applied because they have published information which describes it. There remain, however, frequent intimations in the policy statements of politicians and of government bodies shaping science and technology policy that mechanistic models of information transfer have not been abandoned. Mowery and Rosenberg (1979) have argued strongly against the certainty embodied in the policies of some governments that "demand-pull" is what must be heeded in attempts to encourage innovation. They seem to have suggested (Mowery and Rosenberg, 1979, p.150) that government policy faces fewer problems in encouraging the diffusion of innovations than in provoking their initial adoption, since "encouragement of the diffusion of innovations . . . seems to be an area in which one can indeed rely upon the more conventional market incentives designed to produce a demand-pull for a proven innovation."

Nelson and Winter (1977, p.73) have addressed policy issues related to the dilemma about the relationship of science to technology, and identify as a key question "to what extent are the directions in which science advances inevitable and to what extent can these be molded by conscious policy?" In partial answer, Nelson and Winter continued:

It is apparent that the evolution of basic scientific understanding has a certain logic, and momentum, of its own. To try to guide that evolution with any precision or to believe that improvements of fundamental understanding can be won simply because the payoffs are high, is foolishness. However, the fields of aerodynamics and applied thermodynamics did not evolve as rapidly and fruitfully as they did merely because they were "ripe" and groups of academics were interested in them. Rather, they were carefully nurtured and funds and institutions provided for their development.

Researchers into technological innovation frequently recommend nurturing policies to governments, as Mowery and Rosenberg (1979, p.149) put it, "directed toward increasing both the frequency and the intimacy of interactions" among all the groups involved in the process. Johnston (1976) stressed the importance of the technological infrastructure in the " 'transfer' model for radical innovations" which he proposed. He remarked (Johnston 1976, p.162) that "for a technologically innovatory industry, one of the important factors determining their rate of advance is the existence of a fully developed and efficient technological infrastructure into which the majority of companies are coupled." Johnston (1976, p.164) saw value in specific government action to maintain and develop appropriate technological infrastructures.

Innovations research has so far proved capable of offering broad policy guidelines to governments; it is still a long way from producing certain prescriptions, because, as Mowery and Rosenberg (1979, p.149) have acknowledged, "we do not yet understand the characteristics of the innovation process sufficiently well, nor do we possess the necessary knowledge base in certain areas of substantial social utility."

Some of the assumptions, concepts, and measurements of innovation research which have affected the strength of its knowledge base and the rate of its accumulation are addressed in the final section of this review.

VI. CONCLUSIONS

A. Assumptions, Concepts, and Measurements

This review promised and has delivered ample evidence of the lack of synthesis in the innovations literature. Some of the causes of lack of internal consistency are explored a little further here, and some of the effects of lack of integration of insights from related research fields are explored in the next part of this Section.

1. The information concept

Nowhere is the lack of consensus on important concepts in the innovations literature more obvious than in the concept of information. Problems of formal definition were addressed in Section I.B, and Arrow (1962, p.615) has pointed to "enormous difficulties in defining in any sharp way an item of information and differentiating it from other similar sounding items." The operational definitions of information used in innovation studies indicate that this warning has not been sufficiently heeded. Utterback (1971, p.124) defined information as "discrete pieces of technical information that had an important effect on the initiation or on the course of a development." Gibbons and Johnston (1974, p.225) justified their division of information into pieces as follows:

> In order to describe the characteristics of this information (that which contributed to the resolution of technical problems) we had to isolate "units" of information. While it was clear from the outset that the information would not fall readily into comparable and internally homogenous units of equal "size," nevertheless in practice it was found possible to sub-divide information into units on the basis of a general coherence in terms of content and source.

Myers and Marquis (1969) not only made the judgement that some pieces of information were more important than others but allowed only one "major information input" to each innovation. They were, however, willing to admit inputs on non-technical information. Gibbons and Johnston (1974) counted only technical information inputs. Langrish et al. (1972) referred to "important ideas" reaching firms.

While some innovations researchers have had a disconcerting habit of referring to "units" of information, they have contented themselves with epithets such as "important" and "major" to measure the importance of elements of information. But studies tend to have assumed that respondents shared the frame of reference of their inquirers, which is at odds with the obvious fact that inquirers do not share each other's. For example, Gibbons and Johnston (1974) classed handbooks in firms as external sources of information, whereas Ettlie (1976) classed technical manuals held in the firm as internal sources. Langrish et al. (1972, p.7) noted that data gathered from different people in a firm about origins of an innovation were not necessarily the same. At the very least, these problems with the concept of information must raise questions on the findings of many studies relating to information inputs. Mowery and Rosenberg (1979) have raised many more.

Lamberton (1971, p.10), an economist, has suggested that the concept of a "bit" of information can be dangerous, because it can suggest a quantitative approach to what is a qualitative problem. A similar warning could be applied to references to "units" of information. The tendency of economists, however, has been rather to ignore, than to attempt to quantify, elements of information. Newman (1976) has pointed out that the widespread assumptions in economic models about the market's perfect knowledge of, and instant and costless access to, information need to be abandoned.

The doubts and problems which surround the concept of information help explain why the understanding of technology has come to be based on the assumption Burns (1969, p.13) identified, and why his criticism of this basis is valid. Burns complained of:

the basic assumption of technology as an assemblage of pieces of information which can be extracted or expelled from one sector of organized creativity and transferred to another to produce different outputs.

2. Measurement of effectiveness

Problems of measurement and enumeration of information inputs also apply, of course, in assessment of the potential value of information, and of the impact of information on technological innovation. If we work from the assumption underlying that about technology, criticized by Burns above, we are led readily to the belief that if information is available it will be used, and that the availability of information creates understanding. The further observation that, even if understood, information is not necessarily perceived as relevant, takes us back to arguments already covered in Sections II.C.1 and IV.B.

In assessment of the effectiveness of information in technological innovations, it is surprising that there has been so little emphasis on unsuccessful attempts to innovate. Project SAPPHO (1972), remarkable for its equal emphasis on successful and unsuccessful innovations, revealed interesting evidence of instability in the measures apparently important to success. "Coupling with technological and scientific community" was superior in the more innovative of 13 of the 29 pairs of firms SAPPHO examined, equal in 15 of them, and in one pair the "failure" rated higher than the "success" in the pair. It is worthy of remark that the SAPPHO researchers were far more cautious in their conclusions than many who have considered only successful innovations. But other questions also quickly arise related to measurement of the effectiveness of the innovation process itself. To address them requires some examination of the innovation concept.

3. The innovation concept

The concept of innovation in the literature has often not been adequate to support any but superficial inquiry into the process. Freeman (1977, p.230) noted that some writers had begun to query the realism of attempting to distinguish and measure discrete units of technological change. Layton (1977, p.202) found it necessary to point out that:

innovations are themselves rather arbitrary entities, which may be useful for some purposes but not all. Innovations are not uniform, atomistic units. One innovation may represent only a minor modification of another.

Mechanistic thinking about the complex process of technological innovation is of much greater significance than the inconsistencies in terminology discussed in

Section I.B. Mowery and Rosenberg (1979, p.144) have severely criticized studies which "adopt a 'black-box' explanation of the innovation process: inputs in, innovations out." Such thinking is most readily detectable in TRACES (1968), Battelle (1973), and HINDSIGHT (1969). Definition of the "events" they studied is sufficient to account for the differences in their results. Mowery and Rosenberg (1979, p.111), however, have also criticized artificial division of the innovation process into, for example, "recognition" and "problem-solving" phases. They have contended that such stages cannot be clearly distinguished, as the entire innovation process is one of loosely-directed search for information leading to problem-solving.

While there has been widespread acknowledgment in the literature that the process of innovation is both complex and iterative, this is still not universally reflected in the design of empirical studies. To the exaggerated pursuit of linearity may be added the fact that the tendency to regard technical data as the only type critical to the innovation process has not been eradicated.

4. Summary

Mowery and Rosenberg (1979, p.146) have summarized their arguments on the innovation process thus:

> The innovation process surely comprises an area of economic behavior in which uncertainty and complexity are absolutely central characteristics of the environment; empirical approaches to the problem must therefore take far greater cognizance of the processes which underlie the output of innovations. Rather than focussing exclusively upon innovational outputs at widely separated times, a more fruitful approach might be that of tracing the growth and evolution of a given organizational form involved in the research and innovation processes, in an effort to provide a somewhat deeper analysis of the evolution of the information flows and processes which are responsible for success (or failure) in the production of innovations over a period of time; changing the unit of analysis in this manner might yield a richer set of conclusions and studies than is currently the case.

This passage brings into sharp focus the importance of organizational variables in the innovation process, but it may be remarked that underlying the innovation process is a communication process, and that the motives of economic behavior are not readily separable from the totality of human behavior. Innovation research may, therefore, find nourishment not only in the study of organizations but also in communications studies and in studies of information use.

B. Connections with Related Research

1. Communications research

Creighton and Jolly (1981) have recognized that:

> A basic principle underlying the movement of knowledge into use is that all parties involved are both generators and users of information and play a part in the effectiveness of knowledge movement.

Such recognition, welcome in the innovations literature, would now seem old hat in the communications literature. In a fine analytical review of communication gaps and inequities, Dervin (1980, pp.96–97) has traced the gradual abandonment by communications researchers of the concept of "information as being able to drop into receivers like bricks into buckets," through a change from attempting to predict information use "as a straightforward, unchanging, mechanistic process to a process that is now beginning to be seen as occurring at specific points in time, space, and as changing over time and space." Dervin (1980, p.102) stated that progress had been made in synthesis of the observations of empirical research into communication failures by researchers willing to give "full recognition of the need for user-constructed perceptions of situations and more fundamentally full recognition of and allegiance to the ideas of user-constructed information."

Dervin (1980, p.104) has also claimed that "for the first time hypotheses are emerging, predicting the conditions of information use rather than assuming it will be used and then trying to comprehend why it isn't."

The separation of communications research from innovations research is indicated by the fact that only the names of Ronald G. Havelock and Everett M. Rogers appear in both Dervin's bibliography and that appended to this review. Dervin's review addressed the communication of all types of socially important information to citizens in developed and developing countries, often through the mass media. Both her theoretical arguments and the problems of the innovations literature identified in this review make it impossible to dismiss her analysis as inapplicable to research on the adoption and diffusion of technological innovation.

2. Information use studies

"Information use studies" is an imprecise term used to refer to a disparate collection of literature. Pursued from as many different disciplinary bases as innovations research, information use studies have concentrated on identifying the characteristics of various groups as information users. Some of these studies have focused on the professions; others have covered specialties within professions. Some have looked at the members of particular communities and at particular industries and types of firms. Some have looked at the users of a particular information service, whether a library, type of library, or an indexing or abstracting service. The purpose of many of the studies has been to improve information services generally to a group or to improve a particular information service.

The earliest studies tended to be of scientists and engineers, while later studies have spread to cover virtually every profession. A useful guide to the evolution of these studies has been provided by Crawford (1978).

Like innovations research, information use studies have suffered from a weak basis in theory. The principle of least effort enunciated by Zipf (1949) has been used to explain information use, embellished with insights on the operation generally of the accessibility factor in determining use of information channels.

Rosenberg (1967), in a useful empirical study of scientific organizations in industry and government, has demonstrated that for their professional members too, the accessibility of information channels is a more important determinant of use than the quality of the information carried.

Some cognizance has been taken by innovations researchers of information use studies of engineers and scientists, to which indeed some of the innovations researchers have contributed. T. J. Allen is one of these. But it is readily apparent that information use studies have not progressed any further than innovations research in explaining the behavior of their subjects. These studies have, however, tried to come to grips with distinctions between information needs, information wants, and information demands. In this they may be said to have progressed a little further than some of the discussion of needs/means in the innovations literature.

But the useful insights which information use studies seem capable of offering to innovations research lie in understanding the relationships between formal and informal channels of information, and of the interaction between sources and channels. Line (1980, p.264), who has been responsible for large studies on information requirements and the design of information services in the social sciences, has pointed out that:

> Alongside the informal system, and behind it in the sense that personal information services may be largely based on formal secondary sources, is the formal system. . . . Indeed there are limits to how far the informal system can be developed or improved without introducing some formality, which might thereby deprive it of some of its special and attractive features.

At the same time, information use studies, which are increasingly looking at the introduction and use of new services based on innovative information processing technology, could be about to enter innovations research territory without necessarily being aware of what has already been learned there. It could also be suggested that the quality of research emanating mainly from those who design and manage information services could be enhanced by the greater awareness of economic and especially of market factors, which is found in the literature on technological innovations.

C. The State of Knowledge

The literature on the adoption and diffusion of technological innovation has not produced a critical mass of data which is about to impel new paradigms. The literature has, however, amassed much useful data from which sensible guidelines can be extracted for all involved in the innovation process, including managers and policy-makers in research institutions, industry, and government. Innovations researchers should of course heed their own insights and exploit opportunities for personal involvement to ensure that the innovations in systems and organizations which they propose have maximum chances of being adopted.

The innovations literature has reached a stage where it is capable of self-criticism and thus capable of resolving some of its own anomalies. There are also avenues which remain largely unexplored. There appears, for example, to have been little formal study so far of the contribution made to the innovation process by publicity and public relations sections of research institutes, universities, and research companies.

It seems most unlikely that any of the models of the innovation process proposed by individual researchers will gain widespread acceptance. Any breakthrough to stronger theoretical positions seems rather to depend on the widespread acknowledgment by innovations researchers of the relevance of the deeper insights into the nature of information and of human communication offered by communications researchers, and into the dynamics of organizational behavior offered by management scientists. It seems not unduly pessimistic to remark that most researchers have not yet fully taken into account the complexities and uncertainties of the innovation process identified by Schon (1967).

Conditions in the innovations research business ought to be buoyant. Never has the choice and application of effective and appropriate technology been more obviously important to human welfare. Yet, of all people, innovations researchers ought to be aware that returns from investment in research are very difficult to demonstrate. In confronting this problem, they are addressing the problems not only of all researchers but of all human societies.

REFERENCES

Allen, T. J. (1966). Performance of information channels in the transfer of technology. *Industrial Management Review 8*, 87–98.

Allen, T. J. (1967). Communications in the research and development laboratory. *Technology Review 70* (No. 1), 31–37.

Allen, T. J. (1975). ''Transferring Technology to the Firm: Report of a Pilot Study in Irish Industry. Cambridge, Massachusetts: Alfred P. Sloan School of Management, Massachusetts Institute of Technology. (Working Paper No. 815–75.)

Allen, T. J. (1977). ''Managing the Flow of Technology: Technology Transfer and the Dissemination of Technological Information within the R & D Organization.'' Cambridge, Massachusetts: MIT Press.

Allen, T. J., Utterback, J. M., Sirbu, A. M., Ashford, N. A., and Hollomon, J. H. (1978). Government influence on the process of innovation in Europe and Japan. *Research Policy 1*, 124–149.

Arrow, K. J. (1962). Economic welfare and the allocation of resources for invention. *In* National Bureau of Economic Research, ''The Rate and Direction of Inventive Activity: Economic and Social Factors,'' pp. 609–626. Princeton, New Jersey: Princeton University Press.

Baker, N. R., Siegman, J., and Rubenstein, A. H. (1967). The effects of perceived needs and means on the generation of ideas for industrial research and development projects. *IEEE Transactions on Engineering Management EM-14*, 156–163.

Battelle Memorial Institute. (1973). "Interactions of Science and Technology in the Innovative Process: Some Case Studies." Columbus, Ohio: Battelle Memorial Institute. (Final Report on Contract NSF-C 667.)

Beer, S. (1970). Managing modern complexity. In "The Management of Information and Knowledge: A Compilation of Papers Prepared for the Eleventh Meeting of the Panel on Science and Technology," pp. 41–62. Washington, D.C.: Committee on Science and Astronautics, U.S. House of Representatives.

Bierfelder, W. (1976). Innovation in acceptable doses: Problems of supplementing educational technology innovations in firms. R & D Management 6, 183–187.

Blandin, J. S., and Brown, W. B. (1977). Uncertainty and management's search for information. IEEE Transactions on Engineering Management, EM-24, 114–119.

Bowman, W. H. (1978). Importance of patents and information services to research workers. Journal of Chemical Information and Computer Sciences 18, 81–82.

Burns, T. (1969). Models, images and myths. In W. H. Gruber, and D. G. Marquis (Eds.), "Factors in the Transfer of Technology," pp. 3–23. Cambridge, Massachusetts: MIT Press.

Carter, C. F., and Williams, B. R. (1957). "Industry and Technical Progress: Factors Governing the Speed of Application of Science." London: Oxford University Press.

Churchman, C. W., and Ratoosh, P. (1961). Innovation in group behavior. In "Proceedings of the Second International Conference on Operational Research," pp. 122–127. London: English Universities Press.

Collins, H. M. (1974). The TEA set: Tacit knowledge and scientific networks. Science Studies 4, 165–186.

Cooper, A. C. (1971). Spin-offs and technical entrepreneurship. IEEE Transactions on Engineering Management EM-18, 2–6.

Crawford, S. (1978). Information needs and uses. Annual Review of Information Science and Technology 13, 61–81.

Creighton, J. W., and Jolly, J. A. (1981). The linker role in innovation. (Paper presented at the Conference on Learning Technology for the 80's, Orlando, Florida, Society for Applied Learning Technology, Warrenton, Virginia.)

Czepiel, J. A. (1974). Word-of-mouth processes in the diffusion of a major technological innovation. Journal of Marketing Research 11, 172–180.

Davies, S. (1979). "The Diffusion of Process Innovations." Cambridge, England: Cambridge University Press.

Dervin, B. (1980). Communication gaps and inequities: Moving toward a reconceptualization. Progress in Communication Sciences 2, 73–111.

Ettlie, J. E. (1976). The timing and sources of information for the adoption and implementation of product innovations. IEEE Transactions on Engineering Management EM-23, 62–68.

Evans, D. G., Higgins, R. S., and Shedden, I. W. (1972). Dewatering Victorian brown coal—an innovative idea. In "Development and Innovation for Australian Process Industries: Papers of the Australian Chemical Engineering Conference," pp. 56–60. Newcastle, New South Wales: The Conference Committee.

Feller, I. (1979). Three coigns on diffusion research. Knowledge: Creation, Diffusion, Utilization 1, 293–312.

Freeman, C. (1974). "The Economics of Industrial Innovation." Harmondsworth, England: Penguin Books.

Freeman, C. (1977). Economics of research and development. In I. Spiegel-Rosing and D. de S. Price (Eds.), "Science, Technology and Society: A Cross-Disciplinary Perspective," pp. 223–275. London: Sage.

Ganz, C. (1980). Linkages between knowledge creation, diffusion, and utilization. Knowledge: Creation, Diffusion, Utilization 1, 591–612.

Gibbons, M., and Johnston, R. D. (1972). "The Interaction of Science and Technology." (Final Report of a Study Carried Out for the Economic Benefits Working Group of the Council for Scientific Policy.)

Gibbons, M., and Johnston, R. D. (1974). The roles of science in technological innovation. *Research Policy 3*, 220–242.

Grabowski, H. G., and Vernon, J. M. (1979). "The Impact of Regulation on Industrial Innovation." Washington, D.C.: National Academy of Sciences.

Havelock, R. G., with Guskin, A., Frohman, M., Havelock, M., Hill, M., and Huber, J. (1969). "Planning for Innovation through Dissemination and Utilization of Knowledge." (Report from Center for Research on Utilization of Scientific Knowledge, University of Michigan, Ann Arbor, Michigan.)

Hayward, G., Allen, D. H., and Masterson, J. (1976). Characteristics and diffusion of technological innovations. *R & D Management 1, 15–24.*

Hill, C., and Roessner, J. D. (1980). "Government Policy, Technological Innovation and Alternative Energy." (Final Report of the Innovation Task Force, SERI Solar/Conservation Project.)

Holland, W. E. (1972). Characteristics of individuals with high information potential in government research and development organizations. *IEEE Transactions on Engineering Management EM-19*, 38–44.

Holt, K. (1978). Information inputs to new product planning and development. *Research Policy 7*, 342–360.

Jervis, P. (1975). Innovation and technology transfer—the roles and characteristics of individuals. *IEEE Transactions on Engineering Management EM-22*, 19–27.

Johnston, R. (1976). Government policy for technology transfer: An instrument for industrial progress. *R & D Management 6*, 159–164.

Johnston, R., and Gibbons, M. (1975). Characteristics of information usage in technological innovation. *IEEE Transactions on Engineering Management EM-22*, 27–34.

Katz, R., and Allen, T. J. (1980). "An Empirical Test of the Not Invented Here (NIH) Syndrome: A Look at the Performance, Tenure, and Communication Patterns of 50 R & D Project Groups." Cambridge, Massachusetts: Alfred P. Sloan School of Management, Massachusetts Institute of Technology. (Working Paper No. 1114-80.)

Kelly, P., and Kranzberg, M. (1975). "Technological Innovation: a Critical Review of Current Knowledge" Vol. 1, "The Ecology of Innovation." Atlanta, Georgia: Advanced Technology and Science Studies Group, Georgia Tech.

Kolm, J. E. (1978). Innovation in Australian industry. *In* "The Resources Challenge: Technological Thrust, Social Impact," pp. 322–330. Surfers Paradise, Queensland: The Conference Committee. (Papers of the Sixth National Chemical Engineering Conference.)

Kolm, J. E. (1979). Science and technology transfer to Australia; benefits costs and problems—the chemical industry. *In* A. T. A. Healy (Ed.) "Science and Technology for what Purpose? An Australian Perspective." Canberra, Australia: Australian Academy of Science.

Lamberton, D. M. (Ed.), (1971). "Economics of Information and Knowledge: Selected Readings," Harmondsworth, England: Penguin.

Langrish, J., Gibbons, M., Evans, W. G., and Jevons, F. R. (1972). "Wealth from Knowledge: Studies of Innovations in Industry." London: Macmillan.

Layton, E. (1977). Conditions of technological development. *In* I. Spiegel-Rosing and D. de S. Price (Eds.), "Science, Technology and Society: A Cross-Disciplinary Perspective," pp. 197–222. London: Sage.

Lazarsfeld, P. F., Berelson, B., and Goudet, H. (1944). "The People's Choice: How the Voter Makes up His Mind in a Presidential Campaign." New York: Columbia University Press.

Line, M. (1980). Secondary sources in the social sciences: The need for improvement and the role of librarians. *Behavioral and Social Sciences Librarian 1*, 263–273.

Machlup, F. (1962). "The Production and Distribution of Knowledge in the United States." Princeton, New Jersey: Princeton University Press.

Maguire, C., and Kench, R. (1974). "Information and the Small Manufacturer: Report of a Survey of the Information Needs of Small Manufacturers in New South Wales." Kensington, New South Wales: University of New South Wales.

Maguire, C., and Kench, R. (1981a). "The Diffusion to Industry of University Research: A Study of Two Projects at the University of New South Wales." Kensington, New South Wales: School of Librarianship, University of New South Wales.

Maguire, C., and Kench, R. (1981b). The role of publication in the dissemination of applied research at Australian universities. *Journal of Research Communication Studies 2*, 219–235.

Maguire, C., and Kench, R. (1981c). "Sources of Ideas for Applied University Research and Their Effect on the Application of Findings in Australian Industry." Unpublished.

Mansfield, E. (1968). "Industrial Research and Technological Innovation: An Econometric Analysis." New York: W. W. Norton.

Marquis, D. G., and Allen, T. J. (1966). Communication patterns in applied technology. *American Psychologist 21*, 1052–1060.

Menzel, H. (1967). Planning the consequences of unplanned action in scientific communication. *In* A. de Reuck and J. Knight (Eds.), "Communication in Science: Documentation and Automation," pp. 57–71. London: J. & A. Churchill.

Mowery, D., and Rosenberg, N. (1979). The influence of market demand upon innovation: A critical review of some recent empirical studies. *Research Policy 8*, 102–153.

Myers, S., and Marquis, D. G. (1969). "Successful Industrial Innovations: A Study of Factors Underlying Innovation in Selected Firms." Washington, D.C.: U.S. Government Printing Office. (NSF69-17; GPO 1969 0-354-703.)

Nelson, R. R., and Winter, S. G. (1977). In search of useful theory of innovation. *Research Policy 6*, 36–76.

Newman, G. (1976). An institutional perspective on information. *International Social Science Journal 28*, 466–492.

Ozanne, U. B., and Churchill, G. A. (1971). Five dimensions of the industrial adoption process. *Journal of Marketing Research 8*, 322–328.

Pavitt, K., and Walker, W. (1976). Government policies towards industrial innovation: A review. *Research Policy 5*, 11–97.

Pelz, D. C., and Andrews, F. M. (1966). "Scientists in Organizations: Productive Climates for Research and Development." New York: John Wiley.

Persson, O. (1981). Critical comments on the gatekeeper concept in science and technology. *R & D Management 11*, 37–40.

Porat, M. (1977). "The Information Economy: Definition and Measurement." 9 vols. Washington, D.C.: U.S. Department of Commerce. (Office of Telecommunications Special Publication 77–12.)

Price, D. J. deS. (1967). Research on research. *In* D. L. Arm (Ed.), "Journeys in Science: Small Steps—Great Strides," pp. 1–21. Albuquerque, New Mexico: University of New Mexico Press.

Project HINDSIGHT. (1969). (Final report of Project HINDSIGHT. Office of the Director of Defense Research and Engineering, Washington, D.C.)

"Project Sappho: A Study of Success and Failure in Innovation." (1972). Sponsored by the Science Research Council and carried out at the Science Policy Research Unit, University of Sussex, by a team consisting of B. Achilladelis, P. Jervis, and A. Robertson, with contributions from R. Curnow, C. Freeman, J. Fuller, and A. Horsley. 2 vols.

Rice, R. E., and Rogers, E. M. (1980). Reinvention in the innovation process. *Knowledge: Creation, Diffusion, Utilization 1*, 499–514.

Roberts, E. B., and Frohman, A. L. (1978). How federal agencies approach research utilization. *Technology Review 80* (No. 5), 33–39.

Roberts, E. B., and Peters, D. H. (1981). Commercial innovation from university faculty. *Research Policy 10*, 108–126.

Roberts, E. B., and Wainer, H. A. (1968). New enterprises on Route 128. *Science Journal 4* (No. 2), 78–83.

Rogers, E. M. (1962). "Diffusion of Innovations." New York: Free Press.

Rogers, E. M. (1976). Communication and development; the passing of the dominant paradigm. *Communication Research 3*, 213–240.

Rogers, E. M., and Shoemaker, F. F. (1971). "Communication of Innovations: a Cross-Cultural Approach." New York: Free Press.

Rogers, E. M., Williams, L., and West, R. B. (1977). "Bibliography of the Diffusion of Innovations." Monticello, Illinois: Council of Planning Librarians. (Exchange Bibliography 1420–1422.)

Rosenberg, N. (1972). Factors affecting the diffusion of technology. *Explorations in Economic History 10*, 3–33.

Rosenberg, V. (1967). Factors affecting the preferences of industrial personnel for information gathering methods. *Information Storage and Retrieval 3*, 119–127.

Rosenbloom, R. S., and Wolek, F. W. (1970). "Technology and Information Transfer: A Survey of Practice in Industrial Organizations." Boston, Massachusetts: Division of Research, Graduate School of Business Administration, Harvard University.

Rothwell, R., and Robertson, A. B. (1973). The role of communications in technological innovation. *Research Policy 2*, 204–225.

Rubenstein, A. H. (1964). Organizational factors affecting research and development decision-making in large decentralized companies. *Management Science 10*, 618–634.

Rubenstein, A. H., and Ettlie, J. E. (1979). Innovation among suppliers to automobile manufacturers: An exploratory study of barriers and facilitators. *R & D Management 9*, 65–76.

Rubenstein, A. H., Buel, W. D., Kegan, D. L., Moore, E. A., Moor, W. C., Rath, G. J., Thompson, C. W. N., Trueswell, R. W., and Werner, D. J. (1970). Explorations on the information-seeking style of researchers. *In* C. E. Nelson and D. K. Pollock (Eds.), "Communication Among Scientists and Engineers," pp. 209–231. Lexington, Massachusetts: D. C. Heath.

Rubenstein, A. H., Chakrabarti, A. K., and O'Keefe, D. (1974). "Final Technical Report on Field Studies of the Technological Innovation Process: Executive Summary." Evanston, Illinois: Program of Research on the Management of Research and Development, Department of Industrial Engineering and Management Sciences, Technological Institute, Northwestern University. (NSF Grant DA 39470.)

Rubenstein, A. H., Douds, C. F., Geschka, H., Kawase, T., Miller, J. P., Saintpaul, R., and Watkins, D. (1977). Management perceptions of government incentives to technological innovation in England, France, West Germany, and Japan. *Research Policy 6*, 324–357.

Sayles, L. R. (1974). The innovation process: An organizational analysis. *Journal of Management Studies 11*, 190–204.

Schon, D. A. (1963). Champions for radical new inventions. *Harvard Business Review 41* (No. 2), 77–86.

Schon, D. A. (1967). "Technology and Change: The New Heraclitus." New York: Pergamon.

Schon, D. A. (1971). "Beyond the Stable State: Public and Private Learning in a Changing Society." London: Temple Smith.

Schuchman, H. L. (1981). "Information Transfer in Engineering." Glastonbury, Connecticut: The Futures Group.

Shimshoni, D. (1970). The mobile scientist in the American instrument industry. *Minerva 8*, 59–89.

Tobin, R. J. (1978). Governmental efforts to develop and diffuse innovative pollution control equipment. *In* E. T. White, P. Hetherington, and B. R. Thiele (Eds.), "Clean Air - the Continuing Challenge." Ann Arbor, Michigan: Ann Arbor Science Publishers. (Proceedings of the International Clean Air Conference.)

"TRACES: Technology in Retrospect and Critical Events in Science." (1968). 2 vols. Chicago, Illinois, Illinois Institute of Technology Research Institute.

Tushman, M. L. (1977). Special boundary roles in the innovation process. *Administrative Science Quarterly 22*, 587–605.

Tushman, M. L., and Katz, R. (1980). External communication and project performance: An investigation into the role of gatekeepers. *Management Science 26,* 1071–1085.

Utterback, J. M. (1971). The process of innovation: A study of the origination and development of ideas for new scientific instruments. *IEEE Transactions on Engineering Management EM-18,* 124–131.

Utterback, J. M. (1974). Innovation in industry and the diffusion of technology. *Science 183,* 620–626.

Utterback, J. M., Allen, T. J., Hollomon, J. H., and Sirbu, M. A. (1976). The process of innovation in five industries in Europe and Japan. *IEEE Transactions on Engineering Management EM-23,* 3–9.

Von Hippel, E. (1976). The dominant role of users in the scientific instrument innovation process. *Research Policy 5,* 212–239.

Von Hippel, E. (1977). The dominant role of the user in semiconductor and electronic subassembly process innovation.*IEEE Transactions on Engineering Management EM-24,* 60–71.

Von Hippel, E. (1979). "Appropriability of Innovation Benefit as a Predictor of the Functional Locus of Innovation." Cambridge, Massachusetts: Alfred P. Sloan School of Management, Massachusetts Institute of Technology. (Working Paper No. 1084-79 (short form).)

Warner, K. E. (1974). The need for some innovative concepts of innovation: An examination of research on the diffusion of innovations. *Policy Sciences 5,* 433–451.

Wolek, F. W. (1970). The complexity of messages in science and engineering: An influence on patterns of communication. *In* C. E. Nelson and D. K. Pollock (Eds.), "Communication Among Scientists and Engineers," pp. 233–265. Lexington, Massachusetts: D. C. Heath.

Wolek, F. W., and Griffith, B. C. (1974). Policy and informal communications in applied science and technology. *Science Studies 4,* 411–420.

Zaltman, G., Duncan, R., and Holbeck, J. (1973). "Innovations and Organizations." New York: John Wiley.

Zipf, G. K. (1949). "Human Behavior and the Principle of Least Effort: An Introduction to Human Ecology." New York: Hafner.

8

Consumer and Social Effects of Advertising

Charles K. Atkin
Department of Communication
Michigan State University
East Lansing, MI 48824

Advertisers spend more than 50 billion dollars per year to influence consumer purchases of products and services. Newspapers attract the greatest advertising expenditures, primarily for local retail advertisements. In second place is television, primarily promoting convenience goods consumed by the mass public. Radio and magazines, featuring ads for specialty items aimed at specific market segments, carry somewhat less advertising.

What is the impact of this pervasive stream of commercial messages? Examination of advertising effects is central to the study of mass communication for several reasons: ads constitute a significant proportion of mass media content, ranging from one-seventh of television airtime to two-thirds of newspaper space, which outweighs more frequently studied content categories such as news, violence, and political messages; advertising provides an important context for applying principles of persuasion derived from social psychology and mass communication theory; advertising plays a prominent role in the average person's daily life, as hundreds of messages are encountered each day and many are utilized for consumer decision-making; and advertising messages produce intended and incidental social effects, aside from product orientations.

This review examines key concepts and comprehensively surveys research evidence dealing with the effects of advertising on product knowledge, attitudes, and behavior. The assessment of consumer impact is supplemented with a brief overview of socially significant consequences of advertising. The primary focus is on adults; the extensive literature on children's advertising effects is summarized by Atkin (1981a).

Advertising is one form of communication for which the classic sender-oriented perspective is still appropriate. Advertisers treat the audience as receivers, and attempt to manipulate source, message, and channel factors to achieve maximum impact on the audience. Thus, conventional learning theories predominate in this field, although there is increasing acknowledgment of the active role of the consumer in processing commercial information.

The discussion of consumer effects begins with an examination of the output variables that advertisers are seeking to influence, and continues with an outline of the models of advertising persuasion. A sampling of concrete research evidence illustrating the effectiveness of advertising is presented next, followed by a systematic analysis of the key input factors that determine impact on the consumer.

I. TYPES OF ADVERTISING EFFECTS

Before reporting the impact of advertising, the criterion variables must be carefully defined. The ultimate goal of advertising is the sale of products and services. However, consumer purchase behavior is influenced by a number of marketing factors aside from advertising, such as price, quality of the product, competition, packaging, personal selling, and availability. The study of advertising must focus on a variety of intermediate responses that lead up to purchasing; these are more appropriate communication goals.

The first set of variables encompasses information processing of consumers in their reception and perception of advertising stimuli, particularly cognitive responses. The second set of variables includes a range of outcomes in the learning and yielding hierarchy.

There are a number of outcomes resulting from consumer information processing that contribute to the ultimate impact on purchase behavior. Impact may be considered at the cognitive learning level (e.g., awareness, knowledge acquisition), at the affective level (e.g., generic product desirability, brand preference), and behavioral enactment. Depending on the receiver's pre-existing needs, involvement, cognitions, attitudes, and behavior patterns, advertising may influence one or more of the following specific outcomes:

a. Attain Exposure: An initial prerequisite for any further impact is reaching the receiver with the message at a minimal level of contact, such that the advertisement is discriminated and noted.

b. Attract attention: the second reception variable is attention, the stimulation of cognitive engagement and decoding of the message content; attentiveness to specific portions of the message as well as the overall advertisement have important implications for learning.

c. Provide enjoyment: an entertaining advertisement increases affective arousal that helps assure attention and may produce a pleasant experience that transfers to the item advertised.

d. Produce comprehension: to avoid misinterpretation, the material in the ad must be clear and understandable at the cognitive perceptual level.

e. Facilitate acceptance: an advertisement that engenders trust in the claims and agreement with the value of benefits is more likely to influence the formation of favorable beliefs and attitudes about the product.

f. Create awareness: it is important that consumers know that the item exists, especially when a new brand is fighting for entry into a crowded market or a unique new product is being introduced.

g. Increase recognition: if consumers are familiar with a brand's appearance, packaging, or trademark, it will facilitate causal choices among alternatives encountered in the marketplace.

h. Raise name identification: not only should a brand be among those that are recognized, but it is preferable if the brand name achieves a prominent mental position relative to competitors. This "top of mind" salience is advantageous when there are marginal substantive differences among brands.

i. Augment knowledge: this form of information gain involves creation of factual linkages between the product and attributes of an objective and verifiable nature, such as size, flavor, calories, mileage, and price.

j. Cultivate beliefs: advertising claims typically attempt to convince the consumer to believe that the product is linked to valued attributes of an intangible or subjective nature (e.g., tastes fresh, smells good, looks stylish, exudes sex appeal). Although it is more difficult to persuade consumers that such benefits really occur, success at this stage clearly contributes to positive attitudes.

k. Re-order attribute salience: once beliefs are established, the strategist wants to stress the importance of those attributes on which the brand is seen to be superior, so that factor is given greater weight in the decisional matrix. The cumulative impact of the attributes emphasized in the generic stream of messages for all brands may lead consumers to adopt problem-framing criteria for judging brands in a product class.

l. Enhance attitudinal image: at a minimum, the advertiser seeks to place the brand within the spectrum of acceptable brand alternatives; inculcating highly positive brand attitudes is even more desireable. This can be accomplished by cognitive changes at the recognition, identification, knowledge, and belief levels, through direct endorsement by an esteemed source, via paired associations with irrelevant but valued symbols, or as a result of sheer frequency of exposure to the advertised product. Achieving consumer confidence in the company and affect toward the promoted item strongly increases the disposition to purchase behavior.

m. Change relative preference: not only should the consumer like the brand itself, but it should also be perceived as preferable to alternative options. This may require dramatization of marginal differences among substantively identical brands, or a direct challenge to a competitor's product. Advertising is designed to provide some basis for the consumer to feel that the brand is superior to the rest of the field.

n. Elicit generic needs: although advertising is primarily aimed at producing differentiated brand responses, one key goal is to evoke needs for the general class of product or service. Ads may seek to increase the acceptability of drinking alcohol, reinforce the desirability of eating cereal for breakfast, or arouse anxieties about personal hygiene. To the extent that basic wants and needs are intensified, then a specific brand is more likely to be purchased.

o. Motivate action: when a consumer feels a need for a product or has a favorable disposition toward a brand, the advertiser's task is to activate these latent tendencies. This may involve convincing the consumer to replace the current model with a new one, reawakening interest in an item that hasn't been used lately, or triggering purchase with a special sale offer. The message serves to overcome inertia by activating the underlying receptivity of the receiver.

p. Facilitate intentions: in situations where the consumer already has a clear intent to buy, the advertisement helps to consummate the overt behavior. A mere announcement may remind the consumer to implement an intention, and practical guidance information in an ad can provide directions about where and when to carry out the purchase.

q. Reinforce purchase: advertising may also serve to consolidate post-purchase evaluation, especially for an item bought on a trial basis. The messages encountered subsequent to a purchase provide the consumer with a rationale to justify the action and to facilitate acceptance of the product. At a broader level, ads reinforce feelings of satisfaction with brands that are currently consumed. Such reinforcement increases the likelihood of repeat buying in the future.

r. Stimulate consumption: for a consumable item already in the consumer's possession, continual advertising encourages a higher rate of usage through reminders to eat, drink, smoke, wear, or clean with the product, and through suggestions for new uses. This will accelerate the eventual replacement of the product with another purchase.

s. Generate interpersonal communication: unique advertising style or convincing arguments can arouse interpersonal discussion of the message or product. This extends the range of impact through the trusted word-of-mouth channels, and the recommender may become more favorable through public commitment to the endorsed brand.

Of course, not all of these variables come into play when consumers respond to advertising, and there is not a uniform sequence of stages for information processing. Indeed, there is considerable controversy about which of these outcomes are necessary or sufficient for impacting buying behavior. For example, enjoyment of an ad hardly guarantees that the product will be purchased, or even that the content will be cognitively acquired (Bogart et al., 1970; Ramond, 1976). Knowledge gain may not translate into positive attitude change, and behavior may occur without recall of factual material from advertising (Greenwald, 1968; Haskins, 1964). Furthermore, there have been extensive challenges to the assumption that attitude change is a strong predictor of corresponding behavior change. The next section examines the process of consumer response to advertising messages, focusing on different patterns of response according to the level of involvement in consumer decision-making.

II. MODELS OF ADVERTISING RESPONSE

The consumer is a sophisticated and efficient information processor trying to absorb and utilize available messages pertinent to product selection decisions. Several scholars have presented conceptual frameworks for describing cognitive mediation that occurs in consumer information processing, including stimulus perception, conscious evaluation, and memory (Chestnut, 1980; Wilkie and Farris, 1976).

Analysts have recently drawn a major distinction between levels of psychological involvement in the decision. Many consumer choices are trivial and minimally ego-involving for the individual who has weak brand commitments (Robertson, 1976). Consequently, the consumer does not become engrossed in the information processing task and tends to be a passive receiver of ads for these products.

For important decisions, the consumer gets involved as an active seeker and evaluator of information, carefully considering various options along certain decisional criteria. The role of advertising is considerably different in this context.

A. High Involvement Learning

Classic advertising theories were developed to describe the mental stages experienced by a consumer during a highly involving decision process. Models proposing that the advertising message moves the consumer through a sequential series of responses culminating in a purchase are classified as the "hierarchy of effects" approach. The labels for this process vary, but each begins with cognitive learning and progresses through attitudinal reactions to behavioral consequences. The oldest scheme is AIDA, which stands for Attention, Interest, Desire, and Action. Lavidge and Steiner (1961) proposed a more elaborate sequence of Awareness, Knowledge, Liking, Preference, Conviction, and Purchase. Another well-known model developed by Rogers and Shoemaker (1971) suggests that innovation adopters pass through four stages: Knowledge, Persuasion, Decision, and Confirmation. These conceptions are most closely tied to psychology learning theories (Ray, 1973), and assume a rational, discerning, and active effort on the part of the receiver. These cognitive-affective-behavioral approaches posit the consumer devoting attention to the ad, critically perceiving the content (perhaps derogating the source, ignoring certain appeals, and challenging some arguments), evaluating the personal relevance of the benefits offered, forming an attitude, and executing a purchase (Ramond, 1976).

In the past decade, the attitude model of Fishbein has been applied to this process (Fishbein, 1967; Glassman and Pieper, 1980; Guerrero and Hughes, 1972; Lutz, 1975). The consumer's attitude toward the brand is a function of beliefs regarding linkages from the advertised item to various attributes, and the values for those attributes. Advertising strategies usually take the consumer's pre-existing value system as a given, recognizing that there are deeply ingrained global wants which translate into specific desires regarding valued attributes. The advertiser focuses on formation and change of beliefs, attempting to convince the consumer that the product possesses the desirable attributes and doesn't have unattractive features. An alternative strategy is to raise or lower the salience of positively or negatively valenced attributes.

Advertising researchers have explored the cognitive impact of advertising in recent years. Studies show that consumers are often influenced by advertising claims, including the exaggerated puffery regarding subjective qualities of the advertised item (Rotfeld and Rotzoll, 1980). Indeed, inferential beliefs are drawn by many consumers beyond the literal content, and implied claims are readily accepted (Shimp, 1978). Although some conscious discounting occurs, there is a tendency for consumers to expand on what the advertisement says at the manifest level (Rotfeld and Preston, 1981).

Reception and perception of advertising messages have also been tentatively explored in a few studies. Krugman (1968) examined thinking reactions to ads, which he defined as connections tying the content to the consumer's personal life; thoughts occurred to a very limited degree, varying with channel and structure of the message. Several researchers have proposed that different types of ads and various aspects of the advertising message may be distinctively processed by the more verbal left brain than the visually-oriented right brain (Krugman, 1977, 1980; Rossiter and Percy, 1980; Vaughn, 1980; Weinstein et al., 1980). Although data are lacking or inconclusive, there are indications that the left brain processes verbal information such as advertising copy in a conscious and selectively attentive manner, while the right brain absorbs a large amount of visual imagery from TV and print displays at a more affective level. This has implications for the low involvement model discussed below.

One other high-involvement model deserves brief mention. The behavioral-affective-cognitive perspective reverses the conventional sequence to account for situations where advertising is sought out after purchase to bolster that act. This approach is derived from Festinger's (1957) cognitive dissonance theory, which predicts than an ego-involving decision between comparable alternatives tends to generate psychological discomfort and defensiveness. Specifically, purchasers try to convince themselves that they have done the right thing by subsequently changing to a more favorable attitude toward the chosen brand and by selectively learning supportive information about it from advertisements (Ehrlich et al., 1957). Few researchers have followed up on this notion in the past decade, however.

B. The Low-Involvement Model

When the consumer doesn't particularly care about a minor product decision, another sequence of stages seems to occur. This is the cognitive-behavioral-affective model based on theoretical ideas of Krugman (1965). Under low involvement conditions, the individual acquires a minimal brand familiarity at the cognitive level, but does not form a distinct attitude toward it. The advertising attracts attention and, through constant repetition, some perceptions of the product slowly sink in; the messages are passively processed without much critical resistance. Then, when an item is encountered in a store, it is recognized and a trial purchase is made. As a consequence of the overt behavior, along with subsequent experience and advertising, the consumer eventually develops an attitude. Because information is not actively sought out by the consumer, intrusive or entertaining commercials are best suited for this model. Since the decision isn't treated very seriously, emotional appeals may be more appropriate.

III. EVIDENCE OF ADVERTISING INFLUENCE

To provide concrete evidence of the impact of advertising, findings from a number of studies are reviewed for several key outcomes. Most of the data deal with purchase behavior; brief summaries of evidence are also presented for advertising reception (exposure and attention) and cognitive learning. These findings illustrate the degree of advertising effects; the following section examines the factors that determine effectiveness, going beyond description to explanation.

A. Reception of Advertisements

How many advertisements do people receive in a typical day? There are many methods used to estimate the quantity of advertising exposure. One simple approach is to calculate the total opportunity for exposure in the course of watching, listening, and reading entertainment and news content in the mass media; the best estimate is that the average person encounters between 250 and 300 ads per day (Britt et al., 1972).

However, actual exposure to advertising messages is considerably lower than this inflated calculation. Bauer and Greyser (1968) instructed a sample of adults in the use of a mechanical counter to record the number of ads they consciously noticed in a typical day; the total was about 75 advertisements.

In a survey of newspaper readers, Lynn (1981) found that ads were read regularly by three-fourths of the sample; this is only slightly lower than regular readership of national news and local government news. Substantially more women than men read newspaper ads, but other demographic differences were minor.

Special efforts have been made to measure how much people pay attention to TV commercials. Steiner (1966) asked a group of college students to surreptitiously observe the advertising viewing of their relatives over a period of time; 90 percent of those watching a TV program sat through the subsequent commercial, with about half paying close attention. Attention declined 10 to 25 percent for later ads in a cluster.

Another researcher mounted a photographic device near the TV set to monitor viewing responses. Full attention was given to ads about half the time, representing a slight drop from attention levels during the lead-in programming (Allen, 1965). Using an aided-recall technique, Hsai (1974) showed TV viewers still pictures of ads that appeared the previous day. The sample reported watching about half of the ads embedded in shows they had seen.

These studies indicate that people occasionally talk, read, eat, and walk out during commercials, just as they do when programs are on, but at a slightly higher rate of inattention. The overall picture that emerges from the data suggests that people pay fairly faithful attention to the stream of messages on their television screens. It appears that a larger number of print ads are read each day, especially in newspapers, but there is little published research on radio commercial listening.

B. Cognitive Effects

There is little doubt that advertising has a strong impact on awareness, knowledge, and name identification. Some examples of informational learning can document this type of effect.

When Crest toothpaste received an endorsement from the American Dental Association in 1960, a single print ad publicized this information. A survey two weeks later showed that almost half of the sample recalled this claim (Bogart, 1967). Several weeks after Bell Telephone introduced its "finger-walking" campaign, one-third of the sample could complete the yellow pages slogan; eventually, more than two-thirds of the public had learned this unique phrase (Dunn, 1974). When Northwestern Mutual Life discovered that the company ranked 34th in name familiarity among the nation's insurance companies, they spent a million dollars on TV advertising during the 1972 Olympics telecasts. Soon afterwards, the familarity rating had jumped to third place (Gunther, 1974).

Among a sample of adults interviewed in the late 1960s, 80 percent knew that United Air Lines flew through "friendly skies," 51 percent crowned Budweiser as the "king of beers," and 19 percent associated General Electric with "progress is our most important product" (Larson and Wales, 1970).

In the early 1970s, Exxon used saturation advertising in all media to introduce its corporate name change. After a month, 90 percent of the population were aware of the new name, and half could play back the reason for the change (Enis, 1978).

Since it is unlikely that these types of brand information were learned from sources other than media advertising, the high figures indicate substantial effects. Further evidence comes from a correlational survey which showed a strong positive association between alcohol advertising exposure and brand awareness (Atkin and Block, 1981). Respondents highly exposed to alcohol ads on TV and in magazines were much more able to recall brand names, identify slogans and symbols, and know key claims featured in the advertisements. For example, twice as many persons in the high exposure group as the low exposure group wrote Cutty Sark when presented with the phrase "old sailing ship," and more than twice as many identified Tanqueray as the brand of gin sold in fat green bottles.

These learning effects are primarily cumulative, building steadily over frequent repeated exposures over months or years of advertising. Recall of particular advertisements, however, is not impressive (Bogart, 1973). For instance, when researchers telephone TV viewers minutes after a commercial break, less than one-fifth can correctly name the sponsor of the last ad that they saw (Ramond, 1976).

C. Effects on Purchase Behavior

The fundamental question of how much advertising influences sales is not easy to answer. The amount of scientifically valid evidence about the sales effectiveness of advertising is remarkably meager, although proprietary research might provide a more impressive case. The published literature includes studies featuring a variety of research methodologies.

The first set of findings is based on surveys correlating buying behavior and advertising received or disseminated. One study found that women who saw ads for various products were more than twice as likely to purchase the advertised items as non-exposed women (Stapel, 1971). Similarly, housewives who changed supermarket patronage were more exposed to newspaper ads for the adopted store than the previously preferred store (Atkin, 1962).

Adults who were highly exposed to liquor advertisements in magazines were much more likely to drink each of 10 types of advertised liquors (Atkin and Block, 1981). For beer, those viewing the most commercials reported consuming about twice as much advertised beer as low-exposure adults.

As with most correlational studies, it is difficult to trace causality back to the advertising, however. It is possible that brand preferences might be the cause of advertising exposure rather than the consequence, or that some underlying factor might be accounting for the apparent relationship.

Correlations can also be observed at the aggregate level of analysis, without tracing the relationship among individuals in society. In general, those brands that advertise the most also have greater sales than their less advertised competitors. A review of the research literature shows that the amount of brand advertising is positively associated with brand sales for a number of products, such as beer, candy, soft drinks, drugs, cigarettes, and paints (Peles, 1971; Telser, 1962; Sexton, 1971). The same pattern has been demonstrated for product categories; when the drug or coffee or beer industries as a whole began advertising more, overall sales rose (Bourgeois and Barnes, 1979; Sexton, 1971). Again, it is difficult to infer causality in this situation; it is possible that sales success enables greater expenditures for advertising, or that unmeasured contaminating factors are responsible for the relationship between advertising and sales.

To overcome these limitations of survey methodology, researchers have relied increasingly on field experiments and quasi-experiments to trace the precise causal impact of advertising. Field experimentation has been used by Anheuser-Busch on a major scale to assess the consequences of altered levels of advertising volume in 27 markets. Researchers increased the advertising budget 50 percent in nine areas, decreased it by 25 percent in 9 other districts, and maintained it at the same level in control markets. While sales remained unchanged in the control condition, the higher expenditure resulted in 7 percent more sales; inexplicably, there was a 14 percent increase where advertising was cut back (Ackoff and Emshoff, 1975). Subsequent experiments in other sections of the country revealed small but significant gains in Anheuser-Busch's beer sales when advertising was increased.

Dupont conducted field experiments to test effectiveness of advertising for their non-sticking Teflon cookware. In cities that received heavy advertising, the sales figures were three times as high as in locales receiving light advertising (Becknell and McIssac, 1963). One petroleum that doubled advertising for 3 years in one set of cities found a 36 percent sales increase over control areas with normal advertising (Bogart, 1967).

A more refined type of field experiment features different advertising treatments for subgroups of individuals in the same market. During the 1960s, the city of Milwaukee was divided into a number of equivalent districts. Different editions of the newspaper were delivered to the districts in order to test the impact of various strategies. A Western city has been wired with a "split cable" television system, so randomly assigned subsets of homes receive different versions of TV commercials. In each system, precise comparisons have demonstrated significant sales impact and provided information useful for formulating national strategy decisions (Rhodes, 1977; Sunoo and Lin, 1978; Ule, 1966).

Magazines are especially flexible in accommodating different ads for various subgroups of the overall readership. For several years, one auto manufacturer deleted its ads from each issue sent to 100,000 subscribers. Compared to other subscribers who received the normal dose of ads, car registration figures indicated that the unexposed persons bought significantly fewer autos (Bogart, 1967).

An extreme example of this experimental approach is the painstaking measurement of the impact of a single newspaper advertisement. For a number of paired package goods, researchers randomly inserted a test page in the newspaper advertising either one brand or the competitor. Interviews with housewives the next day showed that .5 percent had bought the advertised brand, while .44 percent had purchased the unadvertised alternative (Bogart et al., 1970). Even such a small difference can be critical to the sponsoring company when generalized to the national market.

There are other methods that fall short of true field experiments, but such quasi-experiments provide useful evidence in some cases. The simplist approach is to assess sales changes when advertising starts or stops. For example, a long New York newspaper strike provided an opportunity to analyze what happens when some advertising temporarily disappears. A study found that one-third of the sample bought less clothing and household goods during the months of the strike, and many complained about the difficulty of locating bargains. City-wide sales figures showed that purchases of these items lagged behind the previous year, but returned to normal soon after the strike settlement (Simon and Marks, 1965).

A labor strike against General Motors caused major changes in the quantity of auto advertising, allowing comparisons between changes in advertising expenditures and sales. For five auto models that sharply decreased spending, average sales declined 20 percent. Modest decreases in spending led to sales equal to the previous year, and the models that substantially increased advertising had sales increases averaging 20 percent (Buzzell and Baker, 1972).

Clearly, advertising works; the next question is how.

IV. KEY PREDICTORS OF EFFECTIVENESS

The research evidence presented in the previous section indicates that advertising has significant impact, but provides few hints about the reasons for success. Each of the elements in the mass communication model can be manipulated by the advertising strategist seeking to achieve the optimum approach: different sources can deliver the message, various message appeals and styles can be created, varying frequencies of repetition can be used, certain media channels can be selected, and specific target subgroups of receivers can be identified. These factors must be considered in interaction with each other, so that the appropriate combination of source, message, and channel variables can be utilized to reach different sets of consumers.

A rapidly increasing body of academic and commercial research relates to these issues. Many of the studies have isolated individual components of the multi-faceted advertising stimulus systematically to ascertain how effects operate, and a few investigations have examined complex combinations that facilitate impact. This section describes theory and evidence regarding source credibility, message appeals (focusing on fear appeals and comparison claims), style of presentation, quantitative factors (mechanical elements, volume, repetition, and timing), media channels, the role of the receiver, and reception environment of mass media and interpersonal influences.

A. Impact of the Source

The sponsoring company is the ultimate source of any advertising message, but the individual models featured in the advertisement serve as the more visible communicator in many cases. Credibility has been the most thoroughly studied source quality. Theorists emphasize that credibility is not a property of the sender, but must be attributed by the receivers of the message. For example, Orson Welles may be perceived as a highly credible product endorser by some consumers, while others may hold him in low repute.

A number of dimensions of source credibility have been identified; the three factors pertinent to advertising persuasion appear to be trustworthiness, competence, and dynamism (or attractiveness). Early research by Hovland and his associates demonstrated that a highly credible source is more persuasive than a less credible sender (Hovland and Weiss, 1951; Hovland et al., 1953). Subsequent reviews of the literature have revealed considerable evidence that the source associated with a message makes an important difference (Hass, 1981; McGuire, 1969; Sternthal et al., 1978).

The sources that companies use to present their advertising message can be grouped into three categories representing the major dimensions of credibility: famous spokespersons (dynamic), professional models (competent), and ordinary individuals (trustworthy). Of course, each presenter may be perceived to have credibility on more than a single dimension.

1. Famous Spokespersons

Many advertisements rely on a well-known person to serve as an endorser of the product; this is particularly the case for television commercials, where about one-fifth of the ads feature a famous name (Celebrities in TV ads, 1978). Athletes and entertainment celebrities are thought to be highly persuasive sources. Friedman and Friedman (1979) found that celebrities work best for products with high psychological or social risk, and generate greater message recall regardless of product. Singer Johnny Cash produced desired attitudinal impact in a major Amoco advertising campaign, and former athletes have been credited with the recent sales success of Miller Lite beer (Celebrities in TV ads, 1978). Actor Al Pacino produced greater impact on attitudes toward a wine brand than did an expert or peer source tested in an experiment by Friedman et al. (1977).

In a series of experiments by Atkin and Block (1981), alcohol advertisements featured testimonials by either a celebrity (actor Telly Savalas, model Cheryl Teigs, and basketball player Happy Hariston) or a non-celebrity. The celebrity sources were rated more positively along a number of scales, and evaluation of the product was more favorable, particularly among teenage respondents.

Unfortunately, the published literature yields little other evidence regarding the impact of famous endorsers or the reasons why they are influential. It appears that celebrities who attract attention to the advertisement in the cluttered stream of messages are perceived as more entertaining and, possibly, are seen as trustworthy. Although celebrities are paid handsomely for their endorsements, many people believe that such major stars don't really work for the money, and consequently they attribute the testimonials to genuine affection for the product (Kamen et al., 1975).

2. Professional Models

Most ads use professional actors to demonstrate, consume, handle, or discuss the product. These characters are selected to represent various aspects of credibility, particularly competence. The prototype competent source has authoritative appearance and manner; for products aimed at the general public the model is likely to be male, middle-aged, upper-middle class, white, tall, deep-voiced, and somewhat handsome. If it is more important to establish trustworthiness, models with average characteristics are used, since receivers tend to trust sources similar to themselves (Hass, 1981; McGuire, 1969). When the strategy calls for a dynamic source, a model with compelling demeanor or distinctive physical attractiveness is shown.

The advertising model attribute that has received the most research attention is race. Researchers have compared equivalent experimental ads with white models only, black models only, and both whites and blacks. The weight of the evidence indicates that black models are about equally effective as white models in influencing samples of white consumers, regardless of channel used, area of the country, or type of product (Barban, 1969; Block, 1972; Bush et al., 1974, 1979; Choudhury and Schmid, 1974; Guest, 1970; Muse, 1971; Schlinger and Plummer, 1972; Solomon et al., 1976). Only one study bore out advertiser's pragmatic concerns about alienating the larger white market, as Cagley and Cardozo (1970) discovered that highly prejudiced white respondents reacted negatively to black and integrated ads. A more recent study with prejudiced whites did not replicate this finding (Bush et al., 1979). Several studies report that most black consumers are favorably impressed by black models, particularly those with distinct Negroid features (Barban, 1969; Choudhury and Schmid, 1974; Gould et al., 1970; Kerin, 1979; Schlinger and Plummer, 1972; Szybillo and Jacoby, 1974).

The advertising effectiveness of male vs. female sources has received little research attention. Although more than 90 percent of all voice-over announcers in commercials are male, there are no studies demonstrating that the male voice is more influential. Kanungo and Johar (1975) reported that a male-female pair had greater impact on attitudes and intentions than either a lone male or lone female. Whipple and Courtney (1980) examined the persuasive influence of several test commercials portraying females either in traditional roles (e.g., as housewives concerned with cleanliness or serving the family) or progressive roles (e.g., in professional jobs or being helped with housework by the husband). Evaluations by females of both the ads and products were slightly higher for the progressive version, regardless of attitude toward women's liberation.

3. Ordinary Amateur Sources

The logical extension of the proposition that people are most influenced by sources similar to themselves is the use of "real people" in advertisements. Instead of hiring a professional actress to play an average housewife in a testimonial or slice-of-life commercial for a detergent, an actual housewife is used in the role. It is thought that consumers can derive more personal relevance from testimonials by the obscure than the famous person, since they can believe the recommendations of sources sharing their background characteristics. Empirical application of this hypothesis to advertising messages is not yet available, however.

B. Impact of the Message

The content and structural attributes of a message probably account for the most variation in the performance of advertising. Research relevant to message strategies has been developed by social psychologists and applied advertising researchers. The first portion of this section will examine content appeals and style of presentation; the latter portion will deal with structural factors, such as frequency and timing of the messages.

1. Rational vs. Emotional Appeals

Most discussions of advertising content attempt to distinguish rational and emotional appeals. This usually involves subjective judgement, since it is difficult to achieve consensus regarding the attributes of each type of appeal. One criterion involves the use of factual information to bolster claims; a rational ad presents specific, relevant, and verifiable evidence (Marquez, 1977). In another approach, Bauer and Cox (1963) assert that rational ads are drive-reducing; assuming that a need exists, the message provides the missing solution to the problem. An emotional claim arouses drives and intensifies motivation by establishing a problem where none was previously felt.

Content analysis studies have focused specifically on the amount of informational content presented in advertisements. Marquez (1977) classified about one-third of magazine ads as informational, particularly ads for automobiles and household products. Resnik and Stern (1977) proposed 13 specific informational attributes (e.g., price, performance, availability, taste). Their analysis shows that half of all TV commercials contain one or more attributes. In a replication, Pollay et al. (1980) estimated that 5 out of 6 commercials contain informational material, with an average of 1.7 pieces of information; the two major categories are assertions regarding how well the product performs, and the ingredients/components of the product. Stern et al. (1981) found a similar quantity of informational content in magazine ads, with ingredients/components and price/value/special offers the leading forms of information. These studies have found extremely limited information about product quality, safety, nutrition, taste, research evidence, new ideas, packaging, or operation. In sum, these results indicate that the rational exposition of substantive information about product attributes is minimal. Advertisements tend to emphasize symbolic imagery rather than logical factual descriptions of product substance. According to Bogart (1978), creation of distinctive images is necessary because many companies produce essentially the same commodity.

Although advertising campaigns vary tremendously in amount of information and degree of rationality, there are no published studies that specifically compare the effectiveness of this factor. Applying principles from the social psychology literature, it would appear that rational appeals are most effective for intelligent, well-educated audiences; emotional appeals should be more influential in reinforcing or activating consumers who are already predisposed or in attracting interest of an indifferent audience (McGuire, 1969).

2. Fear Appeals

Social psychologists studying fear appeals have produced complex and confusing findings. Advertisers understandably regard fear arousal as a risky strategy, and use this approach cautiously. The two main advantages of threatening messages are greater attention and anxiety-based drive arousal (Brooker, 1981). However, Ray and Wilkie (1970) point to several counterproductive outcomes: the receiver may defensively avoid exposure, deny the personal relevance of the extreme threat, distort the message, or derogate the source. Persuasion researchers have shown that fear appeals are most successful when there is a simple, direct means of alleviating the induced anxiety, which is usually the case with advertising that offers the product as the easy solution to the problem (Sternthal and Craig, 1974). It is important that the source of the fear appeal be judged as highly credible, however (Powell and Miller, 1967; Sternthal et al., 1978).

One common approach is to raise the salience of physical well-being concerns. In a field experiment, advertising pamphlets for a health maintenance organization manipulated the level of threat. The high fear version was perceived to be more relevant, generated more positive attitudes toward the sponsoring organization, and produced higher intentions to discuss the plan with the family (Burnett and Oliver, 1979). Another experiment, testing toothbrush and flu vaccine ads, showed that mild fear appeals were less effective than straightforward or humorous appeals (Brooker, 1981).

Advertisers have also sought to exploit personal and social insecurities. Rokeach (1968) suggests that ads attempt to associate inconsequential beliefs (e.g., that Brand A is superior to Brand B) with more fundamental beliefs involving negative self-conceptions, such as compulsions, obsessions, self-doubts, and anxieties regarding social acceptance, personal worth, and masculinity/femininity. Although this type of fear appeal is commonly employed, especially in ads for grooming and hygiene products, there is no evidence demonstrating effectiveness.

Audience receptivity to threatening messages varies with demographic and personality characteristics. Research indicates that fear appeals are more effective with persons who have low anxiety, high self-esteem, and low perceived need for the product; older and lower-status persons also appear to be receptive (Burnett and Wilkes, 1980; Ray and Wilkie, 1970; Wheatley, 1971; Wheatley and Oshikawa, 1970). Thus, targeting to market segments is critical in using fear appeals.

The question of fear appeal impact in advertising is far from answered. Research is needed to identify the conditions maximizing influence (i.e., type of product, media channel, and audience segment), the optimum degree of threat, and the information processing mechanisms that govern responses to this type of appeal. Since the basic influence mechanism seems to be motivation to action through increased salience of anxieties, it is possible that fear appeals primarily stimulate generic product consumption (e.g., use of mouthwash or smoke detectors) rather than specific brand preferences within the product class.

3. Comparative Claims

The traditional approach to commercial persuasion is the one-sided argument, emphasizing the virtues of the advertised brand in isolation from the competition. In recent years, there has been a surge in the use of comparative strategies, where the advertiser makes reference to competing brands along one or more dimensions. Some type of comparative assertion was used in about one-sixth of TV commercials and magazine ads during the 1970s (Wright and Barbour, 1975; Brown and Jackson, 1978). The Federal Trade Commission has encouraged this approach because it presumably affords the consumer an opportunity to weigh the advantages of alternative brands in a more rational manner (Barry and Tremblay, 1975; Pride et al., 1979).

Several aspects of comparative advertising have been explicated by Lamb et al. (1978) and Golden (1979). Comparisons can be classified according to directionality; associative comparisons emphasize similarities between the advertised brand and a leading brand, while differentiative comparisons focus on distinguishing attributes on which the advertised brand is superior. The level of specificity of comparisons can vary from vague references (e.g., ''brand X'' or ''leading brand''), to specific identification of the competing brand by name, to elaborate point-by-point comparisons with the named brand across attributes. Finally, where explicit comparisons are drawn, the message may contain varying amounts of substantiation to back up the claims.

Comparative advertising is relevant to the basic issue of one-sided vs. two-sided message strategies, which has attracted considerable attention among social psychologists (McGuire, 1969). Comparative ads are two-sided in the sense that alternative options are mentioned; in practice, however, this strategy is not genuinely two-sided, since unfavorable comparisons are seldom presented.

What are the advantages and disadvantages of the comparative approach? To the extent that a product can be portrayed as superior to the competition or equivalent to the leading brand, comparisons provide persuasive guidance to consumers in the same alternative-choice framework that they are using to select among brands; thus, it can facilitate decision-making. When a new or secondary brand makes concrete reference to the leader, it can benefit from the competitor's heavily promoted good name; this cue may attract attention to the ad, and the famous brand may become more closely associated with the lesser brand in the consumer's mind (Golden, 1979; Murphy and Amundsen, 1981; Wilkie, 1976). The general two-sided approach has been shown to be influential in converting unfavorable receivers (Hovland et al., 1949). Thus, the comparative approach is better suited for high involvement decisions where meaningful differences exist between brands and where consumers are motivated to rationally study the relevant comparison attributes. It is particularly appropriate if the high involvement brand is new or secondary in the market, since these products stand to gain the most from the psychological linkage with the leader, and the majority of receivers are not favorably disposed but are willing to process the information.

On the negative side, there may be counterproductive consequences of high specificity comparisons: the ads may produce information overload that discourages attention or interferes with comprehension; mention of the competing brand may stimulate counterarguing among competitor loyalists who experience dissonance from the challenge; inattentive reception or selective perception may lead to misidentification of the sponsoring brand, resulting in free advertising for the named competitor; and the practice of claiming superiority may strain credulity and undermine the credibility of the advertiser (Golden, 1979).

The research evidence suggests that comparative advertising has only limited effectiveness. Studies have shown repeatedly that ads featuring comparative claims are rated as less believable than straight one-sided claims (Golden, 1979; Lamb et al., 1979; Levine, 1976; Murphy and Amundsen, 1981; Shimp and Dyer, 1978), although respondents did believe comparative claims for high involvement products (Bowen and Chaffee, 1974). Among various comparison executions, associative is more believeable than differentiative, and specific identification is better than not identifying the competitor by name (Lamb et al., 1979).

Recall of brand name or copy points is not consistently greater for comparative than standard claims across four experiments (Jain and Hackleman, 1978; Murphy and Amundsen, 1981; Pride et al., 1979; Shimp and Dyer, 1978). The comparative strategy of identifying the competitor by name tends to produce more recall than unnamed comparisons (Earl and Pride, 1980; Murphy and Amundsen, 1981; Prasad, 1976; Pride et al., 1979), although non-specification was superior for differentiative claims (Pride et al., 1979). Copy recall is greater if comparative ads cite product performance test results to support superiority assertions (Earl and Pride, 1980).

Two studies have shown that specific identification of the competitor serves to publicize the named brand: Jain and Hackleman (1978) found that many people recalled the competing brand name, and Levine (1976) reported that a substantial minority of the audience misidentified the sponsor in ads for low involvement products.

Regarding the impact on brand preferences and purchase intentions, the findings are far from definitive at this point. Bowen and Chaffee (1974) concluded that the comparative approach was effective for highly involving products. Golden (1979) reported that comparative appeals were slightly more persuasive. According to Shimp and Dyer (1978), the comparative approach was slightly more effective for an unknown brand, but less influential for an established brand. Testing the level of specificity, Goodwin and Etgar (1980) found that naming the competitor was less influential than a vague reference. Finally, one pair of experiments by Atkin and Block (1981) simply compared brand evaluations between young people exposed to comparative liquor ads and nonexposed control groups. In each of two comparative ads tested, the exposed subjects were far more positive toward the secondary brand that made a specific comparison with the leading brand in the product category.

In conclusion, the evidence indicates that the comparative approach can be effective under certain conditions: if a new or secondary brand in a high-involvement product category presents an associative comparison with a well-known leading brand that is specifically identified. Despite the extensive research on this subject in recent years, such generalizations must be offered tentatively, because the data are inconclusive and inconsistent. This is an interesting and pragmatically important subject that is conceptually well-developed, but which requires more extensive empirical exploration and replication.

4. Style of Presentation

A variety of stylistic communication devices are used to help convey message ideas in an attractive and engaging fashion. Style is a qualitative message factor largely unrelated to the nature of product attributes; creative personnel in advertising agencies often use music, humor, decorative sex objects, clever play on words, and soft-sell imagery to gain attention, provide enjoyment, and facilitate retention.

Form can be as critical as substance in producing effects, as creative execution is a major predictor of exposure and learning. Bogart (1978) points to extremely high slogan identification for campaigns mounted by Alka-Seltzer and Charmin, while other heavily advertised themes were far less successful. Analyses of Starch readership scores indicate that the type of content (e.g., fear appeal, testimonial) is less closely tied to magazine ad reading than stylistic factors such as special artistic execution and surprising attention-getting devices (Fletcher and Zeigler, 1978; Holbrook and Lehmann, 1980).

Since style of presentation is more closely related to the advertisement than the product, Shimp (1980) has suggested studying the attitude toward the ad as a separate contributor to brand preferences. For substantively undifferentiated products, he argues that the positive feelings evoked by stylistic execution are transferred to the brand through an affect-referral process. This is a mechanism whereby brands are chosen in the marketplace because of elicitation from memory of the overall affect toward the object generated by classical conditioning from advertisement exposure. There is no solid evidence bearing on this notion, however.

This section will focus on two key stylistic factors, humor and sexual suggestiveness. Humor is widely used in contemporary advertising, particularly television commercials (Cantor and Venus, 1980; Kelly and Solomon, 1975). There are several theoretical reasons supporting the use of humorous style: it attracts exposure to the message, reinforces learning and recall of facts presented, creates a positive mood, induces distraction that interferes with counterarguing, and creates a favorable impression of the source (Cantor, 1981; Roberts and Maccoby, 1974; Sawyer and Ward, 1977). On the other hand, humor may prove detrimental by distracting attention from the serious elements of the message, interfering with comprehension, preventing the audience from taking the message seriously, or creating a frivolous image of the source. Furthermore, humor isn't universal and it wears out quickly (Sternthal and Craig, 1973).

The research on the impact of humor is mixed. Murphy et al. (1979) and Engel et al. (1971) cite industry research demonstrating that humorous appeals produce higher recall and brand preference changes. Published reports show that humor increases interest in the message itself (Markiewicz, 1974; Murphy et al., 1979), but there is no evidence that it improves product-relevant orientations. In experiments pitting humorous ads against serious styles of appeal, learning about the product is lower in the humor condition (Cantor and Venus, 1980; Murphy et al., 1979). Across a number of product attitude measures, Brooker (1981) found no difference between humorous vs. straight message presentations. After reviewing the early research literature, Sternthal and Craig (1973) concluded that humor is not superior in producing attitude change. Considering the available research, humor does not seem to be particularly effective in marketing goals. Nevertheless, there may be specific situations where it can be successfully utilized; further research is needed to isolate these conditions.

Suggestive sexuality is another stylistic element that has attracted scholarly interest. Advertisements occasionally use sexy illustrations and suggestive copy, and female models have long been used as decorative sex objects (Kerin et al., 1979). While sexual stimuli may appear to have the same potential to attract attention, distract the audience from the persuasive purpose of the message, or provide a pleasant conditioner, the research shows that this approach may boomerang. Some consumers may be offended by the sensual display (Atkin and Block, 1981; Baker, 1961; Morrison and Sherman, 1972; Steadman, 1969), while others may be so completely distracted that they don't learn the persuasive content (Alexander and Judd, 1978; Steadman, 1969). More subtle use of sex may be more effective (Peterson and Kerin, 1977).

There is considerable variation across audience segments in reactions of sexual themes in advertising; for instance, women were found to be more responsive to suggestiveness of copy and many women evaluated nudity favorably (Morrison and Sherman, 1972). A key factor may be product-model congruence, with more positive impact when the sexual expressiveness is germane to the nature of the product (Kasserm and St. John, 1973; Kerin et al., 1979). When a female was used for purely decorative purposes, there was greater advertisement recognition but no difference in brand name recall (Chestnut et al., 1977). Atkin and Block (1981) reported that a sexually suggestive version of a liquor advertisement was more effective than a non-sensual control version in producing favorable ratings of both the advertisement and the product.

Thus, sexuality in advertising is a risky approach, although it may be influential for certain products and target audiences. More research is needed to determine whether reactions to the advertisement carry over to evaluations of the product, before any definitive conclusions can be drawn.

5. Mechanical Factors

A number of technical aspects of message production have been examined, including size and time length, use of color, illustrations, rate of speech, and physical positioning. Most studies involving mechanical factors have focused on exposure and recall rather than attitudinal or behavioral effects.

Impact increases with greater size of print ads and greater length of broadcast commercials (Barclay et al., 1965; Bogart, 1967, 1973; Hendon, 1973; Simon, 1969; Simon and Arndt, 1980; Troldahl and Jones, 1965; Valiente, 1973). However, the added size or length delivers diminishing marginal returns; for example, doubling the size of a print ad increased the recall by only one-quarter (Hendon, 1973).

Use of color generally enhances effects (Valiente, 1973; Hendon, 1973; Holbrook and Lehmann, 1980; Sparkmann and Austin, 1980), although a black-and-white advertisement among a sequence of color ads may stand out by contrast (Gensch, 1970).

Readership of print ads is slightly higher when a prominent illustration or multiple photos are featured, especially with a bleed to the border of the page (Holbrook and Lehmann, 1980; Troldahl and Jones, 1965; Valiente, 1973). In addition, a larger size picture had more influence on buying intention than a smaller visual depiction (Rossiter and Percy, 1980).

Positioning of an advertisement on the back or inside cover of a magazine, at the beginning of a cluster of commercials, and within rather than between TV programs tends to augment impact (Barclay et al., 1965; Hendon, 1973; Steiner, 1966).

Finally, recent research suggests that time compression is an effective technique for broadcast commercials. Researchers have compressed half-minute ads by 25 percent through electronic removal of millesecond segments of the audio track; the speaker sounds slightly crisper but does not have the hurried tone of a fast-talker. Experimental comparisons against normal-speed executions have shown considerably higher liking and recall for both radio and television ads (LaBarbera and MacLachlan, 1979; MacLachlan and LaBarbera, 1978; MacLachlan and Siegel, 1980). One explanation is that people prefer listening to accelerated rather than normal speech rate, and thus pay more attention and derive more enjoyment from the advertisement. A dissonance theory rationale is that the listener must exert more effort to attend the message, and justifies the investment by liking the message (Miller et al., 1976). In addition, Miller et al. (1976) have found that the faster rate of speech leads to the perception that the speaker is more knowledgeable, thus increasing the believability of the message.

6. Volume of Advertising

The overall quantity of advertising for a brand, or "weight," is represented by the total number of impressions that reach consumers through various media over a period of time. Many experiments have been conducted where the weight was intensified above the normal level. The field experiments described in an earlier section demonstrate varying degrees of effectiveness due to sharp increases in weight (Ackoff and Emshoff, 1975; Becknell and McIssac, 1963; Bogart, 1967). Haley (1978) reviewed a number of studies of package good sales in split-cable or matched checkerboard markets. One product receiving triple weight increased sales by almost one-third; double weight tests generally produce a gain of 15 percent above control markets. Effects of heavier weight tend to be felt immediately, but subsequently lose effectiveness as consumers adjust to the new higher levels. After examining several cases, Simon concluded that added volume is increasingly less efficient, such that advertising produces diminishing returns (Simon, 1969; Simon and Arndt, 1980). Just as with size, doubling the weight dosen't come close to doubling sales.

Two reports describe experiments where weight was reduced for long periods. Ule (1966) reported that sales plunged, while Ackoff and Emshoff (1975) discovered that cutting weight in half resulted in a surprising modest increase in sales. There was no ready explanation for this latter finding, and no other research examining this phenomenon has been published.

One possible side benefit of heavy weight has been suggested by Nelson (1974). He argues that consumers explicitly or implicitly believe that the brand which advertises the most must be the best one in the product category; thus, sheer volume of advertising may indirectly cultivate positive product perceptions.

7. Timing of Message Presentations

The schedule of presenting a given weight of advertising is also an important consideration, since differential allocation of the same number of messages over time results in different patterns of impact. Researchers have focused exclusively on message recall to assess learning and forgetting curves over extended periods. In a year-long field experiment, Zielske (1959) sent 13 ads to consumers either once per week or once per month; the concentrated schedule lead to a rapid increase in recall which decayed rapidly after the 13-week period. The monthly distribution generated a series of gradually increasing peaks and valleys that reached a much lower maximum but persisted longer. In a re-assessment of these data, Simon (1979) estimated that the wider spacing has greater selling power because the average weekly recall over the long run was twice as high, even though the concentrated schedule produced a higher peak. Zielske and Henry (1980) examined data from a number of TV commercial tracking studies, and calculated a similar pattern: concentrated weight generates a much greater but short-lived peak, while spaced distribution of ads persists longer at a lower level of recall.

A modified strategy for timing involves "pulsing" or "flighting" along a sliding schedule; typically, a heavy-weight introductory burst is followed by less intensive reinstatement of the campaign periodically during ensuing months (Greenberg and Suttoni, 1973; Katy, 1980; Strong, 1977; Haley, 1978). This variant allows receivers to learn the message thoroughly through intense practice before wearout sets in, and the effectiveness is sustained by subsequent secondary bursts. There may actually be improvement at the attitudinal level during the hiatus, due to the discontinuation of noxious overexposure to the messages (Ray et al., 1971) or the dissociation of message content from the biased advertiser source via the sleeper effect mechanism (Cook and Flay, 1978; Gruder et al., 1978; Hovland and Weiss, 1951).

8. Repetition

Once a specific advertisement is created, how many times should it be run? For low-involvement situations, the basic strategy is to drum the message into the receivers with frequently repeated presentations. Thus, the uninvolved receiver finds it harder to avoid the advertisement, has a greater opportunity to learn the basic message, and is less likely to forget it.

On the other hand, a much shorter process occurs when the consumer is in a receptive state of mind. Krugman (1972) suggests that three exposures to a commercial may be sufficient in this situation. On the first encounter, the receiver attempts to understand the nature of the novel message; in the second exposure, the receiver evaluates the content to determine personal relevance, and mentally decides whether to try it; the third exposure serves as a reminder to carry out the decision. For a print ad that says something of significance to the receiver, Bogart (1967) argues that a single reading is enough to close the deal.

Since the bulk of the audience typically dosen't care or isn't consciously in the market for a given product, frequent repetition is necessary to get through and create positive impressions or to be available at the right moment for decisional guidance. In addition, repetition can function as a reminder for routine recurrent purchases, and can reassure recent purchasers about the correctness of their decision-making.

The impact of repetition has been investigated at both the cognitive and affective level. Repeated message exposure rapidly increases learning to a plateau that is reached after five or ten exposures; further repetition serves to maintain recall levels until tedium leads to inattention due to wearout, and the decay curve sets in (Appel, 1971; Axelrod, 1980; Craig et al., 1976; Grass and Wallace, 1969; Greenberg and Suttoni, 1973; Sawyer, 1981).

In terms of attitudes, the evidence indicates that liking continues to increase with higher levels of repetition. Two psychological theories have dominated thinking on the relationship between frequency and liking for a stimulus. Zajonc (1968) proposed that "mere exposure" to a repeated presentation of a novel stimulus leads to greater familiarity, such that the individual becomes more comfortable and favorable toward it. Berlyne (1970) advanced a two-factor theory: with increased repetition, uncertainty and conflict regarding a new stimulus is reduced through positive habituation, but the simultaneous operation of the tedium process generates disliking for it. Since the habituation factor plays a relatively stronger initial role, liking increases at first and then declines.

In laboratory experiments, Zajonc and his associates use a procedure where different groups of subjects are exposed to simple stimuli (e.g., a face, name, symbol, or foreign word) varying numbers of times. This research shows the evaluative ratings of the object become steadily more positive with increasing exposure. Most of the positive change occurs after the first few exposures, although liking continues to increase over dozens of repetitions. The mere exposure effect is more likely to continue upwards with more complex stimuli (Harrison, 1977; Zajonc, 1968; Zajonc et al., 1971).

Of course, these experimental stimuli are quite dissimilar to actual advertisements. Several studies have used slightly more realistic messages. In a field experiment, Zajonc and Rajecki (1969) placed nonsense words in one-column-inch boxes in a newspaper for varying numbers of repetitions. They found positive exposure effects with increasing frequency. Miller et al. (1971) showed subjects nonsense-syllable brand names in various frequencies, and found that the positive effect transferred to liking for different brand characteristics that were linked to the repeated brand names.

Investigations using real advertisements have also demonstrated increases in affect with more frequent repetition (Axelrod, 1980; Grass and Wallace, 1969; McCullough and Ostrom, 1974; Ray, 1973). After the first few exposures, however, the increment in attitude becomes progressively smaller; an old ad dosen't work as well as when it was fresh (Greenberg and Suttoni, 1973; Simon and Arndt, 1980; Winter, 1973). A number of studies have shown that the effectiveness of a message can be enhanced by using repetition with variation; a basic theme is repeatedly presented, but slight changes in the execution can maintain attention and learning beyond the usual satiation point (Calder and Sternthal, 1980; Craig et al., 1976; Grass and Wallace, 1969; McCullough and Ostrom, 1974).

The nature of the advertisement has also been suggested as a factor determining the potency of repetition. Krugman (1962) argues that receivers need more exposure to highly complex messages in order to draw conclusions about the advocated position. In particular, soft-sell ads have subtle indirect copy themes that rely on pleasing mood and verbal persuasion; repetition should increase impact. On the other hand, he asserts that there is little to learn from a hard-sell ad after the first few exposures, especially when simple ideas are being presented.

A cognitive information processing explanation has recently been proposed to account for wearout at the affective level. In a study using non-advertising persuasive messages, Cacioppo and Petty (1979) reported that attitude change increased from one to three exposures, but declined after five consecutive repetitions. Further research indicated that favorable thoughts increased from one to three exposures because of the greater opportunity to elaborate cognitively and realize the cogency and favorable implications of the arguments; at five exposures, tedium or reactance motivated the receiver to counterargue and attack the now-offensive message. In a similar study of advertisements, Calder and Sternthal (1980) found the same curvilinear pattern for product attitude, and evaluation of the ad itself became slightly more negative with each repetition.

There is surprisingly little research examining the impact of repetition on actual purchase behavior. In one major field experiment, buying of frozen dinners did increase with increments of repetition of newspaper ads up to 20 presentations (Stewart, 1964).

In sum, repetition is another area that is well advanced conceptually, but the applied empirical evidence is not yet definitive regarding the optimum frequency of repetition. In general, repetition with variation seems to produce positive impact up to moderate frequency levels, but there are a number of specific conditions governing the effectiveness. Further research is needed to explore the combination of product, content, timing, channel, and receiver variables that determine the outcome of repetition frequency.

C. Impact of the Channel

Is one mass medium more effective than another? There is no simple answer to this simple question, since the impact depends on the type of product, the nature of the message, the characteristics of the source, and the target audience. Nevertheless, conventional wisdom presumes the superiority of television; when a sample of the general public was asked to identify the most influential advertising medium, the vast majority selected TV (The people's choice, 1976).

Surprisingly, researchers have made few attempts at head-to-head comparisons of channel effectiveness. DuPont examined the attitudinal impact of TV commercials vs. magazine ads promoting the same corporate image themes and found that TV worked much better (Grass et al., 1972). Another study conducted under natural conditions discovered that TV produced more learning than magazines for 6 pairs of parallel ads (Grass and Wallace, 1974). A cross-media comparison of copy recall also indicated the superiority of television (McConnell, 1970).

An investigation, using non-advertising persuasive messages, demonstrated that TV generated more opinion change than radio or print for simplified content presentations; complex versions of the message were more effective in the print modality (Chaiken and Eagly, 1976). Andreoli and Worchel (1978) showed that medium interacts with source credibility, as a high trustworthy source was more influential via television and a less credible source via print.

The impressions and findings favoring television run counter to surveys assessing the public's evaluation of advertising channels. These studies show that people tend to feel that newspapers carry the most informative, reliable, and believable ads, while television and radio rate quite low (Bauer and Greyser, 1968; Becker et al., 1976; Grotta et al., 1976; Larkin, 1979; The people's choice, 1976).

Furthermore, self-reported reliance on different media channels for advertising tends to favor newspapers. Both Lynn (1981) and Hirschmann and Mills (1980) questioned people about sources used for shopping trip decisions; newspapers were the leading medium by a wide margin. When Larkin (1979) asked consumers to identify the "most useful" medium, newspapers were cited by far more people than magazines or television. Newspapers are particularly useful for learning about bargains and price information; however, television is most widely cited as the best source for acquiring information about new products introduced on the market (Larkin, 1979; Lynn, 1981).

Researchers have drawn cross-media comparisons in terms of exposure and cognitive responses. TV has a greater capacity to attract the attention of the audience, particularly for low involvement products, while those reading the print media can easily ignore most of the ads they encounter. However, the intrusiveness of television has the drawback of causing annoyance and irritation among receivers who don't desire to be exposed (Larkin, 1979; Ule, 1969).

The audience of televison viewers is large and diverse; it is the only true "mass" medium well suited for selling products consumed by the broad public. Newspapers, radio, and magazines reach progressively narrower and more specialized audiences. For instance, Rentz and Reynolds (1979) factor analyzed magazine readership patterns among women, and isolated several distinct groupings of periodicals (e.g., home operation, fashion, sensationalistic). Advertisers can use magazine vehicles to target messages to these largely non-overlapping subaudiences.

Television commercials tend to be passively consumed by viewers, while print ads are more actively consulted by readers (Krugman, 1965). Recently, researchers have shown that magazine reading generates more brain-wave activity than TV commercials, as measured by an electroencephalogram recording beta waves (Weinstein et al., 1980). However, this difference in mental activity was not reflected in higher recall scores. Furthermore, the print media allow re-reading, contemplation, and multiple exposures at later points in time. These factors should produce more impact among readers who are reached (Buchanan, 1964; Sawyer and Ward, 1977; Wright, 1974).

The print media are more appropriate for detailed, technical, and lengthy presentations of information, while short and simple messages are better suited for the broadcast media.

Wright (1981) has constructed an elaborate analysis of information processing differences across media channels. He argues that the consumer prefers a message reception environment that is conducive to thought production. The broadcast advertising context severely limits the opportunity for active thinking, however. Commercials present brief and fleeting pre-programmed texts spoken in a continuous linear exposition; there is no chance to slow the pace or refer back to earlier material. There are distracting non-text transmissions, including audio noises, motion pictures, and superimposed words. In addition, the individual may still be processing the preceding message content, or anticipating the next message. All of these factors serve to inhibit decoding and thinking during and after exposure, and produce a mental strain on cognitive responses.

Compared to broadcast commercials, research shows that print ads generate considerably greater numbers of thoughts, support arguments, and mental connections linking the message to personal experience (Krugman, 1966; Wright, 1981). On the other hand, the pace and concurrent distractions of commercials discouraged extensive counterarguing. Wright also found that people cope with the mental strain by letting negative reactions dominate the overall response to broadcast messages. To help avoid this coping mechanim, he suggests that advertisers shorten the text, pause between assertions or reduce distracting visual stimuli.

Beyond the major mass media channels, the little-used medium of cinema deserves brief mention as an advertising vehicle. Cinema advertising has recently been tested in movie theaters across the United States after considerable success in Europe. According to Johnson (1981), this form of advertising is advantageous because of high technical quality of message presentation and the access to a captive audience with desireable demographic characteristics. The research indicates that recall is far greater than for TV commercials, and there is some evidence of attitudinal impact as well.

The predominate theme emerging from conceptualization and research on media channels is that television is not necessarily superior over print or even cinema advertising. Indeed, there are a number of arguments and findings demonstrating that the print media are more effective in many situations. Television has the clearest advantage in terms of attracting attention, especially for low involvement advertisements. Otherwise, newspapers and magazines appear to be more effective in producing cognitive responses and in usefulness for decision-making among target audiences, especially if the product is highly involving and the consumer is seeking guidance.

D. Impact of the Receiver

Although early theories of advertising regarded the consumer as a sitting duck who could be easily hit by a well-aimed shot, more recent perspectives acknowledge the important role of the receiver in determining advertising effects. The receiver isn't always so readily exploited by an all-powerful advertiser source. Bauer (1971) contends that the audience is really obstinate, rather than compliant, noting that the communicator must operate within the range of interests and values of the receivers.

The consumers can assert themselves in several ways. In the low involvement situation where the individual dosen't care about a product decision, many advertising messages are simply ignored or attended superficially. Under more involving conditions, the consumer becomes an active, selective processor of information. Rather than passively absorbing ads, the receiver takes the initiative and reacts overtly to the message (Bauer, 1963; Wright, 1975). This often takes the form of resistance: selectively avoiding ads, challenging claims with counterarguments, or derogating the source (Roberts and Maccoby, 1974; Wright, 1973, 1975). In some cases, the response is more favorable, with message-seeking and support-arguing, depending on the predispositions of the receiver.

Since the overall public has a variety of predispositions, the advertiser seeks to identify how certain subgroups feel, and adjusts strategies accordingly. This usually requires market segmentation, where the audience is divided into target segments according to sex, age, ethnicity, income, occupation, education, personality, lifestyle, or regional locale. With this background information, the selection of source, message, and channel factors can be implemented in a manner appropriate to the intended audience.

A small amount of research has provided evidence regarding the differences in general responsiveness to advertising by various audience subgroups. For example, there are indications that highly educated people are more critical processors of ads, more likely to learn factual information in ads, and less likely to be directly influenced (Larson and Wales, 1970; Peritti and Lucas, 1975; Steiner, 1966); Blacks seem to be more favorably inclined toward TV commercials than print advertising, compared to Whites (Block, 1970). Children are more susceptible to television advertising than are other age groups (Atkin, 1981a).

The basic conclusions regarding the role of the receiver are that consumers differ considerably in their receptivity to advertising; in some situations, ads are eagerly sought out and used to make decisions, while much of the time advertising messages are ignored or defensively resisted. It is clear that even the most well-implemented campaign will not be universally effective, due to resistant or apathetic receivers. Thus, the receiver is an important component of the mass communication process determining the outcomes produced by advertising messages.

E. Impact of Communication Environment

The discussion to this point has considered brand advertising in isolation from other messages that are reaching the receiver. It is important to recognize the context of the advertisement in terms of competing messages and vehicle setting and the network of interpersonal influences.

1. Message Context

The mass media audience is exposed to a ''message stream'' that contains ads for competing brands which may cancel out some of the behavioral effects of a brand's advertising. Laboratory experimenters have exposed individuals to a long series of symbols, with each symbol appearing a different number of times in the stream. When asked to select a symbol afterwards, the preferences were in direct proportion to the relative number of exposures (Wells and Chinsky, 1965).

The repetition research by Zajonc et al. (1971) demonstrates the effectiveness of relative rather than absolute frequency of exposure. Individuals gave more favorable ratings to symbols seen 9 times than those seen 3 times or once; in other experiments, liking increased from 9 to 27 to 81 exposures. However, the most frequently seen symbol in each case (whether 9 or 27 or 81) had about the same high absolute rating, and the least frequently seen symbol (whether 1 or 3 or 9 times) scored equally low. Therefore, it is the share of the stream of symbols that makes the difference, not just the raw number seen.

A field study of brand ads found that brand dominance of the stream was more crucial than absolute volume in producing sales (Geiger, 1971). If 2 brands have approximately equal numbers of ads per week, it matters little whether the absolute rate is high or modest. Thus, an advertiser must maintain parity with the competition to maintain sales. To achieve superior performance, the advertiser must have a proportionately larger share of all messages reaching the receiver about that product, whether the ratio is based of 30 vs. 20 ads per month or 15 vs. 10 ads per month.

Aside from competing brand ads, there are issues relating to the general message context of advertising. Concerns have been expressed about advertisement ''clutter'' created by the large amount of general advertising, particularly on television, where a greater number of shorter ads have been shown per hour in recent years. In an experiment manipulating the number of advertising and promotional messages from 16 to 38 per hour of programming, Webb and Ray (1979) found that low involvement ads were detrimentally affected as clutter increased. The findings indicated that attention rate declined, recall dropped, and positive cognitive responses decreased, although no differences were obtained for the more stable measures of attitude and intention, and high involvement ads were impervious to the cluttered context. This study also showed that the first commercial in a cluster enjoyed a strong advantage over subsequent ads.

The stylistic quality of preceding commercials also influences responses to subsequent ads in the cluster. Ads following a humorous commercial were more favorably received, while those presented after a fear appeal message were evaluated less positively (Brooker, 1981).

In addition, three experiments have examined the impact of television program context. Commercials embedded in a highly engrossing drama were substantially less effective in terms of recall, liking for the ad, and purchase intention, compared to the same ads presented during a less involving situation comedy (Soldow and Principe, 1981). Bryant and Comisky (1978) reported greater recall of an ad placed at a less involving stretch of a drama that at a high point in the action that either preceded or followed the climatic scenes. They argue that viewers with lingering or anticipated affective reactions to the program are less able to learn and store the advertising message content. Finally, humorous ads were better recalled in the context of an action-adventure program than a comedy program, suggesting a contrast effect (Murphy et al., 1979).

In a somewhat different process, certain television programs can create a favorable mood that enhances the impact of the commercials embedded in the show. One research study showed that recall of commercials was almost twice as high when carried in a favorite program than in programs rated as fair or poor (Clancy and Kweskin, 1971). For the print media, the editorial climate surrounding the advertisement can carry over to the ad itself. In an experiment, Winick (1962) informed consumers that an ad had appeared in either a contemporary magazine or a traditional magazine; when attributed to the latter vehicle, the company was perceived as reliable, ethical, and sound, while the message supposedly advertised in the contemporary periodical lead to perceptions of the company as youthful and aggressive.

These findings demonstrate the need to take into account the contextual setting of a given advertising message. Apparently, people are influenced in different ways by the same message content, depending on competing ads, preceding ads, and the vehicle carrying the ad. More conceptual development is needed to understand how and why the environment shapes reactions.

2. Interpersonal Influences

Mass media advertisers have long recognized that "word of mouth" advertising is a very potent force shaping certain purchase decisions. First, interpersonal communication can serve a relay function, so a mediated ad can indirectly reach a wider range of receivers than actually see the message. Katz and Lazarsfeld's (1955) study of consumer decisions found that opinion leaders passed along advertising information via a two-step flow to followers.

More typically, advertising reaches consumers directly and stimulates interpersonal discussion that modifies the eventual outcome (Day, 1971). People refer to the reactions of others before forming their own beliefs and enacting purchases, especially for high risk decisions about products that are expensive, innovative, or conspicuously consumed (Woodside and Delozier, 1976). This interpersonal dependence may be based on "reality testing" when the receiver is unsure whether to believe or act on an advertising message, or be due to conformity pressures to acquire socially acceptable products. A special case of interpersonal communication about advertising occurs when co-viewers of TV commercials make comments while viewing the advertisements. In Steiner's (1966) observational study of viewing behavior, one-seventh of the viewers talked about an average commercial while it appeared.

Studies of face-to-face communication about advertising and purchasing show that discussants add personal evaluations to the information that they exchange (Arndt, 1968; Day, 1971; Robertson, 1968; Steiner, 1966). The key factor is the favorable vs. unfavorable tenor of the interpersonal comments. Arndt (1968) reported that those receiving positive word-of-mouth evaluations were three times as likely to purchase a food product as those hearing negative remarks. It appears that product-relevant discussions are closer to a reciprocal "opinion sharing" between the two parties, rather than the strict one-way flow of opinion leadership proposed by Katz and Lazarsfeld (1955).

Although interpersonal communication can clearly play a significant role in determining advertising effects, the research applied to advertising is sparse compared to other types of media content. There is much to be learned about which decisions are discussed, the nature of the comments about ads and products, and how advertising can stimulate word-of-mouth discussions.

V. SOME SOCIAL EFFECTS OF ADVERTISING

Although the intended effects of advertising focus on consumer behavior, social scientists and humanists are interested in analyzing the broader consequences of advertising for individuals in society. Aside from influencing orientations toward products, advertising may have a variety of secondary or "side effects" that are socially significant. Discussions of these social impacts can be characterized as predominatly speculative, apprehensive, and value-laden: the commentary is seldom documented by empirical evidence, many observers utilize an implicit hypodermic needle conception of the powerful media and defenseless audience, and ideological judgements play a role in determining which effects are considered harmful or beneficial. Of course, most of the critical analysis has dealt with outcomes that are thought to be socially or psychologically undesirable. This section will cover three basic categoreis of effects: social roles, social problems, and psychological orientations.

A. Social Role Learning

Mass communication researchers have devoted considerable attention to the role of the media in the formation of social role perceptions, attitudes, and behavior, particularly among young people. Advertising depicts a rich array of characters in various roles: women and men, Blacks and Whites, old and young, rich and poor; in addition, there are portrayals of drinkers, smokers, workers in varied occupations, players, and those who are physically attractive and others who are physically ill. It is not surprising that research interest has broadened beyond entertainment content to include the social role learning from advertising messages. Most of the scholarly work focuses on sex roles.

Since the late 1960s, enormous attention has been devoted to the roles portrayed by women in TV commercials and magazine ads. The traditional stereotypes have been attacked by feminist groups such as the National Organization of Women and government panels such as the U.S. Commission on Civil Rights; a United Nations report blamed ads for "perpetrating the derogatory image of women as sex symbols and as an inferior class of human being (Lundstrom and Sciglimpaglia, 1977).

Numerous content analysis studies reviewed by Atkin (1981b) have documented a pattern of depictions familiar to any TV viewer or magazine reader: women are underrepresented in jobs outside the home and appear in a narrower range of primarily subservient occupational roles; women tend to be depicted in the home setting as a housewife or mother; women are centrally concerned with attracting and serving men; women are seldom the voice of authority in TV commercials; women are frequently used as sex objects; and women tend to be characterized as passive, dependent, submissive, and unintelligent.

A few researchers have moved to the next stage of studying actual reactions to such ads and learning by the audience. A survey in the early 1970s discovered that women were generally satisfied with role portrayals, regardless of their opinion on the issue of women's liberation; they preferred to see females in traditional roles, especially for appropriate homemaker-oriented products (Wortzel and Frisbie, 1974). A later survey of men and women by Lundstrom and Sciglimpaglia (1977) reported that almost half of the respondents felt female depictions were offensive; furthermore, almost half agreed with statements that ads "suggest that women are fundamentally dependent on men," "treat women as sex objects," "suggest that women don't do important things," and "suggest that woman's place is in the home." One team of researchers asked college students to give their impressions of several TV commercials presenting common negative stereotypes of women. Recognition of stereotyping was limited among males in this sample, especially for ads where women were portrayed as fulfilling domestic tasks; there was considerably greater sensitivity among female respondents and individuals supporting principles of the women's liberation movement (Lull et al., 1977).

There are four noteworthy experiments examining social effects of sex role depictions in TV comercials. Tan (1979) exposed high school girls to either 15 neutral commercials or 15 beauty-oriented ads for cosmetic or personal hygiene products, which featured sex appeal, youthfulness, or physical attractiveness to sell the item. When asked what characteristics are important for a women to achieve popularity with men, the experimental group was significantly more likely than the control group to cite a pretty face, slim body, youthful appearance, sex appeal, and glamour, relative to substantive factors such as intelligence, articulateness, and education.

Jennings et al. (1980) argued that the domestic, male-dependent image of females in commericals serves to undermine women's self-confidence in the public domain and their ability to make independent judgements. The researchers created one set of commercials where women portrayed traditional roles catering to men in a subservient manner; a second set of ads using the identical vignettes depicted male and female characters in reversed roles. College women exposed to the counterstereotyped versions displayed significantly more independence of judgement in a conformity test and more self-confidence in delivering extemporaneous speeches, compared to the control group who viewed the traditional ads. In a similar study, Jennings et al (1980) found that college women exposed to reversed sex role commercials expressed significantly more career aspirations.

In an experiment with young children, Atkin and Miller (1975) manipulated the depicted occupation of a woman endorsing the product. Compared to the non-exposed control group, children seeing the commercial character in a non-traditional role such as judge or appliance repairperson were much more likely to believe that these occupations were appropriate for women.

Although counterstereotypes can raise the consciousness of some persons, the preponderent content of advertisements remains traditional. Thus, the major effect of such depictions on sex role learning is probably reinforcing of conservative stereotypes.

The research on other demographic roles is less extensive. Regarding Blacks, findings reviewed by Greenberg and Atkin (1982) indicate that a major increase in the frequency of portrayal occurred in the 1960s. While less than 1 percent of advertising characters were Black two decades ago, by the 1970s more than 10 percent of TV commercials contained Blacks and about 5 percent of newspaper and magazine ads depicted Blacks. Most still appear in ads with a large number of characters; for example, there were about 4 characters per TV ad with Whites only, compared to an average of 14 characters if the ad contained one or more Blacks (Bush et al., 1977). Pierce et al. (1977) found that Blacks in TV commercials tend to be relatively dependent, subservient, and less authoratative and knowledgeable than Whites. The possible impact of this content has yet to be explored by social scientists, however.

Likewise, there is nothing beyond content analyses to examine the role of older people in advertising. The research indicates that elderly people are substantially underrepresented in TV and magazine advertising, and tend to be depicted in an unflattering manner (Atkin, 1976; Gantz et al., 1980).

Aside from demographic roles, the projection of distinctive brand images in advertisements may have an influence on people's social role conceptions of the type of person who consumes a particular brand. From advertising, the public can gain impressions about the kind of individual who drives a Mustang, drinks Chivas Regal, sends Hallmark cards, smokes Marlboros, wears Calvin Klein jeans, or uses some other conspicuously consumed product. This phenomenon has been illustrated with the ''shopping list'' experimental technique where subjects are asked to evaluate a consumer based on the items included on a hypothetical shopping list. Reid and Buchanan (1979) showed woman cat owners a 40-item list that either included Morris the Cat's ''Nine Lives'' cat food or a less distinctively advertised competing brand. In describing the personality of the grocery shopper, the women in the ''Nine Lives'' condition gave far more positive comments. Similarly, Woodside (1972) found that users of an aggressively advertised leading beer brand were rated much more favorably than the hypothetical purchaser of a declining brand.

Portrayals across brands in a given product category may also shape generic perceptions of product users. For instance, liquor advertisements typically depict flattering images of liquor drinkers, regardless of the brand promoted. In a survey of teenagers and young adults, those who were highly exposed to magazine liquor advertising tended to hold more favorable perceptions of whiskey drinkers on the following attributes: friendly, relaxed, fun-loving, happy, manly, successful, sophisticated, and good-looking (Atkin and Block, 1981). Thus, it appears that there is considerable social role learning that occurs in addition to the learning about product attributes.

B. Psychological and Social Problems

Advertising may have some minor but significant impact on several of the societal problems that concern the public. In terms of social behavior, Atkin (1981a) summarizes a number of studies showing that Saturday morning commercials contribute to parent-child conflict over food and toy purchases, and that ads may produce aggressive behavior through frequent modeling of aggression and creation of frustration due to unfulfilled expectations generated by exaggerated product claims. Research by Atkin and Block (1981) indicates that alcohol advertising leads to earlier experimentation with drinking during the teenage years, and contributes to excessive and problem drinking behavior to a limited extent. Concerns that proprietary medicine advertising would increase usage of illicit drugs have not been borne out, however, as several studies show no relationship between exposure to these ads and a favorable inclination toward marijuana, amphetamines, or barbituates (Atkin, 1982). While some commentators have speculated about the impact of provocative advertising on basic sexual attitudes and behaviors, there is no empirical research on this subject.

There is a long list of psychological consequences that have been attributed to advertising, but solid evidence is generally lacking. There are some data indicating that materialism is slightly associated with advertising exposure among young people, according to studies reviewed by Atkin (1982). It appears that unhappiness is produced among some children when their own social or psychological condition is less satisfactory than the lifestyles and situations portrayed in TV commercials, or when actual experience with products falls short of high expectations derived from attractive advertising presentations (Atkin, 1981a).

Many critics have charged that ads heighten anxieties and insecurities by magnifying latent fears about personal shortcomings and social disapproval. The only evidence related to this issue comes from studies of proprietary drug advertising, which does appear to increase concerns about getting sick (Atkin, 1978; Robertson et al., 1979).

The notion that advertising creates cynicism, skepticism, and distrust, due to deceptive claims, has yet to be documented beyond findings that people occasionally disbelieve the content of advertising itself. Attacks by social critics regarding the inculcation of artificial or bogus wants and desires that wouldn't be felt without the presence of advertising also lack empirical support. Finally, the idea that ads increase dissatisfaction among low-income people who can't possess attractively advertised luxury items hasn't been adequately tested, nor has the argument that ads produce demands for instant gratification. Many of these topics are difficult to study, since they involve vague concepts and subtle and gradual processes. There are a number of challenging research problems that remain for researchers to explore in the area of advertising's social impact.

REFERENCES

Ackoff, R. L., and Emshoff, J. R. (1975). Advertising research at Anheuser Busch, Inc. *Sloan Management Review 17*, 1–15.

Alexander, M. W., and Judd, B. (1978). Do nudes in ads enhance brand recall? *Journal of Advertising Research 18* (No. 1), 47–50.

Allen, C. L. (1965). Photographing the TV audience. *Journal of Advertising Research 5* (No. 1), 2–8.

Andreoli, V., and Worchel, S. (1978). Effects of media, communicator, and message position on attitude change. *Public Opinion Quarterly 42*, 59–70.

Appel, V. (1971). On advertising wear out. *Journal of Advertising Research 11* (No. 1), 11–13.

Arndt, J. (1968). A test of the two-step flow in diffusion of a new product. *Journalism Quarterly 45*, 457–465.

Atkin, C. K (1976). Mass media and the aging. *In* H. J. Oyer and E. J. Oyer (Eds.), "Aging and Communication," pp. 99–118. Baltimore, Maryland: University Park Press.

Atkin, C. K. (1978). Effects of drug commercials on young viewers. *Journal of Communication 28* (No. 4), 71–79.

Atkin, C. K. (1981a). Effects of television advertising on children. *In* A. Dorr and E. L. Palmer (Eds.), "Children and the Faces of Television: Teaching, Violence, Selling," pp. 281–305. New York: Academic Press.

Atkin, C. K. (1981b). Changing male and female roles on television. *In* M. Schwarz (Ed.), "Television and Teens: The Experts Look at the Issues," pp. 47–55. Reading, Massachusetts: Addision-Wesley.

Atkin, C. K. (1982). Television advertising and consumer role socialization. *In* "Television and Behavior: Ten Years of Scientific Progress." Washington, D.C.: Government Printing Office.

Atkin, C. K., and Block, M. P. (1981). "Content and Effects of Alcohol Advertising." Springfield, Virginia: National Technical Information Service. (PB-82123142.)

Atkin, C. K., and Miller, M. (1975). "Effects of Television Advertising on Children." (Paper presented at the Annual Conference of the International Communication Association, Chicago, Illinois.)

Atkin, K. L. (1962). Advertising and store patronage. *Journal of Advertising Research 2* (No. 6), 18–23.

Axelrod, J. N. (1980). Advertising wearout. *Journal of Advertising Research 20* (No. 5), 13–20.

Baker, S. (1961). "Visual Persuasion." New York: McGraw-Hill.

Barban, A. M. (1969). The dilemma of "integrated" advertising. *Journal of Business 42,* 477–496.

Barclay, W., Doub, R., and McMurtrey, L. (1965). Recall of television commercials by time and program slot. *Journal of Advertising Research 5* (No. 5), 41–47.

Barry, T. E., and Tremblay, R. L. (1975). Comparative advertising: Perspectives and issues." *Journal of Advertising 4* (No. 1). 15–20.

Bauer, R. A. (1963). The initiative of the audience. *Journal of Advertising Research 3* (No. 3), 2–7.

Bauer, R. A. (1971). The obstinate audience: The influence process from the point of view of social communication. *In* W. L. Schramm and D. Roberts (Eds.), "The Process and Effects of Mass Communication," pp. 326–346. Urbana, Illinois: University of Illinois Press.

Bauer, R. A., and Cox, D. (1963). Rational vs. emotional communications: A new approach." *In* L. Arons and M. A. May, (Eds.), "Television and Human Behavior," pp. 140–154. New York: Appleton-Century-Crofts.

Bauer, R. A., and Greyser, S. (1968). "Advertising in America: The Consumer View." Boston, Massachusetts: Graduate School of Business Administration, Harvard University.

Becker, L. B., Martino, R. A., and Towners, W. M. (1976). Media advertising credibility. *Journalism Quarterly 53,* 216–222.

Becknell, J. C., and McIsaac, R. W. (1963). Test marketing cookware coated with "teflon." *Journal of Advertising Research 3* (No. 3, 2–8.

Berlyne, D. E. (1970). Novelty, complexity, and hedonic value. *Perception and Psychophysics 8,* 279–286.

Block, C. E. (1970). Communicating with the urban poor: An exploratory inquiry. *Journalism Quarterly 47,* 3–11.

Block, C. E. (1972). White backlash to Negro ads: Fact or fantasy? *Journalism Quarterly 49,* 258–262.

Bogart, L. (1967). "Strategy in Advertising." New York: Harcourt, Brace & World.

Bogart, L. (1973). Consumer and advertising research. *In* I. S. Pool and W. Schramm, "Handbook of Communication," pp. 706–721. Chicago, Illinois: Rand McNally.

Bogart, L. (1978). Is all this advertising necessary? *Journal of Advertising Research 18* (No. 5), 17–26.

Bogart, L., Tolley, S. B., and Orenstein, F. (1970). What one little ad can do. *Journal of Advertising Research 10* (No. 4). 3–13.

Bourgeois, J. C., and Barnes, J. G. (1979). Does advertising increase alcohol consumption? *Journal of Advertising Research 19* (No. 4), 19–30.

Bowen, L., and Chaffee, S. H. (1974). Product involvement and pertinent advertising appeals. *Journalism Quarterly 51,* 613–621.

Britt, S. H., Adams, S. C., and Miller, A. H. (1972). How many advertising exposures per day? *Journal of Advertising Research 12* (No. 6), 3–9.

Brooker, G. W. (1981). A comparison of the persuasive effects of mild humor and mild fear appeals. *Journal of Advertising 10* (No. 4), 29–40.

Brown, S. W., and Jackson, D. W. (1978). Comparative advertising: Examining its nature and frequency. *Journal of Advertising 6* (No. 4), 15–18.

Bryant, J., and Comisky, P. W. (1978). The effect of positioning a message within differentially cognitively involving portions of a television segment on recall of the message. *Human Communication Research 5*, 63–75.

Buchanan, D. I. (1964). How interest in the product affects recall: Print ads vs. commercials. *Journal of Advertising Research 4* (No. 2), 9–15.

Burnett, J. J., and Oliver, R. L. (1979). Fear appeal effects in the field: A segmentation approach. *Journal of Marketing Research 16*, 181–190.

Burnett, J. J., and Wilkes, R. E. (1980). Fear appeals to segments only. *Journal of Advertising Research 20* (No. 5), 21–24.

Bush, R. F., Gwinner, R. F., and Solomon, P. J. (1974). White consumer sales response to Black models. *Journal of Marketing 38* (No. 2), 25–29.

Bush, R. F., Hair, J. F. Solomon, P. J. (1979). Consumers' level of prejudice and response to Black models in advertisements. *Journal of Marketing Research 16*, 341–345.

Bush, R. F., Solomon, P. J., and Hair, J. F. (1977). There are more Blacks in TV commercials. *Journal of Advertising Research 17* (No. 1), 21–25.

Buzzell, R. D., and Baker, M. (1972). Sales effectiveness of automobile advertising. *Journal of Advertising Research 12* (No. 3), 3–8.

Cacioppo, J. T., and Petty, R. E. (1979). Effects of message repetition and position on cognitive response, recall, and persuasion. *Journal of Personality and Social Psychology 37*, 97–109.

Cagley, J. W., and Cardozo, R. N. (1970). White response to integrated advertising. *Journal of Advertising Research 10* (No. 2) 35–39.

Calder, B. J., and Sternthal, B. (1980). Television commercial wearout: An information processing view. *Journal of Marketing Research 17*, 173–186.

Cantor, J. (1981). Modifying children's eating habits through television ads: Effects of humorous appeals in a field setting. *Journal of Broadcasting 25*, 37–47.

Cantor, J., and Venus, P. (1980). The effect of humor on recall of a radio advertisement. *Journal of Broadcasting 24*, 13–22.

Celebrities in TV ads spotlighted as key trend. (1978). *Advertising Age* (Feb. 27), 32–33.

Chaiken, S., and Eagly, A. H. (1976). Communication modality as a determinant of message persuasiveness and message comprehensibility. *Journal of Personality and Social Psychology 34*, 605–614.

Chestnut, R. W. (1980). Persuasive effects in marketing: Consumer information processing research. *In* M. E. Roloff and G. R. Miller (Eds.), "Persuasion: New Directions in Theory and Research," pp. 267–283. Beverly Hills, California: Sage.

Chestnut, R. W., LaChance, C. C., and Lubitz, A. (1977). The "decorative" female model: Sexual stimuli and the recognition of advertisements. *Journal of Advertising 6* (No. 4), 11–14.

Choudhury, P. K., and Schmid, L. S. (1974). Black models in advertising to Blacks. *Journal of Advertising Research 14* (No. 3), 19–22.

Clancy, K. J., and Kweskin, D. M. (1971). TV commercial recall correlates. *Journal of Advertising Research 11* (No. 2), 18–20.

Cook, T. D., and Flay, B. R. (1978). The persistence of experimentally-induced attitude change. *Advances in Experimental Social Psychology 11*, 1–57.

Craig, C. S., Sternthal, B., and Leavitt, C. (1976). Advertising wearout: An experimental analysis. *Journal of Marketing Research 13*, 365–372.

Day, G. S. (1971). Attitude change, media and word of mouth. *Journal of Advertising Research 11* (No. 6), 31–41.

Dunn, S. W., and Barban, A. M. (1974). "Advertising: It's Role in Modern Marketing." Hinsdale, Illinois: Dryden Press.

Earl, R. L., and Pride, W. M. (1980). The effects of advertisement structure, message sidedness, and performance test results on print advertisement informativeness. *Journal of Advertising 9* (No. 3), 36–45.

Ehrlich, D., Guttman, I., Schonbach, P., and Mills, J. (1957). Postdecision exposure to relevant information. *Journal of Abnormal and Social Psychology 54,* 98–102.

Engel, J. F., Wales, H. G., and Warshaw, M. R. (1971). "Promotional Strategy." Homewood, Illinois: Richard Irwin.

Enis, B. M. (1978). Exxon marks the spot. *Journal of Advertising Research 18* (No. 6), 7–12.

Festinger, L. (1957). "A Theory of Cognitive Dissonance." Stanford, California: Stanford University Press.

Fishbein, M. (1967). Attitude and the prediction of behavior. *In* M. Fishbein (Ed.), "Readings in Attitude Theory and Measurement." pp. 477–492. New York: Wiley.

Fletcher, A. D., and Zeigler, S. K. (1978). Creative strategy and magazine ad readership. *Journal of Advertising Research 18* (No. 1), 29–33.

Friedman, H. L., and Friedman, L. (1979). Endorser effectiveness by product type. *Journal of Advertising Research 19* (No. 5), 63–71.

Friedman, H. L., Termini, S., and Washington, R. (1977). The effectiveness of advertisements utilizing four types of endorsers. *Journal of Advertising Research 17* (No. 3), 22–24.

Gantz, W., Gartenberg, H. M., and Rainbow, C. K. (1980). Approaching invisibility: The portrayal of the elderly in magazine advertisements. *Journal of Communication 30* (No. 1), 56–60.

Geiger, J. A. (1971). Seven brands in seven days. *Journal of Advertising Research 11* (No. 5), 15–22.

Gensch, D. H. (1970). Media factors: A review article. *Journal of Marketing Research 7,* 216–225.

Glassman, M., and Pieper, W. J. (1980). Processing advertising information: Deception, salience, and inferential belief formation. *Journal of Advertising 9* (No. 1), 3–10.

Golden, L. L. (1979). Consumer reactions to explicit brand comparisons in advertisements. *Journal of Marketing Research 16,* 517–532.

Goodwin, S., and Etgar, M. (1980). An experimental investigation of comparative advertising: Impact of message appeal, information load, and utility of product class. *Journal of Marketing Research 17,* 187–202.

Gould, J. W., Sigband, N. B., and Zoerner, C. E. (1970). Black consumer reactions to "integrated" advertising: An exploratory study. *Journal of Marketing 34* (No. 3), 20–26.

Grass, R. C., and Wallace, W. H. (1969). Satiation effects of TV commercials. *Journal of Advertising Research 9* (No. 3), 3–8.

Grass, R. C., and Wallace, W. H. (1974). Advertising communication: Print vs. TV. *Journal of Advertising Research 14* (No. 5), 19–23.

Grass, R. C., Bartges, D. W., and Piech, J. L. (1972). Measuring corporate image and effects. *Journal of Advertising Research 12* (No. 6), 15–22.

Greenberg, A., and Suttoni, C. (1973). Television commerical wearout. *Journal of Advertising Research 13* (No. 5), 47–54.

Greenberg, B. S., and Atkin, C. K. (1982). Learning about minorities from television. *In* G. Berry and C. Mitchell-Kernin (Eds.), "Television and the Socialization of the Ethnic Minority Child," pp. 338–354. New York: Acadamic Press.

Greenwald, A. G. (1968). Cognitive learning, cognitive response to persuasion, and attitude change. *In* A. G. Greenwald, T. C. Brock, and T. M. Ostrom (Eds.), "Psychological Foundations of Attitudes," pp. 147–170. New York: Academic Press.

Grotta, G. L., Larkin, E. F., and Carrell, B. J. (1976). News vs. advertising: Does the audience perceive the journalistic distinction? *Journalism Quarterly 53,* 448–456.

Gruder, C. L., Cook, T. D., Hennigan, K. M., Flay, B. R., Alessis, C., and Halamaj, J. (1978). Empirical tests of the absolute sleeper effect predicted from the discounting cue hypothesis. *Journal of Personality and Social Psychology 36,* 1061–1074.

Guerrero, J. L., and Hughes, G. D. (1972). Am empirical test of the Fishbein model *Journalism Quarterly 49,* 684–691.

Guest, L. (1970). How Negro models affect company image. *Journal of Advertising Research 10* (No. 2), 29–33.

Gunther, M. (1974). Do commercials really sell you? *TV Guide* (Nov. 9), 4–8.

Haley, R. I. (1978). Sales effects of media weight. *Journal of Advertising Research 18* (No. 3), 9–18.

Harrison, A. A. (1977). Mere exposure. *Advances in Experimental Social Psychology 10,* 40–83.

Haskins, J. B. (1964). Factual recall as a measure of advertising effectiveness. *Journal of Advertising Research 4* (No. 1), 2–8.

Hass, R. G. (1981). Effects of source characteristics on cognitive responses and persuasion. *In* R. E. Petty, T. M. Ostrom, and T. C. Brock (Eds.), ''Cognitive Responses in Persuasion.'' pp. 141–172, Hillsdale, New Jersey: Erlbaum.

Hendon, D. W. (1973). How mechanical factors affect ad perception. *Journal of Advertising Research 14* (No. 4). 39–45.

Hirschman, E. C., and Mills, M. K. (1980). Sources shoppers use to pick stores. *Journal of Advertising Research 20* (No. 1), 47–51.

Holbrook, M. B., and Lehmann, D. R. (1980). Form versus content in predicting Starch scores. *Journal of Advertising Research 20* (No. 4), 53–62.

Hovland, C. I., and Weiss, W. (1951). The influence of source credibility on communication effectiveness. *Public Opinion Quarterly 15,* 635–650.

Hovland, C. I., Janis, I. L., and Kelley, H. H. (1953). ''Communication and Persuasion.'' New Haven, Connecticut: Yale University Press.

Hovland, C. I., Lumsdaine, A. A., and Sheffield, F. D. (1949). ''Experiments in Mass Communication.'' Princeton, New Jersey: Princeton University Press.

Hsai, H. J. (1974). Audience recall as tolerance toward television commercial breaks. *Journalism Quarterly 51,* 96–101.

Jain, S. C., and Hackleman, E. C. (1978). How effective is comparison advertising for stimulating brand recall? *Journal of Advertising 7* (No. 3), 20–25.

Jennings, J., Geis, F. L., and Brown, V. (1980). Influence of television commercials on women's self-confidence and independent judgement. *Journal of Personality and Social Psychology 38,* 203–210.

Johnson, K. F. (1981). Cinema advertising. *Journal of Advertising 10* (No. 4), 11–19.

Kamen, J. M., Aghari, A. C., and Kragh, J. R. (1975). What a spokesman can do for a sponsor. *Journal of Advertising Research 15* (No. 2), 17–24.

Kanungo, R. N., and Johar, J. S. (1975). Effects of solgans and human model characteristics in product advertising. *Canadian Journal of Behavioral Science 7,* 127–138.

Kasserm, S., and St. John, D. (1973). Sex in advertising: Its relevance, use, and effects. *Management Decision 11* (Summer), 145–158.

Katy, W. A. (1980). A sliding schedule of advertising weight. *Journal of Advertising Research 20* (No. 4), 39–44.

Katz, E., and Lazarsfeld, P. F. (1955). ''Personal Influence.'' Glencoe, Illinois: Free Press.

Kelly, J. P., and Solomon, P. J. (1975). Humor in television advertising. *Journal of Advertising 4* (No. 3), 31–35.

Kerin, R. A. (1979). Black model appearance and product evaluations. *Journal of Communication 29* (No. 1), 123–128.

Kerin, R. A., Lundstrom, W., and Sciglimpaglia, D. (1979). Women in advertisements: Retrospect and prospect. *Journal of Advertising 8* (No. 3), 37–42.

Krugman, H. E. (1962). An application of learning theory to TV copy testing. *Public Opinion Quarterly 26,* 626–634.

Krugman, H. E. (1965). The impact of television advertising: Learning without involvement. *Public Opinion Quarterly 29,* 349–356.

Krugman, H. E. (1966). The measurement of advertising involvement. *Public Opinion Quarterly 30,* 583–596.

Krugman, H. E. (1968). Processes underlying exposure to advertising. *American Psychologist 23,* 245–253.

Krugman, H. E. (1972). Why three exposures may be enough. *Journal of Advertising Research 12* (No. 6), 11–15.

Krugman, H. E. (1977). Memory without recall, exposure without perception. *Journal of Advertising Research 17* (No. 4), 7–12.

Krugman, H. E. (1980). Point of view: Sustained viewing of television. *Journal of Advertising Research 20* (No. 3), 65–68.

LaBarbera, P., and MacLachlan, J. (1979). Time-compressed speech in radio advertising. *Journal of Marketing 43* (No. 1), 30–36.

Lamb, C. W., Pride, W. M., and Pletcher, B. A. (1978). A taxonomy for comparative advertising research. *Journal of Advertising 7* (No. 1), 43–47.

Lamb, C. W., Pletcher, B. A., and Pride, W. M. (1979). Print readers' perceptions of various advertising formats. *Journalism Quarterly 56*, 328–335.

Larkin, E. F. (1979). Consumer perceptions of the media and their advertising content. *Journal of Advertising 8* (No. 2), 5–7.

Larson, C. M., and Wales, H. G. (1970). Slogan awareness in the Chicago market. *Journal of Advertising Research 10* (No. 6), 38–43.

Lavidge, R. J., and Steiner, G. A. (1961). A model for predictive measurements of advertising effectiveness. *Journal of Marketing 25* (No. 4), 59–62.

Levine, P. (1976). Commercials that name competing brands. *Journal of Advertising Research 16* (No. 6), 7–14.

Lull, J. T., Hanson, C. A., and Marx, M. J. (1977). Recognition of female stereotypes in TV commercials. *Journalism Quarterly 54*, 153–157.

Lundstrom, W. J., and Sciglimpaglia, D. (1977). Sex role portrayals in advertising. *Journal of Marketing 41* (No. 3), 72–79.

Lutz, R. J. (1975). First-order and second-order cognitive effects in attitude change. *Communication Research 2*, 289–299.

Lynn, J. R. (1981). Newspaper ad impact in nonmetropolitan markets. *Journal of Advertising Research 21* (No. 4), 13–19.

MacLachlan, J., and LaBarbera, P. (1978). Time compressed speech in television commercials. *Journal of Advertising Research 18* (No. 4), 38–45.

MacLachan, J., and Siegel, M. H. (1980). Reducing the costs of TV commercials by use of time compressions. *Journal of Marketing Research 17*, 52–57.

Markiewicz, D. (1974). Effects of humor on persuasion. *Sociometry 37*, 407–422.

Marquez, F. T. (1977). Advertising content: Persuasion, information, or intimidation? *Journalism Quarterly 54*, 482–491.

McConnell, J. D. (1970). Do media vary in effectiveness? *Journal of Advertising Research 10* (No. 5), 19–22.

McCullough, J. L., and Ostrom, T. M. (1974). Repetition of highly similar messages and attitude change. *Journal of Applied Psychology 59*, 395–397.

McGuire, W. J. (1968). The nature of attitudes and attitude change. *In* E. Aronson and G. Lindsey (Eds.), "Handbook of Social Psychology," 2nd ed., Vol. 3, pp. 136–314. Reading, Massachusetts: Addison-Wesley.

Miller, N., Maruyama, G., Beaber, R. J., and Valone, K. (1976). Speed of speech and persuasion. *Journal of Personality and Social Psychology 34*, 615–624.

Miller, S. J., Mazis, M. B., and Wright, P. L. (1971). The influence of brand ambiguity on brand attitude development. *Journal of Marketing Research 8*, 455–459.

Morrison, B. J., and Sherman, R. C. (1972). Who responds to sex in advertising? *Journal of Advertising Research 12* (No. 2), 15–19.

Murphy, J. H., and Amundsen, M. S. (1981). The communications-effectiveness of comparative advertising for a new brand on users of the dominant brand. *Journal of Advertising 10* (No. 1), 14–19.

Murphy, J. H., Cunningham, I. C. M. and Wilcox, G. B. (1979). The impact of program environment on recall of humorous television commericals. *Journal of Advertising 8* (No. 2), 17–21.

Muse, W. V. (1971). Product-related response to use of Black models in advertising. *Journal of Marketing Research 8,* 107–109.

Nelson, P. J. (1974). The economic value of advertising. *In* Y. Brozen (Ed.), ''Advertising and Society.'' New York: New York University Press.

Peles, Y. (1971). Economies of scale in advertising beer and cigarettes. *Journal of Business 44,* 32–37.

Peles, Y. (1976). The people's choice, TV is voted best advertising medium. *Broadcasting* (Jan. 12), 29.

Peretti, P. O., and Lucas, C. (1975). Newspaper advertising influences on consumers' behavior by socioeconomic status of customers. *Psychological Reports 37,* 693–694.

Peterson, R. A., and Kerin, R. A. (1977). The female role in advertisements: Some empirical evidence. *Journal of Marketing 41* (No. 4), 59–63.

Pierce, C. M., Carew, J. V., Pierce-Gonzalez, D., and Wills, D. (1977). An experiment in racism: TV commercials. *Education and Urban Society 10,* 61–87.

Pollay, R. W., Zaichkowsky, J., and Fryer, C. (1980). Regulation hasn't changed TV ads much. *Journalism Quarterly 57, 438–446.*

Powell, F. A., and Miller, G. R. (1967). Social approval and disapproval cues in anxiety-arousing communications. *Speech Monographs 34,* 152–159.

Prasad, V. K. (1976). Communications-effectivenss of comparative advertising: A laboratory analysis. *Journal of Marketing Research 13,* 128–137.

Pride, W. M., Lamb, C. W., and Pletcher, B. A. (1979). The informativeness of comparative advertisements: An empirical investigation. *Journal of Advertising 8* (No. 2), 29–35.

Ramond, C. K. (1976). ''Advertising Research: The State of the Art.'' New York: Association of National Advertisers.

Ray, M. L. (1973). Marketing communication and the hierarchy of effects. *In* P. Clarke (Ed.), ''New Models for Communication Research,'' pp. 147–173. Beverly Hills, California: Sage.

Ray, M. L., and Wilkie, W. L. (1970). Fear: The potential of an appeal neglected in marketing. *Journal of Marketing 34* (No. 1), 54–62.

Ray, M. L., Sawyer, A. G., and Strong, E. C. (1971). Frequency effects revisted. *Journal of Advertising Research 11* (No. 1), 14–20.

Reid, L. N., and Buchanan, L. (1979). A shopping list experiment of the impact of advertising brand images. *Journal of Advertising 8* (No. 2), 26–28.

Rentz, J. O., and Reynolds, F. D. (1979). Magazine readership patterns. *Journal of Advertising 8* (No. 2), 22–25.

Resnik, A., and Stern, B. L. (1977). An analysis of the information content in television advertising. *Journal of Marketing 41* (No. 1), 50–53.

Rhodes, J. R. (1977). ''What AdTel has Learned—A Summary of General Findings from Over Two Hundred Advertising experiments.'' (Paper delivered to Annual Advertising Research Conference, American Marketing Association, New York.)

Roberts, D. F., and Maccoby, N. (1974). Information processing and persuasion: Counterarguing and behavior. *In* P. Clarke (Ed.), ''New Models for Communication Research,'' pp. 269–302. Beverly Hills, California: Sage.

Robertson, T. S. (1968). Purchase sequence responses: Innovators vs. noninnovators. *Journal of Advertising Research 8* (No. 1), 47–52.

Robertson, T. S. (1976). Low commitment consumer behavior. *Journal of Advertising Research 16* (No. 2), 19–24.

Robertson, T. S., Rossiter, J. R., and Gleason, T. C. (1979). Children's receptivity to proprietary medicine advertising. *Journal of Consumer Research 6,* 247–255.

Rogers, E. M., and Shoemaker, F. (1971). ''Communication of Innovations.'' New York: Free Press.

Rokeach, M. (1968). "Beliefs, Attitudes, and Values." San Francisco, California: Jossey-Bass.

Rossiter, J. R., and Percy, L. (1980). Attitude change through visual imagery in advertising. *Journal of Advertising 9* (No. 2), 10–16.

Rotfeld, H. J., and Preston, I. L. (1981). *Journal of Advertising Research 21* (No. 2), 9–17.

Rotfeld, H. J., and Rotzoll, K. B. (1980). Is advertising puffery believed? *Journal of Advertising 9* (No. 3), 16–20.

Sawyer, A. G. (1981). Repetition, cognitive responses, and persuasion. In R. E. Petty, T. M. Ostrom, and T. C. Brock (Eds.), "Cognitive Responses to Persuasion," pp. 237–261. Hillsdale, New Jersey: Erlbaum.

Sawyer, A. G., and Ward, S. (1977). Carry-over effects in advertising communication: Evidence and hypotheses from behavioral science. In D. G. Clarke (Ed.), "Cumulative Advertising Effects," pp. 73–170. Cambridge, Massachusetts: Marketing Science Institute.

Schlinger, M. J., and Plummer, J. T. (1972). Advertising in black and white. *Journal of Marketing Research 9*, 149–153.

Sexton, D. E. (1971). Overspending on advertising. *Journal of Advertising Research 11* (No. 6), 22–25.

Shimp, T. A. (1978). Do incomplete comparisons mislead? *Journal of Advertising Research 18* (No. 6), 21–27.

Shimp, T. A. (1980). Attitude toward the ad as a mediator of consumer brand choice. *Journal of Advertising 10* (No. 2), 9–15.

Shimp, T. A., and Dyer, D. C. (1978). The effects of comparative advertising mediated by market position of sponsoring brand. *Journal of Advertising 7* (No. 3), 13–19.

Simon, J. L. (1969). New evidence for no effect of scale in advertising. *Journal of Advertising Research 9* (No. 1), 38–42.

Simon, J. L. (1979). What do Zielske's real data really show about pulsing? *Journal of Marketing Research 16*, 415–420.

Simon, J. L., and Arndt, J. (1980). The shape of the advertising response function. *Journal of Advertising Research 20* (No. 4), 11–28.

Simon, L. S., and Marks, M. R. (1965). Consumer behavior during the New York newspaper strike. *Journal of Advertising Research 5* (No. 1), 9–17.

Soldow, G. F., and Principe, V. (1981). Response to commercials as a function of program context. *Journal of Advertising Research 21* (No. 2), 59–65.

Solomon, P. J., Bush, R. F., and Hair, J. F. (1976). White and Black consumer sales response to Black models. *Journal of Advertising Research 13*, 431–434.

Sparkmann, R., and Austin, L. M. (1980). The effect on sales of color in newspaper advertisements. *Journal of Advertising 9* (No. 4), 39–42.

Stapel, J. (1971). Sales effects of print ads. *Journal of Advertising Research 11* (No. 3), 32–36.

Steadman, M. (1969). How sexy illustrations affect brand recall. *Journal of Advertising Research 9* (No. 1), 15–19.

Steiner, G. A. (1966). The people look at commercials: A study of audience behavior. *Journal of Business 39*, 272–304.

Stern, B. L., Krugman, D. M., and Resnik, A. (1981). Magazine advertising: An analysis of its information content. *Journal of Advertising Research 21* (No. 2), 39–44.

Sternthal, B., and Craig, C. S. (1973). Humor in advertising. *Journal of Marketing 37* (No. 4), 12–18.

Sternthal, B., and Craig, C. S. (1974). Fear appeals: Revisited and revised. *Journal of Consumer Research 1* (No. 3), 22–34.

Sternthal, B., Phillips, L. W., and Dholakig, R. (1978). The persuasive effect of source credibility: A situational analysis. *Public Opinion Quarterly 42*, 285–314.

Stewart, J. P. (1964). "Repetitive Advertising in Newspapers." Boston, Massachusetts: Harvard University Graduate School of Business Administration.

Strong, E. C. (1977). The spacing and timing of advertising. *Journal of Advertising Research 17* (No. 6), 25–31.

Sunoo, D. and Lin, L. Y. S. (1978). Sales effects of promotion and advertising. *Journal of Advertising Research 18* (No. 5), 37–40.

Szybillo, G. J., and Jacoby, J. (1974). Effects of different levels of integration on advertising preference and intention to purchase. *Journal of Applied Psychology 59*, 274–280.

Tan, A. S. (1979). TV beauty ads and role expectations of adolescent female viewers, *Journalism Quarterly 56*, 283–288.

Telser, L. G. (1962). Advertising and cigarettes. *Journal of Political Economy 70*, 471–499.

Troldahl, V. C., and Jones, R. L. (1965). Predictors of newspaper advertisement readership. *Journal of Advertising Research 5* (No. 1), 23–27.

Ule, G. M. (1966). Two years of the Milwaukee ad lab: First report. *Proceedings of Advertising Research Foundation Annual Meeting 12*, 58–65.

Ule, G. M. (1969). The Milwaukee advertising laboratory—a continuing source of advertising serendipity. *Proceedings of Advertising Research Foundation Annual Meeting 15*, 71–76.

Valiente, R. (1973). Mechanical correlates of ad recognition. *Journal of Advertising Research 13* (No. 3), 13–18.

Vaughn, R. (1980). How advertising works: A planning model. *Journal of Advertising Research 20* (No. 5), 27–33.

Webb, P. H., and Ray, M. L. (1979). Effects of TV clutter. *Journal of Advertising Research 19* (No. 3), 7–12.

Weinstein, S., Appel, V., and Weinstein, C. (1980). Brain-activity responses to magazine and television advertising. *Journal of Advertising Research 20* (No. 3), 57–63.

Wells, W. D., and Chinsky, J. M. (1965). Effects of competing messages: A laboratory simulation. *Journal of Marketing Research 2*, 141–145.

Wheatley, J. J. (1971). Marketing and the use of fear- or anxiety-arousing appeals. *Journal of Marketing 35* (No. 2), 62–64.

Wheatley, J. J., and Oshikawa, S. (1970). The relationship between anxiety and positive and negative advertising appeals. *Journal of Marketing Research 7*, 85–89.

Whipple, T. W., and Courtney, A. E. (1980). How to portray women in TV commercials. *Journal of Advertising Research 20* (No. 2), 53–59.

Wilkie, W. L., and Farris, P. W. (1976). "Consumer Information Processing." Cambridge, Massachusetts: Marketing Science Institute.

Winick, C. (1962). Three measures of the advertisng value of media context. *Journal of Advertising Research 2* (No. 2), 28–37.

Winter, F. W. (1973). A laboratory experiment of individual attitude response to advertising exposure. *Journal of Marketing Research 10*, 130–140.

Woodside, A. G. (1972). A shopping list experiment of beer brand images. *Journal of Applied Psychology 56*, 512–513.

Woodside, A. G., and Delozier, M. (1976). Effects of word of mouth advertising on consumer risk taking. *Journal of Advertising 5* (No. 3), 12–19.

Wortzel, L. H., and Frisbie, J. M. (1974). Women's role portrayal preferences in advertisements: An empirical study. *Journal of Marketing 38* (No. 4), 41–46.

Wright, P. L. (1973). The cognitive processes mediating acceptance of advertising. *Journal of Marketing Research 10*, 53–62.

Wright, P. L. (1974). Analyzing media effects on advertising responses. *Public Opinion Quarterly 38*, 192–205.

Wright, P. L. (1975). Factors affecting cognitive resistance to advertising. *Journal of Consumer Research 2*, 1–9.

Wright, P. L. (1981). Cognitive responses to mass media advocacy. *In* R. E. Petty, T. M. Ostrom, and T. C. Brock (Eds.), "Cognitive Responses to Persuasion," pp. 263–282. Hillsdale, New Jersey: Erlbaum.

Wright, P. L., and Barbour, F. (1975). The relevance of decision process models in structuring persuasive messages. *Communication Research 2,* 246–259.

Zajonc, R. B. (1968). Attitudinal effects of mere exposure. *Journal of Personality and Social Psychology 9* (No. 2, Pt. 2), 1–27.

Zajonc, R. B., and Rajecki, D. (1969). Exposure and effect: A field experiment. *Psychonomic Science 17,* 215–216.

Zajonc, R. B., Snap, W. C. Harrison, A. A., and Roberts, P. (1971). Limiting conditions of the exposure effect: Satiation and relativity. *Journal of Personality and Social Psychology 18,* 384–391.

Zielske, H. A. (1959). The remembering and forgetting of advertising. *Journal of Marketing 23,* 239–243.

Zielske, H. A., and Henry, W. A. (1980). Remembering and forgetting television ads. *Journal of Advertising Research 20* (No. 2), 7–13.

Author Index

Subject Index